GREEN GROCERIES

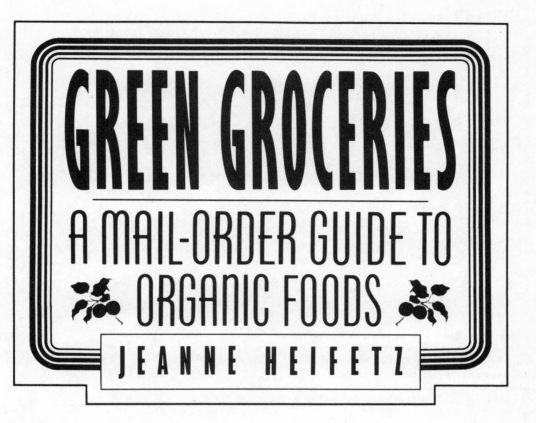

GREEN GROCERIES

A MAIL-ORDER GUIDE TO ORGANIC FOODS

JEANNE HEIFETZ

HarperPerennial

A Division of HarperCollins*Publishers*

HarperCollins books may be purchased for educational,
business, or sales promotional use. For information, please call
or write: Special Markets Department, HarperCollins Publishers,
Inc., 10 East 53rd Street, New York, NY 10022. Telephone:
(212) 207-7528; Fax: (212) 207-7222.

FIRST EDITION

DESIGNED BY JOEL AVIROM

Library of Congress Cataloging-in-Publication Data

Heifetz, Jeanne, 1960–
    Green groceries : a mail-order guide to organic foods /
Jeanne Heifetz. — 1st ed.
        p.   cm.
    Includes index.
    ISBN 0-06-273135-1 (paper)
    1. Natural foods—United States—
Directories.   2. Groceries—United States—
Directories.   3. Mail-order business—United
States—Directories.   I. Title.
TX369.H45   1992
381′.456413′029473—dc20   91-55501

92 93 94 95 96 DT/CW 10 9 8 7 6 5 4 3 2 1

ENTS

ACKNOWLEDGMENTS

First and foremost, thanks go to Laurie Colwin and Juris Jurjevics. Laurie helped hatch the idea; Juris shepherded me through the legal maze that is a publishing contract, and then in his finest imitation of Simon Legree cracked an invisible whip and shouted, "Write faster!"

Pat Seppanen taught me everything I know about planning, organization, and Pendaflex file folders.

I could never have done any of this without the computer system designed by my father, Simon Heifetz, whose wizardry made my research possible and who provided "software support"—including some days I'm sure both of us would rather forget. For the graveyard shift, thanks to Guy Gallo, who answered computer questions at hours most sane people would be asleep.

I owe a debt to Daniel Siktman and John Cawthron, the UPS men who cheerfully delivered packages of organic food day in and day out. They always showed up at my door when they said they would—I never had to spend a day waiting around for them to arrive. I wish I could say the same of the U.S. Mail—our local post office is notorious, prompting a cover story in our local weekly titled, "What's Happening to the Mail?" Countless pieces of mail got lost during the months I spent doing research.

Many thanks to the growers themselves, who patiently explained what they did and why they did it to someone who didn't know the first thing about farming—sort of a telephone version of the Fresh Air Fund. I'm also grateful for their encouragement, which always seemed to come when I most needed it. Organic growers tend to be very nice people, and I've made some great telephone friends I hope to meet in person someday.

Thank you to all the friends who put up with the index cards and pens I put next to their plates: Susan Bandler, Ellen Belknap, Ori Ben-Yehuda, Marlene Booth and Avi Soifer, Kenny Breuer and Rochelle Hahn, Susan and Priscilla Cobb, Margarita Crocker, Sharon Daniel, Michael Downing (a man of inimitable vocabulary), Maggie Elliott, Alan Gerber and Rachel Wiseman, Jocelyn Gordon and Bruce Mallory, Melinda Gould, Roger Gould, Lizzie Leiman, Noah Lumsden, Sophie Lumsden, Arnie Miller, the Osler family, Dave Rich, Philip Rosenthal, Judy Sirota Rosenthal, and Eva, Sylvia, and Ariel Rosenthal, Jeff Saver and Kay Young, Adrienne Shishko and Joel Sklar, Amira and Rafi Soifer, Cindy Spiegel, and Katie Towler.

Thanks to Sheila Gillooly and Rick Kot at HarperCollins, who—when you finally get through to them on the phone—are wonderful to work with.

Finally, special thanks to Tom Gould for adjectives, reassurance, and for baking and cooking long into the night.

INTRODUCTION

The idea for this book grew out of a conversation with Laurie Colwin, who is both a wonderful cook and a concerned parent. Laurie's daughter was then four. The headlines were full of the risks associated with Alar, a chemical sprayed on apples to control ripening and enhance redness. Laurie had successfully campaigned to get her daughter's school to buy only Alar-free apple juice; at home, she was trying to cook with organic ingredients whenever possible. Over dinner one night, she told me that some things were easy enough to find at a local health-food store, but other ingredients seemed impossible to locate. "Wouldn't it be great," I said, after devouring a slice of her delicious bread, "if you could have one book that listed all the mail-order sources of organic food?" "Yes," she said. "Why don't you write it?" This is the result.

When I started this project, I liked the idea of buying organically grown food, and did so when it was convenient. I wasn't a fanatic by any means, and didn't stare glumly at my plate in restaurants wondering what had gone into my food. The more I talked to organic growers, however, the more compelled I felt to buy organic. About halfway through the project, I found myself feeling a little heartsick when I bought conventionally grown foods. Of course, I still go to restaurants, but I do wonder about the ingredients—and wish I didn't have to.

WHY ALL THE FUSS?

If you've picked up this book, you're probably not asking yourself this question. But if you need further convincing, I can give you several answers. One—probably the one most consumers are thinking of when they start buying organic food—has to do with your health, and the health of your family.

You first: according to the *New York Times,* "At least 27 pesticides approved for use in the United States are listed by the E.P.A. as probable carcinogens in humans." Of the more than two dozen environmental hazards the EPA regulates, the agency ranks pesticides as the third-greatest cancer risk—greater, for example, than exposure to asbestos. The EPA attributes some 6,000 cases of cancer annually to pesticide residues. Granted, this represents only a small percentage of cancer cases, but these are cases that don't have to exist at all. According to Dr. Robert N. Hoover, an epidemiologist at the National Cancer Institute, "Among the easiest cancers to prevent are those with causes that can be regulated by the Government, like pesticide residues in food." To make matters worse, many pesticides are not even used to protect crops' health. The California Public Interest Research Group found that some 40 to 60 percent of pesticides used on tomatoes, and 60 to 80 percent used on oranges, were for cosmetic purposes. According to their research, the government and the produce industry have established standards for the way produce *looks* that make it extremely difficult for farmers to cut down on pesticides.

And, although cancer gets most of the headlines, greater danger may lie elsewhere. Some 600 pesticides registered with the EPA—not all for use on food—are neurotoxins, according to a report prepared by the Office of Technology Assessment. Even that "not-for-use-on-food" classification can be tricky; for example, cottonseed oil is a food made from a crop that is not classified or regulated as a food.

Antibiotics and hormones in meat present other problems. As the standard method of raising livestock has changed from outdoor grazing, or "free ranging," to cramped quarters, animals become more likely to share diseases. Antibiotics, which have a legitimate use in animals—curing illness—are now given routinely as preventive measures. In 1985, almost ten million pounds of antibiotics were administered to livestock, more than were used to treat human illness in that year. One result has been the evolution of resistant strains of bacteria, including the one that causes salmonella poisoning.

Both hormones and antibiotics are routinely given to meat animals to speed up weight gain. For example, DES, which can cause cancer in the children of women who took it before or during pregnancy, was regularly used as a growth hormone for cattle until it was banned in 1979. In a particularly chilling episode, children in Puerto Rico who had eaten the meat and milk of animals that had been fed artificial estrogens began developing secondary sexual characteristics as early as age one. Today's debate concerns bovine somatotropin, a genetically engineered growth hormone that is supposed to increase cow's milk production by up to 25 percent. The hormone affected the growth rates of laboratory rats, and critics wonder what it might do to humans who ingest it in milk.

As the Puerto Rican experience illustrates, whatever effects agricultural chemicals have on adults, they probably affect children to an even greater extent. As the Natural Resources Defense Council's February 1989 report pointed out, children are particularly vulnerable to pesticide residues because they eat more fruit and vegetables relative to their body weight than adults do. In the well-known case of apple juice, for example, it was determined that children consume more than twenty times the amount of apples and apple products. And, because children's bodies are still forming, they may absorb toxins at four to five times the rate adults do. Yet the government uses adult consumption to set its standards of safety. The NRDC estimated that the risk of pesticides to children was some 460 times greater than the level the federal government considers acceptable.

The added irony is that as Americans have taken the advice of medical experts and increased their intake of fruits and vegetables, the EPA's standards of adult consumption have fallen increasingly out of date. While the National Academy of Sciences' National Research Council recommends that Americans eat five half-cup servings of fruits and vegetables *per day,* the EPA continues to calculate pesticide risks based on an intake of one avocado, one artichoke, one nectarine, one wedge of melon, a quarter of an eggplant, and a handful of mushrooms *per year.*

Finally, there's the issue of detection. According to the General Accounting Office, the investigative arm of the Congress, the FDA's standard tests detect only half the pesticides that may be present in foods. Alar, for example, was not detected by the FDA's methods. The FDA also lacks the legal authority to punish those who market contaminated foods. As the uproar over food safety continues, both the EPA and FDA are tightening their standards and intensifying their inspections. But will that be enough?

Even if we were to gain at least minimal control over the domestic use of pesticides, imported food would pose other dangers. According to the *New York Times,* at least 110 pesticides that are registered for use in five countries that export food to us are not approved for use in the United States. For example, when Uniroyal, the manufacturer of Alar, stopped selling the chemical in the United States, the company continued to sell it abroad.

According to Dan Howell, director of Americans for Safe Food, the Bush administration "is studying ways to convince the public that there is nothing to worry about." He cites Cooper Evans, a special agricultural assistant to the president, whose method of persuading consumers that food is safe is simply to tell them the food is safe "over and over for a number of years."

If you can't rely on federal agencies to guarantee food safety, what *can* you do? The *New York Times*'s Marian Burros offered readers a number of ways to reduce the risks of pesticides, among them, "Grow your own food." (If you're interested, see the "Grow Your Own" section.) If that's not a realistic option, her other suggestions include washing fruits and vegetables "in a diluted solution of dishwashing soap or Ivory soap and water. Rinse thoroughly." This is a time-consuming prospect, and with waxed fruits and vegetables, it's ineffective. If a fungicide is mixed with wax before it's applied to your cucumber, no washing in the world is going to remove it. You'll have to peel it. And even that won't always work. One of the main dangers the National Academy of Sciences has cited is that many pesticides cannot simply be washed off the food. Among the more troubling types of pesticides are systemic: they are absorbed into the whole plant. Aldicarb, for example, is a systemic that can cause nervous disorders, and is routinely used on bananas, potatoes, and melons. And no amount of washing will help you when it comes to antibiotics and hormones in your meat and poultry.

THE BIG PICTURE

I realize that even all this may not be enough to convince you. I still find the risk of agricultural chemicals to my health rather remote (with the exception of hormones and antibiotics which seem a more immediate threat). However, the more I read, the more I realized that buying conventionally grown food was supporting a system that puts the health of American agriculture, and the plant as a whole, at risk. The people who are probably at highest risk for pesticide exposure are not the consumers but the growers. If you've ever read the instructions for the home-use version of these chemicals, you can imagine what the hazards are for people handling concentrated pesticides year in and year out. As one grower told me, "If you go to the shows and see the space suits they sell to use for chemical applications, you wonder why people don't start to think, 'If I need to wear that, what is it doing to food safety? What is it doing to the environment? What is it I'm giving little Johnny to take to school?'" In a *New York Times* editorial, Richard Rhodes quotes one farmer as saying, "The label said to burn my work clothes afterward, and I just decided I didn't want to be around anything that deadly." Pesticide exposure also has political implications: on large-scale farms, the workers in the fields who risk contamination by direct contact with pesticides are often nonwhite, migrant laborers.

Another group at risk are the people whose water supply is downstream from chemical-dependent farms. According to the EPA, drinking wells in thirty-eight states have been contaminated with seventy-four pesticides from agricultural runoff. Agricultural chemicals account for some 50 percent of the surface water pollution in this country. These chemicals can also destroy marine life; or simply make those plants and fish too toxic for humans or other animals to eat; or, in the case of fertilizers, throw off the natural balance by overfeeding one type of life, producing abnormal conditions like algae blooms.

Moreover, the bulk of agricultural chemicals, whether designed to feed plants or kill pests, are petroleum-based. In 1981, farmers were the single largest consumer of petroleum products in the United States. Does it make sense to remain dependent on these chemicals in an era of dwindling and expensive supplies of fossil fuel?

HOW DID WE GET HERE?

Before World War II most farms were relatively small, family-run operations. They grew an assortment of crops to meet the varied needs of local consumers, who ate whatever was in season on these local farms. A farm that produced nothing but tomatoes wouldn't have made sense, because the local markets also wanted lettuce and carrots and potatoes and squash and beans, and so on. In prewar farming, farmers not only grew a mixture of crops; they also practiced crop rotation: crops that removed nutrients from the soil would alternate with crops that would be plowed under to return nutrients to the soil.

After the war, the advent of chemical pesticides, coupled with low transportation costs, made farmers think for the first time of supplying a single crop to a large geographical area rather than a range of crops to a small one. "Monocropping"—growing a single crop or small number of crops on a whole field, year after year—had never been possible before. Chemical pesticides and fertilizers changed all that, making the impossible seem possible.

While poisonous substances like lead and arsenic have been used as pesticides on crops for over 100 years, the current "crop" of chemical pesticides, fertilizers, and herbicides dates to World War II. DDT, the first large-scale commercial pesticide, was first used during the war to kill off disease-carrying insects, and its success at that task inspired farmers to try it back home. As one grower told me, "People defend DDT from the standpoint of protecting the soldiers from malaria and yellow fever, and it's hard to disagree with that. But farmers have been sold a bill of goods."

At the same time, seed companies, which had been developing hybrids since the 1930s, offered what seemed like magic: hybrids could be bred for ease of storage or shipping, or to mature all on the same day, making harvest easier than it had ever been. All of this was a devil's bargain, however, because hybrids often sacrificed nutritional value—as one organic seed supplier puts it, hybrids trade nutrition per acre for yield per acre—needed far more water than the older strains, and virtually ensured that the farmer would have to use chemicals to protect against pests. If every plant is not only the same species, but is generally *identical* to the plants around it, the whole crop shares weaknesses as well as strengths. If one is susceptible to a blight, they all are. If a crop has been bred to ripen all at once for ease of harvesting, any pest attacking at that moment will devastate the entire crop.

By using hybrids, American agriculture began to put its eggs in very few baskets. Ninety percent of our food now comes from fewer than twenty *types* of plants, and even fewer *strains*. Of 30,000 strains of corn, for example, only six are in large-scale use. When so few strains are used, they become sitting targets for pests or disease. (The Irish Potato Famine, which claimed two million lives, illustrates the danger of feeding a nation on a tiny number of genetic strains.

All the potatoes in the country were genetically similar, and all were vulnerable to the same devastating blight. For more on hybrids, see the "Grow Your Own" section.)

With the advent of pesticides and monocropping, farmers stopped rotating crops. Planting the same crop year after year means taking the same nutrients from the soil year after year. Farmers became dependent on synthetic fertilizers to replenish the soil artificially as cover crops had once done naturally. Petroleum-based fertilizers provide nitrogen, potassium, and phosphorus (hence the acronym NPK, from their symbols on the periodic table), but at the expense of the naturally occurring bacteria that produce nitrogen, so the soil becomes entirely dependent on artificial fertilizer to sustain life.

The cycle escalated. Heavy doses of NPK fertilizers made it possible to plant the same crop annually. Pests could now count on a reliable food source so the farmers' dependence on pesticides increased. Because farms were serving the national market, they soon grew too large and too densely planted to weed, so chemical herbicides—weed killers—entered the picture. In this cycle of increasing chemical dependency, the problems created by one chemical were answered by another chemical. Lured by ever-increasing crop yields, farmers got further and further into debt to pay for the costly chemicals necessary to sustain the farm.

As it turned out, the chemicals were far from foolproof. Not surprisingly, as has happened with the overuse of antibiotics in humans, some 600 pests in this country have developed resistance to pesticides. Farmers found that every few years they needed new and stronger chemicals. Crop losses due to pests and weeds have actually *increased* in the past forty-five years. When chemicals in the soil built up to the point that plants' roots couldn't penetrate the layer of chemicals to reach water farmers' yields decreased. In times of drought, these plants become particularly vulnerable.

Meanwhile, aquifers were being drained for irrigation, often a highly subsidized and energy-guzzling endeavor. If this water contains dissolved salts, it tends to leave salt deposits in the soil as it evaporates, which can render the soil unusable, because the high concentration of salt tends to draw water out of the plant, rather than allowing the plant to draw water in. Chemical farming put the soil at risk in another way: as farmers cut down trees to expand farms, the wind shield disappeared, and topsoil began blowing away.

As one organic farmer mentioned in this book has written, our agricultural history raises the question, "Are we treating our soil like dirt?" He went on to observe, "You only have to open your eyes to see the agricultural abuse here in the valley. Every spring tons of valley soil blow away, never to be seen again. The other day, I drove by a fence that was completely drifted over with soils from the adjacent field. Our precious aquifer is contaminated with nitrates and God-knows-how-many agricultural chemicals that are leaching through our sandy soil. We have witnessed the creation of the superbug, immune to the many poisons we have created to kill it. Local farmers tell me that herbicides rarely live up to the claims on the label. [M]any of our soils could be classified as 'dead,' with few worms and little microbial activity. Crops are basically grown hydroponically, with nutrients and chemicals injected through the irrigation system, the soil merely serving as a growth medium."

In layman's terms, he means you could pretty much be farming in shredded cardboard, as long as you injected enough chemical fertilizers into the "soil," applied herbicides to keep weeds away from the "soil" you'd fertilized, and sprayed pesticides on the bugs that were attracted to your crop.

THE ORGANIC ALTERNATIVE

Becoming an organic farmer, particularly if you've been a conventional farmer, doesn't mean that one day you stop using chemicals and suddenly you're organic. It's not just a matter of what you stop doing, but what you *start* doing. If any type of farming bears out the adage that "the best fertilizer is the farmer's foot," it's organic farming. The soil needs constant maintenance and monitoring, not to mention repair, if it's been treated with chemicals for years or decades. Organic growing doesn't mean unscientific growing: it can and usually does incorporate modern research as well as time-honored practices. Organic farming is a year-in year-out commitment to improving the nutrients in the soil and making it "biologically active"— which is a fancy way of saying that plenty of organisms are alive and at work in it.

To organic farmers "soil" is an almost mystical substance. In the words of Jane Mulder, editor of *Organic Food Matters: The Journal of Sustainable Agriculture,* "Organic farmers feed the soil, not the plant. Soil is not dirt. It is a complex, fragile, living community. It teems with life. A tablespoon contains more microorganisms than there are people on the whole planet. In healthy, active soil, air circulates freely, and moisture is retained. The exchanges among plant roots, microorganisms, and larger creatures like earthworms and insects provide nutrients to the growing crop and protection from disease, erosion and drought."

Organic farmers add nutrients to the soil in many ways, among them composting, which uses plant waste, animal waste, and mineral-rich rock dust; and "green manure," which means planting crops, many of which attract bacteria that "fix" airborne nitrogen, and plowing them back into the soil as fertilizer. For the consumer, this means organic foods have drawn a far wider *range* of nutrients from the soil than foods grown with chemical fertilizers.

By rotating crops, organic farmers decrease the likelihood that pests, whether fungi, insects, or microbes, will take up permanent residence—if their food source is unreliable, they're unlikely to settle in for the long term. Organic farmers also used a technique called companion planting: alternating rows of different crops—one crop may provide shade for another, add nutrients to the soil the other crop can use, draw pests away from the other crop, repel pests, or attract the pests' natural predators.

Pest control looks very different on an organic farm and a conventional farm. Instead of waiting to see whether, and where, a given crop has a pest problem, the conventional farmer will spray the entire crop; in the case of apple growers, for example, this can mean ten sprayings a season, and more. An organic farmer will tend to monitor crops much more closely and respond quickly if and when pests appear. Some organic farmers release the pests' natural predators—tiny wasps, for example—into the fields; others literally vacuum insects off the plants. But don't panic if you hear an organic farmer talk about spraying a crop. These sprays, whether fertilizers or pesticides, are biological compounds. Some almost-organic farmers use a method called Integrated Pest Management (IPM), that uses traditional pesticides only as a last resort. They break down in oxygen and sunlight and are not absorbed systemically into the plant. To combat weeds, organic farmers may use mechanical means like flame-burning, or planting cover crops to smother weeds. They may even allow some weeds to grow —both to distract pests from food crops and to plow under to feed the soil.

Organic farmers tend to choose crops that are suited to their soil and climate, instead of imposing a crop on the land willy-nilly and letting chemicals make up for anything that's lacking. For the consumer, that means getting accustomed once again to seasonal, regional eating: an organic farmer can't use the magic of chemicals to grow crops that the land doesn't support naturally.

WHY AREN'T MORE FARMERS GOING ORGANIC?

Organic farming is booming—and yet it still makes up less than 3 percent of American agriculture. No organic crop is in surplus. Yet conventional farmers are often leery of making the transition. As one grower told me, "I have to keep telling conventional growers it's a marketing niche—then at least they'll listen to you. Before I started saying that, they'd see you coming and put a cross in front of your face to keep you away." Unfortunately, agricultural policy in this country makes it difficult for farmers who currently run large, single-crop farms to switch over to multi-crop farming and crop rotation. For one thing, banks' lending policies can restrict a farmer's choices. If the farmer devotes some of his land to a cover crop that nourishes the soil but doesn't produce a cash crop, bankers, looking at the short-term and not the long-term output of the farm, may be unwilling to lend to these farmers.

Many banks will only lend to farmers who are using the methods supported by local county extension agents. The extension services the educational arm of the Department of Agriculture, that works in partnership with land-grant universities, and tends not to get a lot of funding to support research into alternative agriculture; the four-billion-dollar-a-year domestic pesticide industry has an interest in funding research that supports its own products. As a result, the majority of extension agents advocate chemical farming, and bankers follow their lead. Bank loans often won't cover compost, or the equipment a farmer will need to weed mechanically rather than chemically.

Some states, however, are pioneers in supporting organic farming. According to Dan Howell, director of Americans for Safe Food, "Banks are often hesitant to make loans to farmers who want to start organic operations or other non-traditional ventures, [so] several states have established programs to provide below-market-interest financing for alternative farming projects." Texas has officially recognized the importance of these farmers by establishing a legal definition of "transitional organic" to cover the years between abandoning chemicals and receiving organic certification; this allows farmers to get public support—in the form of higher prices—as they wean their fields of chemicals.

States may be supportive, but farmers who receive subsidies can be penalized for switching from one crop to a crop not covered by the subsidy program. For example, farmers who receive the federal subsidy for corn are paid by the bushel. If they cut down on the number of bushels they produce, because they plant another crop on some of their fields, or alternate rows of corn with another crop, their subsidy goes down, even though much of the corn they raise is surplus that only the government buys. In 1989, the National Academy of Sciences recommended changing federal subsidies to encourage farmers to decrease their use of chemical pesticides and synthetic fertilizers. Until the government responds, farmers will continue to be penalized for any decrease in production. As Richard Rhodes pointed out in the *New York Times,* "The No. 1 rule for any farmer who wants to survive economically in farming today is to keep up his crop base—never to plant less acreage to a given commodity that he planted in previous years, a number on which his subsidies are based. If he planted 100 acres of corn each year for the past three years and plants only 95 this year, then his subsidies will be correspondingly reduced. He is effectively penalized for growing less surplus than he has grown in the past."

Farmers who make the transition to organic don't just need funding, however: they also need the benefit of agricultural research. As one grower told me, "If the government had spent the last thirty years on research into nonchemical methods of growing instead of researching high-production chemicals and concentrating on yields, we'd all be a lot better off. They're just now waking up to the fact that consumers want food grown without chemicals." In 1990, only .5 percent of the Department of Agriculture's budget for research and education went to study nonchemical methods of farming.

As I began to research organic farming, I was relieved to learn that, in spite of the risks, going organic is beneficial not only to the consumer, but also to the farmer. Although the initial transition period may be costly, farmers do not lose out by going organic. The National Academy of Sciences reported in 1989 that farmers who use few or no chemicals are usually as productive as conventional farmers. Farmers themselves bear out that claim. A survey of *New Farm* readers found that only 4 percent of full-time farmers had a decrease in net income after cutting their use of chemicals; 32 percent reported an increase in income; and 64 percent experienced no change at all. This is not surprising when you consider that chemical inputs account for between 25 and 55 percent of total farm costs. In fact, many of the growers in this book initially became organic not out of a philosophical commitment, but because they simply couldn't afford the chemicals any longer. Jim Hightower, former commissioner of agriculture in Texas, and a strong supporter of organic farming, has said that "farmers doing this kind of agriculture make money. They pay off their notes; they pay for tractors and they do it without crop subsidies."

So, as one of my favorite T-shirts proclaims, "Don't Panic—Go Organic."

BUT WHAT DOES ORGANIC REALLY MEAN?

At the consumer level "organic" is still easily confused with "all natural," or "health food," both of which are fuzzily defined at best. If there's any single convention about the label "all natural," it's that all the ingredients in that product can be found in nature, and that no substances from the laboratory—the infamous additives or preservatives—have been added during processing. However, "all natural" says nothing at all about how the ingredients were grown; they may have been sprayed with all the chemicals the laboratory has to offer. "Health food" similarly makes no claim about the agricultural methods used to grow the ingredients —if anything, this means only that this type of food—fruit, seeds, nuts, whatever—is healthier for you than, say, a junk-food alternative. Both labels are overused.

The relevant dictionary definitions of organic simply read "designating any chemical compound containing carbon" or "of, having the characteristics of, or derived from living organisms." Since most food we eat was carbon-based living matter at some point, that really doesn't help you very much. What people generally mean by organic is food grown without pesticides, herbicides, or chemical fertilizers; in the case of meat, that the livestock was raised on organically grown feed and given no hormones or antibiotics. What *is* "organic" or "biological" is the material used to fertilize the soil, and control weeds and pests.

Without the word "certified" in front of it, people can use the "organic" label to mean just about anything. "Certified" in front of "organic" adds the guarantee that an *independent* organization has inspected some combination of the produce, the soil, and the grower's methods, and made sure that they met an established standard. Many states have a law governing the use of "organic," but with a few exceptions, these states do not have any mechanism for inspecting farms; they do specify a penalty, often lamentably small, for willfully violating the state statute. Some states only regulate the use of "certified organic"; growers can still use "organic" without meeting any set standard. You may also see the label "Pesticide-free," which is not regulated by any state, and so only represents a grower's assertion that no pesticides were used in that crop year. You should also be aware of the distinction between "organic" and "no detected residues," which means only that no pesticide residues have been found on the produce; it doesn't indicate that the grower has a long-term commitment to organic farming that will benefit the land as well as the consumer.

Naysayers are quick to tell the cautionary tale of Pacific Organic, which had to shut down when it was discovered that the company was taking conventionally grown carrots from Mexico out of their original wrappers and repackaging them with an organic label. However, they had no documentation that they were, in fact, *certified* organic growers.

The "established standard" for certification is not always the same. Each certifying organization has its own list of acceptable and prohibited substances, and methods of monitoring compliance. Many of these lists are similar, and by 1993 will become more so, as the federal law (discussed below) takes effect. What follows is a general overview of what certifiers do. In the Index, you will find a list of the names of the major certifying organizations; you can call them for the specifics of their program, or to check on the status of a specific grower or producer.

At the most basic level, certifying organizations require two things: that no synthetic chemicals be used for a specified period—although some chemicals can stay in the land for more than seven years, three growing seasons is the common waiting period—before sale of the produce; and that the grower actively improve the soil using organic methods. It's important to recognize that organic certification represents *both* an absence of chemicals *and* the presence of an intensive organic program. A few organizations provide for a transitional label for the period prior to certification, so that farmers can let consumers know they've started going organic.

As a consumer, you can help support transitional farmers, who have given up using pesticides and synthetic fertilizers but have not been pesticide-free long enough to qualify for certification. As the inspection coordinator for California Certified Organic Farmers has said, "The transitional farmer needs a break. He is taking a risk. By buying from transitional growers, you will be sending the message that you support the choice they've made, a choice they may feel shaky about." As another grower said, "It's easy to get discouraged in the first few years before you get your land in balance. Things don't automatically look as beautiful as the photos in *Organic Gardening*." It also takes determination to buck tradition. "I've had to get in the five-ton farm truck and drive 93 miles to get organic fertilizer," explained one farmer. "If I were farming chemically, I could just trot down to the co-op eight miles away." Ultimately, you will benefit from supporting these farmers, because the more organic farmers there are, the less of a premium you will pay for organic foods. And, as one grower pointed out, "People are always asking what they can do for the environment. Buying organic food, and paying a little more for it, is a direct contribution, because organic farmers are committed to the health of the environment."

Longtime organic farmers are understandably concerned that some "transitional" farmers may be hopping on the organic bandwagon without seriously intending to remain organic. One grower said that she'd heard of people pouring on the herbicide just before officially entering their "transitional" period, knowing that the chemical would keep on working for many months. I'm hopeful that such organic opportunists represent a very small percentage of the transitional growers, and encourage you to support transitional growers, particularly ones in your local area, whom you can get to know and whose sincerity you can judge for yourself.

Most certifying organizations require growers to join the organization first, and then apply for certification. Both steps involve a fee, which can be on a sliding scale depending on the size of the farm. Growers then complete paperwork that documents what methods and inputs they have used on the farm for a specified period. This can take the form of a sworn and/or notarized affidavit.

After receiving the paperwork, organizations usually send out an inspector (sometimes more than one) to examine the farm, test the soil and water, and often to bring back samples of produce for residue testing. Each organization sets an allowable limit for residue, often based on the safety limits established by the FDA. Certification is often renewed once a year. If chemical use does show up, the farm loses the right to use the "certified organic" label, and may have to go back to square one and go through the transitional period all over again.

Some organizations inspect farms once in a crop year; some inspect as many as seven times. Some make only scheduled appointments; others do "spot" or "surprise" inspections. In most cases, inspectors are independent agents, who must not have a conflict of interest— they can't buy from the farm they're inspecting, be a partner in it, or collect fees as a consultant from it. Some organizations use member farmers to do the certification, on the theory that a farmer is least likely to be fooled by another farmer; in these cases, the organizations make an effort to make sure certifying farmers have no interest in the farms they certify.

Most organizations will only certify an *entire* farm, but a few will certify part of a farm, as long as the produce from the organic portion is kept strictly separate from produce grown with chemicals. Some organizations also certify processors, like grain mills or cheese plants. This is an added protection against adulteration. Some organizations do not certify processors, but require growers to keep detailed records of produce sold to processors or distributors to make sure that those processors or distributors are not using the "certified" label on any other produce or products.

Quite a few organizations require that the farms maintain detailed records that provide for an audit trail of the produce. The theory is that a given acreage with given inputs can only produce a given amount of produce. If a farmer is suddenly selling twice that amount and labeling it "certified organic," some of that produce probably came from somewhere else.

While most certifying organizations tend to be private nonprofit groups made up of member growers, a few are state-run: notably, those of Washington and Texas. One organization, Farm Verified Organic, is a corporation that certifies growers and plants on behalf of the producer of the final product, who is a licensee of the FVO trademark and pays certification costs. For example, FVO might certify 100 apple growers for a single producer of apple sauce. The manufacturer of the sauce pays for all the inspections and can use the FVO label; the individual growers may not use that label, because they have been certified by FVO *for* the sauce producer, not for their own sales.

"Biodynamic" growers follow the agricultural practices of the Austrian philosopher Rudolf Steiner, which not only involve organic methods, but also require a high degree of self-sufficiency (as few inputs as possible should come from off the farm) and a recognition of the relationship between the farm and the cosmos. The biodynamic certifying organization, Demeter, offers three levels of certification: "certified organic," "certified biodynamic," and "Demeter quality."

Many growers in areas that do not have certifying organizations use the standards of the California Health and Safety Code Section 26569.11. To use this label, the law requires that the land be free of synthetic chemicals for only *one* year prior to the sale of produce—a stipulation most growers would consider the equivalent of "transitional" rather than "organic." In 1990, the law was changed to require a three-year period, but that won't go into effect until 1995, by which time the federal Organic Food Production Act will have kicked in, superseding the state law.

THE FEDERAL STANDARD

When the Organic Foods Production Act of 1990 was signed into law, it established certain standards that growers and processors will have to meet in order to use the label "organic" and the seal of the Department of Agriculture after October 1, 1993. (Farmers whose total sales are less than $5,000 are exempt.)

The national program will be devised by the secretary of agriculture in consultation with a National Organic Standards Board established by the secretary. The Board, with some input from the EPA and the secretary of health and human services, will establish a national list of substances that can or can't be used in organic farming.

The law establishes a three-year period before the harvest of a given crop during which the land has to be free of synthetic chemicals. (Some chemicals, of course, stay in the ground for much longer than three years, but this is a good start.) Growers and processors who want to use the organic label will have to develop a written plan of their organic practices. The growers' plan will have to include methods for fertilizing the soil, including crop rotation. Certification will take place annually, as will on-site inspections, and "periodic" residue testing will take place. Farmers will be allowed to have part of their land certified if it is physically separate from any land farmed with chemicals, if machinery and tools are kept separate, and separate records are kept for produce, so that the farmer can't try to sell the produce of the chemical field under the "organic" label and at organic prices.

After harvest, processors can't add any synthetic ingredients, or ingredients that haven't been produced organically, unless allowed by the National List, or unless these ingredients represent less than 5 percent by weight of the final product. They can't add ingredients that contain significant levels of nitrates, heavy metals, or toxic residues—the levels will be set by the individual certification program. They also can't add sulfites, nitrates, or nitrites, which primarily affect smoked meats and wines, where sulfites are produced when sulfur dioxide is added to prevent spoilage. They can't pack or store with fungicides, preservatives, or fumigants, or in containers that previously came in contact with these substances. Any water used has to meet federal safety standards.

There is a procedure for exceptions, and one notable exception is any chemical application made by the federal or state government "emergency pest or disease treatment program," in which case the Board will make a recommendation about exemption. Organic farmers in Massachusetts, for example, were furious when the state began aerial spraying of their land to combat mosquitoes that might transmit a form of potentially fatal encephalitis. One of the growers' major complaints was that nothing had been done during the breeding and hatching phase, when the area affected by spraying would have been quite small. Instead, the state waited to spray until the mosquitoes had become widespread.

Livestock (which under this law includes wild game, poultry, fish, and many other forms of "nonplant" life) must be fed organically grown feed, as defined by the law. Animals can't be fed plastic pellets for roughage, can't be fed manure, and can't be given growth promoters or hormones in any form, including antibiotics. Antibiotics can only be used to treat illness; and no medication, other than vaccines, can be given unless an animal is actually sick. Animals also can't be given synthetic internal parasiticides on a routine basis. In processing, this meat has to be kept separate from meat raised conventionally. Dairy cattle have to be raised in this manner for at least a year prior to the date their milk or any products made from their milk is sold.

The law also provides for foods gathered in the wild, like wild rice, sea vegetables, some wild fruits, and many herbs. Harvesters will have to designate the area they're going to harvest, provide a three-year history of the area that shows that no prohibited substances have been applied there, a plan for harvesting showing that harvesting will not harm the environment and will actually sustain the wild crop, and ensure that processors are not going to add any prohibited substances.

To carry the organic label, imported foods will have to meet requirements, as evaluated by the secretary of agriculture, that are at least equivalent to the domestic requirements. In the case of processed foods (defined as "cooking, baking, heating, drying, mixing, grinding, churning, separating, extracting, cutting, fermenting, eviscerating, preserving, dehydrating, freezing, or otherwise manufacturing, and includes the packaging, canning, jarring, or otherwise enclosing food in a container"), if 50 percent or more of the food's ingredients by weight are organic (excluding water and salt), it can carry the organic label. If less than 50 percent of the ingredients are organic, it can only include "organic" on the ingredients list, next to the relevant ingredients.

The bill allows each state to develop its own certification program as long as it is consistent with the aims and regulations of the national legislation, and if approved by the secretary of agriculture. The states can be stricter than the feds if they choose, but not if the result penalizes the produce of other states with more lenient regulations.

States that do not already have a certifying organization may elect to bring in a certifying organization from another state, or place the responsibility in the hands of the state's department of agriculture. The secretary of agriculture will provide both financial and technical assistance to help set up a certification program. One grower I spoke to was skeptical. "If you give the rules to state government to enforce, that's going to make it worse. Traditionally, the state department of agriculture has been absolutely against everything we stand for, and now we're going to put them in the position of policing organic standards?" Another grower said that the atmosphere of the voluntary, farmer-run organizations was going to be lost. "Our meetings are full of good people—people you'd leave your wallet with. These organizations are self-policing for opportunists. Once the government gets involved, there's a bureaucracy, and a whole new set of hoops to jump through."

In states that already have active programs, the existing certification organizations will, in all likelihood, do this work, but that will be a tough row to hoe: how to certify a rapidly expanding number of organic farms and maintain standards that actually mean something? One grower I spoke to said of outside certification, "It used to be farmers certifying farmers—

who better to catch the cheats than another farmer? But farmers are some of the busiest people in the business community, so people are voting to give the certifying job to a nonfarming entity. With outsiders who are not farmers, it's just so easy to cheat."

Certifying organizations, whether run by the state or not, will have to be accredited by the secretary of agriculture, and provisions have been made for conflict of interest—basically, certifiers can't take bribes, certify operations in which they have a financial interest, or charge outside fees as consultants on organic practices.

Finally, what happens if a grower or processor breaks the law? If you knowingly misuse the organic label, you will not be eligible to be recertified for five years. In terms of fines, the ceiling on the civil penalty is $10,000, which is small potatoes if you're a large-scale potato farmer or even larger potato-chip manufacturer. It remains to be seen whether this will be enough to keep everyone honest.

The Organic Food Production Act is primarily a labeling law. It does not provide money for research into organic agriculture, loans for transitional farmers, or other incentives for farms to become certified. Farmers who choose to go organic will still be taking a risk—and we, as consumers, will have to support them by keeping up the demand for organic food at the supermarket, in restaurants, and in our own kitchens.

HOW TO USE THIS BOOK

If you are trying to convert to organic food, don't be overwhelmed and feel you have to do it all at once. Many parents I've spoken to find the prospect of trying to keep their children's food free from chemicals so daunting that they just give up. "They're going to end up eating all that junk anyway, so what difference does it make what I feed them?" Of course, you can't become the food police and inspect every morsel, but you can focus on the foods they eat most often. If you and/or your children live on hamburgers and hot dogs, you can get organic hamburgers and hot dogs—and buns. If it's pasta and sauce, the same holds true. When it's time to pack the lunchbox, you can make sure the bread that goes into sandwiches is organic, ditto the fruit. Using this book, you'll find you can provide the staples of your children's diet from organic sources.

If you don't already eat a lot of organic food, you may think that if it's good for you it can't possibly taste good. Nothing could be farther from the truth. If anything, organic food will taste *better* than its chemically grown counterparts; some growers attribute this to the mineral-rich soil the plants grow in. Alice Waters, the chef of the trend-setting Chez Panisse restaurant in Berkeley, California, argues that "organic growers give their crops the special attention they require. Their goal is to choose the best varieties, plant them in the best possible conditions, and harvest them when they are perfectly ready. There is an irresistible quality of life and vitality in the food that makes it taste so good." While that may be a bit of poetic license, you will possibly find organic produce fresher, sweeter, and more interesting than what you are used to, partly because organic growers often grow old-fashioned varieties bred for taste, rather than hybrids that simply ship the store well.

It's almost a cliché by now that organic produce is never picture perfect. If the only organic you've seen is in your supermarket, you may have been put off by cosmetic blemishes. One grower I talked to explained that the people who handle the intermediate steps from grower to supermarket often do not realize that organic produce has to be handled differently from the conventionally grown produce, which can comfortably sit in a warehouse for days or weeks without ill effects. Organic produce has to get to market immediately. When the system works, organic produce will be some of the freshest produce you can buy in the supermarket.

In the case of mail order, you are dealing with people who understand the importance of getting the produce to you fast, and what you receive may well look better than anything in the supermarket. (I certainly received plenty of gorgeous produce while working on this book.) You should also regard many of the products in this book as perishable, even when you might not treat their preservative-rich counterparts as such: for example, many of the grain mills listed here recommend refrigerating their freshly ground flour. Fresh produce is obviously the trickiest thing to order by mail, but it is available. Root vegetables and sturdy fruits are relatively dependable. For more perishable fruits or vegetables, try the "Under One Roof" companies, which do this kind of shipping on a regular basis.

I've grouped the growers and companies more or less as you would find them in the aisles of a supermarket. "Under One Roof" is my heading for companies that sell a little bit (or a lot) of a lot of things. The nature of organic farming made organizing the sections a bit difficult: organic farmers tend to grow more than one kind of food. When suppliers sell produce or products in several categories, I've tried to choose the category that covers the majority of what they sell. You'll find cross-references at the end of each section that will direct you to the other growers and companies that sell that type of food.

Each entry will indicate whether the grower/company has a catalogue or a price list you can ask for. "Organic" is becoming big business, but for many growers, it's still a small, family-run operation. In this book, you'll find the whole spectrum of organic growers: some have fax machines, full-color glossy catalogues, and fancy packaging; others have no literature (and in a few cases, no telephone) but invite you to call (or write) to find out what's in season and what they can ship to you. If both an 800 number and another number are listed, as a courtesy to the growers, please use the 800 number for orders, and the other number for inquiries. The list of products reflects what was available in 1990–91. Growers and companies may well carry new items or have discontinued some items by the time you contact them. Some, sadly, may have decided to discontinue their mail-order business.

If the grower or producer has a minimum order, that will be listed. You may decide that for some items you want to form a buying club with friends to buy in quantity and get wholesale prices. On page 291 you'll find a list of growers and companies whose minimum order is large, or which sell items only in bulk. These are useful for individuals with a large storage space, but are more likely to be useful for groups of friends or buying clubs; if you already belong to a buying club or are thinking of forming one, you might consider what they have to offer.

If the entry says "Visits: yes," this means on-farm sales (where the growers may sell more perishable produce than they are able to ship) or a retail store. If you want to visit, please call ahead for hours (which can vary with the season) and directions. If the company sells to local farmers' markets, the locations are given.

Beneath the address, you'll find the name of the certifying organization(s). Certification tends to be renewed annually; some organizations renew all certifications at the same time of year; others renew based on the date of the original application. I verified that the growers were certified by these organizations in 1990, and in some cases, in early 1991 (except for two or three suppliers certified by European organizations). If a grower had certification pending in early 1991, I checked with the certifying organization to make sure that the process had been initiated. You should feel free to use the list of certifying organizations in the Appendix to check whether a grower or producer has received certification since then, or whether a grower or producer certified in 1990–91 is still certified. If the line for certification reads "CHSC," that means that the grower or processor has not actually been certified by an outside organization but asserts that his or her practices meet the standards of the California Health and Safety Code (see above). Because the state doesn't actually go out and certify farms and processing plants, I could not verify these "certifications." The state of California does have a penalty for misuse of this label, however.

Several certifying organizations also certify processing plants and distributors, but unless otherwise specified, in the case of prepared foods like bread or jam, or of distributors (mainly in the "Under One Roof" section), "Certified by" refers to individual *ingredients* or *suppliers* rather than the finished product. I have not checked up on every ingredient (that would be a book in itself), but many processors and distributors have copies of the certification of their ingredients on file, and you can ask to see them. When the Organic Food Production Act takes effect, processors will be inspected to make sure that they are not diluting certified organic ingredients with noncertified ingredients; mixing organic and chemical produce; or treating organic produce with after-harvest chemicals. In the meantime, if you have concerns about mislabeling, you can contact consumer organizations (see the resources listed below) to press for better auditing of organic processors.

If certification reads "SELF," this means that the grower/producer is not certified by an outside agency. This does *not* mean anyone is trying to put something over on you. Many of the growers in this book have no certification even though they've been farming organically for anywhere up to forty-five years. Not being certified doesn't mean having something to hide. Some of these growers live in states that have no certification organizations; others have taken a "wait-and-see" attitude toward organizations that have only been around a few years. In some cases, growers feel their reputation should be sufficient and that the expense of certification is simply not justified. Because of the new federal law, all of these growers will have to make a choice by 1993—either become certified, or not use "organic" on their labels.

As I worked on this book it became increasingly important to me to communicate that your food comes from people, not machines. In the entry itself, you'll find a bit of the history of each farm or company, as well as a description of its produce/products. I hope as you read the entries you get something of the sense of being at a farmers' market: that you are building a relationship with the people who grow your food. Organic farmers are generally a passionate lot. Some of them are out there on the fringes, and some of them couldn't be more mainstream —third- or fourth- or fifth-generation farmers.

At the bottom of each entry, where available, I've listed representative prices. Unless noted, shipping costs are usually added based on your distance from the shipper. Please note that prices are given for 1990, and that for most crops, prices fluctuate from year to year and are generally not set until harvest time.

At the end of many chapters, you will find a few suppliers whose information came in after my deadline. I was not able to interview these suppliers or sample their produce, but I included them so that readers would have access to as many sources as possible.

Finally, even though this book is geared to the mail-order customer, I encourage you to order from the grower nearest you, particularly in the case of perishable foods. Of course, some produce and products are only available from one or two sources. But if you have the choice of buying from a grower near you, the produce will be fresher, and the shorter the distance the goods have to travel, the less you'll pay on shipping (unless shipping is included in the price). You'll also minimize the amount of gasoline used to transport your food. As the cost of energy mounts, it will become increasingly important for all states to have some kind of local agricultural base, and you will contribute to that by supporting local organic agriculture.

Many of the growers and producers listed here also supply stores in their local areas, and some are national suppliers. I urge you to use the local resources available to you: farmers' markets, organic sections of supermarkets, and your local organic and transitional growers. But I hope that after using this book you will feel that even without access to any of those resources, it's easy to stock your cabinets with organic foods.

For more information about organic farming, sustainable agriculture, and/or chemicals in food, here are some resources:

Americans for Safe Food
Center for Science in the Public Interest
1501 Sixteenth Street, NW
Washington, DC 20036
(202) 332-9110
ASF publishes a newsletter, *Safe Food Action.*

Center for Study of Responsive Law
P.O. Box 19367
Washington, DC 20036
The Center has published *Eating Clean,* a guide to food safety and regulatory policy.

Committee for Sustainable Agriculture
P.O. Box 1300
Colfax, CA 95713
(916) 346-2777
CSA has published *Growing for the Future: Organically Grown,* a magazine-format guide to organic agriculture for consumers.

Mothers and Others for Pesticide Limits
Natural Resources Defense Council
1350 New York Avenue, NW
Suite 300
Washington, DC 20005
(202) 783-7800
Mothers and Others has published *For Our Kids' Sake,* a guide to protecting children from pesticides in food. The NRDC has published *Pesticide Alert: A Guide to Pesticides in Fruits and Vegetables.*

National Coalition Against Misuse of Pesticides
530 Seventh Street SE
Washington, DC 20003
(202) 543-5450
Clearinghouse and newsletter.

Public Voice for Food and Health Policy
1001 Connecticut Avenue NW, Suite 522
Washington, DC 20036
(202) 659-5930
Public Voice has published studies on sustainable agriculture and other issues relevant to food safety.

Rodale Institute
Box 323
RD 1
Kutztown, PA 19530
(215) 683-6383
The Institute studies organic agriculture and is associated with the Rodale Press, publisher of *Organic Gardening* magazine.

Finally, if you are or know of an organic grower/retailer who does mail-order sales and is not included in this book, please let me know for the next edition.

Jeanne Heifetz
c/o HarperCollins Publishers
10 East 53rd Street
New York, NY 10022

GREEN GROCERIES

EARTH'S BEST® BABY FOOD
P.O. Box 887
Middlebury, VT 05753

Ingredients certified by: CCOF, FVO, NOFA, OR-TILTH, OCIA, OGBA, OGM, VABF, WSDA, others
Catalogue/price list: see below

VEGETABLES

Carrots · Green beans and rice · Peas and brown rice · Sweet potatoes · Winter squash

FRUIT

Apples · Apples and apricots · Apples and bananas · Apples and blueberries · Apples and plums · Bananas · Oatmeal and bananas · Peaches · Pears · Plums, bananas, and rice · Prunes and oatmeal

JUICE

Apple · Apple-grape · Pear

CEREAL

Brown rice · Mixed whole-grain

Arnie Koss, approaching forty, describes himself as a onetime hippie, chauffeur, Mexican cook, and maker of Shaker-style brooms. But, like many of his generation, Koss is now a parent, and that has brought a new role: president of Earth's Best Baby Food. The Koss brothers (Arnie's twin brother, Ron, is the company's treasurer) founded Earth's Best in 1987, shortly after their own children were born. Arnie Koss had managed a health-food store, where he had seen organic dog food come on the market—but not organic baby food.

The need was so obvious that it's hard to understand why the Koss brothers were turned down by more than 100 bankers, venture capitalists and investors. Once they finally raised start-up money, the Koss brothers didn't have to wait to see results. Their sales hit one million dollars in the first year. Not surprisingly,

Earth's Best has struck fear into the hearts of the Big Three—Gerber, Heinz, and Beech-Nut—because the side-by-side comparison in the supermarket raises the obvious question: If Earth's Best is organic, what does that say about the others?

In addition to requiring independent organic certification, Earth's Best sends field representatives to each farm it buys from, and has produce tested in the laboratory for pesticide residues. The foods are cooked for a short time at a high temperature to preserve flavor and nutrients. No sugar, preservatives, or fillers are added. The juices are made from whole fruit, not concentrate, and filtered just enough to make them suitable for bottles. The cereals are fortified with iron. All foods are kosher.

Earth's Best's literature is sprinkled with praise from parents and pediatricians of the "I've never written to a manufacturer before but I just had to tell you" variety. But don't just take parents' word for it. The *San Francisco Chronicle*'s adult food critic, Michael Bauer, compared Earth's Best to Gerber's, and "in every case, the organically grown product tasted sweeter and fresher." What more could you ask?

Earth's Best is not available directly by mail order from the company, but is available through Simply Delicious (page 278), Rising Sun Organic Food (page 276), and The Green Earth (page 283).

BREAD AND OTHER BAKED GOODS

All breads listed here start off with organic grain, but the similarity ends there: some bakeries use baker's yeast, while others use sourdough starter, also called "natural leavening." Sourdough starter can leaven more than thirty times its weight in dough, and advocates of this method explain that while bakers' yeast breaks down only a part of the wheat berry—the carbohydrate, or starchy portion—sourdough leavening acts on all the elements of the wheat berry, including the grain's bran layer, making its mineral content available for the body to use. Natural leavening combines a number of airborne fermenting agents, which break down complex carbohydrates into simple sugars more completely than yeast does. This ultimately makes a sourdough loaf easier to digest.

Some bakeries listed do not even use flour in the traditional sense. Instead, they allow the grains to sprout, and then grind the sprouts. If you are avoiding yeast, you should look for naturally leavened or sprout breads.

BALDWIN HILL BAKERY
Baldwin Hill Road
Phillipston, MA 01331
(508) 249-4691

Visits: yes
Ingredients certified by: OCIA, OGBA, GAIA, FVO
Catalogue/price list available
Minimum order: 12 loaves (can be an assortment)
Order by: phone, mail
Pay by: check
Ship by: UPS
Place your order on the Friday morning before the week you want it shipped

BREADS

Whole wheat · Sesame · Rye · Salt-free whole wheat · Raisin · French · Rice

In 1970, Dr. Herman Lerner met a bread that changed his life. Lerner, a Boston doctor, was convinced that diet and whole grains were an important part of human health. Then he received the fateful gift: a loaf of whole-grain sourdough from the LIMA bakery in Belgium. It was more delicious than anything he'd ever eaten. Then it was gone. Lerner had never baked before, but he took to the oven to try to reproduce that loaf. The quest eventually brought him to the source: Belgium, and the LIMA bakery.

On his return to the States, Lerner moved to a twenty-acre farm in northern Massachusetts where he set about to create an American version of LIMA, complete with wood-fired brick oven, fueled by remnants from local furniture factories. Today, it's running three shifts a day, 200 loaves at a time.

The *Boston Globe* has "often considered nominating the Phillipston bakery for a Nobel prize in breadbaking" for its "glorious" breads. *Food and Wine* raved. So did *Town and Country*. Julia Child "loves" the bread, says the bakery's manager, Phil Leger. This makes me feel as if I'm jumping on the local bandwagon since I live right down the street from Herself, but honestly, I've been a fan for years.

"Whole wheat" conjures up a tan-colored loaf, but Baldwin Hill's whole wheat is almost pumpernickel-dark, a not-sour sourdough with the rich flavor and dense texture of the best Central European peasant breads. There's no air in this loaf, a meal-in-itself bread that can stand up to sandwiches.

The rice bread, sourdough French, and sourdough rye are lighter in color. The rice bread is mildly flavored, slightly sweet and nutty, almost as moist as a sprouted-grain bread, and slightly spongy. The rye combines the earthy heft of Baldwin Hill's whole-wheat breads with the tang of a classic sourdough rye, making a great sandwich bread. The sourdough French is softer, lighter, and airier than most of the

bakery's breads, with a more obviously sour taste. The sesame wheat has a strong sesame flavor; I gave some to a real sesame fan who called the blend of sesame and sourdough "a real treat," and said it made a light, crispy toast. All of Baldwin Hill's breads are moist enough to hold up to toasting without drying out.

The universal winner was the raisin bread. Raisin fans, take note: three-quarters of a pound of raisins go into each one-and-a-half-pound loaf. I gave some to a neighbor whose sons are raisin-bread lovers. He'd been trying without success to get them to eat organic raisin bread; after one bite of the Baldwin Hill, he said, "Now *this* they'll eat. Where can I get it?" He walked off munching, and I'm not sure there was any left when the kids got home.

All grain, seeds, and raisins in Baldwin Hill breads are certified organic. The grain is ground locally; the water comes from an eighty-foot-deep well, which is periodically tested for bacteria growth (none has ever been found); and only sea salt is used. The bread is kosher.

In 1990, a dozen loaves were approximately $19, plus shipping.

BREAD & STUFF
HC 63, Box 41
Chester, MA 01011
(800) 733-2291
(413) 623-2291
FAX: (413) 623-5867

Farmers' market: downtown Springfield
Ingredients certified by: FVO, CCOF, OCIA
Catalogue/price list available
Minimum order: none
Order by: phone, mail, fax
Pay by: check, money order, COD, Visa, MC
Ship by: UPS
Bread is shipped Mondays, Tuesdays, and Wednesdays

BREADS

Whole wheat · Whole rye · Whole-wheat rice · Peasant French · Sesame · Sesame French · Baguette · San Francisco sourdough · Raisin

COOKIES

Oatmeal raisin · Sesame · Raisin nut · Carob chip

MUNCHIES

Carob chip · Cinnamon raisin

CEREAL

Berkshire Mountain Muesli

Bread & Stuff sells the breads of Berkshire Mountain Bakery, whose head baker, Richard Bourdon, learned his trade in Holland, where he was the head baker of the "first bakery to rediscover and develop this forgotten traditional way of baking." Bourdon continues to bake in the European manner: the French peasant bread, for example, is baked right on the oven floor.

Berkshire Mountain Bakery's ingredients are almost entirely organic, and the grains are ground fresh at the bakery. If you're allergic to wheat, you might try the whole rye, which is entirely wheat-free—the starter is kept on rye flour. The whole-wheat bread is soft and not very dense with a mild sourdough taste; as toast, it is moist and slightly spongy. I much

Bread & Stuff
NATURAL SNACK FOOD
BY MAIL

prefer the San Francisco sourdough, a moist bread with a buttery, chewy crust and just a hint of sourdough tang.

The Berkshire Mountain Pastry Bakery, which produces the cookies, munchies, and muesli in the catalogue, is owned and operated by a Dutch baker, Sjon Welters, whose wife, Miriam, is one of the two founders of Bread & Stuff. Sjon Welters bakes almost entirely with organic ingredients, adds no sugar, and no dairy products. The munchies start with crispy brown rice and add various sweet treats like raisins, almonds, or carob chips. The muesli contains toasted rolled oats and barley flakes, sesame seeds, almonds, date pieces, and raisins.

In 1990, breads ranged from $1.49 to $3.65 a loaf. Cookies were 85 cents each or $7.55 a dozen. Muesli was $3.35 a pound. Bulk orders receive discounts.

BREAD ALONE
Route 28
Boiceville, NY 12412
(914) 657-3328

Visits: yes
Farmers' markets: Greenmarkets in Manhattan
Ingredients certified by: OCIA, OGBA, GAIA
Minimum order: 12 loaves
Order by: phone, mail
Pay by: check, COD, MC, Visa
Ship by: UPS (Second Day Air), FedEx

BREADS

Farm bread · Sourdough rye with caraway · Mixed grain · Miche · Peasant · Raisin pumpernickel · Whole-wheat walnut · Currant buns · *Pain sur levain*

Daniel Leader, the founder of Bread Alone, speaks with delight about his heroes: Parisian bread bakers, those "roly-poly men in worn T-shirts and flour-encrusted sneakers" who "never seem to have enough time to sleep." (The same could be said of Leader, who's up baking at 5 A.M.) "Their passion for bread is boundless—and in my case, infectious. Not only do I bake and talk bread, I dream bread too."

Leader started his cooking career in the early 1970s at the Culinary Institute of America. After graduating, he worked as a chef in New York and in Europe, where he found himself inexorably drawn to the bakeries. He brought their techniques back with him to upstate New York, where he started Bread Alone.

The most important feature of a French *boulangerie,* and by far the largest, says Leader, is the oven. For Bread Alone, Leader imported André LeFort, a third-generation oven builder, one of only two left in Paris, to oversee the building of two brick ovens. At sixty-three, LeFort had never been out of France. He spent over three months building the ovens. It took another two weeks to bring them up to baking temperature without cracking. As in Europe, the floor of each oven is raked like a theater, so that the bakers can see all the loaves at once, and prevent them from scorching. The one all-American note is the source of the wood: the discards of a baseball-bat factory.

Food writer and novelist Laurie Colwin describes Bread Alone as "the bread that made me stop baking. How can you compete?" The *New York Times*'s food writer, Nancy Harmon Jenkins, called the bread "extraordinary, with the crisp, friable crust and the dense, moist crumb of the best European versions." Craig Claiborne gave the bread his "Excellent" rating. But perhaps the highest compliment comes from a "very devout customer," who actually has Bread Alone ship bread to his home in France.

Leader doesn't stint on any of his ingredients. The walnut bread is chock-full of walnuts, the currant buns dense with currants, and the raisin pumpernickel with raisins. The walnut bread is perhaps the most unusual of his breads with a rich flavor more reminiscent of walnut oil than of the nuts themselves. If you have a sweet tooth, don't miss out on the dense, chewy currant buns. Both the walnut bread and the currant buns stand up well to cream cheese.

The raisin pumpernickel has a heady molasses aroma and taste; whether you like the bread will certainly depend on whether you like molasses. The sour rye is a delicious, satisfying whole-grain rendition of a traditional Eastern European rye, with the classic springy texture and rye tang. The miche is a first-rate strong-flavored sourdough.

The farm bread is a great whole-wheat bread with a bit of rye to give it tang, a little less unusual in flavor than some of the others. I found the mixed grain slightly dry and less appealing after the other standouts—one friend called it "relentlessly healthful," but another friend who grew up in Europe said it was her favorite. "The consistency reminds me of German peasant breads, like their linseed bread." Both the farm bread and mixed grain were good toasters and sandwich breads—and passed the test of our local nine-year-old critic with flying colors.

The French *pain sur levain*—sourdough—is Leader's "personal favorite." It's a gorgeous bread to look at: the classic elongated oval shape with two teardrop-shaped slashes in the chewiest of crusts, which has the slight smokiness of the wood fire. Although made with a whole-wheat flour, it's a much whiter bread than the others, with only 20 percent of the bran, and slightly sweet, the kind of bread you really don't want to put anything on except perhaps an equally delicious cheese. I had trouble keeping my friend Tom from eating the whole loaf at one sitting, and when I discovered a day or two later that the loaf was finished, I felt like crying.

Leader maintains his organic standard by making an annual visit to the farmers who grow his grain. Several of his breads—the miche, the sourdough rye with caraway, and the currant buns—begin with a sourdough starter and contain no yeast.

In 1990, breads ranged from $2.25 to $2.65 for a 1.5-pound loaf. The currant buns were $5.95 for a half-dozen.

FRENCH MEADOW BAKERY
2610 Lyndale Avenue South
Minneapolis, MN 55408
(612) 870-4740

Visits: yes
Farmers' markets: Main Minneapolis farmers' market, Saturday mornings
Ingredients certified by: OGBA, OCIA, FVO, CCOF
Bakery certified by: OGBA
Minimum order: $20
Order by: phone, mail
Pay by: check, Visa, MC
Ship by: UPS

BREADS

Whole wheat · Sesame wheat · Summer bread (a light, whole-wheat French) · Whole rye · Winter bread · Walnut rye with raisins · Pumpernickel · Date and almond brioche · Baguettes (summer dough) · Anaheim pepper · French with basil · French with dill · Austrian rye · Brown rice · Minnesota wild rice · Raisin ·

Oatmeal raisin · Sourdough batard · Sourdough baguettes · Sourdough buns

GRANOLA AND CEREAL

Cherry Berry · Cashew-coconut · Homestead · Pistachio-nut · Steel-cut oat · Prairie · Muesli

MUFFINS

Caramel wild rice · Blueberry oat bran · Carrot spice-bran · Raspberry caramel · Corn, jalapeño, and cheese · Sweet potato-prune

OTHER BAKED GOODS

Bagels · Scones · Pizza crust · Cherry-pecan corn bread

FLOUR

Golden white

No, your eyes are not deceiving you; French Meadow's seal really does read "Trans-Antarctica 1990 Expedition Official Bread." The award for "Most Intrepid Fan of French Meadow Bread" goes to Will Steger, the first man to reach the North Pole by dogsled. Before setting out on an Antarctic trek, Steger and his team sampled breads throughout the Midwest, and chose French Meadow as their official loaf.

After Steger's practice run in Greenland, Lynn Gordon, French Meadow's owner and master baker, sent a congratulatory cake to the expedition, and set to work on making a biscuit the explorers could easily carry to the Antarctic. Ten months before Steger was due to set out, Gordon had 200 pounds of bread and 600 pounds of granola air-dropped every 400 miles along Steger's route, where they were stored in underground depots. Steger wrote back that even the year-old bread was great—but unfortunately, the chocolate truffles she'd made as a special treat got lost in a snowstorm. (I think some penguins out there are having one heck of an endorphin high.)

My theory about Steger is that he took French Meadow breads with him to the Antarctic because you'd have to go someplace completely unpopulated to get to keep them all to

yourself. My warning about these breads is that if you serve any to friends, you'd better have a catalogue handy—if you don't give them the chance to order their own, you may find yours missing.

Bon Appétit called French Meadow bread one of the ten best in the country, a "fabulous freshly baked sourdough," and singled out the Minnesota wild rice, Anaheim pepper, seven-grain prairie, ginger carrot, and sourdough French loaves as "favorites—chewy and long-lasting." *Minneapolis St. Paul* magazine awarded French Meadow Bakery first place in the "Fruit Breads" category for the date and almond brioche. "I don't know where the brioche name comes from," said their food writer, "as this loaf contains neither fat nor eggs, but I couldn't stop snacking on it. A solid wheat loaf studded generously with big toasted almonds and chunks of sweet date. The lack of sugar in the dough allows the natural character of wheat, almond, and date to sing out."

I sampled the French bread with basil; the French bread with dill; and the Homestead bread, created for Steger's trek. All three breads had enormous life to them, dense and remarkably moist. Both French breads had perfect, chewy crusts, and the basil, in particular, was a wonderful complement to cheese, tomatoes, and garlic butter. The Homestead was a substantial, first-rate sandwich bread. The sweetness of the grain balanced the sourdough tang; it had none of the dryness multi-grain breads can have.

In 1990, Lynn Gordon was busy expanding her line to include pizza dough, which comes with a recipe for create-your-own pepper pizza, granolas, bagels, tantalizing muffins, and scones. We all have Will Steger to thank for the granolas, concocted especially for his Antarctic trek. Each is a marvelous combination of flavors and textures. The dried cherries and blueberries give an intense zing to the cherry berry granola; the pistachio-nut's combination of maple and nuts tastes completely sinful. I tasted them and a wave of selfishness came over me. I actually hid them on an out-of-the-way shelf. Where did I put my catalogue?

French Meadow Bakery uses no yeast, dairy products, or sweeteners in its breads. The organic grains are stone-ground only hours before going into the bread dough, and you can buy the flour Lynn Gordon uses from the bakery. The water comes from springs in Minnesota and Wisconsin. The granolas and cereals contain organic grains, and as many other organic ingredients as possible.

In 1990, granolas were $3.75 a pound. The breads range from 20 to 24 ounces, and from $2 to $3.50. Muffins were $1.50. Two pizza crusts were $2.75.

MILL CITY SOURDOUGH BAKERY
1566 Randolph Avenue
St. Paul, MN 55105
(800) 87D-OUGH
(612) 698-4705
FAX: (612) 698-7049

Ingredients certified by: OCIA, OGBA, CCOF, FVO
Catalogue/price list available
Minimum order: 6 loaves
Order by: phone, mail, fax
Pay by: check
Ship by: UPS

SOURDOUGH BREADS

French · French peasant · Whole wheat · Wild rice · Brown rice · Sesame · Rye · Finnish rye · Raisin-almond

In 1982, doctors told John Mattox III, an investment banker, that he had lung cancer. They gave him a 5 percent chance of surviving. He had two operations, followed by radiation treatment. Then his wife, Mary Ann, a trained nurse, quit her job to look after him. She began feeding him a macrobiotic, organic diet, and in less than two months, John Mattox had returned to work part-time. While Mary Ann Mattox doesn't say that the change in diet cured her husband, she does believe it played an important part in his recovery. It also changed her life. At the age of fifty, Mattox had discovered what she really wanted to do: bake bread.

Instead of going back to her administrative job, Mattox took her whole-grain bread recipes and founded Mill City Sourdough, which was an almost overnight success. *Minneapolis St. Paul* magazine awarded Mill City's Finnish rye first place in the "Straight Rye" category. "This all-organic loaf has a dense, moist, grainy texture that makes it a pleasure to chew. There's assertive caraway backed by a hint of sourdough. Excellent for sandwiches." The magazine also awarded Mill City first place in the "Sourdough White" category for its French peasant bread. "Dense crust sprinkled with bran; moist, tight, resilient crumb redolent with the aromas of new hay, flavored with deep sour tang and full wheat. A fine example of the kind of bread celebrated in the French countryside, and in America before the Industrial Revolution." Mill City also won first place in the "Sourdough Whole Wheat" category: "Whole wheat flavor dominates sour tang here for good balance in a wonderfully dense and moist loaf."

I sampled the French peasant bread, the French peasant baguette, and the sesame. All

were soft, dense breads, with soft crusts that needed time in the oven to crisp up and create some contrast with the interior. The sesame had a generous helping of sesame seeds—the top of the bread was completely covered—and a pronounced sourdough flavor. Slightly drier than the other two breads, it went well toasted with strong-flavored spreads, like hummus and pickled herring. The French peasant's sourdough flavor made a nice complement to the sweetness of a friend's leek-and-potato soup on a cool fall evening; the slightly dry bread called out for butter or dunking.

All Mill City breads begin with a sourdough starter. Mary Ann Mattox personally buys all the grain that goes into Mill City breads, traveling to OCIA meetings in North and South Dakota several times a year to meet grain growers. The hard winter and spring wheat is stoneground at the bakery, preserving all the grain's nutrients. In breads that call for a lighter texture, Mattox adds some sifted organic flour (without bran). None contains dairy products, sweeteners, or cholesterol. Only the raisin-almond contains oil. The rye bread (not the Finnish rye) contains no wheat flour. The water is purified using a nonchemical system, and the bread is kosher and pareve.

In 1990, the breads, which weigh between 1 and 4 pounds, ranged in price from $2 to $6.

NATURE'S STOREHOUSE
Highway 108
P.O. Box 69
Lynn, NC 28750
(704) 859-6356

Visits: yes
Ingredients certified by: OCIA, FVO, SELF
Catalogue/price list available
Minimum order: $10
Order by: phone, mail
Pay by: check, money order, COD
Ship by: UPS, mail

BREADS

Whole wheat · Sunflower · Jewish rye · Sprouted whole wheat · Date-walnut · Raisin-nut · Herb · Russian black · Barley-soy · Nutty-pineapple, 100% whole wheat · Five-grain · Sourdough French

Shelly Woodward had always been interested in natural foods, and her husband, Doug, loved to bake. The two worked for United Van Lines, but when Nature's Storehouse came on the market, "We just snatched it right on up," says Shelly. From what I could tell over the phone, the Woodwards run Nature's Storehouse like an old-time homey general store—people came in and chatted while Shelly and I talked; there was lots of laughter, and regulars whose purchases were added to a running tab at the register.

Nature's Storehouse had been in business for nine years before the Woodwards bought it, and they inherited bread recipes along with the store. They've improved on the old recipes and added new ones. "All the breads fly out of here," says Shelly, who says that the barley-soy is their best seller. She calls it "our version of a squishy white bread, so kids will eat it. It is a white bread, but it's enriched with barley and soy flours, so parents know they're giving children something that's good for them." All their breads are made with organic flour, but not all flour is certified.

In 1990, breads ranged from $1.20 to $2 for a 1-pound loaf. Shipping additional. The store carries a wide variety of natural foods, including many bulk items, which the Woodwards will ship to people who are interested.

NOKOMIS FARMS
3293 Main Street
East Troy, WI 53120
(414) 642-9665
FAX: (414) 642-4028

Visits: yes, for bread and organic meat
Ingredients certified by: OGBA, OCIA
Bakery, crops, seed cleaning certified by: OGBA
Catalogue/price list available
Minimum order: none
Order by: phone, mail, fax
Pay by: check
Ship by: UPS

KETTLE MORAINE SOURDOUGH BREADS

Country loaf · Whole rye · Wheat and rye · Sesame · Muesli · Wild rice

YEAST BREADS

Whole wheat · Farmer's loaf · Whole-wheat rolls · Wheat and rye rolls

When I first saw the name Kettle Moraine Sourdough, I thought it must be some unusual method of baking bread in a kettle. In fact, a moraine is a geological formation: the Kettle Moraine hills, in southeastern Wisconsin, are not far from Nokomis's 500 acres of cropland, pastures, and woodlands.

Yes, that's Nokomis, as in "By the shores of Gitche Gumee,/By the shining Big-Sea-Water,/Stood the wigwam of Nokomis,/Daughter of the Moon, Nokomis." Nokomis Farms restores dignity to the name, a Native American word for grandmother. In Ojibway legend, say the people at Nokomis Farms, "She was a nature goddess who taught her children knowledge of the kingdoms and nature and, above all, respect for all of creation."

That respect is central to the people at Nokomis Farms, who follow the biodynamic methods of the Austrian educator Rudolf Steiner, and "consider the earth to be a living organism. Like homeopathic medicine, biodynamic processes radiate through the whole landscape." The proof of their methods came in the drought of 1988, "the worst drought in decades. While farmers around us were experiencing disaster, we had excellent yields."

The folks at Nokomis Farms have an ambitious goal: "to heal the earth." Part of that process is "to provide pure, healthy food for our fellow human beings." The Nokomis Farms bakery, founded in 1984, makes "pure, healthy food" using only whole, stone-ground organic grain. The loaves are shaped by hand, not machine.

Although Nokomis Farms ships only to the Midwest, I sampled the Kettle Moraine sourdough wild rice bread, courtesy of The Green Earth (page 283). Unlike other rice breads I've had—and made—this was a dark, rich loaf. The rice keeps this dense bread moist, even when toasted, and gives a slight stickiness to the dough. The sourdough acting on the rice creates a flavor more like rice wine than like rice itself. The bread is a very good keeper, and its moisture makes it an excellent, flavorful toast, with a fine, crunchy crust.

In 1990, breads weighed 20 to 28 ounces and ranged from $1.58 to $1.89. Packages of 6 3-ounce rolls were $1.45. Shipping additional. Because the bread contains no preservatives, Nokomis Farms ships primarily to the Midwest. If you live outside that area, contact The Green Earth (page 283), which will ship Nokomis Farms bread to a wider area by Next Day Air or Second Day Air.

PONCÉ BAKERY
116 West 12th Street
Chico, CA 95928
(916) 891-8354

Visits: yes
Ingredients certified by: CCOF, FVO, OCIA, TILTH, SELF, CHSC
Catalogue/price list available
Minimum order: none
Order by: phone, mail
Pay by: check, COD
Ship by: UPS ground and air
Place orders by noon on Friday for shipments the following Monday; UPS Zone 2 (local) shipments go out on Wednesdays
The bakery is closed December 24–January 1, and July 21–August 19

BREAD

Whole wheat · Light wheat · Sesame wheat · Poppyseed wheat · Whole rye · Raisin rye · Walnut-raisin rye · Barley wheat · Country wheat-rye · Raisin brioche · Almond raisin · Walnut · Brié · Sesame buns · Raisin brioches · Onion-wheat rolls

For Jean Adrian Poncé, "naturally leavened" is not a type of bread—it is the *only* bread. Anything else, says Poncé, is simply lifeless. He will not allow baker's yeast into his building because it might taint his natural leaven.

Jean Poncé prefers "naturally leavened" to "sourdough," which has come to mean a flavor rather than a method of baking. "If a sourdough is sour," says Mimi Tesseidre, Poncé's partner, "that's the fault of the baker. What they call San Francisco sourdough is really a yeast bread with some sourdough and vinegar added to make it sour. A sourdough bread should really be as sweet as possible." As for the white breads that come out of factories by the thousands, the French-born Poncé cannot even bring himself to call them "food," much less "bread."

When Poncé was a young man, his lungs filled with mucus; doctors wanted to operate. Poncé refused, ran away, taking his life—and diet—into his own hands. By eating only whole-grain bread and eliminating dairy products, he brought himself back to health.

In 1964, Poncé came to Los Angeles to visit friends, and decided to stay on. Given his diet, he went shopping for whole-grain bread. He found none. Poncé began to think of opening a bakery and making that bread himself. He studied and experimented. Mimi Tesseidre wrote to friends in France for recipes using natural leaven, but even there no one seemed to know how to make bread without yeast. In 1978, in France for a visit, Poncé came across a group of young people who had bought a bakery in Paris. Poncé studied alongside them as they learned to bake naturally leavened breads from the eighty-five-year-old master baker, who was about to retire.

Poncé returned to the United States and took a job as the caretaker of an estate in northern California's Klamath valley, near the Oregon border. He installed several pizza ovens in the estate's garage, and his baking career was born.

Poncé is scrupulous about his ingredients. All grains are organically grown. Almost without exception, other ingredients are organic, down to walnuts, raisins, almonds, and citrus peel. He grinds grain fresh for each batch of bread, using traditional stone burrs and slow grinding, to avoid heating the grain and destroying enzymes and vitamins. Because he uses whole grains, the oil content of the flour is quite high, and must be used fresh. The bread needs less salt than other breads, says Poncé, because the freshly ground grain is so flavorful. The water is chemically pure, and the salt is sea salt. These breads will keep up to two weeks in the refrigerator.

Some of his breads are rectangular loaves; others are beautiful, European-style rounds and ovals, with the traditional diagonal slashes. I sampled the barley, whole rye, Brié, sesame, onion-wheat roll, and raisin brioche. All of them were robust and dense, with chewy crusts, slightly dry out of the bag, but they came alive when toasted, growing—oddly—softer and moister.

I understood immediately what Mimi Tesseidre had meant about the sourdough taste; these breads were not at all sour, except for the rye, which was almost too sour for my taste. The orion-wheat roll, an organic version of a bulky roll, had plenty of onion flavor. A real sesame lover would miss the crunch of the seeds in the sesame bread: in this version, the seeds are mixed into the dough and almost disappear, creating a fainter taste, like sesame oil, but a great base for peanut butter. The raisin brioche was not a brioche in the traditional sense—not a light, eggy dough, but a dense, chewy one, appealingly full of raisins. My favorites were the barley, an earthy European peasant bread, and the Brié (nothing to do with the cheese), a dense but light golden wheat bread, almost as sweet as zwieback when toasted.

Breads are available in 1-, 2-, 4-, and 6-pound loaves. In 1990, a 1-pound loaf ranged from $1.70 to $3.50. A 6-pound loaf ranged from $7.25 to $8.20. A package of 6 three-quarter-pound buns was $4.20. Shipping additional. The bread subscription club delivers bread to you (or a friend, with gift card) on a schedule of your choice.

SHEPHERDSFIELD BAKERY
777 Shepherdsfield Road
Fulton, MO 65251-9473
(314) 642-1439

Certified by: OCIA, SELF, FVO, GAIA, OGBA
Catalogue/price list available
Minimum order: none
Order by: phone, mail
Pay by: check, money order
Ship by: UPS
Gift packages available; special gifts possible for Mother's Day, Father's Day, birthdays

BREADS OR MINILOAVES

Whole wheat · Cinnamon-raisin · Rye · Potato rolls (sandwich or dinner)

MUFFINS

Cinnamon-date swirls · Poppyseed · Spiced apple-carrot

FLOUR

Stone-ground whole wheat

SPECIALTY ITEMS

Whole-wheat gourmet waffles

The breads from Shepherdsfield Bakery have the feel, smell, and taste of homemade, the kinds of breads you bake for family and friends. It's not surprising that Shepherdsfield Bakery got its start in a small, close-knit community. Debby Mahaney, who supervises the bakery, describes the Shepherdsfield community as a group of about 100 people who have dedicated their lives to the Lord and to one another. The bakers' work, says Mahaney, is part of their commitment to serve the Lord in everything they do.

At first, the bakery's breads went to feed the community's members, but they've developed a loyal following around the country and have won prizes at the Missouri State Fair, including "Best of Class" and "Best of Show," and the "Bread Sweepstakes" award in 1986, 1987, and 1988.

Like the best recipes, Shepherdsfield's breads, muffins, and waffles were developed by trading and swapping and experimenting. Mahaney says that the community's favorite is still the whole wheat, which they developed using bits of *everyone's* recipes.

All the breads are soft but pleasingly dense and moist, make perfect toast, and would be a cinch to get kids to eat. The rye is a completely

satisfying blend of caraway and rye. The cinnamon bread is much more spicy than sweet. The white bread is rich with the extra sweetness of the potato, and the whole-wheat has a hint of molasses.

All three muffins are moist and light. My favorite is the poppyseed, dense and buttery as the best poppyseed cake. The apple-carrot muffin is a sort of generic, healthy spice muffin, dominated by nutmeg, Neither apple nor carrot to squash or pumpkin. The cinnamon-date swirls are handsome little rolls, far lighter than traditional sticky buns, with much more date than cinnamon flavor.

I hate to admit it, but the waffles are better than my own—and I pride myself on my talent with my grandmother's vintage waffle iron. They were crisp on the outside and fluffy on the inside, not at all sticky or doughy. On a busy morning, a first-rate waffle that needs only a few minutes in the toaster oven is a true luxury.

Breads are baked fresh daily, and the waffles are made individually. With the exception of the potato-roll flour, all the flours are stone-ground on the premises and turned immediately into bread dough, so that the oil in the germ remains fresh. The water comes from a 490-foot-deep well whose water has been tested for purity. Thomas J. Mahaney, Jr., of Shep-

herdsfield Bakery, calls the well "one of God's blessings to us, and a vital ingredient in our baked goods." The only sweeteners are local Missouri honey and molasses, or dates and raisins (not necessarily organic). The bread contains no preservatives.

In 1990, 2-pound breads ranged from $2.50 to $2.85. Potato rolls (6 sandwich or 12 dinner) were $2.40. Six muffins ranged from $2.25 to $3.75. Four waffles were $3. Flour was $1 for a 2-pound bag. Miniloaves (12 ounces) were $1.25. Gift packages and assortments ranged from $14 to $50. You can also arrange to have regular shipments of bread weekly or monthly. Shipping additional.

SILL HOUSE BAKERY
40 Sill House
Coxe Farm
Old Lyme, CT 06371
(203) 434-9501

Visits: yes, for salad greens, fresh vegetables, and breads when available
Ingredients certified by: OGBA, OCIA, GAIA
Catalogue/price list available
Minimum order: 7 pounds
Order by: mail
Pay by: Check, money order
Ship by: UPS
Breads are shipped Tuesdays

BREADS OR "POPS" (MUFFINS)

Rye wheat · Rye with seed (sunflower, flax, or caraway) · Wheat with seed · Jalapeño wheat · Rye with fruit (currants, raisin, cinnamon; or currants, raisins, fresh ginger) · Wheat with fruit · Rye croutons · Wheat croutons · Raw rye wafers (sunflower, flax, sesame, caraway, jalapeño) · Raw fruit-sweet rye wafers (currants or raisins, sunflower, flax, sesame seeds, and chia seeds if available)

Ruth Coxe has been in the food business since 1963. Her first shop, in San Francisco's financial district, served submarine sandwiches with organic ingredients, and "Coxe Box Lunches" with names like the Vegetarial and the Fructivorian. Echoing FDR's famous Four Freedoms, her husband, Samuel Coxe, a constitutional lawyer, formulated the Four Health Freedoms: "Freedom from irresponsible endorsement by government of indiscriminate use of drugs; freedom to buy fresh food free of pesticide poisons; freedom to buy prepared food without artificial preservatives added; non-discriminatory freedom for babies to have the God-given right to mother's milk instead of substitutes and supplements. A threat to the four health freedoms threatens all freedoms."

Twenty-eight years later, Ruth Coxe is still fighting for those freedoms, using organic ingredients, and baking breads without yeast, fats, sugar, or salt. Coxe calls her breads "flourless fuel" because the grains have been sprouted in pure well water rather than ground directly into flour. Coxe warns that "flour can be dead and just ferment in the body instead of nourishing it." Sprouting the grains, she says, converts the flour's starch into maltose sugar

and makes the protein easier to digest so that it "tastes like a cake and digests like a vegetable."

The breads are small but substantial, similar in size and chewiness to a fresh bagel (without the hole or the glazed crust). The "pops" are doughnut-hole size, and just as dense and chewy.

You can tell from the handwritten additions to the printed labels that Ruth Coxe is always experimenting. She's found that the sprouted bread has such a strong grain taste that only certain flavors come through. Garlic, for example, didn't work—no matter how much she put in, the garlic flavor was buried. On the other hand, she's had luck with jalapeño peppers, which she likes to combine with sprouted

rye, which has a sweetness that balances the pepper and is "quite satisfying." The one I tried was pretty fiery, and she makes an extra-hot variety for customers on request. The rye "pop" with currants, raisin, and cinnamon was moist and dense, with the rich sweetness of the grain and fruit. My favorite pop contained currants, raisins, and sweet, pungent fresh ginger.

In 1990, a 1-pound package of 3 breads was $2.25. A half-pound package of pops was $1.75. One pound of croutons was $3.50. One pound of wafers was $12. Shipping additional.

SPROUT DELIGHTS BAKERY
13090 N.W. 7th Avenue
North Miami, FL 33168-2702
(800) 334-2253
(305) 687-5880
FAX: (305) 687-3233

Visits: yes
Certified by: OCIA, FVO, CHSC
Catalogue/price list available
Minimum order: $20
Order by: phone, mail, fax
Pay by: check, money order, Visa, MC
Ship by: UPS Second Day Air

BREADS

Sprouted wheat · Sprouted wheat raisin · Sprouted wheat date · Sprouted wheat seed · Sprouted wheat veggie loaf · Sprouted rye seed · Sprouted rye

CAKES

Sprouted wheat fruit and nut · Just Fruit · Go Bananas · Totally Nuts

MUFFINS

Whole wheat · Sesame · Cinnamon raisin · Oat bran · Sunny millet

BROWNIES

Carob fudge · Chocolate fudge

MISCELLANEOUS

Vegetarian sprout burgers

When Steven Bern graduated from college, he got a job offer from the Federal Reserve Bank —but why take banker's hours when you can have baker's hours: up at 1 A.M., at the bakery by 1:30, ten to twelve hours of baking, then paperwork, deliveries, and a few hours of dealing with people on the West Coast?

At Sprout Delights, Bern bakes "the traditional Bible bread of the Essenes," but Bern admits that the Essenes didn't leave anything so clear as a recipe behind in the Dead Sea Scrolls. "It's more of a poetic verse." Bern turned to this ancient method out of frustration with modern bread baking. "Bread used to be called the 'Staff of Life.' Today, most bread is made with bleached and bromated white flour, dough conditioners, preservatives, stabilizers and vitamin fortification. Some call it the 'Staff of Death,' and rightfully so."

By contrast, Bern starts with certified organic grains, which he turns into sprouts.

SPROUT DELIGHTS®

Sprouting, says Bern, doesn't just mean wetting the grains and forgetting about them. Grains sprout at different rates when there's a full moon, or a cold front, or a power outage. If you wait too long, you've got full-blown wheat grass, which is fine for juice, but not for baking. Bern treats the sprouts as fresh, perishable foods; they're never ground in advance. Once ground, they're in the oven within fifteen minutes, and baked slowly at low temperatures "to preserve the delicate flavor and moisture balance."

Sprouting doesn't just improve flavor. It also "increases the protein by up to 20 percent, and converts the starch of the grain's complex carbohydrates to simple sugars, primarily maltose, which increases by up to 600 percent. This is

what gives Sprout Delight breads their sweetness and cakelike consistency." When you taste the bread, you will find it hard to believe that no sweeteners are used in the process.

These breads are small, dense, and moist, more like dessert fruit breads or cakes in texture than like traditional sandwich loaves. I sampled the basic sprouted wheat loaf, whose flavor and texture were reminiscent of a sweet bran muffin, and made a delicious breakfast toast.

If you have a sweet tooth, and want a healthy way to indulge it, a quick glance at the ingredients of Bern's cakes should get your mouth watering: the sprouted wheat fruit and nut contains pineapple, raisins, figs, dates, pecans, almonds, and walnuts. In "Just Fruit," you'll find Hunza mulberries, apricots, dates, and raisins. "Go Bananas" uses whole dried bananas and walnuts to create a sprouted version of banana bread. And, for nut-lovers, "Totally Nuts" has a bit of everything: almonds, pignolia nuts, filberts, sunflower seeds, and pecans.

All grains, and almost all other ingredients, are certified organic. Sprout Delight loaves contain no yeast, and Bern makes several wheat-free loaves. The water is purified and free of chemicals. All baked goods are made without eggs or dairy products, and are kosher and pareve. The vegetarian burgers come baked and ready to eat. The moisture content of the bread is very high, which makes it fairly perishable, but there's good news. In 1990, Bern started shrink-wrapping the bread with a packet that absorbs oxygen. This prevents spoiling, and enables him to ship the bread anywhere.

In 1990, 1-pound breads were $3. A 20-ounce fruit cake was $5. Muffins were $2.25 for a package of 4. Brownies were $1.10 each. A package of 4 sprout burgers was $4. Shipping and handling on all orders was $4. (A free brownie came with the initial order.)

SEE ALSO
Allergy Resources, Loafers' Glory,
Summercorn Foods

CHEESE

The cheeses listed here start with milk from cows or goats that have not been given hormones or antibiotics. In most cases, the animals' feed is entirely organic. When the animals also eat nonorganic feed, that is listed.

BRIER RUN FARM
Route 1, Box 73
Birch River, WV 26610
(304) 649-2975

Visits: "rarely—it's four-wheel-drive access only"
Certified by: OCIA
Catalogue/price list available
Minimum order: none
Order by: phone, mail
Pay by: check, MC, Visa
Ship by: UPS

GOAT CHEESE

Quark · Fromage blanc · Chabis · Banon · Pyramid · Crottin · Bûche · Chèvre blue · Chèvre blanc · Chèvre fudge

Greg and Verena Sava were teaching at a boarding school in Albany, New York when they decided they wanted to go back to the land. They headed for the Appalachians, which reminded Verena of her Swiss homeland, and where—more important—land was cheap. The Savas bought eighty acres by a stream called the Brier Run. Then they bought an old house and used the wood to build a goat shed, a hen house, and, finally, their own home.

Those purchases left them with twenty-four dollars a week. The question was how to make a living from the land. They bought their first goat, Squeaky, from a local preacher. But goats are sociable creatures, and Squeaky let them know that she wanted company. Soon they had five goats, and more milk than they knew what to do with. Cheese was the natural next step, but Greg Sava says he'd rather forget the early attempts: something hard and white, not particularly identifiable as cheese. Then Verena sought the help of a cheese inspector in the Swiss Alps, who sent them some Swiss bacteria. They started making a Swiss cheese, minus holes. The cheese was a local success, but it couldn't really command a price to match the amount of labor involved, so Verena went back to teaching, and Greg moved into chèvres.

Two years later, in 1987, the Savas took their chèvre to the annual meeting of the American Cheese Society. With 135 goat cheeses in the running, Brier Run carried off one blue, two red, and one white ribbon. At the 1990 meeting, Brier Run was rated "Best in Class" for fresh goat cheeses. The executive chef of the National Press Club told the *New York Times*

that Brier Run's chèvre was "the best in the country."

The cheeses cover the range of chèvre textures and flavors, from creamy to hard, from sweet to salty. Some come with organic herbs like basil or lemon thyme, and others with a traditional ash coating. Quark is a light cheese popular in Europe, not unlike thick yogurt. You can spread quark on toast, muffins, or bagels, toss it on pasta, substitute it for sour cream or mayonnaise to garnish soups, salads, and vegetables, fresh fruit, cereals, pies, pancakes, or even make a cheesecake "that won't leave you feeling full and guilty."

At certain times of year, Brier Run also has aged, mold-ripened cheese available. The chèvre blue uses the same mold that goes into Roquefort cheeses, and is a "smooth-textured piquant cheese that goes well with a full-bodied red wine." The chèvre blanc uses the same kind of mold that goes into a Brie or Camembert, which gives the cheese "a distinct but mild flavor and a velvety smooth texture."

The Savas do everything by hand: the only machines in the cheesemaking process are the pasteurizer and the refrigerator. The cheese is processed without preservatives, mold inhibitors, or coloring. In 1990, Brier Run cheese became the first commercial producer of chèvre to be certified organic by OCIA.

In 1990, cheeses ranged from $2.25 to $4.50, plus shipping.

DUTCH MILL CHEESE
State Road I and I-70
Cambridge City, IN 47327-9436
(317) 478-5847

Visits: yes
Certified by: SELF
Catalogue/price list available
Minimum order: none
Order by: phone, mail
Pay by: check, Visa, MC
Ship by: UPS
Cheese can shipped September–May

CHEESE

Butter · Amish · Colby · Hot Pepper · Disco · Cheddar · Farmer's · Swiss · Baby Swiss · Low-salt Baby Swiss · Weight Checker

While most Americans probably associate the Amish with Pennsylvania, the largest settlement of Amish families in the country is in the hills of northeastern Ohio, where Dutch Country cheeses are made.

"The Amish are well known as organic farmers," says Jean Overbay of Dutch Mill Cheese, "but they do not co-operate with the government to be certified. Tasting the product will tell the story." In fact, Amish farmers use even less fossil energy than many organic farmers: not only do they shun petroleum-based fertilizers or pesticides, they also farm without using electricity or gasoline. They grow the cows' feed without any chemicals and milk the cows by hand rather than by machine.

Milk cans are taken daily to the cheese factory, where the workers are also Amish. The milk is not homogenized, but is pasteurized in the cheese-making process. The cheese-making or clotting enzyme comes from vegetables, not animals. All coloring comes from vegetable extract. No preservatives are added.

Dutch Mill sells a range of cheeses, including Butter, which it calls a white "New World Havarti"; Amish, a white brick cheese; a full-cream Swiss and the lower-fat Baby Swiss; and Disco, a mild combination of yellow and white Colbys. The farmer's cheese is low in sodium and cholesterol. Weight Checker, a white cheese, is the lowest of all in fat.

In 1990, a 3-pound wheel was $14.95. A 3-pound variety pack of Colby, Disco, Baby Swiss, and Butter was $15.95. You save on 6 or more wheels shipped to the same address. Shipping included.

Amish Cheese Shop

DUTCH MILL CHEESE

HAWTHORNE VALLEY FARM
RD 2, Box 225A
Harlemville
Ghent, NY 12075
(518) 672-7500
(518) 672-4465
FAX: (518) 672-4887

Visits: yes (hard and soft cheeses, yogurt, granolas, breads)
Farmers' markets: Union Square in Manhattan, Saturdays
Apprenticeships available
Certified biodynamic by: Demeter
Minimum order: 7–10 pounds
Catalogue/price list available
Order by: mail, fax
Pay by: check, money order
Ship by: UPS

CHEESE

Alpine · Raclette

Rudolf Steiner, an Austrian philosopher and educator, envisioned a life in which the arts, agriculture, and education were inextricably linked. Hawthorne Valley Farm, a branch of the nonprofit Rudolf Steiner Educational and Farming Association, brings that vision to life. The 400-acre farm, purchased in the mid-1970s by a group of teachers, includes a private K–12 day school and a visiting students program that gives inner-city children a week-long farm experience.

"Biodynamic farming," the type of agriculture Steiner developed, means more than simply avoiding chemicals. It requires a relationship with the cosmos. The folks at Hawthorne Valley believe that "the ecological relationships with which a farmer works ultimately include not only the whole earth as a living organism but also the realms beyond the earth, from which come the light and warmth of the sun and the rhythmic workings of the stars and planets. Such thoughts, however, are of little value unless grasped in full clarity and concretely applied to the practical affairs of farming."

Those "practical affairs" include making the farm as self-sufficient as possible. Hawthorne Valley's cheese starts with raw milk from the farm's own herd of fifty Brown Swiss and Holstein cows. All the feed comes from the land itself and contains no hormones or antibiotics. The cows graze freely in summer and get daily exercise, even in the coldest weather. The longer the cows are on pasture, say the folks at Hawthorne Valley, the better the cheese. They are milked twice a day, and in keeping with the cyclical nature of biodynamic farming, the whey left over from the cheese-making process goes to feed the farm's pigs and cows.

Tom Myers, the farm's cheese maker, came to Hawthorne Valley in 1980, after an apprenticeship in Switzerland. Myers starts the cheese with live cultures and vegetable rennet. The cheese is kept in a brine bath for a day to form a natural, edible rind, and then aged in the cellars for sixty days to a year.

As befits a Swiss-trained cheesemaker, Myers makes two cheeses that have a Swiss heritage. Hawthorne Valley Farm describes the Alpine cheese as "a firm cheese reminiscent of the mountain cheeses made in Switzerland and France. When young it is very mild; as it matures, the flavor becomes more assertive and complex." The Raclette is "a semisoft specialty cheese with a mild flavor and buttery consistency, made during pasture season only. The traditional Swiss raclette calls for a half-wheel of the cheese to be placed near a fire—or other heat source—until it begins to melt; as it melts, it is scraped with a knife onto a waiting plate."

In 1990, Alpine cheese came in 10- to 14-pound wheels and Raclette in 7- to 10-pound wheels. Both were $4.60 a pound, plus shipping.

LITTLE RAINBOW CHEVRE

Box 379
Rodman Road
Hillsdale, NY 12529
(518) 325-3351

Visits: by appointment
Farmers' markets: Union Square in Manhattan,
Wednesdays, Fridays, Saturdays
Certified by: SELF
Minimum order: none
Catalogue/price list available
Order by: phone, mail
Pay by: check
Ship by: UPS

CHEESES

Chèvre logs · No-salt chèvre logs (plain,
cracked peppercorn, herb roll) · Chèvre with
basil · Chèvre with dill · Chèvre with parsley,
sage, rosemary, and thyme · Chèvre with
garlic · Pepper chèvre · Special herb roll (the
herbs are secret) · *Crottin mediterranéen* ·
Crottin affiné · *Petit crottin affiné* · *Chèvre de
ferme* (plain, with peppercorns, or smoked) ·
Goatsarella · Berkshire Blue · *Chèvre d'amour* ·
Chèvre with grape leaves

Of all the clippings I received while working
on this book, none was as much fun to pull out
of the envelope as the May 1990 issue of *Scho-
lastic News.* Under the heading "A Day at the
Dairy," there's a shot of a ruby-cheeked Daniel
Reed feeding the kids: six brown-and-white
Toggenburg goats, no taller than Daniel's knee,
suck milk through straws from a bright yellow
pail. In other shots, Daniel unloads hay, pours
milk into the cooling tank, and shows off a
wheel of finished cheese.

Daniel has plenty to be proud of: Little
Rainbow Chevre exists because of him. His
mother, Barbara Reed, started making goat
cheese when she discovered that Daniel was
allergic to cows' milk—but loved cheese. They
had the milk—she and her husband had given
their daughter, Robin, a goat—but there
weren't any goat-cheese makers in the area. So
Barbara Reed read up on the subject and
learned by trial and error. Grown-ups who

sampled her cheeses suggested she turn professional, and she did.

The Reeds describe their chèvre logs as their
most popular and versatile cheese, a semi-soft
cheese, "mild and creamy, with a slight nutty
taste," good in hors d'oeuvres, main dishes,
salads, sauces, and desserts. They recommend
the chèvre with parsley, sage, rosemary, and
thyme in stuffed veal or chicken, or with
steamed vegetables; the chèvre with garlic for
pasta, crackers, with tomatoes, or in omelettes;
and the chèvre with the secret "special herbs"
on its own as a sauce for pasta. The *crottin
mediterraneen* is a small, firm cheese marinated
in olive oil and herbs you can add to a salad or
spread on bread. *Gourmet* described the *crottin
affine* as "a softly oozing morsel, worth asking
for." The Reeds recommend eating this ripened
cheese with crackers and wine, "with one of
New York's fine apples, or baked and served
with a salad."

The *chèvre de ferme,* a semihard cheese, aged
over sixty days, can be served sliced or grated
over pasta, and is available smoked. The Berkshire Blue is a blue-veined goat-milk cheese,
aged at least five months. You can also get aged

chèvre, moistened in virgin Spanish olive oil,
rolled in thyme or pepper, and wrapped in organically grown grape leaves.

The cheese is not certified organic, but the
Reeds farm their land in the foothills of the
Berkshire Mountains organically. The milk
contains no chemicals, additives, hormones, or
antibiotics. Their "gentle pasteurization" pro-

cess ensures "the maximum of nutrients, purity, and flavor for our milk and many cheeses," say the Reeds. The cheese is made only from goat milk, cultures, and vegetable enzymes, and contains no additives, coloring, or artificial preservatives.

In 1990, prices ranged from $7.50 to $12 a pound depending on the cheese.

MORNINGLAND DAIRY
Route I, Box 188B
Mountain View, MO 65548
(417) 469-3817

Visits: by appointment
Certified by: OOGA
Catalogue/price list available
Minimum order: 5 pounds
Order by: phone, mail
Pay by: COD followed by 14 days net
Ship by: UPS
Place your order by Saturday for shipments
Mondays or Tuesdays

RAW-MILK CHEESES

Monterey Jack · Hot pepper Jack · Mild pepper Jack · Caraway Jack · Italian Jack · Chives Colby · Garlic Colby · Colby · Dill Cheddar · Mild Cheddar · No-salt mild Cheddar · Medium sharp Cheddar · Ozark Hill Farms goat cheese

When Jim and Margie Reiners moved to the Ozark hills of Missouri in 1977, they worked hard to turn their 200 acres into a self-sufficient organic dairy farm. They started out with a herd of thirty dairy cattle, but found there wasn't much satisfaction in producing a high-quality milk and then having to sell it to "a national corporation that dumped our milk in with hundreds of other farmers' and then marketed it along with the cheese of hundreds of other plants." To feel that their hard work was actually being appreciated by the people who ate the cheese, they built their own cheese house—against the advice of some commercial cheese makers, who said their small-scale operation would never work.

The Reiners's seventy Holstein cows graze year-round on unsprayed, untreated pastureland. While other dairy farmers use cottonseed as a protein supplement, the Reiners don't, because they're concerned about the extremely heavy—and unregulated—use of herbicides and pesticides on cotton, a nonfood crop. They do not use antibiotics. If necessary, Margie Reiners, who is the head milker on the farm, supplements the cows' diet with homeopathic remedies. Morningland Dairy also does not use any fly sprays on or near the cows, another practice they say is "encouraged by public officials." Nor do the Reiners give the cows any artificial growth hormones.

Only raw, unpasteurized milk goes into the cheese, which preserves the natural digestive enzymes in the milk, and only vegetable rennet is used to solidify the milk. In cooking, the cheese never exceeds the natural body temperature of the cows it came from. The cheese itself contains no synthetic proteins, no preservatives or artificial coloring. Except for the caraway seeds, the herbs that go into the cheeses come from Margie Reiners's own organic herb garden.

In 1990, cheese was available in small pieces, regular pieces, 5-pound, 10-pound, and 40-pound blocks. Prices per pound ranged from $2.63 to $4.03 for small pieces and decreased for larger quantities. Five percent discounts on orders over 40 pounds, additional 5 percent on orders over 250 pounds. Shipping additional.

ORGANIC VALLEY

P.O. Box 159
LaFarge, WI 54639
(800) 526-9388
(608) 625-2602

Visits: yes
Member farms certified by: OCIA, OGBA
Cheese plant certified by: OCIA
Catalogue/price list available
Minimum order: none
Order by: phone, mail
Pay by: check
Ship by: UPS, Second Day Air

RAW MILK CHEESE

Mild Cheddar · Sharp Cheddar · Colby ·
Monterey Jack · Muenster · Low-fat, low-salt
Cheddar

PASTEURIZED

Mozzarella · Provolone · Pepper Jack

PASTEURIZED GOAT-MILK CHEESE

Feta · Cheddar

OTHER DAIRY

Nonfat, noninstant dry milk

MEAT (MANY CUTS AVAILABLE)

Chicken · Pork · Beef · Lamb

FROZEN VEGETABLES

Sweet corn

Organic Valley opened for business in 1988 as the Coulee Region Organic Produce Pool Cooperative (CROPP). "Coulees," explains Organic Valley's Harriet Behar, are deep narrow valleys characteristic of the dairy country of the upper Mississippi River valley. "Small family farms are the norm here, with each 120- to 2,000-acre farm usually having less than 50 percent tillable land. Living in an economically poor, rural area, the farmers of the coulee region are always searching for a way to earn a living from the land."

The cooperative got started as a way to encourage these small farmers to practice sustainable agriculture. By 1990, the cooperative had almost seventy members, ranging "from Amish to back-to-the-landers, to growers with generations of farming experience," says Behar. From its offices in a former creamery in the tiny town of LaFarge, Wisconsin, population 600, the cooperative acts as a "clearinghouse for political action," says Behar, "but also for giving practical technical assistance to interested farmers." While academic institutions have tended to advocate the use of chemicals, Organic Valley does exactly the opposite, by sponsoring classes at the local vocational-technical college in organic vegetable production.

The animals' feed comes from land that's been free of chemicals for at least three years. The cows are cared for "humanely and conscientiously on small family farms" where they have free access to exercise, fresh air and fresh water. They are given no growth hormones and are free of trace antibiotics or other drugs.

In 1990, cheese was available in units of 8 ounces, 1 pound, 5 pounds, and 40 pounds. Prices ranged from $2.65 to $3 for eight ounces and decreased with larger orders. Twelve 8-ounce packages ranged from $16.10 to $18.20. Whole chicken was $1.79 a pound, and parts ranged from $1.61 to $5.06 a pound. Beef was $2.58 a pound for ground beef and $6.47 a pound for T-bone steak. Other cuts ranged from $1.50 to $5.39 a pound. Pork ranged from $2.47 to $3.23 a pound. Shipping additional.

SHELBURNE FARMS
Shelburne, VT 05482
(802) 985-8686

Visits: yes; tours available; inn on site
Certified by: SELF
Catalogue/price list available
Minimum order: none
Order by: phone, mail
Pay by: check, cash, Visa, MC, Amex
Ship by: UPS, parcel post
Sampler and gift packages available

CHEESE

Medium Cheddar · Sharp Cheddar · Extra sharp Cheddar · Smoked Cheddar

At the turn of the century, the land overlooking Lake Champlain that is now Shelburne Farms was the estate of William Seward and Lila Vanderbilt Webb. Frederick Law Olmstead advised the Webbs on landscaping; the entire property is on the National Register of Historic Places.

In the 1950s, the Webb family turned the estate into a working farm, but the following generation faced the hard choice of dividing or selling the property. They chose a third option, turning Shelburne Farms into an independent, nonprofit educational institution, managed by the Webbs' grandson, Alec. Every year, almost 5,000 students and teachers participate in programs whose purpose is "to teach and demonstrate the wise use of natural and agricultural

SHELBURNE FARMS

resources, in the belief that we must all become better stewards of our planet."

Among the agricultural ventures on the farm is the making of what its master cheesemaker, Bill Clapp, calls "a true farmhouse Cheddar," because it starts with the milk of the farm's own herd of Brown Swiss cows. Clapp oversees the making of over 400 pounds of cheese each day. After the cheese is cheddared—a process of separating the whey from the mats of curds—and aged for anywhere from six months to two years (for the extra sharp), it's hand-dipped in wax. The medium Cheddar is also available smoked—the smoking is done by the monks of a local monastery. Ippy Patterson, author of *The Ideal Cheese Book,* called Clapp's Cheddars "one of the finest" in Vermont, praising its texture as "firm and grainy with a pleasant nuttiness." The American Cheese Society awarded Clapp the "Best in Show" blue ribbon for 1990.

Shelburne Farms gives its cows no hormones, and feeds them grass and silage from the farm, which uses no pesticides, no chemical fertilizers, and no herbicides; they are also occasionally given grain from off the farm.

In 1990, cheese was available in 1 pound, 2 pounds, 3 pounds, and 9 pounds. A pound of Cheddar ranged from $8 to $10, and prices decreased for larger quantities. A sampler of 4 1-pound blocks was $35. A year-round bimonthly shipment of cheese (2- or 3-pound blocks) ranged from $90 to $144. Shipping is included, except outside New England: Second Day Air adds 20 percent to your order. The catalogue also contains other Vermont specialties.

YERBA SANTA GOAT DAIRY/ POE ORCHARDS
6850 Scotts Valley Road
Lakeport, CA 95453
(707) 263-8131

Visits: yes
Certified by: CCOF
Catalogue/price list available
Minimum order: none
Order by: phone, mail
Pay by: check
Ship by: UPS, FedEx

HERBED SOFT CHEESES

Dill Onion · Parsley Garlic · Cracked Black Pepper · Plain

CHEVITOS (MINIWHEELS)

Feta-type · Muenster-type

SHEPHERD'S CHEESE

Dry · Extra Dry · Private Reserve

NUTS

Poe walnuts

Chris and Jan Twohy started keeping goats because the only land they'd been able to afford was "more hillside than bottomland," says Jan Twohy. "Goats don't mind climbing hills." They named their dairy after the "Saintly Herb," a shrub native to the chapparal of northern California. According to the Twohys, "Goats find Yerba Santa desirable and nutritious. The plant, in combination with the many other native shrubs and wildflowers, lends a subtly sweet flavor to their milk."

The Twohys' Alpine Chèvre line includes soft, semisoft, and hard cheeses. They have four herbed soft cheeses: Plain, which they recommend on toast or an English muffin with jam; Dill Onion for dips and sauces, particularly on fish; Parsley Garlic, for salad dressings and dips; and Cracked Black Pepper, "a real treat when melted into an omelette."

Chevitos are tangy, slightly salty mini-wheels, and come in a crumbly feta-type cheese; and a surface-ripened "rich-flavored" semisoft Muensterlike cheese that's aged at least two months. The Twohys also make wheels of hard cheese: Dry ages for three to six months, is easy to slice, and fairly mild; Extra Dry is a grating or slicing cheese, aged more than six months, with more flavor than the Dry; Private Reserve takes wheels from the "most outstanding flavored batches of the year" and ages them at least a year.

The Twohys also sell Poe walnuts (no relation to Edgar Allan), a spherical walnut grown almost exclusively in the Lake County region. According to Jan Twohy, the county went through a phase of planting these trees on any available site. "Walnuts were supposed to be an absentee crop—you just come in and pick up your walnuts, and that's it. Of course, it's not quite that simple." The Poe's lower yields and thick shell discouraged many commercial growers, but the shell also makes the Poe less vulnerable to insects and disease than other California varieties, making it ideal for organic growers.

For an organic farmer, Chris Twohy has an unusual off-farm job: he works for the county agriculture department. Most organic farmers, says his wife, Jan, would consider him the enemy. "In his job, he's forced to read a lot about chemicals and their uses. He can see the pitfalls and benefits of both sides. For us, organic is a good way to go."

The walnuts are certified organic; the cheeses are not. The goats graze on hillside rangeland and valley pastureland; all forages and hay, and most of the grain they eat comes from the farm itself, which is certified organic. The goats are not fed any artificial feed supplements. Some grain does come from off the farm and is not certified. Jan Twohy hopes that by 1991, they will have found a reliable source of organic grain and will be able to certify the cheese.

In 1990, the cheeses ranged from $5.25 to $6.56 a pound. Chevitos (wheels of 12 to 14 ounces) ranged from $5 to $5.28. Shipping additional.

SEE ALSO
Old Mill Farm

CULTURES AND CULTURED FOODS

GEM CULTURES
30301 Sherwood Road
Fort Bragg, CA 95437
(707) 964-2922

Ingredients certified by: CHSC
Catalogue/price list available
Minimum order: none
Order by: mail
Pay by: check or money order
Ship by: UPS, first class mail
Recipes available

STARTERS AND CULTURES

Tempeh · Koji · Miso · Amazake · Shoyu · Tamari · Natto · Seed miso · Nigari · Terra alba · Viili · Kefir · Sourdough (wheat or wheat-free rye)

Betty Stechmeyer and Gordon McBride, a husband-and-wife team with forty years of professional experience culturing micro-organisms between them, founded GEM Cultures in 1980 to introduce people to the wide—if microscopic—world of culturing foods from scratch.

GEM Cultures' first—and still most popular —product was tempeh starter. Tempeh, a cultured soybean cake from Indonesia, is the richest vegetable source of complete protein— more than twice that of tofu. Stechmeyer describes tempeh as firmer than tofu, with "a mushroomy smell, a mild flavor, and an after-bite redolent of ripe Camembert." Cooked tempeh can have the flavor of chicken or veal, and can be marinated, baked, or even dusted with flour, dipped in egg, and fried like a cutlet. Thin sticks of tempeh can be stir-fried, or deep-fried like french fries. Dry-roasted tempeh makes a snack or topping. The tempeh starter has a six-month shelf life and will make tempeh in twenty-four hours.

Moving into Western cultures, GEM sells several self-renewing cultures (certainly not a very capitalist notion—buy one and never have to buy again) including viili, a sweet, cultured-milk product from Finland. Viili came into the McBride family over eighty-five years ago, with one of Gordon's Finnish ancestors. Unlike yogurt, viili doesn't require an incubator or sterile jars; the culture only takes twenty-four hours at moderate room temperature to set, and any kind of milk—even soymilk—will do. A tablespoonful of the cultured viili becomes the starter for the next batch. In Scandinavia, viili is a breakfast food or summer cooler, with fruit, powdered ginger, cinnamon, cereal, or honey and wheat germ. Stechmeyer likes to use viili in place of cream, or whisk it briefly to thicken, and turn it into a base for low-fat salad dressings, or in muffins, quick breads, and pancakes. I found viili on its own delicious and slightly sinful; both taste and texture were reminiscent of sweetened sour cream, the kind you might find atop a cheesecake.

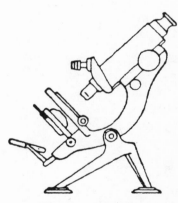

GEM CULTURES

Stechmeyer and McBride know that in many cases they are dealing with first-timers, and their instructions are extremely straightforward. They can send you recipes and also sell a variety of books on cooking with cultured foods. Betty Stechmeyer is an extremely cheerful and generous correspondent; if there is anything related to food cultures you're having trouble locating, she will try to help you find it.

All the ingredients meet the California Health and Safety Code organic standards.

In 1990, starter kits began at $2.25 for 3 1-pound batches, and went all the way up to $60 a kilo of starter "for community or professional use." Self-renewing cultures —viili, sourdough, and kefir—were $5.50. Shipping is included, but there is a "small-order charge" for orders under $10. The company also sells Mendocino Sea Vegetables (page 241).

MALACHITE SCHOOL & SMALL FARM
ASR Box 21 Pass Creek Road
Gardner, CO 81040
(719) 746-2412

Visits: yes; Fall Festival, educational field trips, bed-and-breakfast farmstays, hostel programs, and retreats
Certified by: SELF
Catalogue/price list available
Minimum order: none
Order by: phone, mail
Pay by: check, money order
Ship by: UPS, parcel post

CULTURES

Sourdough starter

SWEETENERS

Honey

GRAIN

Quinoa

The Malachite School & Small Farm starts with a simple idea: whether you are a vegetarian or a meat eater, all human life ultimately depends on "green life" to convert sunlight, water, and soil into food and energy. "We believe that our future as humans is linked to the soundness of our agriculture," say Isabel and Stuart Mace, who founded the Malachite School & Small Farm in 1979 on the site of an overgrazed, abandoned farm. "How we conduct our agriculture ultimately rests with the philo-sophical recognition that life is a gift and that we are guests at life's banquet. We need to mind our manners on the land that sustains us."

The Malachite School teaches people to mind their manners by offering hands-on training in sustainable agriculture to students who range in age from young children to Elderhostel groups. About 70 percent of the food served at the Malachite School is grown organically on the farm, and all of the baking is done in the farm's old kitchen. For breads, the bakers often use sourdough starter, whose lineage dates back 100 years. The starter was brought out of Alaska (where sourdough fueled the gold rush) around 1950. "The more it's used," says Isabel Mace, "the better it gets." One two-ounce package is "guaranteed to make 7 billion pancakes or 7 million loaves of bread."

The school also grows quinoa (pronounced "keen-wah"), an Andean grain that is 22 percent protein and ideal for the elevations of the Colorado Rockies (for more on quinoa, see Ancient Harvest Quinoa, page 123). The folks at Malachite will send you an information sheet and recipes with the sweet, nutty-flavored grain, which can be used anywhere you'd use rice, and some places, like cold dishes, where you wouldn't. They also sell their own honey, gathered from wildflowers in the high mountain valleys near the school, which is unprocessed, so it contains more nutrients than a processed honey.

In 1990, 2 ounces of sourdough starter was $4.50; quinoa was $4.50 for 1 pound and $9 for 3 pounds. Honey ranged from $4 for a 12-ounce squeeze bottle to $7.50 for a quart, and $7 for a 1-pound flint glass honey jar with cork (replica). Shipping included.

SOUTH RIVER MISO
South River Farm
Conway, MA 01341
(413) 369-4057

Ingredients certified by: various
Catalogue/price list available
Minimum order: none
Order by: phone, mail
Pay by: check, USPS money order
Ship by: UPS
Shipping October 1–May 1

MISO

Three-year barley · Two-year barley · Black soy
barley · Sweet-tasting brown rice · Golden
millet · Chick-pea · Adzuki rice · Black soy
brown rice · Dandelion leek

STARTER

Brown-rice koji

In Japanese mythology, say South River Farm's
Christian and Gaella Ellwell, "miso was a gift
to mankind from the gods to assure lasting
health, longevity, and happiness." In worldly
terms, miso starts with beans and grains that
are cooked, fermented, and aged, then used as
a base for soups, stews, sauces, and pickles.
Miso contains "all of the essential amino acids,"
say the Ellwells, which makes it an alternative
to animal protein. They see miso as part of a
larger commitment to finding alternative food
sources "in a time of food crisis and waste, of
need and greed. Good miso makes a grain- and
vegetable-centered diet a gentle, practicable,
healing revolution."

Even if you're not a vegetarian, if you're
looking for those gifts of the gods, particularly
health, the Ellwells advise you not to buy commercially made miso, which is pasteurized, "destroying the very micro-organisms that make
miso so beneficial: natural digestive enzymes,
lactobacillus, and other micro-organisms that
aid in the assimilation of all foods."

The Ellwells make their miso entirely by
hand. They're found that "working directly
with the miso, without the intermediary of the
machine, brings us into greater harmony with
the ingredients and the natural forces at play in
their transformation." First, they cook the
beans in pure, deep-well water, over a wood
fire in a massive masonry stove. This stage
alone takes twenty-four hours. When the beans
are completely soft, steamed grain is inoculated
with spores of *Aspergillus oryzae,* and begin to
ferment into "sweet, fragrant koji." Next, the
koji is mixed with the soybeans and sea salt
using "the age-old process of foot treading."
But not to worry—"We wear plastic foot cov-
erings to satisfy modern standards of hygiene."

Like wine, the miso ages over a period of
years in wooden vats. The Ellwells gauge the
age of each batch by the number of summers
through which it has fermented, "because fermentation is most active during the summer
months." Each container is labeled with the
month and year it was made.

The flavor of the miso depends on the type
of bean and grain used, and the number of
years of aging. All beans and grains are organically grown, "in most cases from farmers with
whom we have direct personal contact." The
bran layer of the grains is polished just enough
to allow the fermentation process to take place.
The russet-colored barley miso won *East West*
magazine's "Most Hearty Miso" award. The
Ellwells recommend it as a base for soups and
stews. The sweet-tasting brown-rice miso is a
lighter, caramel color, with a low salt content.
The Ellwells call it a "versatile miso, perfect for
lighter cooking styles, for all kinds of sauces,
spreads, and salad dressings, and for pickling
tofu and root vegetables."

The champagne of misos is the dandelion-leek, which combines dandelion greens from the farm's own bottomland with kelp—courtesy of Maine Seaweed Company (page 240)—and wild leeks from a "well-protected natural colony in the unspoiled woodland of our valley," whose flavor is "a cross between a scallion and a mild garlic." The leeks and dandelions are steamed briefly; the kelp is pressure cooked, and all three are pickled for one summer in a base of three-year brown-rice miso.

If you're not a miso aficionado, the samplers give you a chance to try out the various flavors. Each one-pound tub comes printed with a basic miso soup recipe, and you can improvise from there. I sampled the golden chick-pea and the velvety brown three-year barley, using the basic recipe. The chick-pea made a delicate broth, a background for the flavors of the fresh greens I'd used (leeks and onions). The three-year barley had a richer, sweeter flavor, without being heavy. Both misos came in plastic containers, one of which had opened slightly during shipping, but only a tiny bit of miso was lost.

All misos are available in 1-gallon, 2-gallon, or 5-gallon pails. In 1990, a 1-gallon pail ranged from $27 to $49.05. Larger pails are more economical. Koji was $4.50, and less for larger orders. Shipping additional. Samplers (4 1-pound containers) ranged from $21.50 to $26, including shipping.

SEE ALSO
MacDonald Farm, Summercorn Foods

DRIED FRUIT

Dried fruit is routinely treated with chemicals—not only in the fields and orchards but once it's been picked and dried. These chemicals may be pesticides or fungicides or preservatives, like sulphur, to make the color of the fruit glow and the texture of the fruit soft. Even organically grown fruit can be fumigated in a warehouse if it doesn't come directly from the grower to you.

The dried fruits listed here are not only grown organically, but also stored and processed without chemicals. And, since you are ordering directly from the grower, you know that the fruit has not been stored in a warehouse—and fumigated—somewhere between the grower and you.

AHLER'S ORGANIC DATE & GRAPEFRUIT GARDEN

P.O. Box 726
Mecca, CA 92254-0726
(619) 396-2337

Visits: yes
Farmers' markets: Santa Monica, California, at 2nd and Arizona, Wednesdays
Certified by: CHSC
Catalogue/price list available
Minimum order: none
Order by: phone, mail
Pay by: check, money order
Ship by: UPS, parcel post

DATES

Khadrawi · Halawi · Deglet Noor · Zahidi

DATE PRODUCTS

Crystallized dates · Ground dates · Coconut-date balls · Snowballs (dates, walnuts, and coconut)

FRESH FRUIT

Marsh white grapefruit (February 1–July 15)

A "date garden" in a town called Mecca conjures up a Middle Eastern paradise. But the idea of harvesting dates in 110-degree weather is a little less than heaven. It's hard work, as Fred Wendler discovered when he took over from the Ahlers who'd planted the dates in 1955. For years, Wendler and his wife, Betty Lou, used to buy dates from the Ahlers when they were in the area on vacation. When the Ahlers' children encouraged them to retire, the Wendlers bought the place. "They stayed on for about six months to show us what to do." Wendler, who'd always enjoyed gardening, had only had a half-acre's worth of responsibilities before. Now he had sixteen acres of trees that needed de-thorning and pollinating, not to mention dates that needed picking. "I continued to work as a surveyor, but after that six months, I could see I would need to be here full-time."

The Ahlers had been growing without chemicals, and the Wendlers were happy to continue the tradition. "Frankly, I wouldn't fool with this if I had to do all the things the big date growers do," says Fred Wendler. "Spraying with sulphur and malathion, and all that—I just wouldn't do it. You hardly know a person who's completely healthy; something's always wrong with them."

The Wendlers don't sulphur their dates or add any other preservatives. "As soon as our dates are picked we put them on hardware-cloth trays in single layers and set them on metal-top tables in the sun. After three or four hours in the hot sun and clear air, at 100 to 110 degrees, our dates are all clean and cured.

We package them in cardboard and cellophane —no plastic." Ahler's dates should be kept refrigerated, or even frozen for longer storage. Dates can last for a year in the refrigerator and up to ten years in the freezer.

All the fruit is graded and packed on site. The Wendlers grade their dates as "Finest Soft," "Fine Soft," "Medium Soft," and "Bread Dates, a chewy, dry date, favored by sportsmen and children, that can be carried loose in your pocket."

In 1990, dates ran between $2 and $3.50 a pound, plus shipping. The Wendlers did not have grapefruit available in 1990, because of a fire.

COVALDA DATE COMPANY
P.O. Box 908
Coachella, CA 92236-0908
(619) 398-3551
(619) 398-3441
FAX: (619) 398-1615

Visits: yes
Certified by: SELF
Catalogue/price list available
Minimum order: 1 pound
Order by: phone, mail, fax
Pay by: MC, Visa, check, money order
Ship by: UPS, USPS
Gift packs and samplers available
Recipes available with SASE

DATES

Bread · Sugar-tip bread · Deglet Noor choice, · Deglet Noor fancy · Deglet Noor pitted · Barhi · Halawi · Honey dates · Khadrawi · Medjool choice · Medjool fancy · Thoori · Zahidi

DATE PRODUCTS

Coconut datelets · Carob-pecan datelets · Individual date pieces · Date-almond confection · Datettes (chopped date pieces) · Creamed dates (date butter) · Date chips · Date-pecan logs · Stuffed dates

DRIED FRUIT

Apples · Apricots · Black Mission figs · Calimyrna figs · Peaches · Pears · Thompson seedless raisins

NUTS AND SEEDS

Almonds (in shell or meats) · English walnuts (in shell or meats)

SWEETENER

Raw date sugar

Charlotte Stocks, who runs Covalda today, describes its founders—her parents, Lee and Ruth Anderson—as "pioneers." In the early days, back in the 1920s, the Anderson family lived in a cabin with canvas sides and palm-frond shingles. They had no refrigerator, and the lids on the pots had to be tight to keep out the desert sand.

When Lee Anderson started Covalda (short for Coachella Valley Dates), he was a veteran of World War I with only 600 dollars in his pocket, all that remained after the bank foreclosed on a citrus grove he'd started before going off to war. (The banker had promised Lee Anderson that the bank would look out for him, because he was fighting for his country.)

Anderson cleared 100 acres in the Coachella valley, where temperatures can break 120 degrees, with a four-horse team, and planted 4,000 date palms. In later years, Anderson captured several first prize ribbons at the National Date Festival in Indio, California, and continued to come to work every day until his death, at age 101, in 1989.

Charlotte Stocks won't say the dates are responsible for her father's longevity, but she does say that he ate them every day, and points out dates' nutritional value. "Dates are high in potassium, high in B vitamins, very low in sodium, and a high-fiber food. People think of them as a holiday item, but they really should be considered an everyday food. With milk or cheese, as the ancients used them, they provide a wonderfully balanced diet." She even recommends date and lettuce sandwiches.

If you're not already a date connoisseur, Covalda will send you a sheet that classifies its dates by appearance, texture, taste, and uses. If you're looking for an organic sweetener, date sugar is made from tree-ripened organic dates, naturally dried, pitted, and ground into a powder; it can be used on fruit or cereals and in cooking.

I sampled the Medjool and Halawi dates, the date-pecan logs, and the datelets. Both varieties of dates were tender and moist. The Medjool was sweeter and softer, with a stronger date flavor; the Halawi had more of a brown-sugar flavor, drier and chewier than the Medjool. As one friend said, the Medjools were "a date to be reckoned with," large enough to stuff with whole or chopped nuts for a contrasting texture. I gave both varieties to an Israeli friend to try—a man sparing of his praise—and he pronounced both "luscious" and "impressive," and proceeded to finish off the Medjools.

The date confections brought an immediate smile to the face of everyone who tried them. One friend bit into a datelet and said, "I think I've died and gone to heaven. Why would anyone eat anything else?" I was torn, myself, between those and the date-pecan logs, which add texture to the equation. If you have anyone with a sweet tooth on your gift list—who doesn't?—and you want to send a good-and-good-for-you treat, this is it.

The dates are grown without chemicals and are not treated with any preservatives, detergents, mold inhibitors, or fungicides, and are frozen if necessary to stop insect action. Lee Anderson, also a pioneer in organic growing, crusaded against laws that would have made

spraying of dates—probably with malathion—mandatory. Covalda is not certified organic, but Charlotte Stocks says, "We pioneered this field—we invented it. The least they could do is grandfather us in," she says with a laugh.

In 1990, dates ranged from $1.75 to $3.95 a pound depending on the variety. An assortment totaling 12 pounds was $29.25. (Smaller samplers are available.) Date sugar was $3.35 a pound. Other dried fruit ranged from $2.30 to $7.70 a pound. Nuts ranged from $1.64 a pound to $4.58 a pound. Many items are less expensive in bulk. The catalogue also lists some nonorganic dried fruits.

FOUR APOSTLES RANCH
P.O. Box 908
Indio, CA 92202
(619) 345-6171

Visits: by appointment only
Farmers' markets: six in California—call for locations
Certified by: CCOF
Catalogue/price list available
Minimum order: none
Order by: phone, mail
Pay by: check, money order
Ship by: UPS, parcel post
Sampler and gift packs available
Dates are shipped October–March; the ranch does sell out, so order early for holiday gifts

DATES

Jumbo Medjool · Choice Medjool

DATE PRODUCTS

Pieces · Coconut snowballs

FRESH FRUIT

Pomegranates

I owe an apology to Four Apostles Ranch for putting them in the Dried Fruit section—the dates they sell are so fresh, so plump, so free of fiber, so soft, well, I could go on, but you get the idea. "Most people think that the dried, sulphured, fumigated deglets on the supermarket shelves are dates," says Four Apostles' Rosalind Milliken. (She makes deglet sound like an age-old Middle-Eastern insult, doesn't she?) "It's the difference between a raisin and a grape, or a plum and a prune."

Four Apostles Ranch was once a stagecoach stop on the Bradshaw line. The Four Apostles, four wild date palms the stagecoach drivers used to steer by, or no longer standing, but Brad and Rosalind Milliken are raising "an oasis" of Medjool date palms in their stead.

Four Apostles is a small family farm, says Rosalind Milliken. "We do not grow great quantities. Dates are the most dangerous and labor-intensive crop grown, and we do all the work ourselves." Rosalind Milliken explains that because date picking is such hard work, commercial growers have to pay a picker twenty dollars every time they send one up into a tree. To save money, growers let the dates dry

out on the trees, so they can pick them all at once. Because they leave ripe dates on the trees, they have to spray very heavily, to keep away insects and prevent the dates from souring.

Unlike these growers, the Millikens start picking the moment the dates are ripe. "My husband goes up in the trees and my older sons go out with him. It's very hard work, because the humidity is running about 70 percent, and the temperature is between 105 and 110. It's like doing hard physical labor inside a sauna." Once they pick the dates, the Millikens put them immediately into a freezer van that brings the dates down to zero within hours, which protects against pests and spoilage but doesn't affect the nutrients (by law, they must either

freeze or fumigate). Commercial growers, says Milliken, stack their dates in boxes and fumigate them once a month. When they get an order, they take the dates inside and steam them up. "They look beautiful," admits Milliken, "but then they start sugaring within a few weeks and look awful." Four Apostles' unpreserved dates need to be refrigerated, and so are shipped only during the cooler months.

Brad Milliken, whose background is in anthropology, has traveled to Yemen to consult on organic date growing for the country's department of agriculture. Milliken was allowed to visit parts of the country normally closed to outsiders; was the guest of honor at a sheik's wedding; and became a fast friend of the minister of agriculture, who didn't want him to leave, says Rosalind. "He offered to buy Brad a big farm, a big house, and get him a wife." Needless to say, she took a dim view of this offer, but was very proud of his work there, which will enable the Yemeni date growers to increase their income some 2,000 percent, and decrease their exposure to toxic pesticides. Previous consultants, says Rosalind Milliken, had encouraged the Yemeni date growers to use enormous amounts of chemicals, even though growers live and sleep right under their trees and drink the groundwater. Moreover, she says, growers often couldn't read the English or German directions and so vastly overused the chemicals. The Yemenis often lost much of their crop to spoilage and had ended up being net importers of dates; Milliken arranged for them to use the freezers at an import-export firm, and explained that as organic growers they would have an enormous export market. Brad Milliken offered them the benefits of his years of experience as an organic grower who had never borrowed money to pay for tools, and so had developed many low-cost methods that were easily transferable to the small-scale farms in Yemen. He encouraged them to return to many traditional practices, some of which, like using sesame oil sprays to discourage pests, he has brought back to Four Apostles.

Back at the home ranch, says Rosalind Milliken, the crop is increasing every year. "Our customers are growing along with our crop. I just got a phone call from a woman in Hawaii who had received two pounds of dates for Christmas. She ordered 400 pounds as gifts."

In 1990, a 1-pound tin of jumbo Medjools was $12 and a 2-pound tin was $22. A 2-pound tin of choice Medjools was $15. Twelve pounds of choice Medjools, loose pack, were $70. A 2-pound tin of date pieces or coconut snowballs was $12. All tins are less expensive in cases of 4 or 8. A sampler pack totaling 8 pounds was $57. Pomegranates will be available in 1992.

GLACKIN'S ORGANIC ACRES

RR 1, Box 604
Richland, MO 65556
(314) 765-3934

Visits: yes; surplus garden vegetables
Certified by: SELF
Minimum order: none
Order by: mail
Pay by: check
Ship by: parcel post

DRIED FRUIT

Persimmons

GRAIN FOR SPROUTING

Corn

Hugh Glackin, the proprietor of Glackin's Organic Acres, turned 85 in May, 1990. While he doesn't claim to possess the secret of longevity, he says, "It might be of interest to know that I eat lots of maize, both green and mature, ground dry or sprouted, a clove of garlic daily, and a sprig of parsley. At eighty-five, I am a healthy, busy person occupied from seven to noon inside, and outside five hours. I do the gardening, gathering, processing, and also conservation work around the farm."

Most of Glackin's 400 acres are planted in trees for timber. "After fifty years planting trees," says Hugh Glackin, "I still think trees are most important for the survival of all life's species." His land has been registered as a certified Backyard Wildlife Habitat—a sort of minirefuge—by the National Wildlife Federation. Glackin's is not certified organic, but Hugh Glackin has used nothing but natural fertilizers for fifty years.

Hugh Glackin says that his sun-dried persimmons are a source of fiber and vitamin C, and compares them to dates. I found them softer and grainier than dates, and a slightly darker flavor, with a hint of coffee. They're not seeded, says Glackin, "because we haven't found a practical way of removing the seeds." This is a real obstacle if you want to use these as easy snacks—where dates have only one large pit, the persimmons tend to have four for the same amount of fruit. They may be more useful for baking—you could pit them with a knife and then use as you would other dried fruit.

In 1990, 2 pounds of dried persimmons were $4 plus postage. Glackin also sells Nutra Greens, a concentrated food supplement, made from the pulverized leaves and stems of alfalfa, comfrey, carrot, and turnip, dried in partial shade.

GOURMET FRUIT BASKET
SIMONE FRUIT COMPANY

8008 West Shields
Fresno, CA 93722
(209) 275-1368
FAX: (209) 275-0860

Visits: yes; fresh fruit during harvest season
Farmers' markets: Marin County and Oakland
Certified by: CCOF
Catalogue/price list available
Minimum order: 4 pounds
Order by: phone, mail, fax
Pay by: check, money order
Ship by: UPS, air freight
Gift baskets available

DRIED FRUIT

Calimyrna figs · Black Mission figs

JAM

Fig

If you've ever eaten a fresh fig right off the tree, you'll know why Laureen Simone feels sorry for the people "back east" who don't get to have really ripe figs—"You don't even need to make them into jam," she says. "You can just spread the fig right on toast." The bad news for those of us "back east" is that ripe figs don't travel well. The good news is that dried figs and fig jam do.

Simone, who runs the Gourmet Fruit Basket, is the third generation of Simones in the fig business. Simone's grandfather emigrated from northern Italy to California, where he started growing figs. Eventually Laureen's father joined the business, as did Laureen and her brothers. The trees have always been cared for organically, and don't really need chemicals. "Although the fruit is quite fragile," says Laureen Simone, "figs are hearty trees."

Simone sells two organic figs, Calimyrna, a California variety propagated from Smyrna stock; and Black Mission, which are dark purple when fresh. The California Fig Advisory Board recommends the Calimyrna's "nut-like flavor and tender skin" for eating out of hand, and the Black Mission both for eating as-is and for cooking. The Simones sent me the Advisory Board's little booklet, "The Love Life of a Fig," to explain where little figs come from. It's a priceless document, with headings like the titles of 1950s television serials: "Papa Needs Some Help," "Mama Does All the Work," "A One-Track Mind," "The Maid Is Betrayed," and "She Lives and Loves in Vain."

In 1990, Calimyrna figs were $3 a pound. Black Mission figs were $2 a pound. You save by buying in bulk.

GREAT DATE IN THE MORNING
P.O. Box 31
Coachella, CA 92236
(619) 398-6171
FAX: (619) 398-6087

Certified by: CCOF
Minimum order: 5 pounds
Order by: phone, mail, fax
Pay by: check
Ship by: UPS, parcel post

DATES

Deglet Noor (pitted or whole) · Black · Black Precioso · Barhi · Medjool · Khadrawi · Halawi · Zahidi

DATE PRODUCTS

Date-coconut rolls · Date-almond rolls · Dry date pieces · Soft date pieces

Jim Dunn is the philosopher-king of dates: our conversation, ostensibly about dates, covered everything from Beowulf to Joseph Campbell to Vladimir Horowitz. Dunn, who has a degree in philosophy from UCLA, has been in the date business since 1969, when he was living in Santa Cruz. One of his friends had lived in the date-growing part of California and suggested to Dunn that they buy some organic dates and citrus and bring them back to the Santa Cruz Community Foods Co-op, which another friend had helped found.

"So we came up and got some dates we thought were organic. The saleslady was very nice, but she knew very little. Organic, shmorganic. To her, organic meant it grew in the ground. We were very specific about no pesticides, no chemical fertilizers. She assured us, and we believed her. Later it turned out that the dates had been sprayed every year. Now I farm that very same land organically—so even though those first dates we ate weren't organic, dates from the same trees are organic now."

Dunn grows a wide variety of dates. He describes the Deglet Noor dates as "very sweet and soft, with the highest sugar content of any commercially produced date." The Medjool is

known for "its remarkable size, often larger than a prune. It's naturally soft and high in invert sugars." The Barhi is traditionally eaten in the Middle East and the Indian subcontinent in a "bright yellow, hard form, when it's low in sugar, and has a starchy, astringent consistency." Dunn sells the dates in this stage, but has found "they're worth much more fully ripened, because the Barhi is such a fine date."

In 1990, a 5-pound box of dates ranged from $9.50 to $17, depending on the variety. Five pounds of date pieces were $9.50. You save by buying in bulk.

HAWAIIAN EXOTIC FRUIT COMPANY
Box 1729
Pahoa, HI 96778
(808) 965-7154
(808) 965-9021

Visits: yes
Certified by: CHSC
Catalogue/price list available
Minimum order: 5 pounds
Order by: phone, mail
Pay by: check
Ship by: UPS, parcel post

DRIED FRUIT

Silk fig banana (Apple banana) · White pineapple · Papaya

VEGETABLES

Purple taro root · Chinese taro root · Purple sweet potatoes

SPICES

Young Japanese yellow ginger root, (July–October) · Mature Japanese yellow ginger root (December–May) · Turmeric root

Andy Sarhanis, a Massachusetts native, moved to Hawaii fifteen years ago and is an unabashed booster of Hawaii's exotic fruits. According to Sarhanis, the Apple banana, also known as the Silk Fig and Sugar banana, is simply "the most delicious banana in the marketplace." Unlike commercial bananas, which are "drenched with deadly fungicide every three weeks," these are grown organically in mineral-rich soil. They are also allowed to ripen naturally, not "cut weeks before maturity and gassed to induce ripening." When dried, these bananas make a sort of natural candy—with something like the consistency of saltwater taffy, a stiffness that softens as you chew. The flavor is sweet but not strongly fruity; I could taste hints, as the fruit's various names suggest, of apple, banana, and fig.

White pineapple, says Sarhanis, is "so delicious and mild that after one bite you don't ever want to go back to a Dole pineapple." Un-

100% Organic
White Pineapple

like the chunky store-bought variety, this dried pineapple comes in very thin slices, as beautiful as exotic flowers. Unlike the dried banana, which provoked mixed reactions among my friends, the dried pineapple was an unqualified hit, and completely addictive. It had none of the heavy sugared taste or stringy texture of commercial dried pineapple: the strong, tangy flavor was quite close to fresh pineapple.

Hawaiian Exotic Fruit also sells young ginger root, which is "juicier, less fibrous and pungent" than mature ginger, says Sarhanis. The young root is the preferred stage for pickling. "In Asian countries, like Thailand, the delicate flavor of young ginger is preferred for many culinary uses," says Andrew Sarhanis. The young ginger must be refrigerated to maintain its firmness. I sampled the mature ginger root, a brilliant yellow color and extremely pungent, as fiery and almost as sweet as candied ginger. A tiny bit goes a very long way in a stir-fry or soup.

In 1990, a 5-pound box of dried bananas was $40; dried white pineapple was $50; fresh turmeric root was $45. Young yellow ginger root was $85 for 15 pounds, and mature ginger root was $70. All prices included shipping. Everything is available in larger quantities; price per pound decreases. Andy Sarhanis is interested in developing mail-order sales of fresh white pineapple if demand is high enough; let him know if you are interested. He also sells medicinal herbs.

PATO'S DREAM
60-499 Highway 86
Thermal, CA 92274

Visits: write for an appointment
Farmers' market: Fullerton, Wednesdays;
Alhambra, Sundays
Certified by: CCOF
Minimum order: 4 pounds
Order by: mail
Pay by: check
Ship by: UPS, parcel post
Orders accepted only August 15–
November 15

DATES

Halawis (September) · Deglet Noor
(October–November)

When I first wrote down the name Pato's Dream, I thought it might be a typo for Plato's Dream, but no. A somewhat breathless Doug Adair (it was 6:45 A.M. and he was racing to get his daughters ready for school) explained that he'd been very active in the United Farm Workers organizing grape pickers. "There's no nickname in Spanish for Doug. 'Pato' is 'Duck,' which comes pretty close. It was either that or 'Perro'—'Dog'—and I decided I'd rather be the duck." (His partner, Francisco, is "Conejo"—"Rabbit.")

"Pato" Adair moved to the Coachella Valley in 1976 to work with grape pickers for the UFW. "I bought a little ranch, basically five acres and an old house, and it had five old date palms on it. I was talking to a friend of mine about them, and he said, 'My brother is a palmero—he can tell you if the palms are any good.' So his brother came and looked at them and said he couldn't tell because the palms hadn't been worked in so long and hadn't been irrigated." Adair suggested that he work the palms for a few years, and keep any dates he got.

Today, Francisco Paniagua and Doug Adair are partners in Pato's Dream, and hope that five acres of dates will soon be able to support their two families. Meanwhile, Francisco Paniagua also works on another date farm, "where he has a union contract and union benefits," says Adair, with satisfaction.

Pato's Dream is a small farm, with no outside employees. For this reason, it accepts mail orders only for a few months each year, does not pack its dates in fancy gift boxes, and can't take orders over the phone.

Pato's Dream has been following CCOF guidelines since 1984. After picking the dates, the partners do not wash, steam, or rehydrate the fruit, nor do they fumigate them or add any preservatives. As proof that the fruit comes directly from the tree, they say: "You may want to wash off the desert dust before use."

Personally, I didn't see a speck of dust. What I did see was a box crammed full of Halawi dates—the folks at Pato's Dream go for quantity, not presentation—and the result is a date lover's delight: a solid box of dense-pack dates, sweet, soft, and with a hint of caramel.

In 1990, a 4-pound box was $16. You save by buying in bulk. Shipping included.

SOWDEN BROS.

8888 Township Road
Live Oak, CA 95953
(916) 695-3750
FAX: (916) 695-1395

Certified by: FVO
Catalogue/price list available
Minimum order: none
Order by: mail, fax
Pay by: check in advance
Ship by: UPS, parcel post

DRIED FRUIT

Prunes

FRESH FRUIT

Fuyu persimmons · Kiwi (fall only)

When they were children, Buzz and Bud Sowden worked in the orchard they now own. Some of the trees in their orchard are older than they are. Even though the Sowden brothers are charter members of Farm Verified Organic, Buzz and Bud Sowden "didn't set out to save the world" when they started farming organically, says Buzz Sowden. They started farming without chemicals in 1981 out of necessity—the orchard was "going broke." At the end of the year, the brothers took a look at the orchard and saw that the trees they hadn't done anything to were in better shape than the ones they'd been farming. Now they farm 140 acres of prunes organically, and are proud of having been the first to sell organic pitted prunes and organic prune juice (unfortunately, the juice can't be shipped). Today, says Buzz Sowden, the orchard is in great shape: the sugars are up in the fruit, and the quality of the fruit is "perfect."

STAR VALLEY FARM

2985 Mix Canyon Road
Vacaville, CA 95688
(707) 448-5303

Certified by: CCOF
Minimum order: none
Order by: phone, mail
Pay by: check
Ship by: UPS

DRIED FRUITS

Faye Elberta peaches · French prune plums · Royal Blenheim apricots

NUTS

Walnuts

Richard Schieffer was working as a secondary-school teacher when he decided to change professions. "I was sitting in my living room and asked myself, 'What does the world really need?' The answer was food. I had always liked fruit, so that's what I chose." In 1982, Schieffer started growing fruit in Pleasant valley, fifty miles east of San Francisco. According to Schieffer, "Fruit from this valley was shipped east 120 years ago via the new transcontinental railroad. We're still harvesting fruit from trees that are over seventy years old."

In the future, Schieffer fears that it will become unusual to have agricultural land so close to a big city. Right now, Pleasant valley is zoned for agriculture as a "rural/residential area, but we're right in the path of residential development. The town has drawn up a plan to

annex the valley and put in a golf course and quarter-acre lots," says Schieffer. "There are billions to be made in development, but in twenty years, I bet there will be plenty of people who will be glad to have pockets of agriculture this close to residential centers."

In 1990, dried peaches and apricots were $6 a pound. Prunes were $2 a pound. Walnuts were $4 a pound. Shipping additional.

THREE SISTERS
JOE SOGHOMONIAN, INC.
8624 South Chestnut
Fresno, CA 93725
(209) 834-2772
(209) 834-3150

Visits: yes
Certified by: CCOF
Catalogue/price list available
Minimum order: 5 pounds (raisins)/20 pounds (grapes)
Order by: mail
Pay by: check
Ship by: UPS, parcel post

RAISINS

Thompson seedless · Zante currants

FRESH GRAPES

Thompson seedless (August–September) · Champagne (August) · Ribier (September)

Joe Soghomonian's parents settled in California in 1935, and he's already wondering whether his young daughters—the "Three Sisters" of the label—will be the third generation of Soghomonians to grow fruit on his land. The children already play a crucial role. "We want to pick the grapes at their sweetest," says Joe Soghomonian. "We feed them to my daughter—if she eats one, and then eats another one, we know it's time to pick."

The three sisters know their grapes. I sampled Soghomonian's Thompson raisins, which were plumper, meatier, and juicier than any

raisins I'd ever eaten. They were a universal hit with friends and relatives, and even one formerly raisin-hating cousin. The remarkable thing about the raisins, which everyone noticed, was that they didn't have the dry, sugared quality of commercial raisins, so the fruit's flavor came through. "You can really tell they started as grapes" was the universal response.

In addition to the familiar Thompsons, Soghomonian grows Champagne grapes, which become Zante currants when dried. These tiny grapes, properly known as Black Corinth, are about a third to a fourth the size of other table grapes.

Soghomonian has been farming for more than twenty-five years, and had left chemicals behind entirely by 1981. "It's the best thing I ever did—that, and quit smoking."

In 1990, a 5-pound bag of Thompson raisins was $6.25. A 25-pound bag of Zante currants was $27.50. Shipping additional. Fresh grapes can be shipped within California by UPS or Greyhound bus or air freight out of state. In 1990, they ranged from 20 to 23 pounds per box, for $15 plus shipping.

TIMBER CREST FARMS
4791 Dry Creek Road
Healdsburg, CA 95448
(707) 433-8251
FAX: (707) 433-8255

Visits: yes; tours available
Farmers' markets: Veterans' Memorial Building in Santa Rosa, Wednesday and Saturday mornings
Certified by: CHSC
Catalogue/price list available
Minimum order: none
Order by: phone, mail, fax

Pay by: check, Visa, MC, Amex
Ship by: UPS, parcel post, FedEx
Recipes available
Gift packs available

DRIED FRUIT

Golden Delicious apples · Bartlett pears · French prunes (extra large, large, medium, and pitted) · Blenheim apricots · Dates · Muir peaches · Thompson raisins · Monukka raisins · Mission figs · Calimyrna figs · Mixed fruit (whole or diced)

FRUIT BUTTERS

Apple · Pear · Plum

"I love to eat, and I eat to live well," declares Ronald "Rancher" Waltenspiel. Waltenspiel, who's been growing organically since 1957, has become famous for the flavor of his dried fruit, which he attributes in part to the timing of the harvest: at Timber Crest Farms, says Waltenspiel, they wait to pick the fruit until it is completely ripe and has its maximum amount of sugar. After working as hard as he does to farm organically, says Waltenspiel, there's no point in harvesting fruit while it's still green. Waltenspiel's best-selling fruits are his dried apricots and prunes.

Waltenspiel farms 300 acres of fruit trees, growing apricots and peaches in the Sacramento valley, and prunes, apples, and pears in Sonoma County, where he also grows wine grapes for a nearby winery. Waltenspiel was drawn to organic farming when he noticed that no pesticide he used worked for very long—pretty quickly, the insects developed a resistance to it, and he'd have to turn to something new, something stronger. The escalation showed no sign of stopping.

To learn how to grow organically, Waltenspiel turned to older, retired farmers, to find out what the wisdom had been in the days before chemical farming. He admits that not everything he's tried worked, and that he's had years of low yields—or no yields. But when it works, says Waltenspiel, there's nothing magical or mystical about it; organic farming is just

plain good farming, and constant monitoring to make sure the trees stay healthy.

Once the fruit is picked, it's kept in cold storage and never fumigated. The fruit is washed in water without chemical detergents or mold inhibitors. After the fruit is dried, no sulphur dioxide is added, which means that it will probably be chewier and darker than the dried fruit you may be used to, but the lushly illustrated catalogue will show you exactly what you're getting. The butters are made with organically grown fruit, apple- and lemon-juice concentrate, and cinnamon—no sugar, pectin, or sulfites.

In 1990, 5 pounds of dried fruit ranged from $14.95 to $34.93. Fruit butters were $4.12 for a 9-ounce jar. Shipping in continental U.S. included. All fruits are available in smaller quantities, at a higher price. The catalogue also lists many nonorganic foods including dried tomatoes, which have won raves from the *Los Angeles Times*, the *New York Times*, and the *San Diego Union*.

VAN DYKE RANCH
7665 Crews Road
Gilroy, CA 95020
(408) 842-5423

Visits: yes
Farmers' markets: Downtown Gilroy at 5th and Monterey from 3 to 7 A.M.; dried fruit, capers, persimmons
Certified by: CCOF
Catalogue/price list available
Minimum order: 5 pounds
Order by: phone, mail
Pay by: check
Ship by: UPS
Shipments go out every 2 weeks

DRIED FRUIT

Royal Blenheim apricots · Bing cherries

Betty Van Dyke's family has raised cherries and apricots in California for seventy years. Van Dyke's grandfather, John Mardesich, a Yugoslav immigrant from a fishing village on the Adriatic, started farming with five acres in the Santa Clara valley in the 1920s. Her father, Nick, expanded the ranch. Development forced the family to relocate in Gilroy—the Garlic Capital—where Betty Van Dyke has managed

the ranch since 1970, continuing to farm organically as her father and grandfather did. The fourth generation, Betty's sons, Kurt, Eric, and Peter, are now partners in the ranch.

The Van Dykes are constantly on the lookout for possible drift from spraying on nearby farms, and even refuse to allow the county to spread herbicides on the road in front of their land, which has branded them as eccentrics in their community, but their produce has drawn such illustrious customers as Chez Panisse's Alice Waters.

Apricots come in extra choice, fancy, extra fancy, and jumbo. In 1990, prices ranged from $4 to $5 a pound, depending on the grade. Bing cherries were $3.50 a pound. Prices drop for bulk orders. Shipping additional.

ZEBROFF'S ORGANIC FARM
RR 1, Barcelo Road
Cawston, BC
Canada, VOX ICO
(604) 499-5374

Visits: yes; fresh fruit, vegetables, eggs, and meat
Certified by: SOOPA
Catalogue/price list available
Minimum order: none
Order by: phone, mail
Pay by: check
Ship by: parcel post
The Zebroffs advise you to order early; most of the produce is committed before the end of June

DRIED FRUIT (AUGUST)

Apricots · Cherries · Peaches · Prunes

DRIED VEGETABLES (AUGUST)

Tomatoes

APPLES (SEPTEMBER–OCTOBER)

McIntosh · Red Delicious · Golden Delicious · Spartans · Transparents · Gravensteins · Wealthy · Cox Orange · Crab · Newtowns · Granny Smith

SWEETENER (SEPTEMBER)

Honey · Caramelized honey

JAM (AUGUST)

Apricot

JUICE (STARTING IN NOVEMBER)

Apple

In southern British Columbia, about twenty miles north of the United States border, George and Anna Zebroff's family farm overlooks the isolated, irrigated semidesert Similkameen valley, surrounded by mountains. "It's a wonderful view in all the seasons," says George Zebroff. "Mount Chopska, a U.S. mountain, paints a magnificent landscape for us in the southern direction."

The Zebroffs have been growing organically since 1973. "The health and well-being of our own children was uppermost in our decision," say the Zebroffs. "Happily, our children could always chew on a blade of grass when they played in the orchard." The components of their eleven-acre farm sustain one another. Chickens and waterfowl fertilize the soil, keep pests under control, and get rid of fruit that drops to the ground. Their food comes mainly from the organic orchard.

The Zebroffs primarily sell fresh fruit, but they also sun-dry some of their harvest and use "electric/wood backup when the sun is not shining." The dried fruit contains no sulphur or other additives. The Zebroffs also turn their apricots into jam, using only their own fruit, honey, and a no-sugar pectin. Their honey comes from bees that are given no antibiotics, and fed no white sugar syrup as a substitute for their own feed. The meadows where the bees forage have not been treated with either chemical fertilizers or herbicides. The honey is cleared by settling, not "excessive heat," which means it isn't raised above body temperature during extraction, and nutrients, like enzymes, have not been destroyed.

If you live relatively close by, the Zebroffs can ship perishables by refrigerated truck. Otherwise, they will ship nonperishables. You can discuss shipping possibilities of goods not listed above with them.

Dried fruit and vegetables are available starting in August in 1-pound, 2-pound, and 5-pound packages. Honey is available by the case of 500-gram, 1-kilogram, or 12-pound jars. Jam is available by the case of 250-gram or 500-gram jars. Juice is available by the case of 1-liter or 2-liter bottles.

SEE ALSO
Adaptations, American Spoon Foods, The Apple Farm, Camas Grain, Cottage Garden Herbs, Diamond K Enterprises, Dirnberger Farms, Eagle Organic and Natural Food, Glaser Farms, Glorybee Natural Sweeteners, Minnesota Specialty Crops, North Valley Produce, Specialty Organic Source, Starr Organic Produce, Inc.

DRIED VEGETABLES AND MUSHROOMS

**AMERICAN FOREST
FOODS CORP.**
Route 5, Box 84E
Henderson, NC 27536
(919) 438-2902
(919) 438-2674
FAX: (919) 492-1170

Visits: by appointment
Certified by: SELF
Minimum order: 1 case/1 pound bulk
Order by: phone, mail, fax
Pay by: check
Ship by: UPS, parcel post
Recipes available

DRIED MUSHROOMS

Shiitake · Oyster

In 1984, Toby Farris moved from Chicago to North Carolina in search of trees—specifically oak trees, because oak logs make ideal homes for shiitake mushrooms. Shiitake, whose name comes from the shiia tree, an Asian relative of the oak, is Asia's most popular mushroom, and Japan's leading agricultural export. In 1984, the Japanese shiitake industry was valued at 1.62 billion dollars. Farris wondered what it could be worth here.

In a six-year study, Farris had discovered that a single cord of wood converted to shiitake growing had a value of 1,750 dollars. Farris hoped to turn the mushroom into a windfall for southern farmers, who could add it as a winter crop to their summer harvest. In 1985, he and his partner, Marlene Smith, received a USDA Small Business Innovative Research grant. They started a mushroom farm in a rural area not far from the high-tech Research Triangle Park. Farris became a shiitake evangelist, giving seminars, public demonstrations, and even introducing the Asian mushroom at the North Carolina state fair. His work promoting shiitake mushrooms garnered him the Governor's Entrepreneurial Excellence award.

American Forest Foods

If you'd rather eat than grow shiitake, American Forest Foods can send you dried shiitake that rehydrate in forty minutes in warm water. The mushrooms come with serving suggestions, which include adding the meaty shiitakes to soups, sauces, and to fresh or frozen vegetables while cooking. For barbecue fans—this sounds more like the state fair—the whole caps can be basted with olive oil and grilled. For a more Asian dish, AFF recommends stir-frying the caps with freshly ground ginger and minced garlic, then adding seafood, and a splash of soy sauce or light wine. A variant on traditional bread stuffing for turkey from AFF includes shiitake mushrooms, celery, and onions.

The mushrooms have been certified by OCIA in the past; in addition, AFF has had its mushrooms tested by the North Carolina Department of Agriculture, which found no pesticide residues.

Mushrooms are available in premium/gourmet grade and regular grade/institutional. In 1990, a pound (bulk) of mushrooms ran between $23 and $25. A case of smaller packages ran between $42.75 and $65, depending on the size of the packages and grade of mushrooms.

CAPAY FRUITS AND VEGETABLES
Star Route, Box 3
Capay, CA 95607
(916) 796-4111

Farmers' markets: Berkeley, Tuesday afternoons; San Rafael, Thursday and Sunday mornings; Davis, Saturday mornings; dried tomatoes and fresh produce
Certified by: CCOF
Catalogue/price list available
Minimum order: none
Order by: phone, mail
Pay by: check, money order
Ship by: UPS
Recipes available

DRIED VEGETABLES

Sun-dried tomatoes · Sun-dried tomatoes in olive oil

Remember when the green-and-white ecology sign was almost as common as the peace sign? Back in the 1960s, Kathleen Barnes was an

"ecology major," so it's not surprising that when she and Martin Barnes started farming, in 1975, they did so organically. The Barneses grow a variety of truck crops, but they grow Roma tomatoes specifically for drying. The tomatoes are picked ripe and dried on wooden trays. No salt is added to the tomatoes; you can buy them plain or in olive oil (the oil is not necessarily organic). Although Capay Fruits and Vegetables will send you recipes with your order, Kathy Barnes prefers her dried tomatoes straight, with just the olive oil they're packed in.

HARDSCRABBLE ENTERPRISES, INC.
Route 6, Box 42
Cherry Grove, WV 26804
(304) 567-2727
(202) 332-0232

Certified by: SELF
Catalogue/price list available
Minimum order: 4 1.5-ounce packages
Order by: phone, mail
Pay by: check
Ship by: UPS
Recipes available

DRIED MUSHROOMS

Shiitake

Paul and Nan Goland live in a large one-room cabin in the mountains of West Virginia with no electricity or running water, heated by a woodstove. Paul Goland originally went in on the cabin with some friends as a summer retreat. In time, the others gave up on the inaccessible location, and Goland bought them out.

Goland first learned about shiitake mushrooms from *Organic Gardening* magazine, and decided to try growing them. To give you a sense of his level of expertise when he started, the native Los Angeleno had to ask a neighbor to point out an oak tree.

Goland harvested his first mushroom in 1981. It was also his only mushroom that year, but he's basically an optimist. After all, growing shiitake mushrooms doesn't require constant attention. You bore holes in a log, inoculate the holes with spawn, seal the holes, and store them in well-ventilated shade while the shiitake colonizes the log. Today, Paul Goland has a steady crop of shiitake, and works hard to convince people that anyone can do it. He does advise people not to repeat his biggest mistake: he'd chosen a tree up a road that even his four-wheel drive truck had trouble negotiating.

You may be familiar with shiitake mushrooms from oriental cooking, but they also work well in sautés, soups, and omelettes. The article that first captured Goland's interest de-

scribed their taste as a combination of filet mignon and lobster, with a hint of mushrooms and garlic. In addition to their culinary allure, the mushrooms contain protein and B-vitamins. If you need inspiration, Nan Goland has developed a booklet on cooking with shiitakes.

Although not certified organic, Hardscrabble grows mushrooms with "completely organic methods and procedures": without chemicals, fertilizers, herbicides, fungicides, or pesticides. It also sells spawn for gardening and commercial growers, as well as books on growing shiitake mushrooms.

In 1990, 4 1.5-ounce packages of shiitake were $14, plus shipping. You save by buying in quantity.

L'ESPRIT DE CAMPAGNE
P.O. Box 3130
Winchester, VA 22601
(703) 722-4224

Farmers' markets: Eastern Market in Washington, DC; Alexandria Farmers' Market
Certified by: SELF
Catalogue/price list available
Minimum order: $25
Order by: phone, mail
Pay by: check
Ship by: UPS
Recipes available

DRIED VEGETABLES

Tomato halves in olive oil · Minced tomatoes in olive oil

The "Campagne" in "L'Esprit de Campagne" is a farm in the Blue Ridge Mountains, but the French name comes as no surprise when you learn that Joy Lokey, part of the husband-and-wife team that runs L'Esprit de Campagne, has a *Grand Diplôme* from the Cordon Bleu cooking school in Paris. When she married Carey Lokey, she was a caterer, and he was a woodworker. They wanted to find a business they could start together, and L'Esprit de Campagne fit the bill.

The Shenandoah valley, explains Carey Lokey, used to be a large tomato-growing region. "When the larger companies moved west for the Agri-Biz centers of the irrigated desert, they switched to mechanical harvesters. They opted for tomatoes that de-stem easily, ship well, store well—and have no taste."

Sure he could do better, Carey began experimenting, while Joy tinkered with seasonings. He was convinced he could grow "a perfect tomato," and she was convinced they could improve on imported dried tomatoes. Carey finally settled on the Roma variety, a nonhybrid American seed. He says the Roma is ideal for drying because it's all meat, with much less water and fewer seeds than other varieties. In "Agri-Biz" land, tomatoes are picked green and artificially ripened with ethylene gas, which reddens the tomato but keeps the low sugar-to-acid ratio of an immature tomato. The tomatoes that go into L'Esprit de Campagne's products are picked by hand, so their sugar level is much higher.

The Roma tomatoes dry in a system of low-heat stainless-steel wind tunnels designed by Carey. Once the tomatoes are dried, Joy's recipe involves minimal salting, packing in extra-virgin olive oil that is processed without chemicals, adding L'Esprit's own rosemary and marjoram, dried fennel from Greece, and dehydrated garlic.

Joy Lokey recommends using dried tomatoes wherever you use fresh—pasta, soups, stews, chili, gumbo, salads, stir-fry, ratatouille, frittatas—but if you're feeling timid about experimenting, she will happily send you recipes. She's worked up a tomato-based pesto, a tomato-based mayonnaise, quesadillas, mozzarella-and-tomato salad, chèvre-and-tomato

pizza, as well as recipes for chicken scallopini, lamb chops, shrimp with tomatoes, and many others.

She acknowledges people don't automatically reach for dried tomatoes the way they do for tomato sauce or ketchup, but says that once people taste them, they're sold. Among her converts are Florence Fabricant, food writer for the *New York Times,* who rated L'Esprit's dried tomatoes the best of the four brands she sampled, with the "fullest flavor." *Food and Wine* observed that "unlike most sun-dried tomatoes, which are very salty, these are sweet with real tomato flavor."

In 1990, a case of 12 8-ounce jars ranged from $42 to $45. A single 64-ounce jar ranged from $25 to $26.50. Shipping additional. Be sure to specify organic tomatoes when you order, because they are labeled separately. L'Esprit also sells dried apples and cherries, not organically grown, but unsulphured, with no sugar or chemical preservatives.

MOUNTAIN SPIRIT ORGANIC FARMS
MEALS FOR TWO
HCR 02, Box 68
Moyers, West Virginia 26813
(304) 249-5139

Certified by: VABF
Farmers' market: Charlottesville
Order by: mail only
Pay by: check, money order

DRIED VEGETABLES

Carrots · Potatoes · Onions · Beets · Tomatoes · Peppers

MEALS FOR TWO

Pancake mix and maple syrup · Dried beets, apples, and sunflower seeds · Vegetable/pasta soup · Herb tea

Not only have Kip and Odette Mortenson been organic farmers since 1976, they're also backpackers who've made several cross-country trips. "Every time we'd go on a trip we were faced with what was out there to buy," says Kip. "There wasn't much selection, it was pretty expensive, and none of it was organically grown."

The Mortensons started making a dehydrated soup mix, which they still sell. Although Mountain Spirit is primarily a livestock operation, they'd gotten into vegetable production and had found themselves with good produce that wasn't always market quality because of its appearance. Rather than canning or freezing, they decided to try using small, electric dehydrators. "As far as I can tell," says Kip, "of all the methods of food preservation, dehydrating maintains the highest level of nutrients and vitamins, because it involves the least processing."

Today, they've expanded their offerings into Meals for Two, complete vegetarian meals for two people for a day of camping or hiking. Breakfast contains a buckwheat pancake mix that's half buckwheat flour and half whole-wheat flour—both grown and stone-ground on the farm—with a little salt and baking powder. All you need to add is water. You need a little cooking oil, or a teflon pan. They also include a half-pint of maple syrup. "Depending on how thick you make the batter," says Kip, "you get six to eight pancakes from the mix." For midday snacks, they include sunflower seeds, and dehydrated beets and apples. Dinner is one of their vegetable soups, with spinach, beets, carrots, onions, and other vegetables from the farm. They've made it richer by adding seasonings and veggie spiral pasta made from organic durum wheat (not their own—West Virginia is not durum-wheat country). "If you made it as a soup," says Kip, "this would serve four adults. But if you don't add as much water, it's a heartier meal for two. The dried soup comes in a Mason jar for easy preparation. They also include Mountain Spirit Herbal Tea Blend, a peppermint/spearmint combination.

You can also buy individual dried vegetables, herbs, and tea. Call or write to find out what's available—the Mortensons are constantly expanding their list. They may have meat available in the future.

In 1990, the Meals for Two was $22, including postage.

PANACEA PLANTATION
57 Brookside Lane
Mansfield Center, CT 06250
(203) 429-3122

Visits: yes
Certified by: NOFA-CT
Minimum order: none
Ordered by: phone, mail
Pay by: check
Ship by: UPS

DRIED VEGETABLES

Tomatoes · Hot peppers · Sweet peppers · Onions

Kathorin Stuart was working on a master's degree when she decided that as long as she wasn't working, she'd better start growing her own food. She had gardened all her life, and what started as a hobby suddenly became a business, when she found herself producing far more food than she and her family needed. She and her husband, a welder and mechanic, then started selling the surplus.

Kathorin Stuart grows almost all her own plants from seed, and dries vegetables for use in soups, stews, and sautés. The Stuarts are just getting into mail order and are interested in

expanding their business to suit the needs of their customers. If there are herbs or produce you are particularly interested in, talk to them in the summer or fall and they can plant for the following season. If you want other dried vegetables, Kathorin can try to dry them for you.

LATE-BREAKING INFORMATION

FOREST RESOURCE CENTER
Route 2, Box 156A
Lanesboro, MN 55949
(507) 467-2437

Certified by: OGBA
Catalogue/price list available
Minimum order: 12 grams (dried);
3 pounds (fresh)
Pay by: check, money order, MC, Visa
Ship by: USPS, UPS

DRIED VEGETABLES

Shiitake mushrooms

FRESH VEGETABLES

Shiitake mushrooms

Forest Resource Center sells sliced, freeze-dried shiitake, which rehydrate instantly and are microwaveable. Where other dehydrated vegetables take twenty to thirty minutes to rehydrate, "and taste woody," say the folks at Forest Resource Center, these take two to three minutes in the microwave, "and you can't tell they're not fresh. You can upgrade a soup, sauce, or gravy instantly." If you insist on fresh, however, the company will sell you that, too, shipped Next Day or Second Day Air.

In 1991, a 12-gram bag of dried mushrooms was $4.35; a 30-gram bag was $10. A 3-pound box of fresh mushrooms was $28.50. Shipping additional. You save by buying in bulk.

SEE ALSO
American Spoon Foods, Big River Nurseries, Cottage Garden Herbs, Emandal—A Farm on a River, Gaeta Imports, Greek Gourmet, Ltd., Munak Ranch, Silver Creek Farm, Trout Lake Farm, Williams Creek Farms, Zebroff's Organic Farm

THE APPLE FARM

18501 Greenwood Road
Philo, CA 95466
(707) 895-2333

Visits: yes
Certified by: CCOF
Catalogue/price list available
Minimum order: none
Order by: phone, mail
Pay by: check
Ship by: UPS
Gift boxes and samplers available

APPLES

Golden Delicious · Sierra Beauty · Rhode
Island Greening · Jonathan · Swaar · Fall
Pippin · Splendour · Winter Banana · Arkansas
Black

CHUTNEY

Green tomato and red chili · Apricot, apple,
and almond · Gingered pear with apples and
nuts · Quince and apple with candied ginger

DRIED APPLE WREATH

Jonathan · Rome

JAM

Santa Rosa plum · Apricot · Pomegranate jelly

SWEETENER

Apple cider syrup (pure reduced cider)

When Don and Sally Schmitt bought land on
the Navarro River, it was covered with ancient
apple trees, but their first task was to make the
land, a former labor camp for a nearby farm,
habitable. Their daughter, Karen Bates, and her
husband, Tim, constructed a modern-day version of an adobe house, with two-foot-thick
earth walls that keep it cool in summer and
warm in winter.

Then it was time to address the apples, with
the help of a neighboring family who had 100

years of apple-farming experience among them.
The Bates-Schmitt clan say that the local climate was on their side. The "morning fogs and
hot afternoons" produce fruit that is "remarkably tender skinned and intensely perfumed."

The Bateses now cultivate these "antique"
apple varieties—types of apples that, but for a
few devoted growers, would soon be extinct,
like the Sierra Beauty, which they describe as
"firm to crisp, with a puckery tart flavor"; the
Winter Banana, "soft and delicate, with a banana flavor"; and Arkansas Black, "crisp, hard,
and mildly sweet."

The assortment I received contained Jonathans and Red Delicious, which didn't have the
lacquered look of store-bought Reds. Both were
sweet and flavorful, the Jonathans particularly
intense. The Pippin added a note of tartness
reminiscent of a McIntosh. The Swaar was the
most unusual apple, with a pear's dense flesh
—if I'd closed my eyes, I'd have sworn it *was* a
pear. The Rhode Island Greening was my favorite, a sweet apple with a tart skin. The folks at
Apple Farm particularly recommend it for baking, because it doesn't shatter in pies.

The star at The Apple Farm is the Golden
Delicious. If you're like me, you think of
Golden Delicious as bland, mealy, overinflated
apples without much to recommend them, but
The Apple Farm will change your mind. Their
firm, crisp, refreshing Golden Delicious, sweet
without being cloying, even have a tiny bit of
tartness in the skin. "This is a genuine apple,"
pronounced one friend who tasted them. I'd
recommend them as eating apples even if

THE APPLE FARM

Bates and Schmitt

Goldens are not your usual choice. None of the "antique" varieties was as good an eating apple as the Golden, but combined in an apple crisp, they were fabulous, so if you're interested in having both eating and cooking apples, the mixed box is the way to go.

The Apple Farm's dried apple wreaths are made from Rome or Jonathan apples, unwaxed and completely edible. The apples are sliced extremely thin, dried over an apple-wood fire (of course). The skins are left on, and the red-and-white wreath looks like an Elizabethan collar ruff.

The cider (which the farm doesn't ship) is made from two-thirds Golden Delicious and one-third tart green apples, usually Fall Pippins or Rhode Island Greenings. The farm does ship cider syrup, which is reduced cider, skimmed of solids, and good for topping ice cream, waffles, French toast, or pancakes. The cider vinegar in the sampler is "a natural end product of the cider," say the Bateses; they store the fermented vinegar in oak barrels, adding a live vinegar culture, and let it rest until the following season, when it's bottled.

Karen Bates comes from a family of cooks and hoteliers, so it's not surprising that some of The Apple Farm's fruit ends up cooked in tantalizing-sounding chutneys. Karen recommends using the green tomato chutney with poultry, or in an omelette with sour cream; the apricot chutney over ginger ice cream with toasted walnuts; the quince on a ham sandwich; and using pear chutney to fill baked apples. Chutneys are also mixed with brandy to glaze an apple tart.

All apples and pears are certified organic; other ingredients of the chutneys are organic whenever possible, as are the fruits that go into the farm's jams and jellies. Karen's parents have plans afoot to start a small inn and culinary arts school at the farm—stay tuned.

In 1990, a box of 40 apples—all Goldens, or 1 layer of Goldens and 1 layer mixed varieties in season—was $30. A box of 3 1-pint jars of chutney (the farm's choice) was $30. The Apple Farm sampler (1 pint of cider syrup, 1 pint jar of chutney, a fifth of cider vinegar, a dried wreath, and 28 Golden Delicious apples) was $55. Shipping included. Apples and samplers are available September 1–October 31. Chutney, cider syrup, and vinegar can be shipped year-round as long as supplies last. Supplies of vinegar are particularly limited. If you add your name to the farm's mailing list, you'll receive a yearly reminder of apple season.

DAISY DELL FRUIT FARM
13041 Vincent Road, Route 6
Mount Vernon, OH 43050
(614) 397-6226

Visits: yes; pick-your-own apples; cider
Certified by: SELF
Certification pending from: OEFFA
Minimum order: 1 box
Order by: mail
Pay by: check
Ship by: UPS
Gift boxes available September–June, anywhere in the eastern U.S.

APPLES

Red Baron · Jonathan · Red Delicious · Yellow Delicious · Criterion · Gala · Matsu · Empire · Jonagold

Richard Bowsher was working as a "one-man contractor band" when he planted his apple orchard back in 1981. "I was completely green. I knew absolutely nothing about it. I just knew I had a field up there that wasn't doing anything, and that I should put something on it other than grass. *Now* I'm getting close to knowing enough to get started."

Daisy Dell was hard hit by a freeze in the fall of 1989, so the only apples available in 1990

were Red Delicious. The apples I sampled came well packed in the apple version of a cardboard egg carton, filled with excelsior. They had a few superficial blemishes, and one apple out of the twenty-two had a rotten spot. The Red Delicious apples were crisp and sweet, if a little watery. I'm not a Red Delicious fan myself, but they made a fine applesauce.

In 1990, a 1-layer box of apples was $18 and a 2-layer box was $25. By 1991, Bowsher expects to be selling pasteurized cider, cider jelly, and apple butter. All will be certified organic. Ask about availability.

DHARMA FARMA
HC 68, Box 140
Green Forest, AR 72638
(501) 553-2550

Visits: yes
Certified by: OOGA
Catalogue/price list available
Minimum order: four-fifths bushel
Order by: mail
Pay by: check
Ship by: UPS

APPLES

Akane (mid-August) · Gala (late August) · Grimes Golden (late September) · Liberty (late September) · Starkspur Winesap (late October) · Arkansas Black (early November) · Granny Smith (November)

PEARS (SEPTEMBER)

Moonglow · Warren · Honey Sweet · Magness · Orient · Harrow Delight

Dharma means "right living," or "truth in action," says Ned Whitlock, who lives and farms on an isolated mountaintop in Arkansas that's never been "poisoned by chemicals." Whitlock came to the woods right after college, and began farming organically as part of "right living" or "truth in action."

Whitlock planted his twelve-acre orchard of apples and pears in 1981 but says it's "a whole lot easier to imagine a full-blown orchard than to make one." He sells his apples in two grades: #1 and #2, which are sound, with minor cosmetic blemishes that make them a better value.

Whitlock describes his Akane apples as "deep red, with a sprightly flavor, a Japanese Jonathan style." The Galas are "red-orange over yellow, crisp, dense, with a sweet aromatic flesh. They keep three months when cooled." The Starkspur Winesap is "red, a sweet-tart blend, an excellent keeper." The Arkansas Black is "dark purplish red, with firm, yellow flesh, a distinct aromatic flavor, and a good keeper."

I sampled the Liberty and Grimes Golden apples, both grade #1 and grade #2. They were all small apples, and the blemishes on the #2s

were negligible. The Liberty had an excellent, crisp texture, with a flavor that started off tart and ended up sweet, more intense than a Red Delicious, closer to a McIntosh or Macoun. Liberty apples, says Whitlock, can store up to four months if kept cold. The Grimes Golden had a blush of pink on the yellow skin, the same very crisp flesh as the Liberty, with a flavor approaching a Granny Smith but softened by the sweetness of a Golden Delicious. Both were good eating apples, but their tartness would make them excellent in pies.

In 1990, four-fifths of a bushel ran from $33 to $40 for #1 apples and $20 to $27 for #2 apples. Shipping additional. Pears will be available in 1992.

ECOLOGY SOUND FARMS
42126 Road 168
Orosi, CA 93647
(209) 528-3816
(209) 528-2276

Certified by: CCOF
Catalogue/price list available
Minimum order: 1 box
Order by: phone, mail
Pay by: check
Ship by: UPS

FRUIT

Navel oranges (January–March) · Valencia oranges (April–September) · Kiwi (November–April) · Asian pears (August–October) · Fuyu persimmons (October–January) · Plums (June–July)

When Norman Freestone dropped from 160 pounds to 120, it was obvious something was wrong. The longtime farmer had become allergic to "just about everything." He had to wear a mask everywhere he went. "I'd become an alien in my own environment."

The names for this condition vary—"environmental sensitivity" is one—but Freestone has no doubt about the cause. Farmers using agricultural chemicals are "dealing with nerve

Organically grown: Oranges, Kiwifruit, Asian Pears, Fuyu Persimmons, Plums

toxins, in small amounts over a long period of time. It can strike in different ways—an inability to digest food, insomnia, headaches. Many farmers just don't make the connection between pesticides and how they feel. If they get headaches or insomnia, they say it's just aging."

Not everyone is affected, admits Freestone. "My neighbor can say to me, 'I've been using pesticides a lot longer than you have, and I'm not sick,' and he's right. But it's kind of like a platoon commander asking his sergeant who's just come back from recon. patrol, 'How is it out there?' and the sergeant saying, 'Well, only two of my soldiers got shot.' So the platoon commander says, 'That's not bad. I guess it's safe out there.' "

Doctors told Freestone that the only cure was to move to an unpolluted area like the coast or the mountains. Instead, Freestone stayed put, stopped using chemicals on his farm, and started growing almost all his own food. "It's taken about ten years, and even so, I'm not completely back to square one. On a good day, I can run three to five miles, but I still have to wear a mask when I travel."

Among Freestone's unusual fruits are the Fuyu persimmon, which he describes as crisp, like an apple, sweet, and high in vitamin C and beta carotene. He also grows Asian pears, which are like an apple-pear cross. The Asian pears I sampled had a crisp, freckled golden brown skin; the flesh was extremely juicy, crunchy, and with the slight graininess of a pear and a lighter version of a pear's sweetness, slightly perfumed and honeyed. Only one pear arrived slightly bruised. The rest arrived in perfect shape. Freestone says the pears can also last for weeks at room temperature.

Ecology Sound Farm stores its fruit without chemicals. If any waxes are used, they are natural waxes without fungicides.

In 1990, a box of 33–36 kiwis was $15, a box of 24 Asian pears or Fuyu persimmons was $15, a box of 75 plums was $15, 88 Navel or Valencia oranges were $17.

GOLDEN ACRES ORCHARD
Route 2, Box 2450
Front Royal, VA 22630
(703) 636-9611

Visits: yes; juice and cider vinegar
Certified by: SELF
Catalogue/price list available
Minimum order: 1 bushel
Order by: mail

Pay by: check
Ship by: UPS
Shipping from the fourth week of September until Christmas

APPLES

Golden Delicious · York Imperial · Jonathan · Winesap · Red Delicious · "Brand X" (variety unknown)

Golden Acres doesn't sell "perfectly waxed apples," says its owner, Scottie Thomson, "but we pick out the best fruit to pack. Our customers are educated—we've even had one letter from a customer thanking us for the beautiful fruit and saying that she was glad she found a worm —just one, in a bushel of fruit—because it proved there was nothing harmful in them."

Golden Acres Orchard is a family-run operation that has been in business since 1945. It's a small orchard of thirty-seven acres, and Scottie Thomson says that in contrast to the big growers in the country, who have 500 or 1,000 acres, she and her son "put up every gallon of juice we sell." Thomson's regular customers become friends. Every year, she sends out a personal letter—or a card if the crop is small— telling them what's available. If the crop is very small, she sells only to regular customers.

Thomson does not use the word "organic." The apples are "biologically grown," she says. "We monitor the orchard very carefully. There's no set pattern of what we use, but we maintain healthy trees and organically rich soil. The soil has been tested and is very rich in trace minerals. My conscience wouldn't let me sell an apple for a child to eat if I thought there was anything harmful in it. When our four young men were young, they went barefoot in the orchard just as God intended."

In 1990, a bushel of apples cost $38.50 east of the Mississippi, and $42.50 west of the Mississippi. Prices include shipping.

GREEN HILLS FARMS
P.O. Box 663
Temecula, CA 92320
(818) 788-3690

Farmers' markets: CCOG Farmers' Markets in Los Angeles
Certified by: SELF
Catalogue/price list available
Minimum order: 6 pounds
Order by: mail
Pay by: check, money order
Ship by: UPS
Fruit is available October 15–December 15
Recipes available

PERSIMMONS

Hachiya · Fuyu

When Bud Weisenberg bought the land for Green Hills Farms, it was certainly hilly, but it had never been all that green. Nothing had ever grown on those twenty acres, part of a former Spanish land-grant ranch, except wild chapparal. Weisenberg, an engineer by training, was undaunted. By using drip irrigation, which delivers water to the trees slowly to prevent run-off or evaporation, he's been able to turn the hills green with avocados, grapefruit, lemon, and two varieties of persimmons. Since 1975, says Weisenberg, he hasn't used chemical insecticides. "We just let the good bugs eat the bad bugs."

The Hachiya persimmon is an acorn-shaped fruit that has to be completely soft before you eat it—if you've ever eaten one too early, the astringent taste probably made you swear off persimmons forever. But if you wait until they are as soft as an overripe tomato, the flesh is as sweet and smooth as pudding, and you'll be hooked. Once a Hachiya's ripe, you can freeze it, then puree it to use in fruit cake or cookies, eat it partially thawed like sherbet, or let it thaw all the way.

Unlike Hachiyas, Fuyus can be eaten when still quite firm, as long as they are completely orange. Fuyus, also known as Japanese tomatoes, are far more familiar in Japan than in the

United States (and are tomato-shaped). Their other names, Persapple and Possum Apple, suggest their crisp, applelike texture, which makes them ideal for fruit salads. The entire Fuyu is edible except for the stem and a few thin seeds.

Green Hills ships both varieties with ripening instructions and recipes.

In 1990, a box of 6 pounds of persimmons was $14.95, plus $2 for shipping and handling.

GREEN KNOLL FARM
P.O. Box 434
Gridley, CA 95948
(916) 846-3431

Certified by: CCOF
Catalogue/price list available
Minimum order: 7.5 pounds
Order by: phone, mail
Pay by: check
Ship by: UPS
Gift boxes available throughout the winter

FRUIT

Kiwi

Gridley, California, is the kiwi capital of America. In 1939, the "mother" and "father" plants of all Gridley's kiwis were brought to this country from New Zealand, and nurtured at the Chico Experimental Station. According to Mark Nielson, owner of Green Knoll Farm, Gridley's climate is ideal for kiwis. "It's one of the few areas in the country with this combination of hot summer weather and adequate chilling hours." When Nielson, a carpenter, moved to Gridley from the "big city" ten years ago, he wanted to get involved with what was going on in the local area. In Gridley, that means kiwis.

Nielson sent me a tray of forty-two kiwis, which all arrived in good condition. I kept the tray in a cool pantry, where they ripened at different speeds over the next month, a relief because I had imagined all forty-two ripening at once. Nielson includes ripening tips with each tray—you can speed up the process by placing them in a sealed plastic bag at room temperature. Kiwis ripen even faster in the presence of other fruit, so you can hurry them along by putting an apple, banana, or pear in the bag with them. When ripe, the fruit was very firm and bursting with juice. Comments included "succulent" and "refreshing."

The fruit will keep up to four months in the refrigerator if sealed to keep in moisture. Kiwis have more vitamin C than oranges, says Nielson, and are high in potassium. They also contain an enzyme similar to the enzyme in papayas, and so can be used as a marinade to tenderize meat.

In 1990, a 7.5-pound tray of kiwis was $18, including shipping.

JAVIANJO KIWIFRUIT
9650 McAnarlin
Durham, CA 95938
(916) 342-1069

Visits: yes
Farmers' market: Heart of the City in downtown San Francisco
Certified by: CCOF
Minimum order: $10.95
Order by: phone, mail
Pay by: check
Ship by: UPS

FRUIT

Kiwi

For Nancy L. Batha, kiwis are more than a fruit. They represent financial independence. When her husband died, Batha was a Montessori teacher and had "a little music school" in

her home. She found herself, like many widows, trying to figure out a way to pay the bills. She thought of selling off some land, but instead, she planted kiwis on one acre of the two-acre parcel around her house. "It grew so well, I just fell in love with it. Instead of splitting off that acre and selling it, I thought, 'Well, I can always do that later if it doesn't work out." But it did work out.

At first, Batha took her kiwis to someone else to package and market, but she soon discovered she could get three times as much by doing the marketing herself. She bought a second two-acre parcel and planted kiwi even more densely there. "I was actually able to pay off the mortgage with the kiwi money." Today, even though Batha has as friend who helps her with the kiwis, it's important to her to remain "independent in the business, as a woman."

In 1990, a 2.5- to 3-pound gift pack was $10.95, a 5-pound gift pack was $14.95, and a 7.5-pound gift pack was $18.95. Shipping included. Prices decrease on larger orders.

JOHNSON'S KIWIS AND PRODUCE
515 Chandon Avenue
Gridley, CA 95948
(916) 846-6511

Visits: by appointment
Certified by: CCOF
Minimum order: 7.5 pounds
Order by: phone, mail
Pay by: check, money order
Ship by: UPS
Shipping November–June

When you drive into Gridley, California, says Brad Johnson, "there's a big sign that says we're the sister city of Tepuke, New Zealand." The sign pays homage to Gridley's most famous crop: kiwis. Johnson's father bought his first land in the area—three acres—in 1950. "After I got out of school," says Johnson, "my father said he had a piece of ground, and if I wanted to do something with it, I could. I was interested in vegetables, but I was really green—we had grown up with orchards, and I didn't know anything about vegetables. I learned a lot the hard way—the expensive way. My father's been real supportive, sometimes to his detriment. He's been real generous helping all of us get started. He lets us use his land, his house, his tools, his shop."

Brad Johnson started growing kiwis from nursery stock in 1975 and planted the kiwis on his own land in 1978. He has been organic from day one. "I didn't really like working with chemicals. I just wanted to grow a good product without them. I like doing the best I can to make good soil. Now it's a more popular thing —back then everybody laughed."

In 1990, a 7.5-pound tray of kiwis was $12 plus shipping. Because packing small orders is time-consuming, Johnson prefers to ship every 2 weeks to allow orders to accumulate.

LONE PINE FARM
P.O. Box 38
Inglefield, IN 47618-0038
(812) 867-3149

Visits: yes; wide variety of fresh produce
Certified by: SELF
Minimum order: none
Order by: phone, mail
Pay by: check
Ship by: UPS

FRUIT

Pureed persimmons

VEGETABLES

Beets · Broccoli · Cauliflower · Cabbage · Sweet
Spanish onions

NUTS

Pecans

In the wild, says Marvin Lundy of Lone Pine Farm, persimmons can be "pretty peppery." Lundy grows a domesticated, grafted version of the fruit, which can be used in puddings, cookies, and in bread like zucchini. Lundy makes a persimmon puree, which he ships frozen. Mine arrived wrapped in a shipping bag, much newspaper, a box, more newspaper, and a second box. The puree was still cold, but not frozen—

LONE PINE FARM
P.O. Box 38
Inglefield, IN 47618-0038

NATURAL FOODS
ORGANICALLY GROWN

if you live any distance from Lone Pine Farm, you will probably want to use the puree soon after you receive it, and not risk refreezing it.

On the spoon, the puree tasted as rich as apricots, but sweeter, nothing at all like the

astringent, puckery taste I had associated with fresh persimmons. I could easily imagine stirring it into yogurt, or using it as a sauce for pancakes, oatmeal, or other hot cereals. I used it to make Lundy's recipe for persimmon-date bread, a rich, dense, wonderful, almost black fruit bread, in which the persimmons were again reminiscent of apricots. One change I would suggest is that two loaf pans work better than one for the quantity he gave me—I had to put a cookie sheet under the loaf pan and got some de facto drop cookies to go with the bread. When I reported this to Mr. Lundy, he said he uses a three-quart loaf pan; if you use his recipe, you might want to do the same.

Marvin Lundy has been growing organically for forty years. Rodale started publishing *Organic Gardening* in 1942, and Lundy has been a subscriber since 1943. Indiana does not yet have a certification program so, says Lundy, "I sure more than qualify, and yet don't have it. But that doesn't bother me at all. We're known by our customers for our quality and taste."

In 1990, 2 pints of persimmon puree were $3, plus shipping. Lone Pine Farm has many vegetables available; if you're reasonably close, you might want to talk to Lundy about shipping more perishable items.

MUNAK RANCH
3770 North River Road
Paso Robles, CA 93446
(805) 238-7056

Visits: yes; peppers, tomatoes, apple cider
Farmers' markets: Paso Robles (Tuesdays), Atascadero (Wednesdays), Santa Barbara (Saturdays), Monterey (Thursdays), Santa Cruz (Saturdays), San Luis Obispo (Thursdays), Morro Bay (Thursdays), and Cambria (Fridays)
Certified by: CCOF
Minimum order: none
Order by: phone, mail
Pay by: check
Ship by: UPS
Fresh fruit is available June–November; sun-

dried tomatoes may be available after November

APPLES

Red Delicious · Gold Delicious · Gala · Granny Smith · Newtown Pippin · Winesap · Jonathan · Mutsu · Rome Beauty · Gravenstein

MELONS

Boule D'Or · Valencia

DRIED VEGETABLES

Sun-dried tomatoes

Ed and Pearl Munak were "city people" before they started Munak Ranch. Pearl Munak had worked as a union organizer; Ed Munak had been a systems engineer. Today, they are both full-time farmers in Paso Robles, about halfway between Los Angeles and San Francisco.

The Upper Salinas valley is a "very special place," according to Pearl Munak, combining hot, sunny days and cool nights. "This climate enables plants to absorb the rays of the sun and to manufacture them into fruit sugars during the cool periods. The result is unusually sweet fruit. The evidence of the taste buds can be verified objectively by the use of a refractometer, a precision instrument that measures soluble solids—mostly fruit sugars—in fruit. We also search out the best-tasting varieties from all over the world. If we don't think it tastes better than what you can get elsewhere, we don't grow it." Pearl Munak is particularly proud of the many "antique" varieties of russet apples they grow, "which have been nearly abandoned for growing because of their appearance, but taste wonderful."

In addition to apples, they grow several kinds of melons, some of which are hardy enough to ship, at least for short distances. The Boule D'Or, says Pearl Munak, is gold on the outside and green on the inside, a sweet melon with "a refreshing component." The Valencia looks like an acorn squash, dark green on the outside, with a sweet green or white flesh on the inside.

In 1990, a 40-pound box of apples was $23, plus shipping.

PARADISE RANCH/VALLEY CENTER PACKING COMPANY
28425 South Cole Grade Road
Valley Center, CA 92082
(619) 749-5464

Certified by: Quality Assurance Labs, International
Certification pending from: CCOF
Minimum order: 30 pounds
Order by: phone
Pay by: check
Ship by: UPS

FRUITS

Star Ruby grapefruit (July) · Valencia oranges (April–December) · Navel oranges (December–May) · Asian pears (September) · Tangelos (end of February–April)

I gave a Valencia orange from Paradise Ranch to a friend who took one bite and said "Heaven!"—and I hadn't even told her the name of the ranch. Don't be surprised if the skin on these Valencias is paler than the neon-orange you see in the supermarket. It may even shade into yellow and green, but the fruit is ripe, juicy, and extremely sweet. "They may not win the award for best looking," said my friend Tom, "but they may well win the award for sweetest—and I'm a Florida orange man myself." They also made a superb orange juice: thick, sweet, and refreshing.

Rudy Monica and Rocky Calamia are the "two buddies" behind Paradise Ranch. Monica

VALLEY CENTER PACKING CO., INC.
ORGANICALLY GROWN CITRUS
28425 S. Cole Grade Rd., Ste. B
Valley Center, CA 92082

had owned a health-food store and Calamia had been a distributor of organic foods. Together they bought a "suitable-for-export Sunkist grove," says Monica, and started the transition to organic growing. Monica is particularly proud of the "beautiful, thin-skinned Valencias," the Star Ruby grapefruit, and the navel oranges. "We've got the best-tasting fruit in the business." I haven't tasted all the fruit in the business, but Monica may be right.

Although Valley Center Packing primarily deals with large orders (54 boxes of fruit), it also prepares gift boxes of 30 pounds of whatever fruit is in season. In 1990, a 30-pound box of fruit was $20 plus shipping.

RIVER BEND ORGANIC FARM
2363 Tucker Road
Hood River, OR 97031
(503) 386-8766

Visits: yes; wide variety of fresh produce; fresh apple juice
Certified by: OR-TILTH
Catalogue/price list available
Minimum order: none
Order by: phone, mail
Pay by: Visa, MC, check, money order
Ship by: UPS, US Postal Air, FedEx
Quantities are limited, so order early

PEARS

Royal Cascade · Comice · Bosc · D'Anjou

APPLES

Royal Gala · Criterion · Red Delicious · Golden Delicious · Granny Smith · Jonagold · Empire · Newtown Pippin

JAMS AND SYRUPS

Huckleberry syrup · Huckleberry honey · Huckleberry jam

Kaye and Bob White bought their farm in Oregon sight unseen. They were living in Arizona, where Kaye was working at Citibank, and Bob was making custom guitars, when they decided to move their family (including three teenage children) to a twenty-eight-acre farm on the banks of the Hood River. And quite a sight it was: a valley in the Cascade Mountains with Mount Hood to the south and the Columbia River to the north.

The rich volcanic soil of the Hood River valley, say the Whites, watered by Mount Hood's eleven glaciers, has been famous for fruit since the 1880s. The Whites grow the traditional fruits of Washington: apples and pears, including some unusual varieties, like the Royal Cascade, a pear they describe as a "red beauty" that combines "the delicate texture of the Comice with the fruity flavor of the Bartlett." Their Comice, the "Cadillac of pears," are "so juicy you need a bib," and they recommend the Bosc as the best pear for cooking.

The Royal Gala is the Whites' favorite apple, "exceptionally sweet-tasting, lightly flavored, and crisp." The Criterion is a yellow apple with a slight red blush, "so juicy it's like drinking a glass of cider." Jonagold is a cross between a Golden Delicious and a Jonathan, a big gold and red apple that "slightly tart and yet sweet." The Empire is a cross between a Red Delicious and a McIntosh, and the Newtown Pippin, "the best in the West for pies," has a "smooth, tart flavor." By 1991, River Bend was selling jams, syrups, and other food products made from organic ingredients under its own label.

In 1990, a 5-pound box of pears ranged from $17.95 to $22.95. A 5-pound box of apples ranged from $16.95 to $23.95. You save by buying a 10-pound box. The Holiday Sampler, one of each variety of apples and pears, was $22.95. A gift crate of huckleberry syrup, honey, and jam was $31.95. The farm also sells conserves from Cascadian Farm (page 172). Shipping was $3.95 per delivery, or $4.50 for 10-pound boxes. The catalogue also contains other products made by cottage industries, but not necessarily organic.

ROYAL ORGANIC
Star Route 1
Royal, WA 99357
(509) 346-2428

Certified by: WSDA
Minimum order: none
Order by: phone, mail
Pay by: check, money order
Ship by: UPS, parcel post

FRUIT

Red Delicious apples

BEANS

Pinto

GRAIN

Triticale (wheat-rye cross)

Peat Eriksen's great-grandfather was injured in the Danish-Prussian war and "resented the king's pittance he got as a thank-you so much that he uprooted the whole family," says Eriksen, whose voice still bears traces of the Scandinavian Midwest, where his great-grandfather settled. "They homesteaded in Nebraska where there were a few stops along the railroad. I guess they just got off and walked—there wasn't much out there. Grampa had older brothers to take care of the farm, so he took off and went west. He purchased this land in 1912 from a railroad real-estate company. At the time the land was covered with prairie grass. Elk and deer and buffalo would range up here."

The name Royal Organic comes from the land, known as the Royal Slope, a gentle, south-sloping bench of soil with long growing hours and many frost-free growing days. Even at the turn of the century, says Eriksen, books talked about the remarkable quality of the fruit and vegetables grown in the area. But the big change for the land came in the late 1960s, with a federal irrigation project that made water from the Grand Coulee Dam, built during the Depression, available to farmers.

Peat Eriksen came back to the family farm in 1973. "After high school I went on a mountaineering expedition to Alaska and much of Canada. I had never been back East and what I saw scared me. The earth seemed more limited to me. I became concerned that the ecology of the land was being ignored. You could say that was my practical education."

Eriksen started farming without much formal training, so he felt free to choose organic methods. Eriksen believes deeply in the nutritional superiority of organic produce, which he feels gets more vitamins and enzymes from the living soil. "When you eat a meal of organic food, you're not hungry afterwards. When you're finished, you're finished. Your body isn't looking for other nutrients it didn't get. People who are overweight may have the problem that they're always hungry because they're not getting what they need. But you don't have to be a nutritional scientist," Eriksen says. "Your taste buds will tell you the difference. I get compliments all the time. My beans have a slightly sweet flavor, and they're full and robust—they don't just taste like filler. The flavors are full and satisfying."

For grains and beans, the standard bag is 25 pounds, but Royal Organic is happy to break that down into smaller amounts. Royal Organic also sells vegetables, which vary from year to year, so call or write to find out what's available.

S. M. JACOBSON CITRUS
1505 Doherty
Mission, TX 78572
(512) 585-1712

Certified by: TDA
Catalogue/price list available
Minimum order: quarter-bushel
Order by: mail
Pay by: check
Ship by: UPS
Shipping period generally runs November–
March, but varies with weather and ripeness

FRUIT

Marrs oranges · Clifford Navel oranges · Ruby red grapefruit

Stanley and Marina Jacobson came to Texas in 1981, but couldn't afford a farm until the big freeze of 1983 brought the price of land within reach. The Jacobsons—he from New York, and she from Houston—started learning from scratch, taking lessons from neighbors.

They started from the ground and worked up; if you make the soil healthy, they reasoned, you get healthy trees, and when you have healthy trees, you have fewer pests. Even when bad weather has given them smaller fruit than usual, the taste has remained "sweet and juicy," which the Jacobsons attribute to organic growing. "An organic farm has self-contained fertility and a natural balance."

The Jacobsons were among the first organic growers certified by the state of Texas, and had to endure "a few chuckles" from conventional farmers. The relatively small size of the orchard —750 trees on seven acres—makes it easier for them to practice organic methods.

Because the bulk of S. M. Jacobson's sales are through mail order, "the fruit stays on the tree until we get your order," says Stanley Ja-cobson. "Tree-ripened citrus gets sweeter and juicier as winter nights are cool and days are sunny. Most citrus hits the market much earlier than ours, but the extra growing time makes better fruit. We don't pick green, nor add color. We start to ship in late November. Typically, early season fruit will have a tinge of green but taste sweet and delicious. The fruit is best after December 1st."

The grove was badly hit by the freeze in the winter of 1989, but the Jacobsons expected to be back in business by 1991. In the future, Mr. Jacobson also expects to grow figs and papayas —"if we can make it through a winter without a freeze!"

In 1989 (the last year before the freeze), a quarter-bushel of fruit (about 13 pounds of oranges, grapefruit, or mixed fruit) ranged from $12.75 to $19.75, depending on the destination. A half-bushel ranged from $18 to $28. Four-fifths of a bushel (38 pounds) ranged from $23.75 to $36.75. All prices include shipping.

S.M. Jacobson Citrus
1505 Doherty
Mission, TX 78572

SEASIDE BANANA GARDEN
6823 Santa Barbara Avenue
La Conchita, CA 93001
(805) 643-4061

Certified by: SELF
Farmers' market: Ventura, California.
Catalogue/price list available
Minimum order: 5.5 pounds
Order by: phone, mail
Pay by: check, money order
Ship by: UPS Second Day/Next Day Air
Shipping every Tuesday

BANANAS

Manzano · Blue Java (Ice Cream) · Brazilian · Mysore · Cardaba · Cavendish

When the box arrives from Seaside Banana Garden, you open it up, dig around in the shredded newspaper, and pull out odd-shaped packages wrapped in last week's funnies that contain bananas in sizes and colors you've never imagined. What you get depends on what the company is shipping the week you order. The bananas in my sampler ran from a brilliant lime green, to a pale green with white racing stripes, to a banana dark as a cucumber at one end and rhubarb pink at the other. The smallest almost fit in the palm of my hand; the largest could run neck-and-neck with a midsummer zucchini. Luckily, the samplers also come with ripening instructions. After a long weekend, the striped banana was completely yellow, with only the faintest hints of white streaks, and a blush had spread the length of the formerly dark green Jamaican Red.

What's even more amazing about this variety is that you're not supposed to be able to grow bananas, a native of tropical southeast Asia, in the continental United States. But that didn't stop Doug Richardson, a landscape contractor whose specialty was edible landscaping. Richardson planted his eleven-acre banana garden seventy-five miles north of Los Angeles, and patiently endured the comments of passers-by, who would go out of their way to tell him he simply couldn't grow bananas there. Richardson says the microclimate was on his side: 300-foot cliffs protect the plants from wind damage, and the Pacific Ocean, which gives Seaside its name, holds heat, keeping the plantation ten degrees hotter than neighboring towns.

Richardson and his partner, Paul Turner, grow some fifty varieties of bananas, from which the sampler is selected, but say none of them should be confused with the "industry standard" for bananas in this country, "high-yielding varieties with a pleasant but very mild flavor, bordering on bland." Brazilians, I'm told, dismiss the fruit we eat as "water bananas."

All the Seaside bananas had a more intense, fruity flavor than any bananas we are used to, a snappier texture, and less of an astringent aftertaste. I would recommend trying the bananas at differing degrees of ripeness to see how you like them best—sort of like finding out whether you like three-minute, five-minute, or hard-boiled eggs.

At first, the Ice Cream banana was both sweet and flavorful with a frothy texture, unlike any banana I'd ever eaten. A few days later,

the flavor was milder, and the flesh was completely creamy. The texture of the Brazilian was the complete opposite, with smooth, solid, substantial flesh; where a supermarket banana breaks easily, the Brazilian only bends. The flavor, a strong blend of sweet and tart flavors, was an idealized version of an ordinary banana. A few days later, the Brazilian banana was all sweetness, with none of the tart flavor remaining. The Iholena was closest to the ordinary banana, although fluffier and coarser, very sweet both out-of-hand and cooked.

The Mysore was an extraordinary pale apricot color; the flesh both sweet and tangy— Richardson describes it as "strawberry citrus flavor." At one end, you could actually see and taste the seeds, which had a slight crunch. The Cardaba was a bit like pineapple in flavor, with a soft flesh and pronounced seeds, and remained tangy when cooked.

The Ae Ae, which I only tried cooked, was spectacular—almost like fresh cooked peaches. The Manzano, which Seaside describes as "the favorite dessert banana around the world," took a full three weeks to ripen, and had a mild sweetness. Unlike the others, the Jamaican Red was not at all sweet, close to a plantain in texture—almost crunchy—with a mysterious musky flavor that drew the following attempts to identify it: vanilla, malted milk, coconut. If you have any better ideas, let me know.

Imported bananas are picked unripe in order to endure the long shipboard trip to American markets. They're also sprayed heavily, both to prevent premature ripening during shipment and to kill bugs. By contrast, the Seaside Banana Garden's bananas ripen on the trees and are not sprayed, either on the trees or after being picked. Pests that might threaten the plants in the tropics are killed off by the colder winters of California, and because they're flown straight to you "as soon after harvest as possible," they don't need to dip the bananas in a fungicide, "as is done with all the imported bananas."

In 1990, the sampler box was $35, including shipping, west of the Mississippi, and $40 east of the Mississippi. Seaside also sells a wide variety of banana plants for growers.

SLEEPY HOLLOW FARM

44001 Dunlap Road
Miramonte, CA 93641
(209) 336-2444

Visits: yes; pick-your-own apples; picnics welcome; mountain spring water available (free)
Certified by: CCOF
Catalogue/price list available
Minimum order: 2 ounces (herbs)/40 pounds (apples)
Order by: phone, mail
Pay by: check
Ship by: UPS, parcel post
It's best to reserve apples by August 1

APPLES

Jersey Mac (July) · Earliblaze (July) · Gala (August) · Red Delicious (September) · Golden Delicious (October) · Blushing Gold (October) · Arkansas Black (November)

CULINARY HERBS

French tarragon · Oregano · Sweet marjoram · Sage · Lemon thyme · Bay leaves · Basil · Rosemary · Peppermint

MIXED HERBS

Italian herb mix · Soup pot mix · Stew pot mix

Dave and Lee Duncan had both worked in public health before they started their orchard, so it was natural for them to become organic growers. They're the only organic orchard in the area, and they soon learned why. The hard clay and granite soil of the mountains in Miramonte made organic growing much more difficult than they'd imagined. "All the growers around here just pour on the chemical fertilizers," says Lee. "We looked at their trees and assumed ours would grow the same way."

Lee Duncan's degree is in agriculture, but Dave's is in history, and when he quit his job to work on the orchard, he'd never farmed before. "We had to learn everything the hard way," says Lee. They deliberately chose varieties that would ripen at different times of year so that the two of them could manage the orchard themselves.

The Duncans recommend that you order your apples early and choose the apples that suit your needs. The Jersey Macs are tart, red eating apples, similar to McIntosh. Galas are "a really pretty yellow orange," says Lee Duncan.

The Gala is an "exceptionally firm," medium-sized apple, with a flavor like a Golden Delicious, but "spicier," say the Duncans. If you're planning to store your apples, you might want to choose Earliblaze, a tart cooking apple with "the best storage life of all the summer apples." Lee's favorite is Blushing Gold, which is "shaped like a Golden Delicious but has more snap and is more solid. I tell people they can put it in plastic and put it in the refrigerator, and it will last until spring. It retains its aroma and taste—it may get a bit shriveled, but it still has its taste." Arkansas Black is "our Christmas apple. It's a lovely deep, almost black red. It's very crisp and firm and can be kept in cold storage for nine months."

In 1990, dried herbs were $2 per ounce, and fresh herbs were $2 per bunch (spring and summer only). A 40-pound box of apples was $20. Shipping additional.

STARR ORGANIC PRODUCE, INC.

P.O. Box 561502
Miami, FL 33256-1502
(305) 262-1242

Certified by: FOGA, SELF
Catalogue/price list available
Minimum order: none
Order by: mail, phone
Pay by: check, money order
Ship by: UPS
Gift baskets packed to your order; special baskets available for Easter and Passover, and winter holidays

FRUIT

Avocados (August–February) · Apple bananas (year-round) · Pineapple juice oranges (November–February) · Navel oranges (November–February) · Temple oranges (February–March) · Valencia oranges (March–July) · Mineola tangelos (January–February) · Orlando tangelos (January–February) · Grapefruit (white, red, or pink) (January–June) · Limes (year-round) · Mangos (June–August) · Sapodilla (year-round, but irregularly) · Star fruit (July–September)

DRIED FRUIT

Apple bananas · Papayas

"RAWIES"

Mango, coconut, and cashews · Apple banana, coconut, and raisins · Papaya, coconut, raisins, and cashews · Apple banana, oatmeal, raisins, and cashews

CAKE

Fruit-and-nut cake

If you've been eyeing some of the exotic new arrivals in the fruit section of your supermarket and wondering what they taste like, Starr Organic Produce gives you a way to try them—organically. The "Produce Availability Form" gives you a brief description, and Starr also sends out a newsletter to introduce its newest exotic fare.

You might want to sample the sapodilla, which the folks at Starr say has the consistency of an apple, with a light brown flesh, an aroma that combines pears, apricots, and honey. Or perhaps you've been wondering about those brilliant yellow star fruits. The people at Starr say the fruit has a sweet/tart flavor. You can cut ripe star fruit in half and scoop out the flesh, or make the unripe fruits into jam. Starr sells four different varieties of mango, which provides the daily requirement of vitamins A and C, and recommends using them fresh, cooked, frozen, dried, or chilled in salad or dessert. Of course, you can also order the citrus fruit for which Florida is famous, or avocados from some of Florida's 12,000 acres of avocado trees. Starr sells some 100 different varieties of avocados—what you get depends on the time of year you order.

The company also dries some of its more unusual fruits—papayas and apple bananas—and makes "Rawies" from fruit dehydrated at low temperatures. These should be refrigerated, and become soft when heated slightly. Fruitcake has its lovers and haters; for lovers, Starr has a fruit-and-nut cake made entirely from organic ingredients.

All of the fruit, except for some papayas (not listed above), is grown organically, and fruit is

shipped as soon as it is picked. The fruit is not waxed or gassed with any chemicals. Larger groves are certified by the Florida Organic Growers' Association. Smaller growers are self-certified, and their standards are kept on file.

In 1990, 12 pounds of avocados were $15. A 12–15 pound box of mangos was $24.95. A 20-pound box of apple bananas, oranges, grapefruit, or tangelos ranged from $17.50 to $22. A 10-pound box of sapodillas was $25. A 10-pound box of star fruit was $30. A half-bushel assorted gift basket was $35. Shipping additional, except on mangos and avocados. "Rawies" were $2 each. Dried apple bananas were $3 for a half-pound package, and dried papayas were $3 for a quarter-pound package. The fruit-and-nut cake was $19.95, including shipping. Starr also offers 3-month, 6-month, 9-month, or 12-month pick-of-the-grove plans. Prices were $80, $150, $220, $289, east of the Mississippi and $2 per month extra west of the Mississippi, but produce is not shipped to Arizona, California, Alaska, Hawaii, or Texas. Be sure to specify that you want the "Produce Availability and Order Form" unless you are ordering in large quantities—then ask for the "Wholesale Order Form."

TURKEY RIDGE ORCHARDS

RR 2, Box 264CC
Gays Mills, WI 54631
(608) 735-4562
FAX: (608) 735-4328

Cheese certified by: OCIA
Certification of orchard pending from: OCIA
Catalogue/price list available
Minimum order: none
Order by: phone, mail, fax
Pay by: check, money order, major credit cards
Ship by: UPS
Gift boxes available

APPLES

William's Pride · Liberty · Freedom · Jonamac · Novamac · Priscilla · Red Free · McShay · Dayton

SWEETENERS

Sorghum · Maple syrup

CHEESE

Cheddar Muenster · Mozzarella · Goat cheese

Turkey Ridge's president, Mike Bedessem, explains that his particular area of Wisconsin is "well attuned to apple growing, the way some climates make areas better for making wines. We grow our apples up on the ridge, where cool nights in the fall give the apples color and flavor. This area's apples have very distinct flavors—that's why the area grows so many varieties."

Turkey Ridge has been organic since its inception in 1988. For one thing, there's no irrigation at Turkey Ridge. "We're not taking a soil not meant to grow apples and growing apples on it," says Bedessem. "We are attempting to pioneer sustainable methods that can be used by the many conventional orchards in our area." The apple varieties at Turkey Ridge are disease- and scab-resistant, which makes them easier to grow organically than "conventional, supermarket varieties." Turkey Ridge Orchards has taken a number of regional specialties, including the cheeses of Organic Valley (page 48), and will mix and match them in gift boxes. The sorghum and maple syrup, from cane and trees on certified land, are available in half-pints, pints, and quarts. "One great thing about sorghum," says Bedessem, "is that it needs no preservatives. It's an easy crop to grow but a difficult crop to harvest. There's a lot of hand work. You just don't see people who've grown it once rushing to do it again."

VALLEY COVE RANCH

P.O. Box 603
Springville, CA 93265
(800) 548-4724
(209) 539-2710

Certified by: SELF
Catalogue/price list available
Minimum order: none
Order by: phone, mail
Pay by: check, money order, Visa, MC
Ship by: UPS
Sampler available

FRUIT

Navel oranges (December 1–March 15) · Valencia oranges (April 1–June 15) · Lisbon lemons (December 1–April 15)

Valley Cove Ranch, in the foothills of the Sierra Nevada Mountains, overlooks the Tule River into the Sequoia National Forest. The grove was planted in the 1950s and became one of the first organic citrus groves in California. "We're the highest altitude citrus growers around," says John Brinkman, the owner of Valley Cove. Height gives him a natural advantage for organic growing—"we're not troubled with sprays drifting down from other growers." His water comes from the Tule River and five lakes on the property. Valley Cove Ranch is not

VALLEY COVE RANCH
P. O. Box 603
SPRINGVILLE, CALIFORNIA
93265

certified organic because it does use weed oil. "We tried to weed mechanically, but with groves this size, it just proved impossible," says Brinkman. "We don't use any other sprays. Natural predators are used to control harmful insect pests." After picking, the fruit is neither dyed nor gassed. No wax preservatives or chemicals are used in storage, nor are the shipping cartons treated with any chemicals.

Brinkman believes that the soil and climate of Valley Cove Ranch produce a "much sweeter fruit than you'll find elsewhere. We ship all over the country, and people tell us they've never really tasted an orange until they've tasted one of ours. I think in our case the taste tells the whole story."

In 1990, a 20-pound carton of fruit ranged from $18 to $26, depending on the destination. A variety carton (navel oranges, a few lemons and avocados, and a pound of walnut meats) is available December 1–January 15. In 1990, an 18-pound variety carton ranged from $20 to $28 depending on the destination. Shipping included. In addition to the principal varieties listed above, Valley Cove Ranch also grows Satsuma mandarin oranges, grapefruit, and avocados. Contact the ranch for availability.

WEISS'S KIWIFRUIT
594 Paseo Companeros
Chico, CA 95928
(916) 343-2354

Visits: yes
Certified by: CCOF
Catalogue/price list available
Minimum order: 2.5 pounds
Order by: mail, phone
Pay by: check, money order
Ship by: UPS
In December, kiwis are only sent to warmer areas of the country.

FRUIT

Kiwi (October–December).

When Gary Weiss retired, he wanted to do something with the small amount of land he had—less than two acres. "I like a challenge," says Weiss, who came to California in 1957, but still speaks with the accent of his native Wisconsin. There aren't too many crops that make sense on a plot that small, but a neighbor of his was growing kiwis, and Weiss thought he'd try it. With homes so close together, he

WEISS'S KIWIFRUIT
594 Paseo Companeros
Chico, California 95928
916 • 343 • 2354

"didn't want to fool around with sprays," so he went organic. His three-quarter-acre plot now bears about 15,000 pounds of organic kiwifruit a year.

Weiss's kiwis were almost twice the size of kiwis I'd gotten in the market. They came well packed and insulated: only one kiwi was slightly bruised. When ripe, the kiwis were extremely juicy (napkin definitely required) and considerably sweeter than store-bought, with almost no acid tang. It turns out that although the Kiwi Marketing Council advises growers to pick when the fruit is at 6.5 percent sugar, Weiss likes to wait until the fruit reaches 7 percent and is "just that little bit better."

Weiss has found that customers often don't know how to ripen kiwis, and includes a flier on ripening with each order—some of mine were ready to eat in two days. He also advises customers in colder climates to order early if they want fruit for Christmas, because the fruit can freeze in transit. If kept completely airtight, however, the fruit can last until March or April in your refrigerator.

In 1990, gift packs of 2.5 pounds were $8.75 east of the Rockies and $9.75 west of the Rockies. Gift packs of 5 pounds were $13.75 east of the Rockies and $14.75 west of the Rockies. Shipping included.

LATE-BREAKING INFORMATION

BLUEBERRY LAKE FARM
621-154th Avenue SE
Bellevue, WA 98007
(206) 747-4599

Certified organic: WSDA
Minimum order: 10 pounds
Pay by: check, money order
Ship by: UPS Next Day Air

FRESH FRUIT

Blueberries (July–August)

FROZEN FRUIT

Blueberries

Call for current prices.

DIRNBERGER FARMS
18900 Southwest 304th Street
Homestead, FL 33030
(305) 245-6837

Certified by: SELF
Catalogue/price list available
Minimum order: 20 pounds
Pay by: check, money order
Ship by: UPS

FRESH FRUIT

Avocado mango · Limes · Navel oranges · Hamlin oranges · Pineapple oranges · White grapefruit · Pink grapefruit · Honeybell tangelos · White sapote · Eggfruit · Apple bananas

UNCOOKED DRIED-FRUIT PATTIES ("RAWIES")

Bananas with coconut, walnuts, raisins · Mango with coconut and cashew · Papaya with coconut, cashew, and raisins · Oat with banana, walnut, and raisins · Mango-oat with cashews and raisins

Fruit is available in 20- or 40-pound boxes, with wholesale prices available for buying clubs. You may mix types of citrus in one box. In 1990, 20-pound boxes of citrus ranged from $12 to $15; 40-pound boxes ranged from $20 to $24. Apple bananas were $20 for 20 pounds. Shipping additional.

FIRST FRUITS ORGANIC FARMS
P.O. Box 864
Paonia, CO 81428
(303) 527-6122

Certified by: Colorado
Catalogue/price list available
Minimum order: 1 gift box (15–20 pounds)
Pay by: COD or payment in advance
Ship by: UPS

APPLES

Jonathan · Rome · Red Delicious · Golden
Delicious · Winesap

PEARS

Bartlett · Bosc

OTHER FRUIT

Cherries · Peaches

Cherries and peaches are shipped by Next Day Air. Fruit
can be packed in 20- or 40-pound boxes, but a gift box
can be 1 or 2 layers of fruit.

GLASER FARMS
19100 Southwest 137th Avenue
Miami FL 33177
(305) 238-7747
FAX: (305) 238-1227

Certified by: FOGA
Catalogue/price list available
Minimum order: none
Pay by: check, money order
Ship by: UPS

FRESH FRUIT

Apple bananas · Avocados (nine months of the
year) · Mangos · Eggfruit · Carambola
(starfruit) · Black sapote · Lichee · Limes ·
Grapefruit · Tangelos · Valencia oranges ·
Navel oranges

DRIED FRUIT

Rawie (dried-fruit cookie)

SEA VEGETABLE

Dulse

In addition to these exotics, Glaser Farms plans to have
papaya in the future. It also sells aloe vera leaves. All
orders carry a handling charge of $3; shipping additional.

NOAH'S ARK
7074 Casitas Pass Road
Carpinteria, CA 93013
(805) 684-5996

Certified by: CCOF
Minimum order: 1 box (30–40 pounds of
fruit)
Pay by: check or money order in advance
Ship by: UPS

FRESH FRUIT

Cherimoyas (November–April) · Kiwi ·
Avocado · Bananas · Pineapple guava ·
Sapotes · Passionfruit

NUTS

Macadamia

Noah's Ark specializes in exotics, like the
pineapple guava, a small, seedless fruit with the
taste of a pineapple.

In 1990, cherimoyas were $3 a pound, plus shipping.

ROSSLOW GROVES
1007 Poinsettia Drive
Fort Pierce, FL 34950
(407) 461-4066

Certified by: FOGA, OCIA
Catalogue/price list available
Minimum order: none
Pay by: COD or check, money order
Ship by: UPS

FRESH FRUIT

Pink grapefruit · White grapefruit · Navel oranges · Orlando tangelos · Tangerines · Mineola tangelos (Honeybells) · Pineapple oranges · Parson Browns · Valencia oranges · Murcott oranges · Temple oranges

The folks at Rosslow Groves say that their Indian River area is known for the sweetest and juiciest citrus in the world. Fruit can be shipped in 20- or 40-pound boxes.

SOUTH TEX ORGANICS
6 Betty Drive
Mission, TX 78572
(708) 585-1040

Certified by: TDA
Catalogue/price list available
Minimum order: 10 pounds
Pay by: check, money order
Ship by: UPS

FRESH FRUIT

Valencia oranges · Navel oranges · Rio Red grapefruit

FRESH VEGETABLES

1015 onions

South Tex Organics will ship in 10-, 20-, or 40-pound boxes. It plans to ship garlic and potatoes in the future.

WILLIAMS CREEK FARMS
P.O. Box 292
Williams, OR 97544
(503) 846-6481

Certified by: OR-Tilth
Catalogue/price list available
Minimum order: $20
Pay by: check, money order, cashier's check;
Visa and MC in the future
Ship by: FedEx, USPS, UPS

APPLES

Empire · Melrose · Cox's Orange Pippin · Newtown Pippin · Red Gravenstein · Winesap · Red Astrakhan

PEARS

D'Anjou · Bartlett · Precoce Morettini · Comice

GARLIC

Braids

HERBS AND SPICES

Kitchen wreath of culinary herbs, peppers, and garlic

FRESH VEGETABLES

Baby lettuces · Gourmet greens

DRIED VEGETABLES

Dried tomatoes

"Our focus here is sustainable agriculture," says Randy Carey of Williams Creek Farms. "That's a lot more than keeping the chemicals and pesticides off. It means insuring that the farm endures for centuries to come."

SEE ALSO
Banwart Family Foods, Blue Heron Farm, Diamond Organics, Eugene and Joan Saintz, Gracious Living Farm, Hawaiian Exotic Fruit Company, How-Well Organics, Mountain View Farm, North Valley Produce, Orange Blossom Farm, Pallan Apple Orchard, Rancho Santa Madre, Ronsse Farms, Sowden Brothers, Sunshower Produce and Juice, Three Sisters, Zebroff's Organic Farm

FRESH VEGETABLES AND MUSHROOMS

Many of the growers in this section do not have catalogues, but will happily ship the hardier vegetables they grow.

ANDERSON ACRES
P.O. Box 168
Dalhart, TX 79022
(806) 384-2084

Visits: yes; okra, melons, hot and sweet peppers
Farmers' market: Dalhart, Tuesday afternoons, Saturday mornings
Certified by: TDA, AGR
Minimum order: 5 pounds
Order by: phone, mail
Pay by: check, money order
Ship by: UPS
Shipping January 1–June

FRESH VEGETABLES

Vine-ripened tomatoes · Cucumbers

Roger Anderson's greenhouse can withstand whatever the Texas weather has to offer, including hail. Anderson has grown tomatoes all his life, but greenhouse growing, says Anderson, gives him "a complete control over the environment that you just can't get outside, and as a result, you get quality you can't get outdoors."

Anderson raises the tomatoes without any chemical fertilizers, herbicides, or insecticides. In addition to state certification, Anderson has a leaf analysis done each week to make sure that the plants are healthy, and to verify that no chemicals are being used. He's also had his tomatoes tested by Consumer Testing Laboratories, an independent lab, and compared with a store-bought tomato. The results showed his tomatoes far outperforming the store-bought on every index, from vitamin A (almost 200 times the amount) to carbohydrates (300 times

the amount) to protein (twice the amount) to iron (30 times) to potassium (five times). And, of course, the store-bought tomato showed traces of paraquat, Round-up (a common herbicide), and 2-4-D.

Although tomatoes seem like a delicate crop to ship, Anderson says he's had no problem shipping to California and New York. He sent me a testimonial from a customer in New York

who said that the tomatoes arrived in perfect shape, and that the last one was was firm and delicious two weeks after it arrived. Anderson guarantees his shipments for full refund or replacement.

Please call or write for current prices.

BANWART FAMILY FOODS
RR1, Box 64
West Bend, IA 50597
(515) 887-6250

Visits: yes
Farmers' markets: Fort Dodge, Walmart parking lot, Wednesdays; Algona, K Mart

parking lot, Saturdays
Certification pending from: Agricultural
Growers' Research
Minimum order: none
Order by: phone, mail
Pay by: check
Ship by: UPS

VEGETABLES

Pumpkin · Potatoes · Onions · Broccoli · Beets · Radishes · Squash · Cabbage · Kohlrabi · Cauliflower · Cucumbers · Carrots

FRUIT

Muskmelon · Watermelon

Ken and Marlene Banwart are bucking tradition by going organic in the heart of the Corn Belt. "Around here," says Ken Banwart, "people think that a lot of people will go hungry if we stop using chemicals. If they forced all the farmers around here to stop, there would definitely be a problem with weeds until they got their fields in balance, but there are alternatives —if they'll listen." After farming for twenty years, Ken Banwart says, "it's always been my gut feeling that the stuff we were using wasn't right." The Banwarts made the decision to give up chemicals when they switched from the traditional crops of the region (corn and soybeans) to truck farming, as a way to get the next generation of Banwarts—all six of them—started on the farm. All except the youngest, born in 1986, do some work around the farm; the oldest is in Future Farmers of America.

The Banwarts are just getting into mail order, and are learning what they can ship easily. They'd like to talk to you about what you most want to buy, to help them plan their crops for the future. By May of 1992, Banwart Family Foods will have been chemical-free for four years, and will be eligible to qualify for organic certification. Until then, the farm is certified transitional. The Banwarts also planned to add herbs in 1991.

Ken Banwart will also make local deliveries at $15 per trip; for example, if he has 6 stops to make, the customer at each stop will owe him $2.50 for delivery.

CROSSROAD FARMS
Box 3230
Jonesport, ME 04649
(207) 497-2641

Visits: yes; 150 varieties of fruits, vegetables, and flowers; specialty is an assortment of salad greens, picked while you wait
Certified by: MOFGA
Catalogue/price list available
Minimum order: $25
Order by: phone, mail
Pay by: money order, bank check
Ship by: UPS
The Pearlmans advise you to order early to avoid disappointment

SQUASH

Buttercup · Delicata · Acorn · Butternut · Red Kuri · Hubbard (blue, green, gold) · Sweet Dumpling · Sweet Mama · Golden Delicious · Spaghetti · Green Hokkaido

OTHER VEGETABLES

Beets · Parsnips · Cabbage · Carrots · Burdock · Jerusalem artichokes · Rutabaga · Potatoes

As a child, I had fantasies of self-sufficiency inspired by *Swiss Family Robinson*, but nothing ever came close to the reality of Crossroad Farms. When Arnold and Bonnie Pearlman moved to Maine from Maryland over twenty years ago, the land that is now Crossroad Farms was all woods. Not a single clearing. The Pearlmans had to use a machete to clear a place to park their van, which doubled as their home until they built a house.

For the first eight years, the Pearlmans worked the land without any power machinery.

That means chopping firewood by hand, digging their gardens with a fork and shovel, and planting trees with the aid of a pick and crowbar. Today, power for their lights comes from batteries charged by windmill; a generator provides the current for power tools and a washing machine.

Eventually, the Pearlmans cleared and planted ten acres of garden and a three-and-a-half-acre orchard. The Pearlmans' children, Delia and Jody, plant, weed, harvest, and bring in firewood. Delia has been running the rototiller since she was ten, and Jody started mulching the potato patch at three.

The Pearlmans are vegetarians and grow "virtually every vegetable that does well in this northern climate, including forty-five varieties of potatoes." If you order potatoes from Crossroad Farms, the Pearlmans will be happy to advise you on how to choose from their forty-five varieties, "from Abinaki to Yukon Gold—yellow, blue, pink, red, and white—tell us what you like in a potato and we'll match your taste to a suitable variety." The family's favorite is the Carole, a large, yellow-skinned and yellow-fleshed potato with a buttery flavor. They also recommend the slightly dry Scotia Blue for baking, and the Lavender Blue (the flesh really is lavender), which has a smoky flavor.

The Pearlmans are intimately acquainted with every vegetable they sell, because the farm provides almost all of their food. Only cooking oils, grains, seeds, nuts, and blackstrap molasses come from off the farm. Without power for a freezer, they don't have frozen food; they don't can, either, except for the few things that can be canned with cold water. In winter, they rely on the root cellar to fill the pot, and the few plants, like kale, that they can pick in the winter snow. As winter comes to an end, says Bonnie Pearlman, and they've run through most of their vegetables, her husband varies the taste by cooking in different pots. Bonnie Pearlman insists that it really does work, and that the family's meals are as pleasurable in the lean times as they are in times of plenty.

In 1990, prices for squash ranged from 70 cents to $1.30 a pound depending on variety. Potatoes were $1.20 a pound. Root vegetables ranged from 85 cents to $2.35 a pound. Prices include shipping and handling, but there is a surcharge west of the Mississippi, and on orders under $40. Ten percent discount for orders over $70.

DIAMOND ORGANICS
45 Pascal Avenue
Rockport, ME 04586
—or—
Freedom California 95019
(800) 922-2396
FAX: (207) 236-0703

Certified by: MOFGA, CCOF, CHSC
Catalogue/price list available
Minimum order: none
Order by: phone, mail, fax
Pay by: check, Visa, MC, UPS COD
Ship by: UPS, Second Day, Next Day Air
Sampler basket available

LETTUCE

Red leaf · Green leaf · Oak leaf (red or green) · Bibb (red or green) · Romaine (red or green) · Butter (red or green) · Lollo rosso · Tango cocarde · Mixed specialties · Mesclun (European salad greens)

FRESH HERBS

Basil · Chervil · Chives · Cilantro · Dill · Mint · Italian parsley · Sage · Oregano · Rosemary · Tarragon · Thyme · Sorrel · Savory · Edible flowers

SPECIALTY GREENS

Arugula · Mizuna mustard · Red mustard · Baby spinach · Garden cress · Baby bok choy · Medium frisee · Mache (corn salad) · Dandelion green · Tatsoi · Radicchio

SPROUTS

Alfalfa · China rose · Sunflower · Spicy mix

VEGETABLES AND GREENS

Artichokes · Bell peppers (red, green, gold) · Blue lake beans · Large bok choy · Broccoli ·

Cauliflower · Bicolor corn · Cabbage (green or red) · Celery · Chard (green or red) · Collards · Cucumbers · Jalapeño peppers · Kale · Anaheim peppers · Shell peas · Snap peas · Snow peas · Spinach · Patty pan squash · Yellow crookneck squash · Salad tomatoes · Cherry tomatoes · Yellow pear tomatoes · Zucchini

WINTER SQUASH

Acorn · Green · Gold · Buttercup · Butternut · Sweet Dumpling · Delicata · Hokkaido · Red Kuri · Kabocha · Spaghetti · Pie Pumpkin

ROOTS AND TUBERS

Beets with greens · Loose beets · Burdock root · Carrots with greens · Loose carrots · Daikon radish with greens · Red radish with greens · Garlic · Onion (red or yellow) · Scallions (red or green) · Leeks · Turnips with greens · Potatoes (russet, red, or yellow) · Jewel yams

APPLES

Red Delicious · Golden Delicious · McIntosh · Gala · Granny Smith · Pippins · Mutsu · Fuji

PEARS

Anjou · Asian · Star Crimson · Bartlett · Bosc

CITRUS

Pink grapefruit · Lemons · Limes · Valencia oranges

OTHER FRUITS

Haas avocados · Bananas · Raspberries · Strawberries · Blackberries · Red or green flame grapes · Kiwi · Melons

Jasch and Kathleen Hamilton describe Diamond Organics as "bringing a European open-air market to your door." In 1984, the Hamiltons began selling the produce of their own half-acre farm and other Maine farms to restaurants and·hotels in the Boston area. The northeastern growing season being what it is, they expanded in 1988 to include growers in California, Washington, and Mexico, and ship directly from the growers to you. Much of the produce is certified organic; if it isn't certified, Diamond Organics requires an affidavit that the growing practices meet the standards of the California Health and Safety Code, and they follow up with a visit whenever possible.

"Our real goal," says Jasch Hamilton, "is to open regionally and buy regional produce and keep shipping costs down by shipping ground service, which will arrive the next day if you're

local. That way we can keep it fresh, native, and organic. The next one we hope to open, by early 1991, will be in Philadelphia, followed by Chicago and then either Florida, Texas, or L.A."

In 1990, a sampler basket containing a selection of specialty lettuces, fresh herbs, edible flowers, apples, pears, citrus fruit, specialty greens, and winter squash ranged from $20 to $38, depending on the destination. Shipping included.

DUTCH COUNTRY GARDENS
RD I, Box 1122
Tamaqua, PA 18252
(717) 668-0441

Visits: yes; wide variety of fresh produce ("We'd rather people visit us and talk with us before buying. We are in this to provide wholesome food to appreciative folks.")
Certified by: SELF
Minimum order: $50
Order by: phone, mail
Pay by: check, cash
Ship by: UPS, parcel post

VEGETABLES

Beets · Carrots · Potatoes (white, red, or yellow)

When Joseph Yasenchak was a little boy, he was "farmed out" every summer to his aunt and uncle's farm, where he was in charge of getting rid of potato bugs and weeds. "Everything was better in those days," he says, unabashedly nostalgic. "The air was better, the water was better. They had a hand-pump that brought water into the kitchen, and a pond with ducks and geese." That early experience gave Yasenchak a love of farming that stuck with him, and when the opportunity came to buy his own farm, he didn't hesitate.

The problem was that the farm "had been a chemical farm, and the land was useless. You could land a B-29 on it, but that's about it. There was no biological life in the soil. There was a pond that was entirely devoid of life. No bugs, no birds, no snakes." Yasenchak brought in minerals and truckloads of leaves, and nourished the soil with cover crops, year after year.

His neighbors said he was crazy, but Joseph Yasenchak has recreated the kind of farm he fell in love with as a boy, and his descriptions of it sound magical: sunflowers fourteen feet high, 100 cucumbers from a single plant, and "watch where you walk, or those pumpkins will get their tentacles out and trip you right up." The land has been clean of chemicals for nearly twenty years. "Not a day goes by that we don't see pheasants, and toads, and turkeys, and mockingbirds—all kinds of songbirds. Deer come down in herds."

Yasenchak says proudly that his "produce has the delicious taste food should have and did have when your granddaddy was a little boy." Yasenchak grows "the world's tastiest potatoes, and the best carrots. Even the carrot tops are edible—the carrot tops from a commercial farmer are almost poisonous. My beets you can peel and eat like an apple. The beets you get from a chemical farmer are like a rock. It would be like chewing on the root of a tree."

Yasenchak uses a refractometer to measure the sugar content of his fruits and vegetables, which "exceeds the range science knows about." Potatoes from a chemical farmer, he says, might register a three, but his have registered as high as nine. This "Brix" reading, explains the former schoolteacher, indicates not only the sweetness of the produce, but its overall health: high sugar also means high mineral content.

GRACIOUS LIVING FARM
101 Mountain Parkway East
Insko, KY 41443
(606) 662-6245

Visits: By appointment; wide variety of fresh produce
Certified by: SELF
Minimum order: none
Order by: phone, mail
Pay by: check
Ship by: UPS, parcel post
"Everything guaranteed 100% or your money back"

VEGETABLES

Broccoli · Cabbage · Carrots · Cauliflower · Cucumbers · Onions · Sweet potatoes · Popcorn · Pumpkin · Winter squash

FRUIT

Watermelon · Cantaloupe · Red Delicious apples · Yellow Delicious apples · Grimes Golden apples · Smooth-skinned kiwi

Paul Patton got serious about farming organically "after being sprayed with the chemicals and poisons in Vietnam—I am disabled from it. I moved to a 100-acre farm last year, and now have a 400-acre farm, mostly hillside, and have a great start on it. It's harder at first to garden organically, but it gets easier every year, because you keep building your soil and getting rid of pests organically."

Kentucky doesn't have state certification. "Colleges here," says Patton, "still teach to poison everything. The University of Kentucky agriculture department wrote and told me I couldn't raise blueberries in Kentucky." Patton, taught to farm by his grandfather "since I was nine years old," proved these experts wrong, and "invited them down to show them my 117 beautiful, four-year-old plants."

In addition to the produce listed above, Patton grows many other fruits and vegetables, but you should discuss with him which can be shipped. He also sells ornamental corn, dried flowers, and grapevine wreaths.

GRAVELLY RIDGE FARMS
Star Route Box 16
Elk Creek, CA 95939
(916) 963-3216

Visits: yes
Certified by: CCOF
Minimum order: none
Order by: phone, mail
Pay by: money order (preferred), check
Ship by: UPS

VEGETABLES

Availability varies

GRAINS

Amaranth · Quinoa

Michael Spurlock spent eight years "in agricultural aviation"—crop dusting—which taught him the risks of chemical farming first-hand. "Some of those chemicals were Class 1 poisons. They'd kill you in fifteen seconds if you got them in your face. And the sad thing is it was all unnecessary, too."

Spurlock's grandparents farmed eighty acres at Gravelly Ridge, which has never had chemicals on it, so Spurlock was able to get certified organic his first year on the farm. Gravelly Ridge Farm is an ideal location to farm organically: an elevation of 1,000 feet on a mountain on the west side of the Sacramento valley. "A creek runs through the farm with snow runoff," says Spurlock. "There are a few people above me, but basically I'm one of the first to use the water."

By 1991, Spurlock plans to have a periodic mailing—probably quarterly—listing the pro-

duce he has available for mail order. He's in a rural area, thirty-five miles from the nearest town, so prefers to wait until he has several orders before going to town to mail them.

GREENSWARD/NEW NATIVES
1255 Hames Road
Aptos, CA 95003
(408) 728-4136

Farmers' markets: Cabrillo College in Aptos, Saturday mornings; Monterey Peninsula College in Monterey, Thursday afternoons
Certified by: CCOF
Catalogue/price list available
Minimum order: $20
Order by: phone
Pay by: check
Ship by: FedEx

SPROUTS

Alfalfa · Clover · Mustard · Bean mix · Buckwheat · Sunflower · Wheatgrass (for juicing)

Sprouts are a health-food staple, but—ironically—they are often grown from chemically treated seeds. What makes Greensward/New Natives unusual, says Ken Kimes, its co-proprietor, is that it only sells sprouts from organically grown seed. Kimes and his partner, Sandra Ward, grow all their sprouts in a greenhouse, without any artificial light.

Perhaps just as unusual is the project they started with—wheatgrass. About ten years ago, Sandra Ward started growing wheatgrass in the

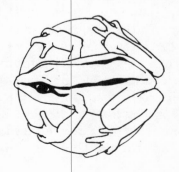

garage of their house, at the request of a juice company Ken had worked for. Wheatgrass juice is extremely high in chlorophyll, explains Kimes. "In the 1930s and 1940s, there was a lot of research into the healing properties of chlorophyll, but when the pharmaceutical companies realized they couldn't patent it, they discontinued the research," says Kimes. Wheatgrass is also high in beta carotene and high in protein, says Kimes. "I've had it tested myself by a research chemist, and he was really surprised."

Kimes admits that wheatgrass isn't for everybody. "It's an extremely concentrated food supplement." For others, it may go along with a philosophical commitment to simplify their lives. "It's the original food on the planet. When you eat it, you're moving way, way down the food chain."

H-S FARMING COMPANY
P.O. Box 724
Healdsburg, CA 95448
(707) 838-4570

Certified by: SELF
Catalogue/price list available
Minimum order: none
Order by: phone, mail
Pay by: check, MC, Visa, COD
Ship by: UPS, parcel post, FedEx
Shipments go out on Mondays and Tuesdays so mushrooms are not in transit over the weekend

FRESH MUSHROOMS

Shiitake · Chinese Cashew · Pearl White · European Brown

After one course in mycology at California Poly San Luis Obispo, Richard Hambright was hooked on mushrooms—the edible variety. The only trouble was that he couldn't find any mushrooms in the store that tasted as good as the wild ones. So in 1976, at the urging of his mycology professor, Hambright tried growing wild mushrooms himself. He read about mushrooms and talked to the experts who grew or foraged for mushrooms. After several years, he had "a 90 percent track record—of failure." Listening to people wasn't helping, so Hambright took to the woods, to listen to the mushrooms. "Thinking like a human wasn't working. I wanted to think like a mushroom, and relate to the environment like a mushroom."

That led Hambright to concentrate on species, like shiitake, that thrived on dead wood. He's been growing these mushrooms and selling them to restaurants, caterers, and markets, since 1981. Hambright thinks that the "cool, moist coast" of Sonoma County gives mushrooms better flavor by slowing down their growth.

Shiitake mushrooms, says Hambright, have a thick cap and a meaty flavor, not unlike lobster. A friend who is allergic to seafood loves shiitake because they come so close to the forbidden foods—without any risk. Hambright also grows seven different species of oyster mushrooms, but says you shouldn't confuse any of his oyster mushrooms with ones you've had in the past. "The oyster mushroom sold in supermarkets is the Phoenix Oyster. It has the least flavor of any cultivated oyster, but it has the greatest yield." By contrast, each variety of oyster Hambright sells has a distinct flavor: "The European Brown has a meaty texture and a mild, nutty flavor. The Pearl White can resemble a Calla lily in shape; it has the same texture as the European Brown, but a stronger, spicy, peppery flavor, and a good bouquet. The Chinese Cashew is a clear yellow color, with coral-like growth, and a cashew-like flavor and aroma."

Although the mushrooms are not certified organic, Hambright says, "we test all raw materials for presence of pesticides. We would discard any lots that showed any level at all, but in sixteen years, we've never had to do this. Our standards are more strict than CCOF or OCIA."

In 1990, a five-pound box of mushrooms was $40, plus shipping. Hambright also sells starter kits for growers.

NEW PENNY FARM

85 Williams Road
Presque Isle, ME 04769
(800) 827-7551
(207) 768-7551

Certified by: OCIA
Catalogue/price list available
Minimum order: 5 pounds (potatoes)
Pay by: check, money order, MC, Visa
Ship by: UPS
Sampler and gift baskets available

POTATOES

Bintje · Carola · Cobbler · Kennebec ·
Katahdin · Russet Burbank · Sangre · Shepody

FRESH VEGETABLES

Fiddlehead ferns (May–June only)

The soil of Aroostook County, Maine, is ideal for growing potatoes, and until the 1950s or 1960s, when states like Idaho began to irrigate intensively, Maine led the nation in potato cultivation with some 200,000 acres producing potatoes each year. Today, only 85,000 acres of Maine are sown with potatoes, and 150 of those acres belong to Chris Holmes of New Penny Farm.

Holmes came to New Penny Farm in 1981, and began building up the soil with clover and other cover crops, supporting the endeavor by continuing to grow conventionally on other land. He saw a future in organically grown potatoes. "After all, people have been growing their own food for thousands of years, and chemicals have only been around since the 1940s. There are alternatives. You just have to work to find them." The relatively low cost of land in Aroostook County made it possible for Holmes to farm organically. "I don't have to plant the same acre year after year. After potatoes, I plant oats, and then clover and other legumes, all of which enrich the soil, so it's three years in between potato crops. If I were near a big city and land costs were high I might have to use the land more intensively. Up here I use a long rotation, and I can afford to experiment on a small scale."

Holmes set out to reintroduce "Potatoes We Knew," the forgotten varieties of potatoes that had made Maine famous but had since gone out of fashion because they were difficult to grow without blemishes and were easily damaged by mechanical harvesting. "Because they bruise easily and have deep eyes, these varieties were only being grown by home gardeners."

His catalogue recommends uses for many of his potatoes whose names may be unfamiliar to you. The Sangre, as the name implies, is a red potato, good for salads; the Kartahdin is good for boiling and a "moist baker"; the Kennebec is a "versatile favorite"; the Shepody is good for baking or mashing; the Cobbler is a trade-off—deep eyes for a particularly flavorful potato; the yellow-fleshed Bintje is a "mealy baker" and the Russet Burbank is "excellent baked or mashed." Holmes's personal favorite is the Carola, a smooth-textured yellow potato "high in solids, and good for baking or mashing." You can mix four varieties in a sampler, or try five in Potato of the Month club, from December through April.

Holmes brushes but does not wash potatoes before shipping them, because washing "increases enzyme activity," which in turn "leads to a more rapid decline in freshness." I sampled the Bintje, moist and smooth but a bit bland, much in need of sour cream or other dressing; the dry but flavorful white Irish Cobbler, a good accompaniment to a rich meat or stew; the mild-flavored, firm, moist Kennebec; and the Carola, an all-around winner with a moist, yellow flesh that needs no addition—the texture is soft, smooth, and buttery, akin to a sweet potato. The Carola needs nothing added. All arrived with eyes, and so required a little more careful preparation than the store-bought variety.

If you like, Holmes will ship your potatoes in an ash-splint basket, made by members of the neighboring Micmac tribe. "Micmac baskets have been the main harvesting tool in this area since the late 1800s," Holmes explains. "When white settlers started to grow potatoes in Aroostook, Indians were already here making baskets from ash. The baskets are part of the tradition." Holmes, who was born in Presque Isle, has worked with the Micmacs as a consultant to help them promote this native craft. "The ones I sell in the catalogue look like the harvest baskets, but they're shaved smooth and made with finer splints."

In 1991, Holmes began shipping fiddlehead ferns, a local delicacy collected on the banks of local rivers.

In 1990, a 5-pound bag of potatoes was $15. The 5-month club was $65, or $90 if the December order was shipped in a handmade Micmac basket. Postage included east of the Mississippi.

ORANGE BLOSSOM FARM
Route 1, Box 94A
Carrizo Springs, TX 78834
(512) 876-2103

Certified by: TDA
Minimum order: none
Order by: mail
Pay by: check
Ship by: UPS

VEGETABLES

Texas spring sweet onions

FRUIT

Washington navel oranges · Ruby red grapefruit · Tangerines · Cantaloupes

Bay Laxson's grandfather grew citrus in the Rio Grande valley. His father was a livestock

ORANGE BLOSSOM FARM
ORGANIC CITRUS, VEGETABLES & LIVESTOCK

CARRIZO SPRINGS, TEXAS 78834

rancher. He combines both on Orange Blossom Farm. Like his father and grandfather, Laxson avoids chemicals. "Many of the older-style growers were not as ready to jump on the bandwagon as we're led to believe today. They stuck to the things they'd been doing forever. Basically, it was the younger people coming out of the university systems after World War II who supported the modern approach, and it just snowballed."

The chemical revolution changed the size and appearance of fruit and vegetables. Laxson admits that when he went organic, "the first winter our fruit was kind of small, but it had real good flavor." A buyer for a natural-foods store in Austin came down and bought out his whole crop, and encouraged Laxson to add vegetables.

Laxson grows two kinds of onions: both the "standard 502," which is a top-shaped, sweet onion, and the "1015y," which Bay Laxson gives "a higher mark in shape—it has the nice, round, baseball shape." The 1015y is "supposed to be the sweetest, but I don't give it that," says Laxson, still a fan of the hardier 502.

If you live within 250 miles of the farm, Laxson can also ship you beef raised entirely on organic feed, and without drugs, except for a seven-way vaccination required by state law.

In 1990, onions were $1 a pound, plus shipping. Laxson may have melons to ship in the future. Citrus fruit is available in 16-pound gift boxes: whole boxes or oranges and grapefruit, or gift packs of all three fruits. Orange Blossom Farm expects to have citrus in 1992. You can put your name on the mailing list and Laxson will let you know when he has fruit available. Orange Blossom Farm also sells short-day and long-day onion plants for growers.

ORGANICLY YOURS/ALDO LEOPOLD AGRICULTURAL INSTITUTE

P.O. Box 1006
Newark, DE 19715
(302) 738-6388

Visits: yes; fairs, festivals, field trips, and workshops
Certified by: NOFA-NJ
Catalogue/price list available
Minimum order: none
Order by: phone, mail
Pay by: check
Ship by: UPS

VEGETABLES

Winter squash · Potatoes · Onions · Turnips · Rutabagas

In 1990, developers were eager to buy the Kranz family farm, but Bill and Ruth Kranz were not so eager to sell. Sure, they could have made a handsome profit, but it would have meant watching land they had farmed for forty-one years turn into a housing development. They wanted the land to be used as they had used it—for agriculture. So they placed fifty acres of their land and a small house in a ninety-nine-year trust, and leased it to Nancy Jones and Paul Keiser.

Keiser had farmed for twenty-five years; Jones, who grew up on a cattle ranch in Bucks County, Pennsylvania, had gardened organically for twenty years, and taught organic gardening for ten. The two have founded the Aldo Leopold Agricultural Institute, named for the author of *A Sand County Almanac,* whom they call "a great American forester, conservationist, farmer, and writer during a period in our history when there were few conservation voices." The Institute sponsors research, demonstration, and cooperative projects, public education, and will act as a consultant on ecological and biodynamic agriculture.

Because of the recent move, Jones and Keiser weren't yet sure what produce they'd have available to ship. For farmers and gardeners, they have Fertrell natural fertilizers and soil aids, herb plants, and books and pamphlets on organic gardening.

REIN FARMS

P.O. Box 10914
Jefferson, LA 70181-0914
(504) 888-5763
(504) 736-8751

Certified by: SELF
Catalogue/price list available
Minimum order: none
Order by: phone, mail
Pay by: check
Ship by: UPS, parcel post

FRESH VEGETABLES

Potatoes · Sweet potatoes · Daikon radishes · Winter squash · Pumpkins

Conrad Rein has a full-time job as an urban planner, but weekends and holidays, and "every other spare minute," he's farming. His grandfather and great-grandfather were truck farmers around New Orleans; his father gardened as a hobby; and he's been gardening since he was "yea high."

Rein, who follows California's organic guidelines, has lately been devoting more of his time to educating both farmers and consumers in Louisiana, where organic farming is fairly rare. Even the local whole-foods markets buy most of their produce from California, Colorado, and Texas. "I'm trying to provide things locally, but that takes educating people too. I'm on the board of the local macrobiotic institute; they support eating locally grown food in season, but even they don't really know what's in season. I have to educate them that you can't grow greens here in July or have corn in December."

Rein is flexible about what he grows: if you talk to him before planting time, he can put in specific crops. "I don't just plant and then try to sell what I have—I try to know in advance what people will want." Let him know early what you're looking for, because he doesn't usually have much of a surplus. Rein doesn't have a price list, but you can send two dollars to receive regular updates on what's available. If you're local, you can participate in his subscription and delivery service—a guaranteed delivery of produce once a week. Contact him for details.

RONNIGER'S SEED POTATOES
Star Route
Moyie Springs, ID 83845
FAX: (208) 267-2762

Visits: yes
Farmers' markets: Bonner's Ferry city parking lot, Saturday mornings
Certified by: SELF
Certification pending from: OCIA, state of Idaho
Catalogue/price list available
Minimum order: $7
Order by: mail, fax
Pay by: check, cash, or money order
Ship by: UPS, parcel post
Shipping September–November and March–May

POTATOES

Anoka · Bison · Desiree · Norkotah Russet · Red Dale · Yukon Gold · Yellow Finn

VEGETABLES

Rutabagas · Yellow onions · Carrots · Beets · Sunchokes (Jerusalem artichokes) · Cabbage ·

GARLIC

German Red

After receiving boxes of produce packed with styrofoam chips, it was a delight to unpack the box from Ronniger's, with produce, still smelling of the earth, wrapped in brown paper bags and bedded in straw. Ronniger's Seed Potatoes is a small, family-operated farm in the northeasternmost part of Idaho, "an hour hike to the Montana state line, and a short half-hour crow flight to the Canadian border," says David Ronniger. The nearest town, Moyie Springs—population 350—is nine miles away. The "thriving metropolis" of Bonners Ferry, with 1,600 people, is twenty miles down the road.

David Ronniger describes himself as a "high-energy person" whose approach to agriculture is "decidedly low-energy." Given his druthers, he'd work the fields with horses rather than a tractor. The Ronnigers have been growing organically since 1966, following the principles of J. I. Rodale, the founder of *Organic Gardening* magazine. "If you treat the soil right, it grows potatoes right," says Ronniger's son, Solomon.

Whatever the Ronnigers are doing to their soil, it certainly produces sweet vegetables. The yellow onions were crisp; the German Red garlic had large cloves whose peel pretty much came off in my hands. Both were markedly sweet when cooked. I have an aversion to beets, but I gave some to a beet lover, who pronounced them sweet and delicious. The carrots, although mild-flavored when raw, with a slightly medicinal taste, were like honey when cooked. They also sell two varieties of Jerusalem artichokes, a relative of the sunflower: Stampede or Fuseau. Both, say the folks at Ronniger's, have a nutty flavor and flesh as crisp as a water chestnut, a sweet vegetable without starch.

But of course, the star is the potato. Ronniger's catalogue is a mine of information about

potatoes, including a history of the potato and an explanation of potato genetics. You can buy a potato cookbook, and a children's book about potatoes, available either in English or in French. Not only does the catalogue contain the largest selection of organic seed potatoes in the United States, you will also find one page of organic eating potatoes for those who can't plant their own.

Ronniger's sells seven varieties for eating. Anoka, an early white-fleshed potato, is "smooth as an egg"; Bison is "simply the best all-around white-fleshed red potato ever developed" (Ronniger's recommends it for baking, boiling, and frying); Red Dale, a white-fleshed red potato, is "the one we grow for our local folks, especially good bakers." Desiree is the most popular red potato in Europe; the Norkota Russet, developed in North Dakota, is a good keeper and "excellent baking, French-frying, chipped, or scalloped." Ronniger's also sells a number of European-style, yellow-fleshed potatoes, whose flavor, according to the staff, is "more intense than whites and has a built-in buttery taste." This is no exaggeration: the Yukon Gold potatoes I sampled—an all-purpose potato that's Ronniger's most popular potato of all—were rich, flaky, and soft, and extremely buttery in flavor, truly delicious without any seasoning at all. Yellow Finn is a close second to Yukon Gold in popularity, and also an excellent keeper.

In 1990, the catalogue was $1, refundable with your first order. Ten pounds of potatoes were $15.50, plus shipping. Jerusalem artichokes were $3.75 for 1.5 pounds, and you save by buying in quantity. Other vegetables were 60 cents a pound, plus shipping. Garlic was $4.25 a pound, or $14.25 for a braid, including shipping. If you order more than $40 worth, Ronniger's will give you a 10% discount. The company sells hundreds of varieties of seed potatoes for growers.

EUGENE AND JOAN SAINTZ
2225 63rd Street
Fennville, MI 49408
(616) 561-2761

Visits: yes
Certified by: SELF
No catalogue/price list available; send the Saintzes a postcard with the items you're interested in, and they'll do their best to fill your order
Minimum order: none
Order by: phone, mail
Pay by: check
Ship by: UPS

FRESH VEGETABLES AND FRUITS

One of Joan Saintz's five children was born with leukemia. By the time the child was three, the doctors said she had six months to live. "That child is now twenty-one," Joan Saintz told me matter-of-factly. "And all I did was change her diet and life-style. I've been growing organically since then." The doctors, she says, now insist the initial diagnosis must have been a mistake. "They call it 'quasi-leukemia.' "

Joan Saintz went to school "in between five children," who now range in age from sixteen to thirty, and by 1980 she had a Ph.D. in nutrition. The basis of the nutritionists' philosophy, says Joan Saintz, is getting people to eat the food that we're biologically adapted to eat, and part of their training is in organic growing. Doctors, she says, think this is all "hooey," but some of the more famous proponents of clean food, says Joan Saintz, include Graham, the inventor of Graham flour; Louisa May Alcott; and Florence Nightingale. "Nutrition fell out of style when drugs came into fashion. Because nutritionists are against bottling and canning food, and against drugs, you have a lot of strong industries lobbying against us."

In addition to growing food without chemicals, Joan Saintz does in-home counseling to help people change their diet and life-style in order to regain their health and maintain a "permanent healthy life."

SEEDS BLÜM

Idaho City Stage
Boise, ID 83706
(208) 342-0858 (help line)
(208) 336-8264 (credit-card orders)

Certified by: various
Catalogue/price list available
Minimum order: none
Order by: mail, phone
Pay by: check, money order, Visa, MC
Ship by: UPS

POTATOES

Bintje · All-Blue · Ruby Crescent

SWEETENER

Sorghum

BEANS

Jacob's Cattle · Molasses Face · Dry Adventist · Black Turtle Soup

FLOUR

Hopi Blue Cornmeal · Bloody Butcher Cornmeal

GARLIC

Braids

When you see the Seeds Blüm catalogue, you know the people who produce it are having an awful lot of fun. The catalogue is a delight to browse in, full of information on cooking as well as gardening, and illustrated not with photographs but with all-singing, all-dancing cartoons of fruits and vegetables that put the California Raisins to shame.

The woman behind the catalogue—and even some of the cartoons—is Jan Blüm. Blüm grew up in a farming community in central California; her parents were professionals, but her grandparents on both sides were farmers. In 1980, she came to Idaho from Los Angeles to work as a caretaker on 600 acres of land. After making the initial adjustment from urban to rural life, Blüm started gardening with a neighbor, who kept telling her about the way older varieties were disappearing—that food just

didn't taste the same anymore. To prove his point, he gave her seeds from plants he'd been given as a wedding present in the 1920s. She was intrigued.

Blüm, who taught vegetarian cooking, started looking for other growers with old-time varieties they'd be willing to share. She ended up with more than 700 varieties of beans and more than 300 kinds of tomatoes. That was fun, but seed saving also had a more serious side: preserving genetic diversity.

Very few species of food crops are actually cultivated on a large scale. A blight on any one of them could put the nation's food supply at risk. Endangered "heirloom" strains may be resistant, but these plants aren't listed in any catalogue. If people stop growing them, they'll simply disappear from the earth, taking that genetic information with them.

Blüm spent a brief apprenticeship at Redwood City Seed Company (page 314), and the folks there encouraged her to go into business. She hated the idea—she hated business. What she loved was gardening. But she gave it a try, figuring that her love of gardening would make her a better adviser to other gardeners than they'd find at most seed companies. Once she wrote her first catalogue, there was no turning back; she was hooked.

At Seeds Blüm, selling seeds is not a one-way proposition: there's a reciprocity between the company and its customers. Many of the seeds in the catalogue originally came from the customers themselves, and customers can become test gardeners, regional advisers, or even seed guardians, who pledge to grow certain varieties every year to keep them alive and well.

As part of the reciprocity between Seeds Blüm and its customers, one grower sends

SEEDS BLÜM
IDAHO CITY STAGE
BOISE, ID 83706

Blüm homemade sorghum, made with a horse-drawn sorghum press that his family has been using since the days Lincoln was president. Sorghum grows in stalks, like corn, which is pressed into juice and then cooked down into syrup. Blüm says she prefers it to honey, molasses, or even maple syrup, on her morning flapjacks.

Naturally, since Seeds Blüm is in Idaho, it has two selections of organic potatoes: Bintje, with a "buttery yellow flesh"; All-Blue, "a beautiful lavender color inside," with a high mineral content and a "lusty flavor"; and Ruby Crescent, which originally came from a Seeds Blüm customer, with a "deep pink skin color, yellow flesh, and a superb flavor." Ruby Crescent is Jan Blüm's personal favorite; the potatoes are "lovely steamed or baked, and I'll wager they make the best hash browns you'll ever get."

In 1990, the catalogue was $3, and thereafter sent free to customers who order during the year. A gift box of 10 Bintje potatoes was $24.95. A gift box of assorted potatoes was $29.95. A 16-ounce jar of sorghum was $13.50. One pound of cornmeal was $7.50. A silk-screened box of 4 1-pound bags of beans was $17.95. A gift box of 1 pound of each cornmeal, with an ironware pan, an ear of red or blue corn, and recipes, was $27.50. A gift box of 4 1-pound bags of beans, 4 spatterware bowls, and red kerchiefs, was $56.95. A garlic braid of 18 bulbs was $19.95. All prices include shipping (slightly more to Alaska and Hawaii). For growers, Seeds Blüm offers only open-pollinated seeds. Many are heirloom varieties, from 65 to 100 years old.

SIMPLY WONDERFUL ORGANIC PRODUCTS
78120 Pitcher Lane
Cottage Grove, OR 97424
(503) 942-2439

Visits: yes; fresh fruits and vegetables
Certified by: OR-TILTH
Minimum order: 1 pound
Order by: phone, mail
Pay by: check
Ship by: UPS, parcel post

POTATOES

Purple Peruvian

HERBS

French tarragon · Oregano · Catnip · Parsley · German chamomile

James Hargreaves was born in England and became an apprentice gardener at fourteen. He met his wife, Gretchen, at a Hari Krishna farm in France where he was the gardener and she was the schoolteacher. They now have four children, and in addition to their responsibilities on their ten-acre organic farm, they are schooling their children at home, with the aid of Gretchen's mother, who lives with them.

For several years, Simply Wonderful made an organic caramel crunch entirely by hand. Not surprisingly, the Hargreaveses found that it just didn't pay. Simply Wonderful was set up to ship the caramel popcorn; shipping vegetables and herbs is a new venture. They will be adding crops each year; you can call to find out what they have available for shipping. Purple Peruvian potatoes are purple all the way through; they are hardy and keep well.

THE SPROUT HOUSE
40 Railroad Street
Great Barrington, MA 01230
(413) 528-5200

Visits: yes
Certified by: various
Catalogue/price list available
Minimum order: none
Order by: phone, mail
Pay by: check, money order, Visa, MC
Ship by: UPS, parcel post
Starter kits, sprouting bags, and baskets available

SEEDS FOR SPROUTING

Alfalfa · Oriental adzuki · Sprouting barley · Sprouting buckwheat · Crimson clover · Chinese cabbage · Onion chives · Sprouting corn · Mexican chia · Fennel · American fenugreek · Brown flaxseed · Garlic · Alaskan green pea · Garbanzo · Green kale · Lentil (red or green) · Sprouting millet · Mung bean · Mustard (brown or black) · Sprouting oats · Sprouting peanut · Whole psyllium · Sprouting quinoa · Icicle radish · Red radish · Bread rye · Sunflower (in shell or shelled) · Yellow soybean · Purple heart turnip · Hard red wheat · Kamut (Egyptian wheat) · Soft white wheat · Triticale (wheat-rye cross)

Hard wheat available in bulk
Wheatgrass available for juice

It's an old story—necessity is the mother of invention. Steve "Sproutman" Meyerowitz suffered from lifelong allergies. He started getting injections when he was five years old. By the time he was twenty-five, he was fed up with being tied to a weekly injection. He started talking to other patients in his doctor's waiting room, and discovered that like his, their conditions had only gotten worse over time. Nobody seemed to be getting better. Meyerowitz decided to take matters into his own hands.

The connection to organic food was "obvious," says Meyerowitz—eliminate any chemicals that might cause allergies. The cheapest

way to get organic foods was to grow them yourself. The only trouble was that he was living in New York City at the time. So he started sprouting mung beans and alfalfa sprouts, and soon took sprouting to "another level—I wondered what would happen if I tried other seeds that were edible as baby plants." Meyerowitz discovered that he could make delicious salads year-round. Then he started sprouting grains and grinding them to make crackers. "People who visited me started asking what I had grow-

ing on the windowsill," and he'd give them some to try. Pretty soon the *Yoga Times* was coming around to interview him, and Meyerowitz was giving up his career in music to teach workshops on nutrition.

Sproutman promises that you too can grow your own sprouts year-'round with no more than nine inches of available counterspace (if you've ever lived in a New York apartment, you know why he's that specific) and two minutes of watering a day—less time, says Meyerowitz, than it takes to check out at the supermarket. Also no bugs and no dirt, and the produce is guaranteed fresh—you pick it just before mealtime. But the idea behind sprouts is not just space-saving: biologists, say Meyerowitz, tell us that a plant reaches its maximum density of nutrients in its first five to ten days of life.

To help you get the most use from your sprouts, Meyerowitz offers a recipe book of sprouted breads and breadsticks, dairyless ice cream, zucchini chips, sprout chowder, sprouted hummus spread, homemade natural sodas, beansprout marinade, banana chip snacks, and even sprout pizza. His list of seeds notes their uses, so you can see which sprouts are appropriate for salads, which for soups and sautés, and which for sprouted breads. His newsletter adds new recipes and gives you other information on the world of seeds and organic growing.

The seeds are all certified organic or from transitional farms and tested for chemical residue.

In 1990, a starter kit with everything you need to start sprouting was $29.95. More elaborate packages with books, cassettes, recipes, ranged from $59 to $139. Seeds are sold by the pound, and ranged from 95 cents to $9.95 a pound, with wheat available in bulk. A beginner's dozen assortment of twelve half-pound bags of seed was $19.95. The Seed Lovers' club offers a discount for bulk purchases. The newsletter also lists air- and water-purifiers; accessories for cooking, drying, and juicing; books, and lectures on tape.

WOOD PRAIRIE FARM

RFD I, Box 164
Bridgewater, ME 04735
(800) 829-9765
(207) 429-9765

Certified by: MOFGA, OCIA
Catalogue/price list available
Minimum order: none
Order by: phone, mail
Pay by: check, money order, MC, Visa
Ship by: UPS
Gift baskets available, as are weekly shipments
of potatoes for 8 weeks beginning in February

POTATOES

Yukon Gold · Kennebec · Reddale · Butte ·
Russian Banana

VEGETABLES

Buttercup squash (September–March) · New
England pie pumpkins (September–April) ·
Dutch yellow onions (September–April) ·
Chantenay carrots (September–May) · Lutz
green-leaf beets (September–May)

SWEETENER

Maple syrup

GRAINS AND BEANS

Jacob's Cattle beans · Whole oat groats · Rolled
oats · Oat bran

GARLIC

Red-skinned Russian (braids or loose)

Jim and Megan Gerritsen have been growing
potatoes in Aroostook, Maine's northernmost
county, since 1976. Potatoes are "one of the
more challenging crops to grow organically,"
says Jim. "They're not grown from true seed,
but propagated from existing potatoes. True
seed doesn't transmit disease, but in potatoes,
whatever affected the last generation will be a
big factor in the next generation." As a result,
says Jim, potatoes are one of the four most
heavily sprayed crops in the country.

The Gerritsens have tried dozens of varieties
of potatoes, and say that Yukon Golds "offer
the best flavor, culinary quality, and versatility
—delicious baked, boiled, fried, or micro-
waved. The Yukon's flesh is European-style,
yellow, rich, and buttery." But you don't have
to be a one-potato eater. Be adventurous—
order a sampler, which mixes Yukons with
Kennebec, "a versatile round white potato";
Reddale, "a beautiful red-skinned potato, great
for boiling"; and Butte, "a handsome russet potato, preferred for baking."

The Gerritsens also grow a rare, heirloom
variety, the Russian Banana, first grown by
Russian settlers over a century ago and passed
down from generation to generation. The Russian Banana, as you might guess, is a yellow-
fleshed potato, and the Gerritsens select "the
smallest and tenderest baby nuggets" to ship.
They recommend steaming the tiny potatoes
until tender and adding herb butter.

The Gerritsens put garlic in the category of
"underutilized vegetables," and offer a red-
skinned Russian variety to remedy that. The
Russian is a "very high quality, good-tasting
garlic," says Jim Gerritsen. "It's also very easy

to peel, because it only has a single layer of
skin."

Wood Prairie also sells a number of other
root crops, including "large, tender, sweet"
Chantenay carrots, another heirloom variety;
Lutz, the "most tender beets you'll ever enjoy";
and Buttercup, the "queen of all squash," with
a green skin and deep orange flesh. The Gerritsens recommend enhancing its already sweet
flavor with butter and maple syrup (I add
brown sugar and sweet spices). You might consider combining their syrup and Jacob's Cattle
beans to make the Mainer's traditional baked-

bean supper. Or, say the Gerritsens, use the beans for chili.

It gets mighty cold up there in Aroostook, and you can buy your potatoes in tongue-and-groove cedar potato barrels that the Gerritsens make themselves "during the cold snowy days of winter."

In 1990, a 5-pound burlap bag of Yukon Gold potatoes was $11. Russian Bananas were $8 for 2.5 pounds. A 10-pound potato sampler was $17. Potatoes are available in gift boxes and barrels. Maple syrup was $6 for 8 ounces. Oats were $4 for 2 pounds. Beans were $8 for 3 pounds, or $9 in a 2-pound gift bag. Garlic braids (18 bulbs) were $17; loose garlic was $6 for 1 pound. Five pounds of onions, carrots, or beets were $8; 8 pounds of squash or pumpkins were $9. You save on many items by buying larger quantities. Seed potatoes are also available for growers.

LATE-BREAKING INFORMATION

HOW-WELL ORGANICS
Route 1, Box 116
Jennings, FL 32053
(904) 938-2046
FAX: (904) 938-2047

Certified by: FOGA
Catalogue/price list available
Minimum order: $25
Pay by: check, money order, MC, Visa
Ship by: UPS

FRESH VEGETABLES

Winter squash · Sweet potatoes · New potatoes

CITRUS

Navel oranges · Tangelos · Grapefruit

GRAINS

Wheat (F) · Rye (F) · Oats (F) · Barley (F) · Corn (F)

How-Well has over seventy varieties of vegetables available throughout the year, as well as a full line of citrus. Grains and flours are available in 10-pound bags. How-Well grinds its grains on site; corn is available as flour or meal.

SEE ALSO
Break-A-Heart Ranch, Forest Resource Center, Green Earth Farm, Jacobs Farm, Lambsfold Farm, Lone Pine Farm, Medicine Hill Herb Farm, Nu-World Amaranth, Inc., Silver Creek Farm, Sonoma Organic Growers, South Tex Organics, Star Route Farms, TKO Farms, Valley Cove Ranch, White Mountain Farm, Williams Creek Farms

GARLIC AND SHALLOTS

Recently, a friend mentioned that she was planting some garlic. "Oh," I asked, "what kind?" She responded, naturally enough, "I don't know. Just garlic." Before I started working on this book, I would have said the same. Now I know there's no such thing as "just garlic."

ARJOY ACRES
HCR Box 1410
Lower Round Valley
Payson, AZ 85541
(602) 474-1224

Visits: yes; pick-your-own produce; wide variety of vegetables
Certified by: SELF
Catalogue/price list available
Minimum order: none
Order by: phone, mail
Pay by: check
Ship by: UPS
Gift boxes available
Recipes available

GARLIC

Silverskin · Italian Red · California Early · California Late (available for shipping after August 1) · Elephant (available for shipping after July 15) · Garlic braids (available August 1)

VEGETABLES

Jerusalem artichokes (November–March)

SAUCES

Swedish lingonberry

BEANS AND SEEDS

Pinto · Kidney · Adzuki · Swedish brown · Swedish yellow peas · Dill seeds

Arne and Joyce Koch have lived at Arjoy Acres, the "Mile-High Home of Healthful Garlic," since 1975. In 1986, Arne, who'd always gardened as a hobby, retired from his job as a systems analyst at Motorola, and took up growing in earnest.

Arne Koch came to this country from Sweden at age twenty-eight on a college scholarship. Koch liked the United States enough to accept a job offer and make it his home, but he still has "loyalties to old memories," says Joyce. In Sweden, brown beans cooked with molasses, vinegar, and brown sugar are traditionally served every Tuesday; yellow pea soup along with pancakes are a Thursday staple. Even the Swedish army serves pea soup on Thursday. Arne Koch grows both these rare beans, as well as dill seeds—Swedes won't eat potatoes without them.

Beans and peas come to you in decorative cloth bags, with recipes. I made the traditional brown beans, and the results were delicious. The beans were sweet and remained firm, even after several hours of cooking. At Arjoy Acres, the yellow peas actually dry on the vine before they are picked. "The peas take a little more soaking than the regular split pea," say the Kochs, "but the finished product, embellished with your favorite seasoning, will make a soup that will give comfort on a cold winter's day." The peas started out white, but turned a lemon-yellow after soaking overnight, and made the base of a gentle, soothing slow-cooked soup.

I also sampled both the Silverskin and Elephant "Healthful" garlics, which come in net

ARJOY ACRES
ORGANICALLY GROWN

110

bags tied with ribbon. The Elephant garlic, not nearly as gargantuan as others I'd seen, was only about three times the size of the Silverskin bulb and close to an onion in flavor. The Kochs say their Elephant is so mild that some people slice it raw and serve it on sandwiches and crackers with cheese. The Silverskin is quite potent and relatively easy to peel.

Arizona has no certification program, but Arne Koch uses no toxic pesticides and only natural fertilizer. "Compost piles are eloquent evidence of our concern for natural ingredients in our vegetable beds," says Koch, "and behind some trees hide the manure piles, a sometimes odoriferous example of Arizona's love affair with the horse."

In 1990, garlic was $3.25 for a half-pound. A 15-inch garlic braid was $15.95. Peas and beans ranged from $1.50 to $2.50 a pound. Jerusalem artichokes were $2.50 a pound. You save by buying in bulk.

CHESAPEAKE CENTER FARM
Route 1, Box 288
Marion Station, MD 21838
(301) 623-3314

Visits: yes; wide variety of fresh vegetables
Certified by: OCIA-PA
Minimum order: none
Order by: phone, mail
Pay by: check
Ship by: UPS

GARLIC

Elephant

When Dale Johnson took early retirement from his job as a professor of sociology at Rutgers, he and his wife, Christine, also a sociologist, looked around for something "worthwhile"—other than academia—to do. Then the farmland and chicken house across the road from their summer home became available, and the idea for Chesapeake Center was born.

The Johnsons had always been organic gardeners, and read *Organic Gardening* "reli-giously," says Dale Johnson. When they took up growing vegetables on a larger scale, however, they started reading the trade publications, and thought that they'd have to forget organic gardening. For the first two years, they used chemicals. "Then we saw that the herbicides didn't really work," says Dale Johnson. "And using broad-spectrum pesticides kills off the beneficial insects, too. By 1985 we were back into real organic farming."

Much of their produce is sold to distributors who supply hospitals, nursing homes, and other institutions. "You'd think the institutions would care that the produce was organic, but our buyers tell us they don't." The only exception, says Johnson, is prisons, where prisoners have been "putting a lot of pressure on to get organically grown food."

In 1990, Elephant garlic was $2.75 a pound, plus shipping. Although Elephant garlic is the only crop Chesapeake Center ships to individuals, it grows a wide variety of fresh vegetables and makes deliveries almost daily to Washington, DC, Baltimore, Philadelphia, and New York. If you belong to a buying club in one of those cities, and order $500 worth of produce, Chesapeake Center can deliver to you.

CHESNOK FARM
RD 1
Marshland Road
Apalachin, NY 13732
(607) 687-6501

Visits: yes
Certified by: SELF
Catalogue/price list available
Minimum order: 1.5 pounds
Order by: mail
Pay by: check, money order
Ship by: UPS
Orders filled August 15–November 30

GARLIC

Carpathian · Elephant · Italian purple · Garlic braids

Mike Wovkulich has been eating garlic daily for the last thirty years. "They say it keeps away a lot of things," says Wovkulich, "including vampires." In keeping with the Transylvanian theme, the name Chesnok comes from a Slavic word for "garlic." Wovkulich has been growing garlic for his own use and protection for the past thirty years, and in the last five years, since he retired as a high-school guidance counselor, he's been growing commercially, using the demanding tasks of cultivating garlic as a way to keep physically active. His wife is responsible for the "artistic" side of the business, which includes braiding the garlic soon after they are picked, while the stalks are green and pliable.

Chesnok Farm is not certified organic, but Mike Wovkulich grows without chemicals, planting his fields in buckwheat and plowing that under before returning to garlic.

In 1990, garlic ranged from $9.50 to $9.95 for 1.5 pounds. Braids were $19.50 for 15 bulbs. You save by ordering in bulk. Shipping included.

CRICKET HILL FARM
670 Walnut Hill Road
Thomaston, CT 06787
(203) 283-4707

Certified by: NOFA-CT
Catalogue/price list available
Minimum order: 1 pound
Order by: phone, mail
Pay by: check
Ship by: USPS

GARLIC

Susanville · German · Italian · Rose Valley Farm Czech · Garlic braids

Brooklyn native David Furman always liked to garden, and has traded a twenty-year career in advertising for farming. His wife, Kasha, continues to work as a graphic designer (she designed the logo of Cricket Hill Farm) as well as working on the farm. Garlic gives them flex-ibility—you don't have to take it to market the day you harvest it—which is important when you have two small boys.

The Furmans chose varieties that work well for New England, says Kasha Furman. "We used California seed, and we were very aware

CRICKET HILL FARM

of the differences of the day lengths and the seasons. All the varieties we grow are pungent, not mild garlics, but they all taste different. If you make a dish with a number of them, you can taste the different flavors." Kasha's favorite is the German, which is particularly long-keeping and strong-flavored. The Furmans also grow over sixty varieties of peonies (one appears as their logo), and have a dried flower business; they weave dried flowers into the garlic braids.

In 1990, loose garlic was $6 a pound. Garlic braids of 15–18 bulbs were $15. Dried flower wreaths are available—prices vary.

EARTHSHINE FARM
11515 S.W. Tonquin Road
Sherwood, OR 97140
(503) 692-1714

Visits: yes, wide variety of salad greens
Farmers' markets: Beaverton, Oregon, Saturdays
Certified by: OR-TILTH
Minimum order: none
Order by: phone, mail
Pay by: check
Ship by: UPS, parcel post

GARLIC

Silverskin · California Early Red · Spanish Roja · Garlic braids

DRIED AND FRESH HERBS

Anise hyssop · Basil · Cilantro · Dill · Lemon thyme · Oregano (several varieties) · Parsley (several varieties) · Peppermint · Thyme · Cayenne peppers · Pepper braids

Earthshine Farm specializes in garlic braids and pepper braids. Tod Elliott and Molly Welch also grow organic flowers, including statice and strawflower, which they braid with the garlic. Elliott had been "into organics and healthy living" for twenty years when he and Welch were inspired to start growing organically by a garlic grower they met at a conference on sustainable agriculture. He gave the couple encouragement—and garlic seed to start them off. Elliott currently works part-time on the farm and part-time in electronics, while Molly Welch is kept busy by their new identical twin daughters.

In 1990, loose garlic was $2.50 a pound. Garlic braids were $12. Cayenne peppers were $2 an ounce dry, and pepper braids were $15. The price of dried herbs depends on the quantity you buy. Shipping additional.

EARTHSHINE Farm

FILAREE FARM
Route 1, Box 162
Okanogan, WA 98840
(509) 422-3030

Visits: by appointment; over 100 varieties of apples, and over 50 varieties of potatoes
Certified by: WSDA
Catalogue/price list available
Minimum order: $7
Order by: phone, mail
Pay by: check, money order
Ship by: UPS
Garlic can be shipped August 15–Thanksgiving; prime season is September–October

GARLIC

Caliente · Carpathian · French Rocambole · German · Israeli · Mexican Purple · Rumanian Red · Russian · Spanish Roja · Yugoslavian · California Early · Chet's Italian Red · Early Red Italian · Genoese Silverskin · Himalayan Red · Inchelium Red · Lorz Italian · Mild French Silverskin · Nootka Rose Silverskin · Oregon Blue · Purple Italian · Susanville

One look at Filaree Farm's catalogue will convince you: there can't be much about garlic these folks don't know. Their catalogue contains a history of garlic, a family tree of garlic, and several pages of instructions on planting, fertilizing, harvesting, and storing garlic, complete with diagrams. Their garlic stock represents a daunting range of garlic-growing regions of the world: France, Spain, Italy, Germany, Israel, Mexico, Rumania, Poland, Yugoslavia, and even Nepal.

Among the more than 200 varieties of garlic grown at Filaree Farm are clones of wild garlic from the Georgian, Turkmen, and Tadzhik republics of south-central Russia. They've never been grown in North America before, but Ron Engeland and Maya Watershine, who have been growing garlic organically for seventeen years, point out that the climate of Okanogan County is very similar to the climate of central Asia, where garlic originated. The county also produces garlic with a distinctive flavor. "We once placed five cloves before a gourmet garlic taster and asked him to identify by taste the one clove that was grown in the Okanogan. He picked the right clove with a great degree of certainty."

I sampled one wild garlic from the Soviet Union, a small bulb with very large cloves that were quite easy to peel. The garlic was full of flavor and completely sweet, without any after-bite. I also sampled a flavorful, but not overly strong silverskin, with large cloves that were relatively easy to peel, and an easy-peeling Lorz Italian, much stronger and slightly bitter.

I also sampled their rich, sweet Spanish Roja, the most popular garlic Filaree sells.

Spanish Roja is a variety of the oldest form of cultivated garlic, with streaked purple bulbs, and large cloves that practically peel themselves. Filaree's is a northwest heirloom variety, brought to the area before the turn of the century by Greek immigrants, and in some places still called "Greek Blue." The flavor, say Engeland and Watershine, "is not overpowered by the sharp bite and metallic aftertaste of so many common garlics. Many garlic lovers view Spanish Roja as a vegetable rather than a mere source of flavoring. It's been described as piquant, poignant, and exquisite."

Availability of varieties varies from year to year. In 1990 garlic was $7 per pound and decreased for larger orders. Filaree Farm also sells an extensive line of seed stock for growers.

HONEY GROVE FARM
P.O. Box 49
Alsea, OR 97324
(503) 487-7274

Visits: yes; raspberries and potatoes
Certified by: OR-TILTH
Minimum order: none
Order by: phone, mail
Pay by: check
Ship by: UPS, parcel post
Garlic is available from the end of July until sold out, usually in December

GARLIC

Elephant · Spanish Roja braids

When the Elephant garlic arrived from Honey Grove Farm, I couldn't resist taking out the kitchen scale. One of the bulbs weighed over half a pound. At Honey Grove Farm, a bulb of Elephant garlic can weigh up to a pound and a half, but Elephant garlic is not just a novelty, says Gisela Green, who with her husband, Salty, has been raising organic garlic since 1972. Its mild flavor means that you can eat a "whole big clove, or two, or three, without being overwhelmed by the legendary 'dragon's breath.'"

Gisela Green recommends baking a whole unpeeled head or individual "toes" with a tablespoon of olive oil poured over it. "At serving time, break open the head, and serve it with a baguette and butter, squeezing each toe onto the bread." I followed her directions; after forty-five minutes, the inside of the cloves were the texture of pureed applesauce, with garlic's heat but without its bite. Spread on rounds of fresh, toasted bread, the sweet, spicy garlic made an excellent appetizer or accompaniment to a meal; with some oregano and basil, you'd have a mini pizza. You could also mix the baked garlic with a baked potato; it would make a great addition to a leek and potato soup.

The chefs she supplies, says Gisela Green, are enthusiastic about how easy the cloves are to peel, and have started to think of garlic more as a vegetable than as a seasoning. (I can easily imagine serving them alongside cooked carrots, potatoes, and onions.) They've even begun using the "pearls"—fresh, unopened garlic flowers—as garnishes.

If you have a microwave, says Gisela Green, you can put the garlic in a dish with white wine or water and steam for ten minutes. The Greens also recommend using Elephant garlic in stir-fries, or even (I find this hard to believe) finely minced in chocolate truffles.

If you want a more potent garlic, or just want to save your Elephant garlic as a conversation piece, the Greens recommend their Spanish Roja, "the gourmet's garlic," with approximately three to five bulbs to the pound,

Oregon Tilth Certified Organically Grown

Salty & Gisela Green
(503) 487-7274

*Elephant Garlic, Spanish Roja
Raspberries, Potatoes & More*

large toes, striped red throughout, and easy to peel.

The Greens also make garlic braids, not your straight-up-and-down variety, but things of beauty, like elaborate hairstyles, in dramatic shapes like cornucopias and figure eights, and bedecked with flowers (including garlic flowers, of course). One of their creations appears on the cover of this book.

In 1990, both Elephant and Spanish Roja garlic were $4.75 a pound. Prices decrease when you order in quantity. Braid prices vary according to size, from $30 to $45.

MEDICINE HILL HERB FARM DBA: COVELO ORGANIC VEGETABLES
23090 Hopper Lane
Covelo, CA 95428
(707) 983-6562

Farmers' market: Willits, Tuesday afternoons
Certified by: CCOF
Minimum order: none
Order by: phone, mail
Pay by: check
Ship by: UPS

GARLIC

California Early White · Garlic braids · Shallots

FRESH VEGETABLES

Jerusalem artichokes · Onions

Tom Palley named his farm Medicine Hill after a local hill known as "place of healing" to Native Americans. Palley came to the Covelo area fifteen years ago to apprentice on an herb farm and has been there ever since. In 1989, Palley started a venture into community-supported agriculture. Currently, some forty-five families have shares in Covelo Organic Vegetables and receive a weekly basket of produce from May to December, a total of some 800 pounds per family. The baskets contains whatever is in season—from arugula to watermelons. While these aren't always the things they might have bought on their own, says Palley, everyone seems pleased to try what he calls the "esoteric vegetables"—like Asian greens that come in season when other vegetables are out.

Palley sent me a braid of garlic, a California white variety that won Palley the blue ribbon at the county fair in 1988. The braid arrived slightly the worse for wear: several bulbs and dried flowers had come off the central braid. I spoke to Palley about shipping, and he's thinking of using net bags or other insulation. The garlic itself, however, was sweet and full of flavor.

Tom Palley is just getting into mail order, and expects to have a catalogue available by mid-1991. He currently grows culinary herbs and plans to build a drying room, so ask him what's available. In 1990, garlic and shallots were $3 a pound. Braids were $12.50. Shipping additional. If you live in Ukiah, Covelo, or Willits and are interested in joining the Community Supported Agriculture Program, call Palley for more information.

MOUNTAIN MEADOW FARM
826 Ulrich Road
Prospect, OR 97536
(503) 560-3350

Farmers' markets: Grants Pass, Saturday mornings; Medford, Thursday mornings; Ashland, Tuesday mornings
Certified by: OR-TILTH
Catalogue/price list available
Minimum order: none
Order by: phone, mail
Pay by: check, money order
Ship by: parcel post, UPS
Garlic can be shipped August–December
Combination sampler available

GARLIC

Silverskin · Rocambole · Mountain Meadow Red Italian · Early Red · Garlic powder · Garlic braids (16, 19, or 22 bulbs of Silverskin)

SHALLOTS

French Red · Dutch Yellow

At the Oregon State Fair in 1985, Mountain Meadow won first and second prize for their Elephant and Mountain Meadow Red Italian garlic; the Elephant also took home the "Outstanding Specimen" award. Mountain Meadow is a one-acre farm in the foothills of the Cascade Mountains in Prospect, Oregon. One acre may not sound like much, but it can produce a ton of garlic—literally—unless the gophers or elks get there first.

With that much garlic around, it's not surprising that Michael Laslovich, Suzanne Nurré, and their two daughters eat as much as thirty pounds of the stuff a year. Laslovich always tosses a bulb in the pot when he's cooking his "Mountain Papa" goulash or "Mountain Papa" spaghetti for the children, and likes to make a garlic-honey glaze for chicken. With that extra dose of garlic, the kids are hardly ever sick, says Laslovich. You might say Jennifer Nicole and Christina Rose live and breathe garlic: not only are they the farm's "top weeders and harvesters," but they also, says their father, probably know as much about garlic as their parents —they're the ones who field questions at the annual garlic festival.

The Mountain Meadow Red Italian is their best seller, a relatively good keeper with strong flavor, large cloves, and—I can attest—extremely easy to peel, as is the Early Red, a juicy garlic that's the source of Mountain Meadow's garlic powder, which packs quite a wallop. It's unusual to find organic garlic powder as well as whole garlic. If you think of garlic powder as something pale or dried out, try Mountain Meadow's version, which is fresh and strong. One or two shakes will garlic up a whole bowl of pasta—add olive oil, grate some cheese, toss, and enjoy.

The individual cloves of Elephant garlic I sampled were each the size of a small egg and extremely easy to peel—the peel literally comes off in your hands. My friend Tom roasted a chicken with a clove of the Elephant garlic inside the body. He surrounded the bird with potatoes, carrots, and unpeeled Silverskin cloves. The Elephant garlic remained firm, and was sweet and mild—close to a cooked onion in flavor. The Silverskin, when cracked out of the skin after cooking, was rich, sweet, and buttery. It's also their best keeper.

Rocambole is the smallest and strongest garlic Mountain Meadow sells (size and potency seem to be inversely related when it comes to garlic); for a small garlic, Rocambole is also very easy to peel. Laslovich calls it a "one-clove" garlic. Forewarned, I went sparingly and found that two cloves provided enough seasoning for several pounds of turkey stuffing. Rocambole doesn't keep very long, so the folks at Mountain Meadow recommend that you use it quickly, or peel it and store in olive oil in a refrigerator or other dark, cool place. I followed their advice, and in a few weeks had a ready-made dressing for potatoes and salads.

Garlic and shallots come packed in net bags. In 1990, garlic and shallots ranged from $3.50 to $4 a pound. The combination sampler of 3 bulbs each of 5 varieties was $8. Braids ranged from $8 to $12. Powder was $3.50 for 3.5 ounces. Shipping additional.

PLUMBOTTOM FARM
Route 3, Box 129
Willow Springs, MO 65793
(417) 962-3204

Visits: yes
Farmers' markets: Willow Springs, Saturday mornings
Catalogue/price list available
Certified by: SELF
Minimum order: none
Order by: phone, mail
Pay by: check, money order, COD
Ship by: UPS

GARLIC

Garlic braids (with or without dried flowers) · Country bunches (with or without dried flowers)

HERBS AND SPICES

Herb bunches · Herb chains · Herb wreaths

Every fall, Kay and Ted Berger plant thousands of bulbs of California Late and Early Red garlic. At harvest time, the Bergers and their daughter, Heidi, harvest, dry, and clean the bulbs by hand, setting the largest bulbs aside to begin the next year's harvest. Then Kay Berger starts braiding. The braid she sent me arrived

well-cushioned and in perfect shape, with a spectacular band of magenta flowers running like a ribbon down the center. The universal reaction was, "You *can't* eat that!" Since I agreed, I can't tell you how the garlic tastes, but even though Kay Berger is proud of her work, she does encourage her customers to eat the garlic—and come back to Plumbottom Farm for more.

Kay Berger also makes herb bunches, fan-shaped bundles of herbs decorated with flowers and a bow; and herb chains secured to a braid of raffia and decorated with dried flowers. The herb wreaths, mixed with dried flowers, are mostly for decoration, but herb bunches can be hung up for decoration in the kitchen and then tossed onto the fire for grilling.

The Bergers have been "strict organic growers" since 1975. The Bergers met or exceeded the standards of the Ozark Organic Growers' Association, by whom they were certified for three years, until the cost of certification "went sky high." Kay Berger said that giving up certification "was a very hard issue for us because of the credibility you get with outside certifiers."

In 1990, a 12-inch garlic braid without flowers was $10 and with flowers was $12. A garlic bunch, plain or with flowers, was $7. Herb bunches were $9.50, and a 22-inch herb chain with flowers was $16. An herbal wreath with flowers, 12 inches around, was $18.50. Shipping additional. The Bergers also sell floral wreaths, amaranth flowers, and scented potpourri.

RATTLESNAKE RANCH
P.O. Box 630
Northport, WA 99157
(509) 732-6163

Certified by: WSDA, TILTH
Catalogue/price list available
Minimum order: 6 pounds
Order by: phone, mail
Pay by: check
Ship by: UPS
Garlic available August–December, while supplies last

Garlic braids available only if you order before the end of July

GARLIC

Spanish Red (medium, large, and jumbo) · Garlic braids

The UPS man really got a kick out of delivering a long, flat box from Rattlesnake Ranch. "I'd like to see you eat that," he said. "It's not the way it looks," I insisted, but he was adamant. "Oh, I'm sure rattlesnake is health food." The long skinny box turned out to contain a garlic braid and a sampler bag of loose garlic from the mountains of northeast Washington just south of the British Columbia border.

Steve Campbell and Hilary Ohm have been growing garlic at Rattlesnake Ranch since 1981. When they arrived, the land was relatively clean forest and brush, which they cleared to plant garlic. Campbell's experience working with apples convinced him that he didn't want to use chemicals. "I've been sprayed on by helicopters plenty of times. It's bodily assault, but you can't prosecute. The farmers put out flags by the orchards they're supposed to spray, but they're in such a hurry, they'll spray even where they don't see a flag, and send the farmer the bill."

Rattlesnake Ranch specializes in Spanish Red garlic, which, says Campbell, is "the best garlic available in the world. The red varieties are all better than the white. Spanish Red is prized by gourmets for its outstanding flavor, and its large, easy-to-peel cloves. Comparisons make all other garlic seem bland and tedious.

Gourmet Spanish Red Garlic

Spanish Red is not usually considered a good keeper, but when stored under proper conditions, in a cool, dry place, it can keep up to a year after harvest." In future years, Rattlesnake Ranch may have other garlics available—they'll be Reds, of course.

Both the loose garlic and the braid come in net bags, so ship well. The garlic braid arrived in perfect shape. It's not the bulbs-down-the-side variety, but a long braid with an oval of bulbs at the bottom, shaped more or less like a snowshoe. The purple streaking on the garlic makes it particularly beautiful as a decoration. All three sizes of loose bulbs were larger than your average supermarket garlic; one bulb of the jumbo was not such smaller than a tennis ball. All were very easy to peel, mild, and sweet.

In 1990, braids were $12.95. Garlic ranged from $3.25 a pound for medium, $3.50 a pound for large, and $3.75 a pound for jumbo. Half-pound sampler bags (minimum of 6 bags) were $2.30 each. All prices drop for larger orders. Shipping additional.

SCHAEFFER FAMILY FARM
HCR 64, Box 221
West Plains, MO 65775
(417) 257-0670

Certified by: OOGA
Farmers' market: (possibly) West Plains, Missouri
Catalogue/price list available
Minimum order: none
Order by: phone, mail
Pay by: check, money order
Ship by: UPS
Garlic braids available from July 1 into the winter as supplies last

GARLIC

California Early White · Silverskin · Italian Red · Garlic braids · Garlic wreaths (plain, with dried flowers, with herbs)

HERBS AND SPICES

Herb wreaths of oregano, thyme, sage, basil, other herbs and dried flowers

Corliss and George Schaeffer are both city-born and have to reach back to their grandparents' generation to find farmers. When they moved to the farm, says Corliss, she'd never gardened in her life, but she liked the idea of farming for a living, calling it an "honest" livelihood. Today, Corliss is the main gardener—George also works off the farm—and does the elaborate garlic braiding. She also makes brooms from broomcorn with braided handles (these can also be shipped).

For the Schaeffers, growing organically is part of making an "honest" livelihood. The Schaeffers started out with a subscription garden, where customers could select a small or large basket of assorted produce delivered once or twice a week for a fixed amount of money. When the Schaeffers' first child, Forrest, was born, they turned to garlic as a crop that might give them a little more flexibility. It's still extremely demanding work—they plant, weed, and harvest by hand, which keeps the size of the patch smaller than most commercial growers'.

In 1990, for orders of 5 or more items, braids ranged from $4.50 to $8 and braid wreaths ranged from $10 to $12.50. Individual items higher. Shipping additional.

SILVER CREEK FARM
P.O. Box 254
Hiram, OH 44234
(216) 569-3487
(216) 562-4381

Visits: yes; fresh produce, lamb, chicken, turkey, and blueberries; stoneware, sheepskins, hand-spun wool and mohair yarns, hand-knit sweaters
Certified by: OEFFA
Catalogue/price list available
Minimum order: none
Order by: phone, mail
Pay by: check
Ship by: UPS

GARLIC

Rocambole · French shallots

FRESH MUSHROOMS

Shiitake

DRIED MUSHROOMS

Shiitake

VEGETABLES

Beets · Carrots · Yukon Gold potatoes · Butternut squash · Acorn squash · Hubbard squash · Giant Blue Hubbard squash · Sweet dumpling squash · Pie pumpkins

Molly Bartlett has been a potter for twenty-five years, and when I reached her by phone she told me she had clay dripping off her hands, a rare occurrence these days. "I used to do a lot of crafts shows, but I've pretty much scaled down—at night, I'm too busy reading farming journals." Molly and her husband, Ted, a professor of medical ethics and philosophy at Case–Western Reserve and Cleveland State, moved to their 125-acre farm in rural Ohio in 1985. Their first task was to renovate the 160-year-old farmhouse; then they began growing specialty vegetables for restaurants. Their neighbors, recalls Ted, wondered what kind of a farm they could possibly be running if it didn't have a single combine. (They might also wonder what kind of farm would play classical music to chickens, but that's another story.) Molly readily admits that a lot of farming "is still Greek to us. We're learning all the time." The next generation has a head start—they describe the youngest of their five children as a "4-H junkie."

The Bartletts "sort of backed into growing organically," says Molly Bartlett. "We decided if we didn't know what something was, we wouldn't use it. When we bought this place, there was a beautiful old apple orchard, very romantic, and we set about reviving it. My husband actually came down with an incredible case of athlete's foot from having to wear rubber from head to toe while spraying the apple trees. We just said, 'Forget it.' We learned as we went along, which is not at all a bad way to go about it. We spent a lot of time talking with

older growers. This is a very rural area of our county, and we're fortunate to have a lot of elderly growers who are organic, even if they're not labeled organic. The more we learn about it, the more appeal it has."

Molly Bartlett says that for most of the restaurants they supply, organic isn't the main selling point. "Most restaurants find it interesting, but what matters to them is that the flavor is superior—I must admit that even I'm a little surprised at that, even though I've been growing organically for ten years. The flavor is significantly different."

The shallots and garlic the Bartletts grow are two ends of a spectrum. The shallots are a sweet, mild cross in flavor between garlic and

onions. They can be frozen and may in fact grow sweeter when frozen. Their garlic is Rocambole, which they chose deliberately because of its reputation as the strongest flavored garlic around.

The Bartletts started growing shiitake mushrooms to extend their growing season into February and March. If you are a newcomer to the joys of shiitake, they will send you recipes for a shiitake quiche, shiitake pilaf, and sautéed shiitake. They recommend the mushrooms not only for taste but for nutritional value, particularly for vegetarians, because they contain all the essential amino acids, as well as being a good source of vitamins.

In the past, the Bartletts have sold their frozen chicken, turkey, and lamb locally, but are willing to discuss shipping.

SUN ANGLE
P.O. Box 669
Redway, CA 95560
(707) 923-2092

Farmers' markets: local crafts fairs; contact the company for information
Certified by: CCOF
Catalogue/price list available
Minimum order: none
Order by: mail
Pay by: check, money order
Ship by: UPS
Shipping in late summer and fall only

GARLIC

California Late · Lorz's Italian · Creole Red · Rocambole

SHALLOTS

Holland Yellow · French Red · Frog Leg · French Epicurean · Grey

Harold K. Neufeld specializes in "heirloom" and imported varieties of garlic, which is fitting for someone descended from a long line of farmers from Bavaria on one side, and Mennonites from Russia on the other. (His father, a doctor, was an "off-generation" of the cycle.) Neufeld says his family also loves garlic—their favorite way to eat it is freshly pressed on toast with a little Parmesan cheese.

Neufeld gets many of his uncommon varieties through members of the Seed Savers Exchange (page 315). In 1990, he planted a bed of two dozen allium from Soviet Central Asia, brought to this country by a member of the Exchange who collected wild garlic in the fields and cultivated garlic from the markets.

The California Late, says Neufeld, is his best keeper, and also probably the hottest garlic he sells, even hotter than the Rocambole. Although Rocambole is supposed to be the most potent of all garlics, Neufeld says he's found an enormous range in garlics called Rocambole: his source sent him some dozen varieties, of which some were "remarkably mild." I had a similar reaction to the Creole Red, which, judging from its name, I expected to be a fire-breather. The garlic had a beautiful deep magenta inner skin, was easy to peel, and flavorful but completely mild. The Lorz's Italian, a mild garlic, had very large cloves; the peel popped right off. The California Late was stronger and richer in flavor and relatively easy to peel.

I was amazed by the variety of colors, flavors, and sizes of Neufeld's shallots. The French Red and French Epicurean had the purple skin and flesh of a red onion, and the Frog Leg had (as the name implies) long, skinny bulbs. When raw, all started out sweet with a fiery afterbite, and a flavor that made ordinary onions seem boring. The French Red and Dutch Yellow had the sweetest and richest flavor when cooked, and the French Epicurean the most pungent.

Sun Angle will start mail order in 1991, so write for a price list.

SEE ALSO
Big River Nurseries, Chesapeake Center Farm, McFadden Farm, Mountain Butterfly Herbs, Sandhill Farm, Seeds Blüm, Williams Creek Farms, Wood Prairie Farm

GRAIN, FLOUR, BEANS, CEREAL, BAKING MIXES, AND PASTA

In this section, you'll see many familiar grains, and may meet some new ones, like amaranth, quinoa, and teff, ancient grains that are new to North America. These grains are all high in protein, and they offer hope for growers in drought-plagued areas, as well as to consumers who are allergic to wheat or other cereal grains. But they don't have to be the only ones to enjoy Ethiopian *injera* bread, made from teff; a stir-fry made with quinoa; or a quickbread baked with amaranth flour.

The flour you'll find here is almost always stone-ground, which is a slow process that doesn't raise the temperature of the grain as it is being milled, leaving the enzymes and other nutrients intact. These flours contain no preservatives, and many are whole-grain flours, containing the bran, or outer layer of the grain. This part of the grain contains the most oil, so treat these flours as perishable—store them in the refrigerator or other cool, dark place. This will protect them from pests (because the grain was never sprayed or fumigated) and also to protect the oil from light and air, which can spoil it. Some of the grains have been flushed with nitrogen, which forces the oxygen out of the bag, and replaces it with nitrogen, to prevent spoilage.

In this section, if a company sells grains, flour, and cereal, whole grains are listed. An (F) following the grain means that flour made from that grain is also available. A (C) means that grits or cereal is available. Other flours and cereals are listed separately.

In many cases, companies mill grain they do not grow. "Certified by" in this section refers to the grain. If the mill is also certified, that is listed separately.

ALLERGY RESOURCES
745 Powderhorn
Monument, CO 80132
(800) USE-FLAX
(719) 488-3630

Sells goods certified by: various
Catalogue/price list available
Minimum order: none
Order by: phone, mail
Pay by: check, Visa, MC, COD
Ship by: UPS

BEANS

Black turtle · Chick-peas · Kidney · Great northern · Pinto

GRAINS

Brown rice (C,F) · Hulled barley (F) · Flax seed Quinoa (C,F) · Popcorn · Buckwheat groats (C,F) · Amaranth (C,F) · Millet (C,F)

OTHER FLOUR

Soy · Corn · Oat · Potato · Navy bean · Rye · Spelt

PASTA

Quinoa

NUT BUTTER

Almond

BREAD

Sourdough rye (100% wheat-free)

SNACKS

Taro chips · Brown-rice crackers

OILS

Fresh cold-pressed flax

Christine Beaman knows first-hand how frustrating allergies can be. "When I was first told I couldn't have dairy or wheat, I thought the world was coming to an end. I was addicted to milk. I had an industrial-size refrigerator to keep my milk really cold." Later, Beaman worked in an allergy clinic, where her job was to find foods and other resources for patients. It was so hard to do that she decided to create Allergy Resources.

Beaman's line fills the needs of people who need to rotate their diets. Human beings were not meant to eat the same foods all the time, says Beaman. "There are so many grains out there—we weren't meant to eat wheat three times a day." (Hence the Allergy Resources "Wheatbusters" logo.) Beaman also points out that farmers may grow varieties of wheat specifically because they endure hard weather, but the very qualities that make them hardy also make them hard to digest.

Because they don't contain wheat or dairy products, many of the foods she carries are not fast movers in the health-food stores, where they often go stale on the shelves. Beaman thinks that her customers get fresher products by buying through her catalogue. She tries to buy organic whenever possible. Anything she's not absolutely sure about, she doesn't list as organic in the catalogue.

In 1990, flours ranged from $3 to $4.50 a pound. Shipping additional. The catalogue also lists a variety of products to reduce allergens in the air and water, and an assortment of books on allergies and rotation diets.

ANCIENT HARVEST QUINOA
P.O. Box 1039
Torrance, CA 90505
(213) 530-8666
FAX: (213) 530-8764

Certified by: SELF
Catalogue/price list available
Minimum order: 1 case
Order by: mail
Pay by: check
Ship by: UPS

GRAIN

Quinoa (F)

PASTA

Rotini · Flats · Spaghetti

WHEAT-FREE PASTA

Elbows · Rotelle · Shells · Garden pagodas

In Inca legend, quinoa (pronounced "keenwa") was left over from a banquet of the gods. The Incas considered quinoa the "Mother Grain," and some scholars believe that Spanish conquistadors deliberately suppressed its cultivation to weaken the Inca empire.

Quinoa did indeed decline under the Spaniards, but remained a staple of the Incas' descendants until recent years. Even though the grain is extremely resilient to drought, it just hasn't been able to compete with the attractions of subsidized, inexpensive North American white flour. One of the founders of Ancient Harvest Quinoa called this the "Wonder Bread Syndrome"—if gringos don't eat it, it can't be worth eating.

But quinoa's nutritional value is a strong argument for making it a part of the gringo diet: it contains roughly twice the protein of other cereal grains, providing all ten essential amino acids. The National Academy of Sciences called quinoa "one of the best sources of protein in the vegetable kingdom." For vegetarians, it's an ideal balance for legumes. Rebecca Wood, author of *Quinoa: The Supergrain,* quotes Duane Johnson, an agronomist at Colorado State University: "If you had your choice of one food to survive on, this would be the best."

The good news is it's also delicious. Once you try quinoa, you'll find yourself reaching for it again and again, as a side dish, like rice, in soups, stuffings, and pilafs. The grain is cooked like rice, and fluffs up to four times its size when cooked. It's easier to cook than rice—no sticking. When cooked, the grain becomes translucent, with a tiny spiral—the grain's germ—curling around it. I first made some without any seasonings as a side dish for chicken; a friend tasted this quinoa porridge right out of the pot and said, "It's very comforting. I could imagine eating a bowl of this on a cold night and then curling up and going to sleep." The next night, we used quinoa as the base for stir-fry, which became a less weighty dish than a fry with rice. The stir-fry was also

good cold the next day, which gives quinoa an immediate advantage over rice. It works very well in cold tabbouleh-like dishes, and makes soup thicker and heartier.

Ancient Harvest combines quinoa with organic durum wheat and sesame to make pasta with up to 50 percent more protein than other pastas. The pasta is also available wheat-free. In general, the pasta is more flavorful than ordinary wheat pasta, but the textures are unusual: the pasta with wheat is slightly gritty; the wheat-free pasta is stickier and sweeter than wheat pasta.

Growers are working to develop a salable strain of quinoa in Colorado. In the meantime, the grain comes from small farmers in the Altiplano regions of the Andes. "To our knowledge," says David Schnorr, the company's president, "the grain is grown without the use of pesticides or herbicides. The company does do random testing that confirms this fact. Efforts to organize a certifiable program are underway now."

In 1990, a case of quinoa pasta ran between $21.50 and $24.25. Grain and flour ran between $50 and $57 for 25 pounds, bulk. Both were also available packed in smaller bags or boxes at a higher cost.

BREWSTER RIVER MILL
Mill Street
Jeffersonville, VT 05464
(802) 644-2987

Visits: yes; cafe opening in 1991
Buys grains certified by: FVO, OCIA, SELF
Catalogue/price list available
Minimum order: none
Order by: phone, mail
Pay by: MC, Visa, check, money order, COD
Ship by: UPS, parcel post

FLOUR

Whole wheat (C) · High-gluten white · Oat (C) · Buckwheat · Rye · Cornmeal

The Brewster River Mill dates back to 1800, and has seen many uses: as a cider mill, a shingle-and-planing mill, and a United Farmers' Corporation way station for milk. In 1977, the Albright family bought the property and began to restore the mill on one of the old stone foundations.

"The project took six years, working eight months out of the year, a few hours a day," says David Albright, who studied old publications about milling to find the appropriate building techniques. "The logs and lumber were gotten locally, mostly from my father-in-law's sugarwoods and a barn he gave us. The windows are

Brewster River Mill

Vermont's Only Steam-powered Gristmill

from recycled Fort Dix Army barracks donated by friends. The structure is post-and-beam with over 200 oak pegs and 600 pounds of old cut nails, square-headed bolts, and cast-iron washers. When different sections of timbers were fitted and ready, many willing townspeople came in the evening and the bents were 'razed' into place."

His wife, Sandy, whose roots in the town go back 150 years, almost as far as the mill itself, would love to return the mill to its original, water-powered form. "We currently power it with a wood-fired 1922 steam engine. It's our dream to put the dam back to utilize the river again."

The Albrights' dedication to authenticity extends to their grain. The cornmeal comes from Indian flint corn, a variety grown in the area for 150 years. In the bag, it's a gorgeous deep yellow flecked with white and bright red, with a rich sweet smell. I made both plain cornbread for stuffing and pumpkin cornbread, first soaking the cornmeal in milk. Both were excellent, moist, buttery cornbreads with real substance and texture, unlike the airy cake- or muffin-like texture of store-bought cornbread. My friend Tom made buttermilk rolls with the Brewster Mill whole-wheat flour and he reported that the dough was very easy to work with and knead. The rolls were light and moist with the full sweetness of the wheat; the universal reaction among friends was "scrumptious."

In 1990, 5 pounds of whole-wheat or high-gluten white flour was $2.75. Two pounds of cornmeal was $1.50. Shipping additional. The catalogue also lists maple syrup, and nonorganic chocolates, and jams and jellies.

CHEYENNE GAP® AMARANTH

HC 1, Box 2
Luray, KS 67649
(913) 698-2292
(913) 698-2457

Visits: by appointment
Certified by: SELF
Catalogue/price list available
Minimum order: 1 pound
Order by: phone, mail
Pay by: check
Ship by: parcel post

WHOLE GRAINS

Black amaranth (F) · Mixed amaranth (mostly white, some red and black)

FLOUR

White amaranth

Amaranth is an ancient Aztec grain that fascinates modern researchers because it not only is high in protein but also contains amino acids the body doesn't manufacture on its own. It is particularly high in the amino acid lysine, which is missing from other cereal grains, so the combination of amaranth with other grains makes a complete protein—like eating eggs.

Marjorie Jones, author of *Super Foods,* says that "the Aztecs dried the seeds, then either cooked them as a hot cereal or ground them into flour. They also discovered that white varieties would pop, as we pop corn. . . . The Indians pulled up the dry plants, laid them on skins, and beat the seeds loose with sticks and clubs. Then they gathered the tiny seeds, dried and stored them for use all year. . . . With some plants, they pulled leaves off the center stalk and cooked them as we cook spinach, collards, and beet or turnip greens." You have to wonder —did those Aztecs leave cookbooks behind?

Cheyenne Gap sells the tiny whole-grain amaranth (the seeds will flow right through a one-sixteenth-inch mesh), which makes several variations on hot cereal. I made a fruit-juice based porridge whose most distinctive quality was the texture: the individual grains never merge, as they do in other hot cereals. On the spoon, they look like tiny translucent bubbles, and have a kind of bounce on the tongue and teeth.

Cheyenne Gap also sells amaranth flour, which is far more versatile. The flour is ground very fine: it takes Cheyenne Gap's Arris Sigle roughly three hours to grind twenty-five pounds of flour to this texture. To keep the flour as fresh as possible, he doesn't start grinding until he receives an order. "We find that when amaranth is used for one-tenth to one-third of the total flour in bread or cake," says Sigle, "the amaranth makes them moist—frosting isn't needed for the cake, and the bread is never dry." I tried it in a banana bread, roughly one to four with whole-wheat flour. It gave a nutty flavor and fine-grained texture to the bread, which, like cornbread, was both moist and crumbly.

By mixing amaranth with other grains you get "an almost perfect protein for humans," says Sigle. He sells a cookbook, called *Baking with Amaranth* by Marge Jones, with recipes for people who have allergies to any or all of the following: corn, wheat, yeast, milk, eggs.

Although Cheyenne Gap is not certified organic, Sigle uses no pesticides or herbicides; he uses a little nitrogen fertilizer on his wheat crop, but none on his amaranth. "I am not an organic grower," says Sigle, "but I try to use the best materials at hand and only those amounts needed to do the job, if they are needed at all."

In 1990, amaranth flour was $3 a pound. Mixed whole-grain amaranth was $2.50 a pound. The price per pound drops if you order in quantity. Shipping additional. Cheyenne Gap® Amaranth also sells seed for planting.

COMMUNITY MILL AND BEAN
267 Route 89 South
Savannah, NY 13146
(800) 755-0554
(315) 365-2664
FAX: (315) 365-2690

Mill and grains certified by: FVO
Catalogue/price list available

Minimum order: $10
Order by: phone, mail, fax
Pay by: check
Ship by: UPS, parcel post

BAKING MIXES

Buttermilk flapjack · Buckwheat pancake · Gingerbread · Cornbread · Oat bran muffin (wheat-free) · Belgian waffle

HOT CEREAL

Mighty mush (wheat, rice, and soy) (available August–April) · Quick rolled oats

WHOLE GRAINS

Hard red spring (bread) wheat (F) · Soft winter (pastry) wheat (F) · Flint corn (F) · Rye berries (F) · Wheat bran

OTHER FLOUR

Buckwheat · Soy · Oat · Unbleached white (with or without germ) · Brown rice · Durum flour

BEANS

Black turtle · Garbanzo · Lentil · Navy · Pinto · Red kidney · Green split peas · Great northern

Community Mill and Bean's master miller, Richard Corichi, has been milling grain on and off since he was seventeen. "He's a self-made person," says his wife, Kit Fallon. "He grew up in New York City and learned to mill as a teenager at a natural-foods bakery in the Adirondacks. He's been independent ever since." In the 1970s, Corichi milled grains on a small scale for Clear Eye, a distributor of organic foods in New York's Finger Lakes region. As the demand for organic flour grew, Corichi realized that it was time to start a separate, but neighboring, mill.

Fallon is proud of the fact that "Community" isn't just a name, but reflects a commitment to the agriculture of the region. All of the grains, with the exception of the hard red spring wheat, are grown locally. "We feel strongly about working closely with our farmers and growers," says Fallon. "We meet regularly with our suppliers to try to answer the questions they have. Most of them are concerned about whether they'll have an outlet for organic grain if we can't take it all. We try to contract for a certain amount in advance, to give them some kind of guarantee."

Community Mill and Bean uses traditional stone grinding, which doesn't overheat the grain, and doesn't destroy the natural enzymes. All grain is milled fresh and to order. The mixes

contain natural or organic sweeteners—Sucanat, maple sugar, or granular honey.

East West Magazine awarded Community Mill and Bean "Best Pancake Mix" for the buttermilk flapjacks, and I could see why. The flapjacks were delicious and fluffy, as dark as buckwheat pancakes, but cornmeal gives them a sweetness all-buckwheat cakes don't have.

When I heard "Oat bran," I thought, "Oh, no, not another leaden health muffin!" But don't let the name fool you. This mix makes a light, spicy muffin you'll eat because it is good, not just because it is good for you. The muffins were a big hit with a two-year-old visitor, who happily left a trail of oat bran crumbs behind him.

The cornmeal was a beautiful deep yellow, and made a very moist cornbread, with a dense, somewhat grainy texture—"a stand-up polenta," said the baker, Tom. Because of the coarse grind, you might want to soak the cornmeal to soften it if you're making something that calls for a more delicate texture.

In 1990, flours and mixes ranged from $1.74 to $3.31 for a 2-pound bag. Beans ranged in price from $3.36 to $5.45 for 2 pounds. You save by buying a box of 6 bags. Flours and grains are also available in bulk quantities, and decrease in price.

CROSS SEED COMPANY
HC 69, Box 2
Bunker Hill, KS 67626
(913) 483-6163

Farm certified by: OGBA
Catalogue/price list available
Minimum order: none
Order by: phone, mail
Pay by: check, money order, COD
Ship by: UPS, parcel post

BEANS AND SEEDS

Adzuki · Mung · Whole green peas · Lentil · Soy · Pinto · Garbanzo · Black turtle · Large striped sunflower seeds (in shell; or roasted and salted) · Hulled raw sunflower meats

GRAINS

Golden amaranth · Barley (whole or hulled) · Whole rye · Oats (whole or hulled) · Hard red winter wheat · Soft white winter wheat · Triticale · Whole buckwheat · Millet (whole or hulled) · Popcorn

SEEDS FOR SPROUTING

Alfalfa · Yellow clover · Red clover · Turnip · Chinese cabbage · Kale · Black mustard · Fenugreek · Radish · Sesame · Small black sunflower

BAKING MIXES

Amaranth biscuit and pancake

The two Cross brothers are "Vietnam-era age," says Dale Cross, and saw first-hand what Agent Orange could do. "We didn't want to get involved with any more chemicals," says Cross. "Everything we grow is organic."

Dale's parents, who founded the Cross Seed Company in 1943, also shied away from chemicals. "We're not wealthy people," says Cross, "and chemicals cost money." Out of necessity, his mother figured out early on how to solve pest problems without chemicals. For tomato bugs, for example, she would grind up a few of the bugs and mix them with pepper, and spray that around the plants. If I were a bug, I wouldn't stick around either. Cross Seed Com-

Selected for PURITY GERMINATION YIELD VIGOR CROSS

pany also buys seeds and grains that meet the standards of the state of California and the state of Oregon.

In 1990, for orders under 5 pounds, beans ranged from 95 cents to $1.45 a pound; whole grains ranged from 85 cents to $1.35 a pound; sprouting seeds ranged from $1.05 to $4.75 a pound; amaranth biscuit and pancake mix was $1.25 a pound. You save by buying in bulk.

DAVID'S GOODBATTER
P.O. Box 102
Bausman, PA 17504
(717) 872-0652
FAX: (717) 872-8152

Ingredients certified by: OCIA
Minimum order: none
Order by: mail
Pay by: check, money order, COD
Ship by: UPS
Recipes available

PANCAKE AND BAKING MIXES

Whole-wheat buttermilk · Buckwheat buttermilk · Wheat-free buttermilk · Wheat-free rice and oats · Premium almond · Premium pecan

About seventeen years ago, Jane and Barry David stopped eating pancakes. They'd started eating natural foods, and had finally broken down and read the ingredients of their favorite pancake mix—"Sugar was the least of the things we knew we should avoid," says Jane David. But they missed pancakes. "So we de-

cided to come up with a mix of our own. It wasn't long before we were having pancakes at breakfast, lunch, or dinner several times a week."

Then the Davids' son was born, and he couldn't eat wheat. "There was this long, sad face at the end of the table whenever we had pancakes." So the Davids came out with wheat-free pancakes. "When he became sensitized to rye, we were back to the drawing board. We knew we could do something with rice flour, but the first couple of attempts were awful. Now we've finally got something we really like. I make layer cakes with it, strawberry shortcake —anything you want to cook that you expect to rise." The Davids have added two nut pancakes, which Jane's mother used to make. My own fond memories of pecan waffles come from a tiny roadside restaurant in North Carolina called the Buttery and Beanery. If you've never had them, you're in for a treat.

David's will send you a folder of recipes for cakes, main-course pies, quick breads, biscuits, fritters, and muffins. The batters contain only organically grown whole grains; the baking powder is aluminum-free. No salt or preservatives are added, and the batters are made under kosher supervision. The reclosable canister adds to their convenience.

David's gets letters from around the country. "We ship to one old lady in California who doesn't get out much and just loves our buckwheat pancakes. When I get her letters," says Jane David, "I know I'm in the right business."

In 1990, the whole-wheat, buckwheat, and wheat-free mixes were $3.69. The rice and oats were $3.95, and the almond and pecan were $4.15. Shipping additional.

DIAMOND K ENTERPRISES
RR I, Box 30-A
St. Charles, MN 55972
(507) 932-4308

Farm and processing certified by: OGBA
Catalogue/price list available
Minimum order: none
Order by: phone, mail
Pay by: check, Visa, MC
Ship by: UPS

GRAINS

Amaranth (F) · Barley (hulled and unhulled)
(F) · Buckwheat (groats or grits) (F) · Corn
(high-lysine or regular) (F,C) · Cracked
wheat · Oats (hulled or unhulled) (F,C—
including baby oatmeal) · Yellow popcorn ·
Brown rice (short-, medium,- and long-grain)
(F,C) · Rye (F) · Triticale (F) · Soft pastry
wheat (F) · Hard spring wheat (F)

OTHER FLOUR

Multigrain · Pumpernickel (wheat, rye, and
cornmeal)

BEANS AND SEEDS

Flax seed (F) · Lentil (hulled or unhulled) ·
Mung · Pinto · Navy · Black turtle · Kidney ·
Soy (F,C) · Brown sesame (unhulled) · Grey-
stripe sunflower · Raw hulled sunflower · Black
sunflower

PANCAKE MIXES

Barley · Buckwheat · Corn · Whole wheat

OIL AND VINEGAR

Sunflower oil

SWEETENERS

Honey

DRIED FRUIT

Raisins

The "K" in "Diamond K" comes from the
Kranzes, Minnesota grain growers who started
milling organic flour in 1970, when they
wanted to bake bread from organic whole-
wheat flour and couldn't find any in the store.
Jack Kranz and his father had been inspired to
go organic after a trip to Texas, where Kranz's
brother-in-law ran a local chamber of com-
merce. He introduced the two to a man who
was raising beef organically. "In the south,"
says Jack Kranz, "most beef cattle are mixed-up
crossed-up breeds, and they generally don't
look too good. These were mixed-up all right,
but they looked good. That impressed my father, and we decided to switch. In the first year,
we got some of the lousiest crops we ever had,
but over the years, we learned how to get good
crops."

Diamond K started out doing specialty milling, and will still do custom grinding for you.

In 1990, whole-wheat flour ranged from 63 cents for 1
pound to $23.47 for 50 pounds.

DO-R.-DYE ORGANIC FARM
Box 50
Rosalie, NE 68055
(402) 863-2248

Visits: yes
Grains certified by: OCIA
Catalogue/price list available
Minimum order: $5
Order by: phone, mail
Pay by: check
Ship by: parcel post, own truck

GRAINS

Oats (groats or hulled) (F,C) · Wheat berries
(F,C) · Rye berries (F,C) · Corn kernel (F) ·
Sweet corn kernel (F) · Blue corn kernel (F)

The Dye family started milling organic grain
in 1978, out of necessity. The Dye children had
developed severe food allergies to chemically
grown and processed foods. "One of them even
became allergic to the coloring they put in butter and oleo," says Richard Dye. "We got a
stone mill and started grinding our own meal
and baking our own bread. That helped. Then

DO-R.-DYE FARM

we started selling to other people whose kids had allergies."

The Dyes purchase most of their grain from Nebraska farmers, and most is OCIA-certified. Although the plant is not certified, the Dyes follow the OCIA guidelines, and the guidelines of the Nebraska Sustainable Agriculture Society.

Grain prices depend on the size of the order. Grains are available in 25 and 50 pounds but can be put in 3-, 5-, or 10-pound bags, for a small surcharge per pound.

EAGLE ORGANIC AND NATURAL FOOD

407 Church Avenue
Huntsville, AR 72740
(501) 738-2203
(501) 442-6792

Visits: yes, in Huntsville and Fayetteville
Buys from growers certified by: CCOF, OCIA, OOGA, affidavit
Catalogue/price list available
Minimum order: none
Order by: phone, mail
Pay by: check, money order, VISA, MC, COD
Ship by: UPS, parcel post, own trucks

BEANS

Anasazi · Pinto · Great northern · Green split peas · Garbanzo · Whole green peas · Green lentils · Mung · Black turtles · Small red · Yellow split peas · Black soy · Navy · Kidney · Adzuki · Baby lima · Soy (C)

GRAINS

Hard red winter wheat (F,C) · Whole soft (pastry) wheat (F) · Whole yellow corn (F,C) · Whole blue corn (F) · Whole white corn (F,C) · Della basmati rice · Della basmati white rice · Brown rice (short-, medium-, or long-grain) (F,C) · Wild rice · Hulled barley (F,C) · Hulled millet (F) · Rye (F,C) · Buckwheat groats (F) · Hulless popcorn · Hulled buckwheat · Amaranth · Sweet brown rice · Oat groats (C,F) · Quinoa · Yellow popcorn

OTHER FLOUR

Unbleached white · Masa harina

OTHER CEREALS

Fiber-7 flakes

BAKING MIXES

Blueberry pancake and muffin · Buttermilk pancake and muffin · Buttermilk biscuit

WHOLE-WHEAT FLATS

Alphabets · Flats · Spaghetti · Lasagna · Fedilini · Spirals · Shells

SEEDS

Sesame (hulled or unhulled) · Alfalfa seed · Sprouting buckwheat · Sprouting sunflower · Hulled sunflower

DRIED FRUIT

Shredded coconut · Thompson raisins · Large prunes

NUTS

Whole almonds

SNACKS

Blue corn chips · Yellow corn chips · Amaranth graham crackers

COFFEE

Cafe Altura medium roast (ground) · Cafe Tierra Guatemalan · Guatemalan blend · Guatemalan French roast · Guatemalan dark roast (regular or decaf) · Guatemalan Viennese blend · German chocolate mint (regular or decaf) · Vanilla almond · Dutch Bavarian chocolate (regular or decaf) · Jamaica rum · French vanilla · Amaretto · Cinnamon Viennese · Kahlua · Golden pecan (regular or decaf) · Swiss chocolate almond (regular or decaf) · Vanilla almond fudge · Irish cream (regular or decaf) · Brandy Alexander (regular or decaf) · After-dinner blend (Swiss Water Process decaffeinated)

HERBS AND SPICES

Peppermint leaf · Sage · Oregano · Raspberry leaf · Spearmint leaf · Lemongrass

CANNED GOODS

Refried beans

In 1973, Kathy Turner and her husband took over a "tiny" grain mill. "You could almost grind by hand. The mill was pretty downgraded. We've really improved it, and now we've got three mills going." All grain is stone-ground, milled to order, and shipped within forty-eight hours. "We knew from our own baking what we wanted in a flour, and what we liked," says Kathy Turner. "For example, we've got the real gritty cornmeal, because that's what we like."

Each grain is ground for a specific purpose. Masa harina, for example, is yellow corn flour ground for tortillas. The Turners grind and sift hard red winter wheat to produce the wheat-dream cereal, "truly the cream of all wheats. This smooth hot cereal can warm any soul on a cold morning." The Turners recommend their cornmeal not only for cornbread and muffins, but also as a batter for frying fish. The Turners also turn corn into grits—"a real southern treat. Use them as a cereal or let them set, pan-fry in slabs, and pour mushroom gravy over them." The Turners have been vegetarians since they met, and for fellow vegetarians, they also sell a range of beans.

The Turners were founding members of the Ozark Organic Growers' Association, and use its standards for grain. Eagle buys processed foods certified by OCIA, and produce certified by CCOF. In addition, it has a four-page notorized affidavit for most of the grains the Turners sell and process.

Grains, flours, baking mixes, and beans are sold in 5- or 25-pound bags, with some smaller bags available. In 1990, a 5-pound bag of flour ranged from $2.20 to $5. You save by buying the larger bags. The catalogue lists some non-organic foods, gardening supplies, vitamins, personal-care items, and pet products. There are incremental volume discounts, with 10% for orders over $60.

Eagle
AGRICULTURAL PRODUCTS

FIDDLER'S GREEN FARM
RFD I, Box 656
Belfast, ME 04915
(207) 338-3568
FAX: (207) 338-4465

Visits: yes; roadside stand; bed-and-breakfast
Ingredients certified by: MOFGA, NOFA, OCIA, FVO
Farm certified by: MOFGA
Catalogue/price list available
Minimum order: none
Order by: phone, mail
Pay by: check, MC, Visa
Ship by: UPS
Gift packages available

WHOLE-GRAIN BAKING MIXES

Pancake and muffin · Buttermilk spicecake and cookie · Bread and biscuit · Oats and barley (wheat-free) pancake and baking · Mandan Bride cornbread

HOT CEREALS

Penobscot Porridge (four-grain) · Toasted oat bran and hot rice (suitable for infants as well as adults) · Oatmeal

FLOUR

Whole-wheat pastry · Whole-wheat bread · Unbleached white · Yellow cornmeal · Wheat bran · Brown rice

PASTA

Whole-wheat spaghetti · Vegetable spirals ·

Sesame rice spirals · Spinach ribbons · Sifted-wheat paella ribbons · Parsley garlic ribbons · Provencale ribbons · Plain ribbons · Soba noodles · Udon noodles

PRESERVES

Orange-rhubarb butter · Apple butter · Blueberry jam · Wild Maine blueberry syrup

SOUP MIX

Beans of Maine

COFFEE AND TEA

Guatemalan medium roast · French vanilla · Decaf breakfast blend · Kukicha tea

SNACK BARS

Oat bran · Strawberry-banana · Spicy raisin

When I started this book I had a list of "Wouldn't it be great if"s—including an organic version of Bisquick. Bisquick biscuits were a staple of my childhood, one of the first things I ever baked for myself, and I'd kept right on eating them even though I'd begun to notice their slightly metallic aftertaste. So I was thrilled to learn that I could check off an item on my wish list with Fiddler's Green bread-and-biscuit mix. This version takes one or two more steps to make, but after tasting the results, I'll never go back. These are fabulous biscuits: buttery, rich, crisp on the outside and flaky on the inside, with a hint of the sweetness of a corn muffin. Unlike Bisquick biscuits, these are also delicious reheated.

The people behind Fiddler's Green are Nancy Galland and Richard Stander. Back in

1977, they had set out to save Galland's Massachusetts farm, which had been in her family for three generations. The town had been laid out so that every settler got a ten-acre parcel, but the town's founders could not have foreseen the day when Galland and Stander would try to use their ten acres to grow organic vegetables while the tobacco and potato farmers on either side of them continued to spray and spray.

Nothing could stop the chemicals from drifting onto their land. When Galland's mother's cat died, the veterinarian blamed the death on pesticide exposure. Galland and Stander stopped farming, and for nine months wondered what to do next. Inheriting land was one thing, but buying land was another, says Galland. Unless you win the lottery. Which, in a sense, they did.

This wasn't your average lottery. They had put their names into the pool of applicants to care for a 115-acre homestead in Belfast, Maine. The former owner, David Kennedy, an oil-tanker pilot, had died when his private plane crashed in fog. His will prohibited the sale of the farm to anyone who would not farm it organically. Kennedy's trustees, a lawyer, a chicken farmer, and an organic gardener, interviewed a host of candidates and chose Stander and Galland. The first year was rent-free, which gave them a chance to get the farm in shape and producing income. After that, they had a lease-purchase agreement, paying rent for five years toward the purchase of Fiddler's Green.

Kennedy had been growing wheat organically for ten years, and had stone-ground the grain into a pancake and muffin mix, still available from Fiddler's Green (Cap'n Dave's Pancakes and Muffins). Galland and Stander expanded into a line of mixes and hot cereals, from certified organic grain.

Breakfast must be the favorite meal at the Stander-Galland home. The *Daily News* called their breakfast products "sensational: all yield fabulous results—tender-crumbed coffee cakes, hearty flavorful pancakes, and light, fluffy biscuits." The *New York Times* called their Penobscot Porridge "one of the finest local versions . . . nutty, grainy, robust, and rib-sticking." The *San Diego Union* said it was "so good it's a pity to wait until fall to try some."

At the Maine Organic Farmers' and Gardeners' Association Fair, I sampled a mild, ginger-flavored raisin-spice cookie made from the spicecake and cookie mix. The texture, more cakey than chewy, made me think I would prefer it as a cake, although Nancy Galland did tell me that the cookie was great with chocolate chips (like coffee, a no-no at the MOFGA fair).

I also took home a bottle of the wild blueberry syrup, which will not last long in your fridge—not because it has no preservatives, but because you can happily finish the bottle at one sitting. Like the best jams, it really shows off the blueberry flavor, is scrumptious on pancakes, stirred into yogurt, or right on the spoon.

Mandan Indian cornbread is Fiddler's Green's newest addition to the catalogue. The grain has been in continuous cultivation for the past 2,000 years by the Mandan Indians of the Dakotas, explain Stander and Galland. The *Boston Globe* found Mandan cornbread "moist and compact and satisfying: it has an earthy quality, a dense crumb, and a rich, deep taste that suggests something more than cornmeal, though it's made entirely of corn."

The Fiddler's Green catalogue includes many perfect gifts: orange-rhubarb butter, made from their own rhubarb, organically grown oranges and raisins, simmered with honey on a wood stove; apple butter from Baldwin apples, simmered with honey, cider, cinnamon, and other spices.

In 1990, baking mixes ranged from $2.84 to $3.25 for 1.5 pounds. Freshly ground flour ranged from $1.35 to $2.45 for 2 pounds. You save by buying larger bags. The catalogue also lists Wood Prairie Farm Yukon Gold potatoes (page 108), Southern Brown Rice (page 224), and Maine Coast Sea Vegetables (page 238).

THE GOOD EARTH ASSOCIATION
Rockcrescent Ridge Farm
202 East Church Street
Pocahontas, AR 72455-2899
(501) 892-9545
(501) 892-8329

Visits: yes; special events on Memorial Day weekend, Harvest Day, and Earth Day; flea and vegetable market the first Saturday of the month April–September; pick-your-own produce
Certified by: SELF
Minimum order: none
Order by: mail
Pay by: check, money order
Ship by: UPS, parcel post

BEANS

Fava · Purple hull peas · Cow peas

GRAIN

Bloody Butcher corn · Indian blue corn · Wheat · Rye · Millet

VEGETABLES

Turnips · Rutabagas

Donald L. Waterworth, Sr., founder of the Good Earth Association, did a lot of traveling when he was in the service. "I saw how people raised food in other parts of the world. They didn't use chemicals, and the food looked so much better—I've never seen prettier fruits and vegetables than in Japan, anywhere." When he retired, Waterworth formed a research group to study the growing methods he'd seen. "We were playing around trying to keep costs down, so we were using old farm equipment, and horses, and doing a lot by hand. Soon people started saying we ought to show off our old machinery. That's how the Living Farm Museum got started."

The Living Farm Museum gives demonstrations of horse plowing, hay baling, wheat threshing, a sorghum mill at work, a grist mill making cornmeal, soap making, and hominy making. The museum's parent organization, the Good Earth Association, is a nonprofit institution dedicated to helping people run low-technology, self-sustaining family farms. One of its fund-raising projects is Hilltop Gardens, which raises money for the association by selling produce. The ten or fifteen participating gardens—it varies from year to year—belong to GEA members, who grow their crops organically. "If any of them have to use chemicals for any reason, we tell people about it. Usually we don't have to tell people because we don't have to do it."

Waterworth advises people who want produce from Hilltop Gardens to let them know well in advance: "Most of it is sold even before it's planted," he says. Bloody Butcher corn, in case you were wondering, is the highest protein corn available. I sampled the fava beans, a traditional bean of Italy and the Middle East, which were meaty, firm, and nutty.

GRAY'S GRIST MILL
P.O. Box 422
Adamsville, RI 02801
(508) 636-6075

Visits: yes
Certified by: SELF
Catalogue/price list available
Minimum order: none
Order by: phone, mail
Pay by: check, Visa, MC ($20 minimum)
Ship by: UPS, parcel post
Recipes available

FLOUR

Johnnycake meal · Whole wheat · Rye

BAKING MIXES

Pancake and waffle · Brown bread and muffin

The milling tradition at Gray's Grist Mill stretches back to 1675, and for most of its life, the mill was central to the town. In this era of store-bought flour, the mill could easily be obsolete. Instead, it's alive and whirring in the hands of Tim McTague, a restoration carpenter who spent two years learning to mill from John Allen Hart, a Gray by marriage and the third generation of Grays to run the mill since 1878. Hart had been the miller for sixty-two years before he retired, and refused to sell until he found someone who could keep it alive as a real, working mill, not just a tourist curiosity.

The mill uses traditional 1,500-pound wheels of granite, powered not by water but by a 1946 Dodge engine salvaged from an old mayonnaise-delivery truck. (McTague jokes that it's more reliable than any car he's ever owned.) The freshly ground meal contains both bran and germ, which gives it more vitamins and flavor than store-bought. McTague cautions that because the fresh-ground grain is oily, it can spoil, and should be kept in the refrigerator, where it will keep for months.

Gray's grinds a number of grains and mixes on its granite stones, but its specialty is Johnnycake meal. Johnnycakes, a staple of the Rhode Island diet, are served not just for breakfast but with every meal. John Allen Hart still eats them almost daily. Since 1878, Gray's has produced the traditional white cornmeal using locally grown Rhode Island White Cap Flint Corn, a strain domesticated by the Narraganset Indians. McTague says he can tell just by smell whether a mill is grinding white or yellow corn: the meal from white flint corn is richer and sweeter.

You don't have to make only Johnnycakes with the meal. McTague uses it to make polenta, spoonbread ("what the angels eat"), muffins, cookies, Indian pudding, and to bread fish and scallops. Gourmet chef Jasper White tops Gray's Johnnycakes with caviar, poached egg and chive. According to White, Gray's Grist Mill is "hardly state-of-the-art, but General Mills's multimillion-dollar operation has never produced flour even close to the quality of Tim the Miller's."

Although not certified organic, the grain that goes into the flour, meal, and mixes has not been treated with herbicides or pesticides. The flours and mixes contain no additives or preservatives. Some conventional fertilizers are used, however.

In 1990, flours and mixes ranged from $6.25 to $6.95 for a 2-pound bag and less expensive in bulk. Shipping included.

GREAT GRAINS MILLING COMPANY
P.O. Box 427
Scobey, MT 59263
(406) 783-5588
(406) 783-5301

Visits: yes
Farm and mill certified by: OCIA
Catalogue/price list available
Minimum order: none
Order by: phone, mail
Pay by: check, money order
Ship by: UPS, parcel post
Recipes available

GRAINS

Whole wheat (F,C)

OTHER FLOUR

Golden wheat · Rye

In Alvin Rustebakke's local supermarket, his Great Grains flour outsells Pillsbury by ten to one. I'm not surprised. A friend and I, both nervous because it had been several years since we'd baked bread, made two completely professional loaves with Great Grains' whole-wheat flour. The recipe called for mixing whole-wheat and white flours. We used all whole-wheat, yet the result was light and golden, soft yet dense, with an even crumb, and all the sweetness of the grain.

Alvin Rustebakke has been growing wheat organically since the 1970s, when he learned that agricultural chemicals showed up in the germ and bran of wheat, the parts of the grain most sought after for their nutrients. He only started milling because he couldn't find organic flour in the local supermarket. "Like many other wheat-growers in northeastern Montana," say Alvin Rustebakke and his wife, Dorothy, "we felt cheated whenever we saw our high-protein hard red spring wheat trucked off to market, while we had to settle for bags of anemic, preservative-laden flour for our own use." They envied the farmers of the 1920s and 1930s who could "haul their grain to a local mill and have it custom ground."

The Rustebakkes bought themselves a kitchen-size stone mill, but say it "had to struggle valiantly to supply our bread-baking family members and our neighbors as well." So in 1979, with the help of two sons and a son-in-law, Rustebakke built a commercial mill next to his wheat fields, and began grinding grain into flour on twenty-inch granite stones.

Golden wheat is Rustebakke's answer to all-purpose flour. It's a fine grind of hard red spring wheat, with most of the bran removed. The flour produces breads that are lighter than whole-wheat breads and have a "light tan color and delicious wheat flavor," says Rustebakke. The whole-wheat flour comes with recipes for pancakes, waffles, and bread, baking tips for

GREAT GRAINS MILLING CO.
Ph. (406) 783-5588
Box 427 · Scobey, Montana 59263

Stone Ground
Golden Wheat Flour

whole-wheat flour, and proportions to use when substituting whole wheat for white flour.

Both flours contain more oil than white flour, and can turn rancid if overexposed to oxygen. To prevent this, all of the flours are packed in plastic barrier bags and flushed with nitrogen (which forces out the oxygen) to preserve their freshness. The barrier bag keeps the nitrogen in and the oxygen out. No chemicals or preservatives are added.

In 1990, a 5-pound bag of golden-wheat or whole-wheat flour was $1.85. A 3-pound bag of rye flour was $1.65. Wheat bran was $1.10 for a 2-pound bag. Prices decrease for bulk orders.

GREEN EARTH FARM
P.O. Box 672
65½ North 8th Street
Saguache, CO 81149
(719) 655-2655

Visits: yes; strawberries, raspberries, vegetables, and herbs
Farmers' markets: call for information
Certified by: state of Colorado, CHSC
Certification pending: OCIA
Catalogue/price list available
Minimum order: none
Order by: phone, mail
Pay by: check, COD
Ship by: UPS, parcel post

GRAIN

Quinoa

VEGETABLES

Purple Peruvian potatoes

Green Earth is a private, cooperative farm in Colorado's San Luis valley whose members include a former dairy farmer, a yoga teacher, a manager with IBM, and a couple who are vintners and raise sheep. One member, Margo Williams, has a master's degree in horticulture and worked several years in the U.S. National Arboretum. What all the members share, says Williams, is a dual commitment: to practice organic farming and to educate people about healing the planet. As Williams puts it, Green Earth aims to provide food for the table *and* food for thought.

Together, the members of Green Earth took a dilapidated 640-acre cattle ranch and turned it into a sustainable farm. The site has turned out to be ideal. Not only was the soil rich to begin with, but the neighboring farm is Coleman's Natural Beef, so they don't have to worry about pesticide drift. Water, which is a precious commodity in the high mountain valley, comes from a creek fed by snows on the 14,000-foot peaks that surround the farm.

Two of the crops they specialize in, quinoa and Purple Peruvian potatoes (say that three times fast) come from another high mountain range: the Andes. Quinoa is an Andean grain that is highly nutritious, with the same protein content as whole milk. It's slightly nutty in flavor, and quite versatile. (For more on quinoa, see Ancient Harvest Quinoa, page 123.) Purple Peruvian potatoes are indeed purple through and through.

In addition to their food crops, they planted 3,000 trees for windbreak and wildlife habitat, and dug a pond that serves both for water storage and filtration and a habitat for wildfowl. "It was fascinating," says one of Green Earth's members, "to watch the pond's inhabitants change from week to week as they flew through the valley during their migration north."

In 1990, quinoa was $3 a pound, and you saved by buying in bulk. Potatoes were $2 a pound. Shipping additional. The farm also sells Calendula Creme, a preparation made from organic herbs to soothe and protect the skin.

HANSON FARMS
P.O. Box 26
Opheim, MT 59250
(406) 762-3265

Visits: yes
Farm certified by: OCIA
Catalogue/price list available
Minimum order: none
Order by: phone, mail
Pay by: check, cashier's check
Ship by: UPS, parcel post

GRAINS

Wheat berries (F) · Barley (whole or hulled)
(F) · Oats (F) · Oat bran · Rye · Flax

Tom Hanson was inspired to go organic by a man who'd started growing organic wheat in 1958. Hanson took his advice, and stopped using chemicals. Hanson's voice is slow and measured, but his convictions come through loud and clear. "I don't see how my God can bless me if I'm out here destroying His land and turning out poison for His people.

"The first year, our production dropped off. The second year the grasshoppers cleaned us out but we didn't touch the land. Our neighbors were furious that we wouldn't spray. They sprayed five times that year. The next year, we seeded our crop, and never had a grasshopper. They sprayed three times, and they were still battling them. They had destroyed all the natural predators. Sure, they saved their crop, but they gave all the profits to the chemical company."

Hanson participates in the FVO certification program, and also buys some transitional grain from farmers in his area. Hanson Farms raises "quality grain, but not a whole lot of quantity. We use the older variety of solid stem wheats that have excellent milling quality, and that just sells itself. The problem with American agriculture is that we've forgotten about quality and just go for bushels." The whole-wheat flour comes from hard red spring wheat and makes "almost a white loaf," says Tom Hanson. He also raises Golden 86 wheat. In 1990, after he

lost his crop to drought, he got a call from a customer asking for some of what little he had left. "It seems his wife bought a bag of it from us two years ago, and now it's all she'll bake with."

All the flour is stone-ground. After grinding, says Hanson, "You really only have about ten hours after milling to use the flour. After that, the oil in the germ goes rancid from being exposed to oxygen." To prevent spoilage, he uses nitrogen, an inert gas, to push the oxygen out. "Our flour has an indefinite shelf life," says Tom Hanson, "and remains as fresh as the day it was ground. Also, our oat products are all alive. They have not been stabilized or steamed to destroy the enzymes. As far as we know, we're the only company offering this to the public."

In 1990, flour ranged from 45 cents a pound to 95 cents a pound for a 2.5-pound bag. You save by buying in larger bags.

HEALTHLAND
HCR 2, Box 271A
Coulee City, WA 99115
(509) 632-8717

Farm certified by: WSDA
Minimum order: 10 pounds
Order by: mail
Pay by: check
Ship by: UPS, parcel post

FLOUR

Hard red whole-wheat bread flour · Soft white whole-wheat pastry flour

CEREAL

Microwavable 100% whole-wheat

JUICE

Wheatgrass

Paul Jorgensen and his brothers grow wheat on land that Jorgensens have been farming since the early years of this century. Their grandfather on one side came from Denmark, a great-grandfather on the other, from Norway. Both ended up homesteading in Washington. Today, Paul Jorgensen, his three brothers, and his father, Ralph, now farm some 7,000 acres in north-central Washington, "in view of the Cascade Mountain range, far from the pollution-producing cities."

In 1990, the Jorgensens farmed about 500 acres organically. The family first used chemicals in the 1940s or 1950s, says Paul Jorgensen. "They were all excited because it doubled their yield. They didn't know about all the environmental problems it would cause." The younger Jorgensens have been experimenting with organics since the mid-1980s. "It's slow going, while we learn how to make it profitable. We can't rush into it because we need to keep our yields up while we build the market for the organic grain. As long as it continues to work, we'll keep doing it."

In recent years, the younger Jorgensens added a stone mill, to mill their wheat into flour. Stone grinding, says Paul Jorgensen, preserves nutrients by not overheating the grain. He reports that "everyone we show the flour to

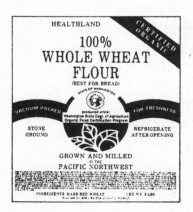

has been excited about it." The soft white flour is good for pancakes and waffles, he says; and the whole-wheat cereal is akin to cream of wheat. Vacuum packing, he says, gives their flour an advantage over other organic grains, because it doesn't need to be refrigerated.

In 1990, whole-wheat flour or cereal was $5 for 5 pounds. You can have a mixed order of 5 pounds of each to meet the minimum. Wheatgrass juice was $1 an ounce, shipped frozen in 32 1-ounce containers. Shipping included.

LIVING FARMS
P.O. Box 50
Tracy, MN 56175
(507) 629-4431
FAX: (507) 629-4253

Visits: yes
Certified by: SELF
Facilities certified by: OCIA
Catalogue/price list available
Minimum order: 1 pound
Order by: phone, mail, fax
Pay by: check
Ship by: UPS, parcel post

GRAINS

Buckwheat (hulled or unhulled) · Corn · Hulled millet · Popcorn · Rye · Hard red spring wheat · Hard red winter wheat · Soft white winter wheat

SEEDS

Alfalfa · Black mustard seed · Flax · Red clover · Radish

BEANS

Adzuki · Black turtle · Lentil · Mung · Pinto · Soy

In the early 1970s, when the organic agriculture movement was "still so small as to be undiscernible," an informal group of organic farmers founded Living Farms in Tracy, Minnesota (population 2,400) to create a marketplace for their organic commodities. Living

Foods of Integrity

Farms buys from both certified and uncertified growers, whose farms range from sixty to 3,000 acres, but all growers must meet the organic standards established by Living Farms for three years prior to the sale of the commodity, and they require annual certification thereafter. The staff of Living Farms travel some 60,000 miles a year to work with farmers, and each lot can be traced from the grower all the way to the customer. The Living Farms facility is certified by OCIA.

In 1990, commodities ranged from 23 cents a pound for wheat to $2.36 a pound for alfalfa. You can buy many commodities in bulk.

M & M DISTRIBUTING
RR 2, Box 61A
Oshkosh, NE 69154
(308) 772-3664

Visits: yes
Farm certified by: OGBA
Minimum order: none
Order by: phone, mail
Pay by: check
Ship by: UPS, parcel post

GRAINS

Whole-grain amaranth (F) · Puffed amaranth

If you know someone who is allergic to nuts, you know that it can be a life-threatening allergy. If you bake for someone who is allergic to nuts, puffed amaranth gives you a way to give cakes and cookies a nutty taste and texture —without danger, because it's not a nut, but a tiny grain that's been popped like popcorn.

Amaranth is an ancient Aztec grain that is getting lots of attention these days (see Nu-World Amaranth, Inc., page 144, and Cheyenne Gap® Amaranth, page 125, for more) because of its high nutritional value, but also because of its resistance to drought, which is what attracted the interest of Mark Jones, says his wife, Marcy Gade Jones. "We're just so dry out here, it's almost a drought. He saw an article on amaranth in *New Farm* and did a test plot of one acre, planting it by hand." Today Mark Jones farms some 400 acres of amaranth, all organically, in part out of concern about the effects of agricultural chemicals on local drinking water, "which is a big concern because the water around here is testing bad."

In 1990, whole-grain amaranth was $1 a pound. You save by buying in bulk. In addition to the amaranth products, M & M sells the Shaklee line of nutritional, household, and personal-care products, which is certified kosher and comes recommended by Greenpeace.

MASKAL FORAGES
1318 Willow
Caldwell, ID 83605
(208) 454-3330

Certified by: SELF
Catalogue/price list available
Minimum order: 2 pounds
Order by: phone, mail
Pay by: check, money order, COD
Ship by: UPS, USPS

WHOLE GRAIN

Brown teff (F) · Ivory teff (F)

In the Amharic language, "teff" means "lost." When mature, the seeds of this indigenous Ethiopian grass fall to the ground, and are so tiny—it takes 150 of them to weigh as much as a kernel of wheat—that they quickly disappear.

In spite of the difficulties of harvesting teff, the grain is a mainstay of Ethiopian culture. It's the country's most nutritious grain—higher in minerals and iron than barley, brown rice, millet, wheat, and oats. Teff is the main ingredient of *injera,* the national bread, a spongy flatbread, two feet in diameter, that serves as plate for the communal meal and individual scooping utensils. Like grapes, teff carries a symbiotic yeast that causes the grain to ferment, making a natural sourdough. The longer the fermentation, the sourer the taste and higher the *injera.*

Wayne Carlson, the founder and president of Maskal Forages, developed a taste for *injera* while working as a biologist on a medical research project in Ethiopia. When he got back to the United States, Carlson began growing teff in his backyard, and now grows several strains in a dry desert valley outside Boise, Idaho. Maskal Forages—named for the Ethiopian harvest holiday, Maskal—is the only commercial grower of teff outside Ethiopia.

Carlson says that the grain's tiny size is part of its appeal to a nomadic culture often threatened by invasion—if you have to move in a hurry, it's not hard to secrete away enough seed to start your crop again somewhere else. Teff is also resistant to drought, which makes it a promising crop for farmers in many parts of the world.

Teff's yeast makes it a good starter for naturally leavened breads, and a good ingredient in flatbreads, quickbreads, and dessert breads. (Be warned that the additives in tap water threaten this yeast, so use pure water if you want to make *injera* or sourdough starter.) I tried teff pancakes, a recipe for Western tastes. They were dense, more like pancakes made from meal than flour, with a sweetness reminiscent of potato flour. The whole grain can be cooked as a cereal. For the novice, the flour comes with recipes for breads, cakes, cookies, stew, and muffins.

Ivory and brown teff are actually two different strains, *not* a polished and a whole-grain version of the same grain. The two differ slightly in nutritional content: the ivory is higher in protein, and the brown is higher in iron. The folks at Maskal Forages say that many of their customers who are allergic to wheat prefer the ivory, because it's a bit lighter and closer to the wheat they've been missing. Others prefer the brown teff, but on its own it produces a dense cake or cookie, and works a bit better when you can mix it half-and-half with wheat.

In recent years, cultivation of teff within Ethiopia has very nearly lived up to its name—"lost." During periods of famine, relief agencies tend to give Ethiopians surpluses of overproduced Western crops, like corn and wheat, which discourages the cultivation of teff. Carlson considers it his mission to maintain the genetic diversity of teff and other food crops from around the world so that if communities ever lose their native crops, Maskal Forages can provide them with healthy, viable seed. In 1987, for example, the company donated 35,000 pounds of planting seed to a relief agency in Ethiopia.

In 1990, teff grain was $3 a pound. Teff flour was $3.30 per pound. Both decrease in price with larger orders. Prices include postage. Next Day or Second Day Air additional.

MORGAN'S MILLS

RD 2, Box 4602
Union, ME 04862
(207) 785-4900
FAX: (207) 785-4907

The Tribute Of The Current To The Source

Visits: yes; eggs, vegetables, local produce
Ingredients certified by: FVO, OCIA
Catalogue/price list available
Minimum order: none
Order by: phone, mail, fax
Pay by: check, Visa, MC
Ship by: UPS

MUFFIN MIXES

Blueberry · Maple cornbread · Orange bran

GRIDDLE-WAFFLE ("GRIFFLE") MIXES

Buttermilk buckwheat · Rice, corn, and oat · Blueberry

FLOURS

Whole-wheat pastry · Sifted wheat pastry · Whole-wheat bread · Whole rye · Yellow corn (flour or meal) · Whole oat · Whole barley · Short brown rice · Millet

Johnnycakes, pancakes made from white flint cornmeal, are a Rhode Island tradition and Richard Morgan, owner of Morgan's Mills, has good reason to be grateful to this "unleavened bread of the New England natives." Without them, William Brewster, one of the original European settlers, might not have survived those first long years; and his descendant—Richard Morgan—would not be around to tell the tale. The hero of the piece is Squanto, known to American schoolchildren as the Pilgrims' friend, who taught Brewster to grind the meal, make the dough, and cook it on a flat rock tipped near an open fire. "The newcomers," says Morgan, "christened it 'Journey Cake,' and Roger Williams pronounced it to be a 'readie very wholesome food.'"

In 1977, Richard Morgan and his wife, Helen, moved to Maine to pursue his dream of a small, self-powered family business that would use passive, nonpolluting energy. Morgan's dream took the form of restoring a mill that had been built in 1803 by John Lermond, the first settler of Union, Maine. The Morgans took several years to put the unused mill back in working order, salvaging granite grindstones from a Vermont mill.

Today, the water-powered mill has exceeded Morgan's dream of being self-powered—not only does it grind the wheat, corn, and rice that go into his flours and mixes, it also provides extra power, which he sells to the Central Maine Power Company to provide electricity for his neighbors.

Griffles have proved to be the mill's most popular product. They too are "an old family recipe," says Richard Morgan, although perhaps not quite so old as the Johnnycakes. The name dates back to his mother's Rhode Island childhood, when one of her siblings—too young or too sleepy to keep griddle cakes and waffles straight—sat down to breakfast and asked "Mom, are we having griffles today?"

Morgan treats all of his flours and mixes as fresh, perishable products. He gets them to stores within a week of grinding, and advises stores and customers to refrigerate them because they contain no additives or preservatives.

In 1990, mixes and flours ranged $2.25 to $4.50 for a 24-ounce bag, and were less expensive in larger bags. Non-organic flours also available. The catalogue also lists other New England specialty foods (not necessarily organic), including seafood, jams, soup mixes, and condiments. The company also sells Maine Coast Sea Vegetables (see page 238).

MOSHER PRODUCTS
P.O. Box 5367
Cheyenne, WY 82003-5367
(307) 632-1492

Certified by: SELF
Catalogue/price list available
Order by: mail
Pay by: check, Visa, MC, money order, COD
Ship by: UPS, parcel post
Recipes available

WHOLE GRAINS

Wheat

Leonard Mosher grows wheat "using modern machinery and an old but proven method—no chemicals" in the plains of eastern Wyoming on land his grandfather started farming around the turn of the century. Mosher first sold his hard red winter wheat for home use when members of the large local population of Latter-Day Saints asked him for some chemical-free wheat to bake bread. It wasn't a particularly high-tech operation. "They got out their trash-cans and bathroom scales and I sold them some." After that, word spread that Mosher had chemical-free wheat for sale.

Mosher sells hard red winter wheat, which is ideal for bread baking, and also sells a variety of mills for home use, so that you can get a whole-grain flour with exactly the texture you want. He adds no preservatives to the wheat, which is packed in airtight bags.

In 1990, 25 pounds of wheat, in 5 5-pound bags, were $14. Shipping additional. Mosher Products also sells grain mills, both electric and hand-powered.

MOUNTAIN PATH FARM
RR 3
Mountain, Ontario
Canada, KOE ISO
(613) 989-2973

Visits: by appointment
Certified by: OCIA
Catalogue/price list available
Minimum order: none
Order by: phone, mail
Pay by: check
Ship by: UPS, parcel post

FLOUR

Hard whole wheat (sifted or unsifted) · Soft whole-wheat pastry (sifted or unsifted) · Sifted rye · Buckwheat · Corn (meal or flour)

GRAINS

Wheat bran (hard or soft) · Wheat kernels (hard or soft) · Cracked hard wheat · Rye bran · Rye kernels

BEANS

Soy · Black soy

Robert Hogg, a poet who has studied with Charles Olson and Robert Creeley, and published five books of poetry, teaches North American literature and modern poetry at Carleton University in Ottawa. He's also a farmer. The two worlds don't really mix, says Hogg. Academics "don't want to hear about people who really *do* farming. It's all very well to write about it, and be bucolic and pastoral. It's another thing to do it."

When Robert and Leslie Hogg went back to the land in 1973 they looked for ways to use their 100 acres and settled on organic grain. Hogg found a historic mill "about halfway between here and Ottawa. The miller was very good; I learned a lot from him about what to expect in the milling process. But the quantity of grain I was bringing there became excessive, and I was told summarily that they wouldn't grind it any more because they were really only set up as a museum."

EGG NOODLES

Linguine · Fettucine · Whole-wheat linguine · Whole-wheat sea shells · Whole-wheat rigatoni

SPINACH PASTA

Fettucine · Linguine

SPICE PASTA

Spinach with spices · Picante · Picante shells · Sweet oregano · Sagee-o

SPAGHETTI

Semolina · Whole wheat · Whole-wheat spinach

TOFU PASTA

Beets and ginger · Lite wheat · Summer herbs and garlic

Luckily, Hogg found a man who had set up a mill but no longer wanted to run it. "Over a summer, I brought the mill back bit by bit—about seventy miles each way—and reassembled it." The flour is freshly ground at a cool temperature on the stone mill. All of the germ and the finely ground bran remain in the unsifted flour; in the sifted flour, the coarser bran is removed. Nothing is added. Hogg hopes that he will soon be able to buy all the grain he needs from other farmers whose organic practices meet or exceed OCIA standards. "Then I'll be back where I started, wondering what to do with the 100 acres."

In 1990, flour, grain, and bran ranged from 75 cents to $1.80 per kilogram for small orders. You save by buying in bulk. Shipping additional.

NEW MORNING FARM PASTA

c/o Crumbs Bakery, Inc.
P.O. Box 315
Athens, OH 45701
(614) 592-3803

Farmers' markets: Athens, on East State Street, Saturdays
Ingredients certified by: OEFFA, CHSC
Catalogue/price list available
Minimum order: 12 pounds
Order by: phone, mail
Pay by: check
Ship by: UPS
Gift sampler available

Joan Kraynanski used to run the largest pasta factory in West Virginia. It was also the only pasta factory in West Virginia. She and her husband, Kip Rondy, got their start in the pasta business when Rondy's Italian-American parents gave them a home pasta maker. Kraynanski started making pasta for the family, then for friends, and then for a local co-op. When she officially went commercial, she moved to a larger machine that could turn out twenty-five pounds an hour.

The business was booming, but they lived in a location accessible only by a dirt road and dry creek bed, so remote that UPS trucks and natural-food distributors couldn't reach them. So in 1986 the second New Morning Farm was born in Ohio, where Joan Kraynanski ran the pasta operation in what used to be a milking parlor. In 1990, Kraynanski moved again, leasing the pasta business to a worker-owned bakery in Athens, Ohio, where she continues to supervise production.

Eggs are the *only* liquid in New Morning Farm's egg noodles. The eggs are fresh out of the chickens, says Kraynanski, and no ordinary chickens, either—these are free-range birds given no antibiotics or hormones and fed organic grain from the farm. Kraynanski actually uses twice the amount of eggs needed to meet the federal standards of what can be called "egg noodles." Naturally, this makes a much richer noodle. But if you're worried about cholesterol, Kraynanski has also branched out into tofu pasta to create a cholesterol-free alternative that remains as close to traditional pasta as possible. The tofu is organic, as are some of the herbs and spices. All the flour is certified organic.

In 1990, pasta ranged from $1.50 to $2.25 for a 1-pound bag. Pasta samplers of 8 varieties of pasta, 8 ounces of each, were $12.95 or $15. Shipping additional.

NU-WORLD AMARANTH, INC.
P.O. Box 2202
Naperville, IL 60567
(708) 369-6819
FAX: (708) 369-6851

Ingredients certified by: OGBA, OCIA, SELF
Catalogue/price list available
Minimum order: 1 pound
Order by: mail, phone
Pay by: check, money order
Ship by: UPS, UPS Second Day Air
Recipes and books on amaranth available; all bread-flour blends come with recipes

WHOLE GRAINS

Seed amaranth (F,C)

OTHER FLOUR

Toasted amaranth bran · Wheat-amaranth · Rice-amaranth · Rye-amaranth · Oat-amaranth · Corn-amaranth

OTHER CEREAL

Amaranth granola

FRESH VEGETABLES

Leaf amaranth

Amaranth may be a new grain crop for North America, but it has an ancient, if lurid, history in the southern part of the New World. Incas, Mayas, and Aztecs all relied on its leaves and grain as staples. The Aztecs used it to pay their annual tribute to Montezuma. And, at least in legend, the Aztecs also mixed amaranth with human blood and honey, shaped the mixture into idols, and ate them. When the Christian Spaniards arrived in the New World, they had some trouble with this practice. They suppressed amaranth, which survived only in small, isolated mountain villages. Today, food researchers are studying the grain's nutritional value, and may perhaps undo the destructive work of the Conquistadors.

Nu-World recommends whole-grain amaranth, with its "earthy flavor," cooked as a cereal or for sprouting. Puffed amaranth, with a "sweet, nutty, toasty flavor," goes well in oatmeal or nut cookies and granola, as a breading

for chicken or pork chops, as a garnish on salad, in place of graham crackers in a pie crust, and as an alternative to high-calorie ground nuts as an ice-cream topping. Toasted amaranth bran flour makes an excellent pizza crust, says Larry Walters, one of the founders of Nu-World Amaranth, and also works well mixed with semolina for homemade noodles.

Nu-World Amaranth particularly recommends amaranth for people on gluten- and wheat-free diets. However, because amaranth contains virtually no gluten, if you want to bake bread, you need to combine it with other flours. Hence Nu-World's bread flour blends, all of which contain whole-grain flours, with all their enzymes intact. An added bonus of mixing other cereal grains is that amaranth is particularly high in lysine, which most cereal grains lack. The combination makes an almost complete protein, like eggs.

Nu-World Amaranth will also ship fresh vegetable amaranth, harvested daily, by overnight air. The fresh greens can be used wherever you would use spinach, both raw in salads and as a cooked vegetable, and are higher in nutrients than spinach, says Walters. I steamed the leaves, which were more tender than spinach and lacked its bitterness.

The company sells both certified organic amaranth and amaranth that hasn't been certified. "All amaranth is basically organic," says Larry Walters, "because it's particularly susceptible to herbicides and pesticides, so they really don't get used." You can specify your interest in organic amaranth, and in organic grains for the bread flour mixtures.

In 1990, whole-grain amaranth was $2 for 1 pound; amaranth flour was $2.50 for 1 pound. Amaranth granola was $2.97 for a 12-ounce package. Puffed amaranth was $1.50 for a 6-ounce package. Toasted amaranth bran flour was $2.50 for 1 pound. All bread flour combinations were $1.35 for a 1-pound bag. Shipping and handling additional. Seed amaranth is available for growers.

WAR EAGLE MILL
Route 5, Box 411
Rogers, AR 72756
(501) 789-5343

Visits: yes; seasonal events; Bean Palace restaurant at the mill
Buys grains certified by: various
Catalogue/price list available
Minimum order: $10
Order by: phone, mail
Pay by: check, money order, COD, Visa, MC, Discover
Ship by: UPS
Gift packages available

CEREALS

Cracked wheat · Yankee corn grits · Wheat bran · Raw wheat germ · Oat bran · Cracked corn and wheat breakfast cereal

FLOURS

Cornmeal (yellow or white) · Whole wheat · Unbleached white · Buckwheat · Rye

MIXES

Biscuits · Cornbread · Buckwheat pancake and waffle · Muffin and pancake · Hush puppies · Fish-fry coating

The "milleress" of the War Eagle Mill, Zoe Caywood, is also, in her spare time, a nature photographer, bird watcher, canoer, fisherman, hunter, and target shooter. Don't get this woman angry: Caywood's skill with the flintlock has won her many awards, "as well as filling the home larder with deer, turkey, squirrel, small game, and a 750-pound buffalo."

This particular buffalo met his end during the sesquicentennial of the state of Arkansas. "I was dressed up in pre-1840 clothes," says Cay-

wood, "and killed him with a flintlock rifle to feed him to the soldiers. We turned him into buffalo stew and buffalo burgers. Then we recreated the burning of the mill by the Confederate army." (They used smoke bombs.)

Today's mill is actually the fourth to stand on its site in the past century and a half. The first was washed away by flood. The second mill was indeed burned on the orders of a Confederate general—to make sure the Union army would get no grain out of it. Today's War Eagle Mill is a reproduction of the third mill, built in 1873 by the son of the original mill owner.

An eighteen-foot redwood waterwheel conveys the power of the War Eagle River to the three sets of stone buhrs that grind the grain without heating it. The whole-wheat flour and cornmeal retain the germ, oil, and bran, which means the whole grains should be kept refrigerated.

After her heroic deeds on behalf of the Confederate army, how can Caywood sell *Yankee* corn grits? Don't Southerners refuse to eat yellow grits? Caywood doesn't sell the white ones, so they don't have much choice. "One time I had a little lady in here, and she wanted to buy them so bad, but she couldn't bring them home, so she had us tape over the word 'Yankee.' "

In 1990, a 2-pound bag of grain or flour ranged from $2 to $2.50. Mixes were $2.50 for 1.5 pounds. You save by buying larger quantities. The catalogue also lists nonorganic foods and many gift items.

LATE-BREAKING INFORMATION

WHITE MOUNTAIN FARM
8890 Lane 4 North
Mosca, CO 81146
(719) 378-2436

Certified by: Colorado
Minimum order: 5 pounds
Pay by: check, money order, credit cards in future
Ship by: USPS
Brochure and recipes available

GRAIN

Quinoa · Black quinoa

POTATOES

Yellow Finn · All Blue · Sangre · Norkota

White Mountain Farm is the world's sole producer of black quinoa, which it describes as chewier and more textured than other varieties. The farm plans to have quinoa flour in the future, and to sell both varieties in boxes of 12 or 16 ounces. The recipes he provides, says White Mountain's Ernest New, are not macrobiotic or exotic—"not what an average person would call far-out. We're Western-style cooks, and believe good food is good eating." You won't find seaweed in these recipes, says New, but he does recommend quinoa sprouted and cooked green like spinach. Celestial Seasonings is even using White Mountain's quinoa in a tea.

SEE ALSO
Arjoy Acres, Bioforce of America, Ltd., Black Ranch, Bread & Stuff, Camas Grain, Chestnut Hill Orchards, Colonel Sanchez Traditional Foods, Fackler Family Farms, French Meadow Bakery, Glorybee Natural Sweeteners, Gravelly Ridge Farms, Hazelridge Farm, How-Well Organics, MacDonald Farm, Malachite School & Small Farm, Montana Flour and Grain, Natural Way Mills, Inc., Oak Creek Farms, Omega Nutrition USA, Inc., Royal Organic, Seeds Blüm, Summercorn Foods, Wood Prairie Farm, Wysong Corporation

CULINARY HERBS AND SPICES

Most herbs sold in this country are imported, and are rarely fresh: they can be in transit and/ or storage for months—or even years. They are often grown in countries that do not regulate agricultural chemicals, and are usually fumigated (often with ethylene oxide, a known carcinogen) and/or irradiated, both on leaving their home port and again on entering the United States.

In this section, you will find culinary herbs that are organically grown or "wildcrafted" (gathered in the wild) in areas that presumably have seen no chemical exposure. Spices are trickier. Most spices come from tropical climates, and aside from Hawaii, the United States doesn't have much in the way of tropical agriculture. Some of the companies listed here also sell imported spices that, while not organically grown, have not been fumigated or irradiated, which is probably as good as you are going to find—for now.

BIG RIVER NURSERIES
P.O. Box 487
Mendocino, CA 95460
(707) 937-5026

Visits: yes; inn, workshops, garden tours
Certified by: CCOF
Minimum order: none
Order by: phone
Pay by: check, Visa, MC, Amex, CB, Diners, Discover
Ship by: UPS, parcel post

DRIED CULINARY HERBS

Basil · Clary sage · Marjoram · Rosemary · Thyme · Sage · Oregano · Pineapple sage · Summer savory · Herb bundles (oregano, rosemary, sage, thyme) · Cayenne braids

TEA HERBS

Angelica · Anise hyssop · Calendula · Catnip · Lemon balm · Red clover · Rosebuds · Spearmint

GARLIC

Garlic braids · Garlic-cayenne braids

DRIED MUSHROOMS

Shiitake

The herbs from Big River Nurseries don't smell like much when you open the plastic bag, but rub a pinch between your fingers and watch out! The aroma will take over your kitchen.

The oregano jazzed up everything I added it to, making a mediocre store-bought (albeit organic) pasta sauce taste homemade, and rescuing a not-in-the-least-bit-organic late-night pizza. The sage was fragrant and delicious in stuffing; the marjoram was particularly heady: slightly astringent, almost alcoholic. Its flavor on chicken was like juniper berries. I had never tasted anise hyssop tea before, but Big River's gently, naturally sweet, soothing anise hyssop quickly became a favorite. The thyme was the only disappointment, not distinguished in any way.

I also sampled Big River's garlic, which didn't look unusual, but minced and baked with potatoes and olive oil, it was sensationally strong. I left the potatoes to cool on a glassed-in porch before tossing them in a vinaigrette, and in minutes, the whole porch was saturated with the aroma.

Big River's head herb gardener attributes the herbs' potency to the fact that she plants thistle between the rows of herbs, a trick she discovered in an herbal. "The thistle actually increases the amount of essential oils in the herbs. It's a bit of a pain to have to work with the thistles, but the results are worth it." She also said that because Big River is a small operation, it can afford to pick the herbs only when they reach their peak of flavor. Big River sells whole, not crushed or powdered, herbs. The oils stay in the leaf until you're ready to use them.

At the turn of the century, the land that is now the Big River Nurseries was called China Garden, after the Chinese growers who grew fruit and vegetables for the logging trade. The fruit trees they cultivated, many of them still bearing fruit today, were brought by ship around Cape Horn.

Jeff Stanford, proprietor of the Big River Nurseries and Stanford Inn by the Sea, has returned the land to farming and is amazed at the demand for Big River's herbs. "We didn't even know what some of them were for—we'd just thought they sounded interesting in the seed catalogue, but we'd tell a store we had them, and they'd get all excited. We bought some herbs in a health-food store in Mendocino, and someone came in and wanted to buy our whole crop. The herbs have just taken off, both as plants and as a product."

In 1990, herbs ranged between $2 and $6.55 for 4 ounces, and were less expensive in bulk. Herb bundles were $5, and wreaths were available at $12, $15, and $35. Dried shiitake was $8 for 4 ounces. Garlic braids were $15, garlic-cayenne braids were $25, and cayenne braids were $35. Shipping additional. Big River also makes nonculinary herbal products like mugwort dream pillows, smudge sticks, rose potpourri, and medicinal herbs.

BIG RIVER NURSERIES
THE STANFORD INN BY THE SEA

COTTAGE GARDEN HERBS/ WINDY RIVER FARM
P.O. Box 312
Merlin, OR 97532
(503) 476-8979

Visits: yes; fresh fruits and vegetables
Farmers' markets: Grants Pass, L Street between 7th and 8th
Certified by: OR-TILTH
Catalogue/price list available
Minimum order: none
Order by: phone, mail
Pay by: check
Ship by: UPS
Recipe books available
Gift combinations available
Apprenticeships available

HERB SPRINKLES (SALT-FREE BLENDS)

English (parsley, sage, rosemary, and thyme) · French (two varieties of basil, savory, thyme, leeks, lavender) · Greek (mint, lemon herbs, and tomato) · Italian (oregano, basil, garlic, dried tomato, and lovage) · Mexican (tomatillos and cayenne) · Riviera (French tarragon) · Scandia (dill, lemon herbs, leeks, parsley) · Sweet Spice (orange balsam, thyme, and other sweet herbs) · Thai (mint, Thai basil, chili pepper, and garlic)

CULINARY HERBS

Anise basil · Lemon basil · Opal basil · Spice basil · Genova basil · Lemon thyme · Thyme · Tarragon · Rosemary · Savory · Greek oregano · Sage · Parsley · Dill · Coriander

TEAS

Happiness (mint, rose petals, chamomile, lemon balm, lavender) · Licorice Stick (licorice basil and applemint) · Oriental Spice (raspberry leaf with spice basil) · Radiance (lemon thyme, lemon balm, sage, blackberry leaf) · Summer Cooler (anise hyssop, mint, lemon balm) · Supermint (spearmint, apple mint, orange mint) · Warmup (anise hyssop, lemon basil, opal basil, southernwood) (available in winter and spring only)

DRIED FRUIT

Apples · Seckel pears · Bartlett pears · Peaches · Plums

DRIED VEGETABLES

Tomato halves · Pimentos · Leeks · Onions · Zucchini

When Peter Liebes was five years old, he visited his grandparents in Oregon and declared that when he grew up, he wanted to be a farmer in Oregon. Forty years later, Peter Liebes and his wife, Judy Weiner, have made the five-year-old's wish come true on the twenty-five-acre Windy River Farm.

When Weiner and Liebes first started selling herbs, their customers mentioned that they were unsure how to combine them. Weiner and Liebes responded with Sprinkles, a line of herb and dried vegetable blends. They don't add salt or MSG, and recommend the Sprinkles as salt substitutes for people on low-sodium diets. Judy Weiner supervises each batch of Sprinkles, making sure that the proportions of herbs are just right.

I sampled the French Sprinkle, and the moment I opened the jar I was transported. These are all the smells of Provence, dried herbs as aromatic straight out of the jar as fresh herbs from the garden, and I was almost tempted to put some in a bowl as potpourri. Just a pinch tossed in soup or on chicken breasts right before serving completely transforms their flavor.

Weiner says that the heavily mineralized local soil, washed down from the ancient Kla-math Mountains, makes their herbs extra strong. Their herbs grow slowly, she says, but with intense flavor. The herbs are harvested (some are "wildcrafted") at the peak of flavor, usually just as they start to flower. They are dried in a solar herb dryer at low temperatures in the dark, so they retain their natural color. Leaves are kept whole to retain their volatile oils. The herb jars come with an inner seal to preserve freshness—if kept away from direct sunlight, they should keep for a year (but I'd be willing to bet you'll use them up first).

The herb teas are packed loose in a resealable bag, and the herbs are left as whole leaves and flowers to preserve their strength and flavor. Weiner recommends "bruising" the leaves slightly before steeping to release their flavor. I sampled the Oriental Spice tea, Cottage Garden's caffeine-free answer to a black China tea. It's a delicate, wonderfully perfumed, extremely satisfying and mysterious blend of flavors (the spice basil stumps everyone) that made me want to sample all the other Cottage Garden blends. I served it to a friend who doesn't normally like herbal teas, and on her second cup she was asking where she could get more. "The smell makes me feel like I've walked into a forest," she said. "I love it."

While Weiner and Liebes sell most of their fruit and vegetables locally, they also have a dehydrator that allows them to sell dried, unsulphured fruits and vegetables that can be rehydrated or used as is. Weiner recommends the dried vegetables for soups and stews. "The zucchini is also a nice snack—it's great trail food for hiking." I sampled the peaches, which are sliced very thin, not the dark brown I was expecting from unsulphured fruit but tan on the outside and ranging from a bright yellow-orange to a dark red on the inside. The fruit is quite chewy, not nearly as soft as commercial dried apricots, for example, but has an intense mix of sweet and tart flavors, and you can soften the fruit in water, if you like.

Weiner says she believes food should be beautiful as well as delicious and healthy, and it shows in everything that comes from Cottage Garden Herbs and Windy River Farm. Every-

thing I tried made me want to take the order form and check off the rest of the list.

In 1990, Sprinkles or single herbs in 3-ounce jars (each contains three-tenths of an ounce to a half-ounce of herbs) were $2.75 each. A box of 4 3-ounce jars or 8 1-ounce jars in a reusable pine crate was $15. Teas (1.5 ounces) were $2.75 each. Six teas (each weighing three-quarters of an ounce) in a reusable silk-screened pine box were $20. Dried fruits were $3 and dried vegetables $3.50 for 3- to 6-ounce cellophane bags.

ELDERFLOWER FARM
501 Callahan Road
Roseburg, OR 97470
(503) 672-9803

Visits: by appointment
Certified by: SELF
Catalogue/price list available
Minimum order: none
Order by: phone, mail
Pay by: check, Visa, MC
Ship by: UPS, parcel post
Recipe books available
Gift sets available in handmade cedar or pine boxes with silk-screened tops

HERBS

Green basil · Greek oregano · Rosemary · Sage · Thyme

HERB BLENDS

Salad bouquet · Fish blend · Poultry blend · Melrose mix · *Bouquet garni aromatique* · *Herbes fines* · Italian blend · Meat and game mix

TEA

Herb and spice (chamomile, pineapple sage, lemon balm, heal-all, mint, and other herbs)

When I think of Oregon, "Mediterranean" is not the first word that comes to mind, but Kelly and John Stelzer attribute their success with herbs to the "Mediterranean climate" of the east slope of Oregon's Southwest Coast range. The Stelzers originally moved to Oregon from the East Coast "because we wanted to be more producers than consumers," says Kelly Stelzer. "We lived in an artificial environment. We had to sign up for exercise classes because we worked so far away from home we couldn't walk to work. Morally, we just decided we needed to make the change."

The Stelzers started out with vegetables, but Kelly Stelzer also planted a small herb garden. "I didn't quite realize how big full-grown herb plants got," she recalls. A friend suggested she take her surplus to the annual Christmas fair at the local fairground, so she bought some bottles and labels, and "sold out as fast as I could get them on the shelf."

The Stelzers grow some fifty varieties of culinary herbs, which they harvest by hand when the "plant's essential oils are at their peak." They air dry the herbs and strip them by hand. "Air-drying and gentle hand-stripping as soon as the air is dry mean that the leaf—we don't include the stems—is fresh and vibrantly green, as it should be. Preservation is not needed because the blends are in the hands of the consumer, on the kitchen shelf, in a matter of weeks." The Stelzers sell only herbs from that year's harvest, recommend using herbs in twelve to eighteen months, and sell refill bags for your glass jars, which are the wide-mouthed corked variety.

The Stelzers established Elderflower Farm as an organic homestead in 1975. While the farm is not certified, they follow the guidelines of the state of Oregon. They also buy some herbs from local organic growers, and have their own certification program for those growers. Some herbs are wildcrafted in their own and nearby forests.

In 1990, bottled herb blends, each containing about a half-ounce of herbs, were $3.95 each, with bagged refills available for $3.50. One-ounce bags of single herbs were $3. Gift sets of 3 jars were $13.95, 4 jars for $16.95, and 5 jars were $19.95. The 9-jar gourmet set with cookbook was $43.95.

McFADDEN FARM
Powerhouse Road
Potter Valley, CA 95469
(800) 544-8230
(707) 743-1122
FAX: (707) 743-1126

Visits: No sales from the farm, but visits welcome
Certified by: CCOF
Certification pending from: CCOF-1991
Catalogue/price list available
Minimum order: none
Order by: phone, mail, fax
Pay by: check, money order, MC, Visa
Ship by: UPS, parcel post

HERBS AND SPICES

Gourmet herb collection (2 types of basil, bay leaf, garlic powder, lemon thyme, marjoram, oregano, rosemary, sage, savory, tarragon, and thyme) · Bay leaf wreaths (November 1–January 31)

GARLIC

Garlic braids

JAM

Wild blackberry

Guinness McFadden is a veteran of more than farming: he's weathered Notre Dame, the Navy, and a year at Stanford Business School. For a man with business school behind him, McFadden took an unusual approach to his workers. He disliked the fact that his crop, wine grapes, meant an annual turnover of migrant workers who arrived at harvest time and then moved on. So he added other crops, like garlic, herbs, and wild rice, that are harvested at other times of year to encourage laborers, and their families, to settle on the farm, and many have stayed ten years and more.

The fill-in-the-gap crops have turned out to be the heart of McFadden's business. In 1987, the permanent committee of the Monde Selection in Brussels awarded McFadden Farm's herbs the gold medal as the world's finest line of dried herbs. You can buy an assortment, or if you prefer a single, and extremely decorative herb, the bay leaf wreath arrives "fresh, green and aromatic"—during which time you can hang it up or wear it as the proverbial crown of laurel. The wreath dries within a few weeks and provides a year-long supply of culinary bay leaves.

All herbs and garlic are grown on acres certified by CCOF or were to receive certification in the spring of 1991. McFadden also grows wild rice with urea fertilizer on acres not certified by CCOF.

In 1990, the Gourmet Herb Collection was $25. Garlic braids ranged from $13.50 to $32.50 depending on size. Wild rice was $4 for a 6-ounce box and $8.50 for a 16-ounce box. Wild blackberry jam was $5 for an 8-ounce jar. Shipping included.

MEADOWBROOK HERB GARDEN CATALOG
93 Kingstown Road
Wyoming, RI 02898
(401) 539-0209

Visits: yes; seasonal workshops
Certified by: NOFA-RI
Catalogue/price list available for $1

Minimum order: $10
Order by: phone, mail
Pay by: Visa, MC, check, money order
Ship by: UPS, parcel post

CULINARY HERBS

Basil · Celery · Chervil · Chives · Comfrey ·
Coriander leaf · Dill leaf · Fennel leaf · Lemon
balm · Lemon verbena · Lovage · Marjoram ·
Oregano · Parsley · Rosemary · Rue · Sage ·
Salad burnet · Savory · Tarragon · Thyme

TEA HERBS

Applemint · Catnip · Comfrey leaf ·
Horehound · Hyssop · Lemon balm · Mullein
leaf · Nettle · Orange mint · Peppermint ·
Rosemary · Sage · Spearmint · Wormwood

HERB MIXTURES

Fish herbs · Hamburger seasoning · Heart's
delight · Poultry seasoning · Salad herbs · Soup
herbs

Meadowbrook Herb Garden's original owner,
Heinz Grotzke, was a follower of the "biodynamic" teachings of the Austrian philosopher
and educator Rudolf Steiner. In Grotzke's
words, biodynamic methods "allow the cosmos
to enter and become part of the field." The Herb
Garden's current owners, Marjie and Tom Fortier, were eager to learn from Grotzke. They
stopped by Meadowbrook one day to ask
Grotzke if he had any work. He didn't, but kept
their number on hand, and when he decided to
retire in 1984, gave them a call.

The Fortiers grow 250 varieties of herb
plants in their greenhouse, and have two acres
of field-grown herbs. They still sell the line of
seasonings and teas Grotzke developed back in
1967, and still follow Grotzke's methods of
biodynamic farming.

Marjie Fortier says that 90 percent of biodynamic farming is "just good growing." She

MEADOWBROOK
HERB GARDEN CATALOG

makes it sound easy, but the Fortiers do much
of their work by hand. They plant seedlings
without machinery, to avoid contaminating the
soil or the plants with oil or gas. They weed
and harvest the herbs by hand and dry them at
low temperatures—generally lower than 100
degrees Fahrenheit. Then they rub the dried
herbs on steel screens to get rid of anything too
large, like stems. Next they shake the herbs in
cloth bags to remove particles that are too small
to have any flavor. Finally, they pack the herbs
in glass—or, in the case of tea herbs, untreated
paper boxes—which helps the herbs retain
their flavor and keep out damaging moisture.

Meadowbrook Herb Garden was certified by
Demeter, the Biodynamic certification organization, for several years before becoming certified by the Rhode Island affiliate of NOFA. In
addition to herbs, Meadowbrook sells imported
spices, which are not guaranteed organic, but
are not fumigated or irradiated.

In 1990, herbs in quarter-cup glass jars were $1.75 each.
The catalogue also lists nonirradiated spices, other food
items (not necessarily organic), health and personal-care
products, fragrances and potpourri, baby-care products,
natural pet-care products, and books on herbs and organic gardening, and herbs from Blessed Herbs in Missouri (page 252). Meadowbrook also sells seeds and
plants for herb gardeners.

MOUNTAIN BUTTERFLY HERBS
P.O. Box 1365
Hamilton, MT 59840
(406) 363-6683

Visits: yes
Certified by: OCIA
Minimum order: 12 packages or $15
Order by: phone, mail
Pay by: check
Ship by: UPS, parcel post
Apprenticeships available

CULINARY HERBS

Basil · Calendula · Chervil · Onion chives ·
Garlic chives · Cilantro · Dill leaves · French
tarragon · Lemon basil · Lemon thyme ·

Lovage · Marjoram · Greek oregano · Parsley · Rosemary · Sage · Winter savory · Summer savory · Thyme

EDIBLE FLOWERS

Assortment · Rose petals

TEA HERBS

Apple mint · Bergamot · Catnip · Chamomile · Lavender · Lemon balm · Licorice mint · Lime mint · Peppermint · Raspberry leaves · Red clover · Spearmint

GARLIC

Loose garlic · Garlic braids (available end of July) · Shallots (available in August)

Suzanna McDougal has set herself a hard task: to support herself on one acre, no bigger than many backyards, in Montana's Bitterroot valley. In her first year at Mountain Butterfly Farm, McDougal foraged for wild sage, and used the sales to support herself while she planted perennials. McDougal had learned about herbs and gardening from her parents and grandparents, and has even managed to grow species that herb books said were "too tender" for the Montana climate.

For the next few years, she worked seven days a week as planter, weeder, harvester, dryer, packager, bookkeeper, and delivery woman. Over the years she's gone from drying herbs in a converted wooden egg-incubator to two solar dryers, small electric dryers, and one "very large" electric dryer (seven feet by seven feet by fourteen feet). The herbs "dehydrate in the dark, with constant warm air movement." McDougal's herbs are neither fumigated nor irradiated. All herbs are available fresh as well as dried, as are bronze fennel leaves, sorrel and sweet cicley leaves and florets.

McDougal sees culinary herbs as a "spark" for the tastebuds, and a particular boon to people who are making a transition to a low-fat, low-salt diet. For example, McDougal likes to add fresh lemon thyme to tunafish, put lemon basil on fish, rice, and potatoes, and use savory in place of pepper.

McDougal also grows medicinal herbs, in which she has a personal interest. In 1987, McDougal was diagnosed with ovarian cancer. After surgery to remove the tumor, her doctors recommended chemotherapy. She refused, feeling just as strongly about healing without chemicals as she does about growing without them. She left her business in the care of two apprentices and started alternative therapy, which included using medicinal herbs with reputations of being tumor reducers. Later that year, doctors found a tumor on her remaining

ovary, but she persisted in her course, and by the end of the year, the cancer was gone. McDougal took up Mountain Butterfly Herbs where she had left it, although not seven days a week—cancer, she says, was a reminder to take time off to play.

In 1990, fresh culinary herbs ranged from 40 cents to $2 per ounce. Fresh tea herbs ranged from 75 cents to $1.50 per ounce. Assorted edible flowers were $1.50 per ounce, and rose petals $2 per ounce. Dried herbs were $1.59 per half-ounce bag. You save on orders of more than a dozen. Shallots were $2.25 a pound, garlic heads were 50 cents a-piece or $2.75 a pound. Garlic braids ranged from $5 to $10. Shipping additional. Fresh herbs are shipped Second Day Air. Medicinal herbs, smudge sticks, culinary herbal wreaths, and dried flowers are also available.

RICHTERS
Box 26
Goodwood, Ontario
Canada, LOC IAO
(416) 640-6677
FAX: (416) 640-6641

Visits: yes; herb talks and guided tours
Certified by: various
Catalogue/price list available
Minimum order: none
Order by: phone, mail, fax
Pay by: check, Visa, MC
Ship by: UPS, parcel post

CULINARY HERBS

Sweet basil · Sweet fine basil · Bay laurel · Chives · Sweet fennel · Juniper berries · Sweet marjoram · Greek oregano · Plain parsley · Rosemary · Garden sage · Summer savory · Winter savory · French tarragon · English thyme · Lemon thyme

TEA HERBS

Alfalfa leaves · Angelica · Lemon balm · Bergamot · Wild bergamot · Borage · Calendula · Catnip · German chamomile · Roman chamomile · Coffee chicory · Hyssop · English lavender · Lemongrass · Linden flowers · Lovage · Applemint · Peppermint · Spearmint · Korean mint · Lemon verbena · Sweet woodruff

HERB BLEND

Mrs. Richter's herb pot (thyme, savory, oregano, basil, and sage)

TEA

Mrs. Richter's special blend

The Richters catalogue doubles as an herbal, giving each herb's history and uses. Did you know, for example, that a pillow stuffed with hops flowers will overcome insomnia? Or that clove-pink, used to flavor ales and wines, including the celebration cups at coronations, earned the name carnation? Or that while va-

nilla grass can cause hay fever, a tincture of its flowers in wine is the cure?

All herbs are grown by certified growers, and have not been fumigated. The Richters also sell some spices, but those cannot be guaranteed free of fumigants. "Virtually *all* herbs and spices sold today are fumigated with a variety of poisonous chemicals, even the herbs at the health-food store," say the Richters. "To prove it, try germinating whole seeds like dill and fennel—they fail to grow because the fumigant destroys the enzymes necessary for germination."

In 1990, packets of dried herbs varied in weight from 10 to 100 grams. The prices ranged from 30 cents to $3.75 for 10 grams. Tea was $3.75 for 20 grams. The cork-sealed ceramic pot of blended herbs was $11, and a refill of herbs only was $4. Honey was $6 for 250 grams and $7.25 for 375 grams. Prices are in Canadian dollars. Shipping additional. The extensive catalogue lists herb seeds and plants for growers, organic plant foods, and medicinal herbs. A gift collection of 12 live herb plants is available in May.

RIVERBLUFF FARM

Route 3, Box 290A
Owensville, MO 65066
(314) 437-4297

Visits: first weekend in December
Farmers' market: Soulard farmers' market in
St. Louis, Agriculture Day in the spring;
Harvest Day in the fall
Certified by: SELF
Catalogue/price list available
Minimum order: none
Order by: phone, mail
Pay by: MC, Visa, check
Ship by: UPS
Gift baskets available, made of twig or
grapevine, with a bed of herbs and everlastings
Recipes available

CULINARY HERBS

Sage · Parsley · Thyme · Oregano · Tarragon ·
Chives · Lavender · *Bouquet garni* · Herb
wreaths

HERB-SEASONING PACKETS

Tarragon mustard · Thyme and basil · Herb
garden · Sage seasoning · Dill seasoning · Bay
leaf

HERB TEAS

Country orchard · Blackberry bramble ·
Victorian bouquet · Riverbluff Farm special
mint

In her former life, Robin Adkison collected antiques. Now she collects herbs. In 1986, Robin and Jerry Adkison shocked their families by selling their new home, withdrawing their life savings, and moving into a dilapidated ninety-year-old concrete farmhouse on a 100-acre farm. To put it mildly, the Adkisons like a challenge, or what they call "a family adventure."

While friends have a somewhat rosy, nostalgic picture of what their life must be like, Robin Adkison often feels like she's reliving the experiences of her great-grandparents, homesteaders in Montana. "Country life can also be drudgery and hard work, setbacks and anxious moments. Moist, crumbly soil with tender seeds nestled precisely in neat rows can become parched, cracked, and thirsty with a long-awaited rain. The lingering moments over coffee are too often times of wondering if we'll make it—or pure procrastination because the house is such a mess, the goats need to be milked, and the day doesn't seem near long enough."

The Adkisons worked hard to recreate the farm's original feel, and today Riverbluff Farm is home to cattle, sheep, goats, and a team of draft horses. Whenever the farm overflows with produce, Robin—a home-economics teacher—starts experimenting. When there was more goat milk than the family could drink, she came up with a line of goat-milk soaps. When the herb garden burgeoned, she developed the herb bundles and blends, and recipes to go along with them. The thyme and basil blend, for example, comes with a recipe for chicken; the sage blend with a recipe for sage bread and for pilaf.

Everything at Riverbluff is done by hand, down to the catalogue, full of recipes in Robin Adkison's script, as though a friend had written them out for you, and tied with a raffia bow.

In 1990, 3-inch herb bundles started at $3; 5- to 6-inch herb bundles started at $6. Half-pint jars of dried herbs were $3.50. The herb-seasoning packets ranged from $3 to $3.50. Teas in a half-pint jar were $3.75, and cost less packed in a cellophane bag. Herb wreaths ranged from $14 to $40 depending on size. The catalogue also contains a wide selection of goat-milk soaps, potpourris, and personal-care products. Robin Adkison also makes a line of herb vinegars, starting with just-picked herbs, which she steeps in champagne white-wine vinegar (not organic) the day they are picked.

ROSE EAGLE ENTERPRISES, INC.
Route 1, Box 135
Firth, NE 68358
(402) 791-5736

Visits: yes; by 1991, the farm may be
producing goat cheese, ice cream, and yogurt
Certified by: SELF
Certification pending from: OCIA-NE
Catalogue/price list available
Minimum order: none
Order by: mail
Pay by: check
Ship by: UPS, parcel post

CULINARY HERBS

Sweet basil · Green bush basil · Thai basil ·
Borage · Fennel powder · Oregano · Green
perilla · Shiso · Pineapple sage · Clary sage ·
Thyme · Lemon thyme · Curled parsley ·
Italian parsley · Epazote · Cilantro

TEA HERBS

Lemon basil · Tulsi basil · Bergamot ·
Chamomile · Anise hyssop · Meadowsweet ·
Clary sage · Pineapple sage · Thyme ·
Strawberry leaf · Catmint · Wild mint ·
Applemint · Bergamot mint · Chocolate mint ·
Pineapple mint · Spearmint · Rose hips

Z. Z. Martin and her husband, Chu-na (an
Aleut nickname, meaning grandfather, picked
up during the time he spent in Alaska), met
over goats. Z. Z. Martin had helped organize
the Nebraska Dairy Goat association, and ed-
ited its newsletter. Chu-na, an engineer "who'd
been around goats all his life," was a charter
member. The two corresponded "about goats
and news of goats" for some time before their
attention turned to other things. Z. Z. and Chu-
na, now "past fifty," have been married for
three years. "We can hold the goats responsible," says Z. Z.

In addition to the goats, they grow garden
produce, fruit, and herbs on the ten-acre Rose
Eagle Farm. Martin has been gardening all her
life, even the years she spent as a city dweller.
Back then, she "wasn't above" using a little fer-

tilizer on her plants, but she's now securely in
the sustainable agriculture camp, where you try
"to produce as much of what you need as you
can right on the farm. You need an animal component, for fertilizer," says Martin. Goats,
which don't take up much room, are the "ideal

animal for sustainable agriculture." And, says
Martin of the "idiosyncratic" animals, "They
kind of grow on you."

In 1990, herb packets of not less than a quarter-ounce
were $1.49 each. Price per packet decreases if you buy in
quantity. Shipping additional. In addition to the tea and
culinary herbs, Rose Eagle Enterprises sells a goat milk
soap and a "vegetarian" bar made with vegetable oils. It
also sells medicinal herbs, other facial products, herbs for
the bath, and fragrance herbs, loose or in sachets.

SEE ALSO
Adaptations, Arjoy Acres, Back of the
Beyond, Bioforce of America, Ltd., Black
Ranch, Blessed Herbs, Circle Herb Farm,
Earthshine Farm, Hawaiian Exotic Fruit
Company, Haypoint Farm, Herb and
Spice Collection, Jacobs Farm, Natural
Way Mills, Inc., Riverview Farm,
Schaeffer Family Farm, Simply
Wonderful Organic Products, Sleepy
Hollow Farm, Smoke Camp Crafts,
Sonoma Organic Growers, Trout Lake
Farm, Williams Creek Farms, Wysong
Corporation

HONEY, MAPLE SYRUP, AND OTHER SWEETENERS

Honey and maple syrup seem organic by definition, but chemicals can enter both processes. Bees can forage for pollen on crops that have been sprayed; the bees themselves can be treated with antibiotics, to protect against disease and mites; and the wax can be treated with moth repellent. Honey can also be filtered and cooked at high temperatures, which doesn't affect the "organic" nature of the honey, but does remove nutrients.

The producers in this section release their bees in uncontaminated areas, but you can't keep bees on a leash, and so you can't know absolutely where the bees have been. Only a few of the producers use antibiotics on their bees, and never during the time when bees are gathering pollen and producing honey.

With maple syrup, producers can spray near the maple trees; put formaldehyde in the tap holes to prevent them from closing; and can use any number of chemicals to remove foam from the sap as it's boiling down into syrup. The producers listed here collect syrup in unsprayed areas, do not put formaldehyde in the holes (this practice is actually illegal in Vermont) or use any chemicals in defoaming.

BROOKSIDE FARM
Tunbridge, VT 05077
(800) 832-9482 (east of Ohio)
(802) 889-3738 (west of Ohio, or in Vermont)
FAX: (802) 889-3739

Certified by: SELF
Catalogue/price list available
Minimum order: 1 pint
Order by: phone, mail, fax
Pay by: check
Ship by: UPS, parcel post

MAPLE SYRUP

Vermont Grade A Medium amber · Dark amber · Cooking syrup

Henry and Cornelia Swayze compare sugaring to winemaking. "No two days' production tastes exactly the same. The syrup made from one grove of maple trees has a different flavor from the syrup made from another grove." The Swayzes should know: they've been sugaring their maples since 1965. They started out mailing syrup to friends, "and then to friends of friends," says Cornelia Swayze. "People got to know our syrup, and ask for it year after year. One thing about our syrup is that the flavor is consistent—our syrup always tastes like our syrup, just like a certain wine always tastes like a certain wine."

The Swayzes maintain the flavor of their syrup by storing all of their syrup in small batches until after the boiling season is over, and then blend "complementary flavors." If they don't like a batch, they don't use it. The blends result in three grades of syrup, differing in intensity. Medium amber syrup has the characteristic maple flavor while dark amber has a maple-caramel flavor. The cooking syrup has "a pronounced caramel flavor, and when used in cooking imparts a stronger maple flavor than the lighter-colored syrups." Cooking syrup is also good on the table, say the Swayzes, when you want to balance other strong flavors, like buckwheat pancakes.

The Swayzes use no sprays in their maple groves, no formaldehyde pellets in the tap holes, no artificial defoamers in the evaporator, and no preservatives in the syrup itself. "We've never used chemicals," says Cornelia Swayze. "The farm is free of anything, except for the minerals that are naturally in the soil, but toxic stuff—forget it." In recent years, the Swayzes switched from glass to polyethylene containers, because of too many experiences of broken containers in the mail. "We rinse out the containers and the plastic lines with boiling water. My daughter, who has a severe allergy to plastic, has never had a reaction to the syrup, but if you do have allergies, you should know the containers are not glass."

If you call, don't be surprised if the person answering the phone says "Gallagher Spring-Tight Power Fence"—it's Brookside Farm. The fence business grew out of their own needs as owners of a flock of some 200 to 300 sheep. Lately, Cornelia has been experimenting with "matted fleece," a way of creating the effect of a sheepskin rug you can sit or walk on without killing the animal, "an ecological, renewable fleece."

In 1990, syrup was $7.35 a pint, and you save by buying in quantity. Cooking syrup was $12.50 a half-gallon. Shipping additional.

GOLDEN ANGELS APIARY
P.O. Box 2
Singers Glen, VA 22850
(703) 833-5104

Farmers' markets: Virginia Beach on Landstown Road
Certified by: SELF
Minimum order: none
Order by: phone, mail
Pay by: check, money order
Ship by: UPS, parcel post
Raw honey is available July–October; supplies are limited

Tulip Poplar honey · Meadow Clover honey · Summer Thistle honey · Virginia Wildflower honey

The Golden Angels Apiary is a small, family-run operation in Virginia's Shenandoah valley, just west of the Blue Ridge Mountains, where Dennis and Neva Whetzel manage 500 colonies of bees "very conscientiously." The Whetzels sell unfiltered honey, which contains the nutrients found in pollen, propolis ("the sticky substance the bees gather from resinous trees like conifers and poplars and use to glue all the parts of their home together to make it stable"), minerals, and enzymes. A coarse strainer allows wax to float to the surface, but nothing else is removed.

The honey is sold both raw and cooked to 135 degrees. Heat destroys the enzymes that cause honey to crystallize, and raw honey will crystallize in two to six months, but crystallized honey, say the Whetzels, "is excellent used in all the normal ways of using liquid honey. Plus, it is easier to measure and doesn't get lost at the bottom of the bowl. Europeans actually prefer it this way."

The Whetzels' honeys cover a range of flavors. They describe Summer Thistle honey as "extremely mild, extra light, good in delicately flavored dishes like fruit salad, on oatmeal, pancakes, muffins, and biscuits." The Meadow Clover is a "good all-purpose honey, for teas, light cakes and breads, sweet potatoes, fruit pies, ice creams." The Virginia Wildflower has a "light amber color and is good in darker cakes, gingerbreads, carrot cakes, cinnamon rolls, chicken, and barbecue sauce." The Tulip Poplar honey, from trees in the foothills of the Blue Ridge Mountains, has the highest mineral and nutritional content of all their honeys, and is a "rich, red-amber honey with a taffy-like flavor, good in fruit cakes, as an ice-cream topping, in granola, and herb teas." The Whetzels suggest dipping a pecan half in Tulip Poplar honey and eating as is.

The Whetzels do not blend their honey with anyone else's honey, and use no chemicals at any time. They do not use antibiotics to treat their bees, either for disease or as a prevention. "We take measures to assure that the bees are not stressed unnecessarily when they are transported. Bees are checked throughout the year, and any affected colonies are quarantined. We isolate, take our losses, destroy infected colonies, and sterilize the equipment." They use an air blower rather than chemicals to force the

bees to leave the supers, the boxes that hold the combs, and do not use ethyl dibromide or moth crystals. Instead, they use a "natural biological control that is harmful only to wax moths and their larvae. It's more labor-intensive, but safe."

In 1990, a 12-ounce honey bear was $1.35. Honey is also available in larger glass containers, but Dennis Whetzel points out that plastic travels better than glass. Golden Angels Apiary sells chemical-free bee pollen, propolis, and beeswax. It also sells orange blossom honey, but this honey comes from Florida.

HAYPOINT FARM
Box 292
Sugar Island, Star Route
Sault Ste. Marie, MI 49783
(906) 632-1280

Visits: yes; cider and fresh herbs
Farmers' markets: Across from the hospital in Sault Ste. Marie, Saturdays; market is "sporadic"
Certified by: SELF
Certification pending from: OGM

Minimum order: none
Order by: mail
Pay by: check, cash
Ship by: UPS, parcel post

SWEETENERS

Maple syrup · Honey

CONDIMENTS

Cranberry catsup · Pumpkin chutney · Maple mustard

CONSERVES

Apple butter (apples, cider, and maple syrup)

DRIED HERBS

Peppermint

Sue Raker has been a forester in Montana, worked on a cattle ranch, and been the boss of a firefighting crew. Raker grew up in Michigan's Upper Peninsula, and in 1986 returned to the UP to farm on Sugar Island, a ferry ride away from Sault Ste. Marie. She has found organic farming in the UP, where being a woman farmer makes her doubly unusual, a lonely business. "There are three or four other kindred souls," she says.

Raker's 120-acre farm sits on a hill covered with hardwoods, overlooking the Laurentian Mountains and Lake Huron. For generations, the local Baie de Wasai Indians have sugared the maple trees on the island. Traditionally, they buried the maple sugar in containers for later use, giving the island its name. Haypoint Farm's maple syrup is tapped by the Baie de Wasai in the traditional manner, with no chem-

icals in the tap holes or in the processing. They boil down the syrup in cast-iron pots over a wood fire.

The honey comes from bees who forage on Raker's own unsprayed land, and on abandoned wild areas. It's a combination of clover, berries, herbs, and even the maples themselves. Raker does have to use antibiotics to protect her bees, but never during the season when they are making honey. Using old Canadian recipes, Raker combines her honey and maple syrup with her own organic produce to make traditional condiments like cranberry catsup, pumpkin chutney, and apple butter.

Raker also sells Cat-A-Tonic ©, which she calls "Herbal Fun for Felines.."

MAVERICK SUGARBUSH
Box 99
Sharon, VT 05065
(802) 763-8680
FAX: (802) 763-8684

Visits: by appointment
Certified by: SELF
Catalogue/price list available
Minimum order: 2 half-pints
Order by: phone, mail, fax
Pay by: Visa, MC, check, COD
Ship by: UPS, parcel post
Quantity available varies from year to year

SWEETENER

Vermont Grade A Medium amber

Arthur Berndt named Maverick Sugarbush for his great-great-grandfather, Samuel Maverick of Texas, "for whom the word maverick was coined." Berndt and his wife, Anne, proudly carry on the family tradition "by being mavericks as sugarmakers," which includes providing a profit-sharing plan for all their full-time employees.

The Berndts see themselves as stewards of their land, 400 acres that form "a natural bowl of gentle and steep hills covered with majestic maples, fields, and streams." They put in only one tap per tree, because they believe that "being conservative now is sensible in the long run."

Conservation is the keynote at Maverick Sugarbush. The Berndts use propane for boiling syrup, "because it's clean energy." They do not use paraformaldehyde tablets, and recount horror stories of other sugarmakers tossing "handfuls of these tablets into storage tanks to combat the onset of bacteria and maintain grade." Their stainless steel pans are welded, not soldered, so the syrup never comes into contact with lead, which is "still widely used in the syrup industry," say the Berndts. "We use an organic defoamer rather than some of the more mysterious substances other sugarmakers use—including nonorganic vegetable oil, lard, and pine boughs." They use brown, not "highly processed," white filters. They don't use plastic jugs because they can't yet be recycled. Their syrup contains no additives: only water has been removed. I found the Medium amber very light and delicate, a good syrup for mild-flavored cereals or pancakes.

Theoretically, say the Berndts, any unfertilized sugarbush is organic, but they work to "give back some of what we take out, using organic fertilizers; we avoid all pesticides." New England's maples have been hit hard by acid rain and air pollution. "It's our belief," say the Berndts, "that many of the nutrients the trees need are present, but simply unavailable. When the soil is too acid, the composting action that

naturally occurs in the forest slows down and important nutrients aren't released." The Berndts have embarked on an "ambitious" plan to heal their land by spraying organic fertilizer on their trees from a helicopter.

In 1990, 2 half-pints were $13, including shipping. Prices decrease if you order in quantity.

MOUNTAIN STAR HONEY COMPANY
140 South Pine
P.O. Box 179
Peck, ID 83545
(800) 437-0660
(208) 486-6821

Visits: yes
Farmers' markets: Moscow, Idaho, Saturdays; downtown next to the Moscow Hotel
Certified by: SELF
Catalogue/price list available
Minimum order: none
Order by: phone, mail, telex
Pay by: check, cash, Visa, MCS, food stamps
Ship by: UPS, parcel post
Gift packs available

SWEETENER

Liquid honey · Honeycomb · Chunk honey · "Honey delight" (creamed honey mixed with wild huckleberry)

MIXES

Cornbread · Split-pea soup · Peasant bean soup

The source of Mountain Star's honey is the star thistle, which produces a heavy, white honey that can last two years without granulating. Kent and Sharon Wenkheimer sell their honey in liquid form, heated just enough to extract and filter it; or still in the comb. Chunk honey combines the two: a chunk of honeycomb floating in liquid honey. According to Richard Taylor, the editor of *Bee Talk*, Mountain Star's honey is "utterly delicious."

The Wenkheimers are also proud of their

"Honey delights," a blend of creamed honey, fruit, and fruit juice. It took them more than a year to come up with the recipe. By the time they sold their first jar, they'd spent $4,000 on the project. It was a good investment—within six months, they'd sold $7,500 worth. Of the six "honey delights," the wild huckleberry is made with organically grown fruit.

The star thistle grows in places that are inaccessible to cultivation, so it's highly unlikely that they've ever been sprayed with anything. As Kent Wenkheimer asked, somewhat bemused, "How do you certify something that grows down the side of a canyon?" Wenkheimer has waged a constant battle against pesticide use by local farmers, because bees working in the field are often the victims of pesticide drift. (Pesticides don't reach the honey; these bees don't make it back to the hive, and the bees within the hive aren't affected.)

Wenkheimer does have to use antibiotics to protect his bees against tracheal mites, but uses it several months before honey collection begins. He uses freezers rather than chemicals to protect combs from wax moths. The Wenkheimers were recently awarded a state grant to help them market their products overseas, and they are using part of the money for a chemical analysis of their comb honey, which is important to their customers in Europe and Japan, who, says Kent Wenkheimer, seem to care more about food safety than Americans. The results of the analysis will also be available for American consumers.

The Wenkheimers have recently branched out into mixes. The cornbread comes from a recipe "my mother made all the time," says Sharon Wenkheimer. "The only thing I've changed is using honey instead of sugar." Most ingredients are organic. She's also come up with two soup mixes: split pea and peasant bean, and will try to use organic ingredients whenever possible.

In 1990, 2.75 ounces of Wild Huckleberry honey delight was $2.75. One pound of honey was $2.40. An 8-ounce round honeycomb was $3. A 1.5-pound jar of chunk honey was $5.75. A 12-ounce honey bear was $1.95. Prices decrease if you buy larger sizes or by the case. Cornbread was available in a case of 24 six-ounce packages for $26.40. Creamed honey is available with other fruits, but they are not organic. The Wenkheimers also sell bee pollen.

OPEONGO MAPLE PRODUCTS
RR 4
Eganville, Ontario
Canada, K0J 1T0
(613) 754-2049

Visits: yes
Farmers' markets: Eganville Maple Festival; summer fairs in Renfrew County
Certified by: SELF
Catalogue/price list available
Minimum order: none
Order by: phone, mail
Pay by: check
Ship by: UPS, parcel post, freight

SWEETENERS

Maple syrup · Maple candy · Maple butter

After the "1812 War with the States," the Opeongo Line, the first pioneer road in the Upper Ottawa valley, provided an inland route to Georgian Bay. "Settlers quickly followed the road," say Dave and June Gardiner, proprietors of Opeongo Maple Products. Early settlers, living in log cabins, boiled sap into syrup in kettles over open fires. The log cabins are still standing, but today's sugarers use modern equipment and stainless steel.

The Gardiners started sugaring in 1973, "just for fun," says Dave Gardiner. "It grew like Topsy. We did twenty trees the first year, and it was so much fun that we did 100 the second, and 200 the third." The Gardiners are up to sugaring 1,200 trees, and it's still fun, says Dave Gardiner, even though sugaring can keep the Gardiners up "boiling sap 'til midnight" during the spring maple run.

The Gardiners also sell maple butter, which contains no butter at all. June Gardiner explains that maple syrup is heated to a certain point and "allowed to sit perfectly still overnight, then beaten" to produce the butter. The Gardiners also make maple candy by cooking the syrup to a higher temperature, beating it, and pouring it into molds.

When the Gardiners first started sugaring, people were just starting to use formaldehyde to keep tap holes open. "I bought 500 tablets," says Dave Gardiner. "I used them in ten trees and didn't use them in the other ten, and I couldn't see a particle of difference, so I just said to heck with it, and I've never used it since." Gardiner is now working to get formaldehyde use banned in Ontario. The trees themselves have no chemicals applied on or near them—the Gardiners grow all of their own vegetables organically—and the area has not been seriously affected by acid rain.

In 1990, maple syrup was $4.50 for a 250-milliliter can. Syrup is also available in jugs. Maple butter was $3.50 for a 100-milliliter jar. You save on both by buying larger containers. Maple candies were 75 cents each or $2.80 for a packaged tray of 3. Shipping is additional, and generally runs 10% of the total.

PRONATEC INTERNATIONAL
P.O. Box 193
Noone Falls Office Bldg.
Peterborough, NH 03458
(603) 924-9452
FAX: (603) 924-6175

Certified by: SELF
Mail-order information: see below

SWEETENER

Sucanat (*Sugar Cane Natural*)

Sucanat, organically grown, evaporated sugarcane juice, is the creation of a Swiss pediatrician, Dr. Max-Henri Beguin. In the 1950s, Dr. Beguin became concerned about his patients' health, particularly the "epidemic" of cavities he was seeing in children. He did some research, and uncovered a study that showed the long-term effects of economic development on Swiss health. With the advent of roads and railroads, the inhabitants of once-remote villages had become less dependent on local crops, eating store-bought white bread instead of whole wheat, and polished white rice instead of whole barley. They were also eating refined sugar for the first time in their lives—at the rate of eighty-five pounds a year.

Dr. Beguin conducted an experiment: he recommended that mothers of his patients replace white sugar, white bread, and sweet syrups

with dark sugar, whole-grain bread, and unsweetened fruit juices. Not surprisingly, the number of cavities fell. With that evidence, Dr. Beguin, his family, and friends founded Pronatec (from Pro Natural Technologies), which trademarked Sucanat and started selling it in Switzerland in 1968.

To make Sucanat, juice is squeezed from fresh organic cane, filtered to remove the cellulose fiber, and then concentrated and dried through a vacuum evaporation process. Nothing is added. The Sucanat process leaves in vitamins and minerals—up to 2.5 percent of Sucanat is mineral salts, vitamins and trace minerals.

Sucanat looks like granulated brown sugar. You can substitute it for white or brown sugar in any recipe—I bake with it frequently—but you may want to decrease the amount in recipes that call for white sugar, because it has the

more potent, slightly caramelized flavor of brown sugar. And if you use Sucanat, you'll be in pretty classy company—the organic sugar can be found in the kitchens of The Four Seasons and Régine's.

Using organically grown cane was "of fundamental importance" to Dr. Beguin, say the people at Pronatec. "With the minimal processing Dr. Beguin had conceived for his sugar, the final product would be highly concentrated, and a concentration of harmful chemical residues was absolutely out of the question." Pronatec works with independent farmers and cooperatives who grow organic cane. Each shipment is analyzed by an independent laboratory and is guaranteed to be free of pesticide residues.

Although Sucanat is not available by mail directly from Pronatec, it is available from Walnut Acres (page 284); Simply Delicious (page 278), Millstream (page 272), Rising Sun Organic Food (page 276), and Natural Beef Farms (page 273).

SANDHILL FARM
Box 115-O
Rutledge, MO 63563
(816) 883-5543

Visits: yes
Certified by: OCIA
Catalogue/price list available
Minimum order: none
Order by: phone, mail
Pay by: check, money order
Ship by: UPS, parcel post

SWEETENERS

Sorghum · Honey

GARLIC

Loose bulbs

CONDIMENTS

Horseradish · Mustard

Sandhill Farm is an egalitarian community of six adults and one child in northeastern Missouri, a "family of friends." Major community decisions are made by consensus, and all members share "philosophical beliefs about living in harmony with the earth and the role of community in the evolution of human consciousness." Since 1980, the community has farmed its commonly owned land—135 acres of gardens, orchard, woods, cropland, hayland, and pasture—organically.

The community grows its own food, and shares responsibility for the farm's animals—

SANDHILL FARM, INC.

cows, chickens, turkeys, ducks, and geese. "We get satisfaction from being able to do things ourselves," say the members of Sandhill, "whether it's making butter and cheese, repairing old machines, inventing new tools, or building our own buildings." Their heat comes from wood, and they are experimenting with solar heating and earth-sheltered construction. The members of Sandhill Farm stress that they like to work *and* to play, and that the two often combine. "We often have high times together making sorghum molasses, ice skating, picking up hay, extracting honey, shelling peas, or taking a solstice walk."

No one on the farm has a regular outside job, and the community's primary income comes from the sale of honey and sorghum molasses. The sorghum harvest takes place every September, and only a few weeks separate the time the cane is ready for harvest from the arrival of the first hard frost. The folks at Sandhill work day and night, cutting the ten-foot stalks of cane, feeding it into a 1902 John Deere Hercules Power Cane Mill, and collecting the juice in stainless steel tanks. They use a kind of clay to filter it: as the clay sinks, it draws with it any plant matter that might make the sorghum bitter. After the juice has settled overnight, they drain off the clear juice, and pipe it into stainless-steel cooking pans, where it is boiled down and skimmed, much like maple syrup. The ratio of juice to syrup is roughly ten to one, but unlike commercial processors, they add no corn syrup to stretch out their yield.

Their honey comes from their seventy hives whose bees gather nectar from a variety of sources, primarily wildflowers, sweet clover, and soybeans, mostly on their own farm, but also on some neighboring farms, which may have been sprayed. They haven't had to use antibiotics with their bees. The honey is raw (uncooked) and contains no additives, so it may crystallize.

The folks at Sandhill Farm also sell two condiments from ingredients they grow themselves: the mustard is made from mustard seed, vinegar, honey, garlic, and spices; the horseradish is made with vinegar, honey, and salt.

In 1990, sorghum was $5 for 1 pound. Honey was $4 for 1 pound. You save by buying in quantity. Garlic was $3.50 a pound. Horseradish and mustard were $4 for 6 ounces. All prices include shipping. Sandhill Farm also runs a mail-order service of books on alternative lifestyles and cooperative living. The catalogue is free. Also, if you are interested in Sandhill's egalitarian life-style, call, write, or stop by for more information.

SCHOONMAKER/LYNN ENTERPRISES
4619 N.W. Barnes Road
Portland, OR 97210
(503) 222-5435

Certified by: SELF
Catalogue/price list available
Minimum order: 2 jars
Order by: phone, mail
Pay by: check, money order
Ship by: UPS, parcel post

HONEY

Fleur des Mediterranees · Montagne · Orangier · Tournesol · Acacias · Spain · Printemps · Lavender

When Karen Schoonmaker was getting ready to go to college, a family friend suggested she might like to spend the summer working on a farm overlooking the Mediterranean. Peter Lynn, whose parents owned the *domaine,* met her at the airport. It didn't take long, says Karen's mother, Dottie Schoonmaker, for the two to fall in love. Karen ended up staying in France for seven years.

Peter and Karen Lynn kept some 200 hives of bees on the *Domaine de Donadei,* or Gift of

God, taking over the work from Peter's father, a Belgian who had been an RAF wing commander—in fact, the commander who took Ernest Hemingway along on a bombing raid during the war. The Lynns set their hives in remote, unpolluted areas, and used vitamin C, rather than antibiotics, to protect their bees from disease. They extracted the honey in old, unheated stone farmhouses, so the temperature of the honey never exceeded 70 degrees, leaving the enzymes in the honey intact.

Each of the honeys has a distinct color and flavor. The *Fleur des Mediterranees* is an early spring wildflower honey that comes primarily from white heather and wild sea lavender. The *Montagne* is a medium honey collected in early June from the wildflowers of the sub-Alpine mountains. In July, some bees go to orange groves on the Italian border and produce the *Orangier,* a light honey; others visit the sunflower fields and produce the *Tournesol* honey, with a "rich, buttery flavor." The light, clear *Acacias* honey comes from the white flowers of the acacia trees. The *Sapin,* a pine honey, is a clear dark amber. Europeans believe this honey

has medicinal qualities that protect the human body during the winter months as pines are protected. The *Printemps* is a blend of the sunflower, acacia, and other light honeys.

Lavender honey is rare and increasingly difficult to get, says Dottie Schoonmaker, because the lavender fields of Provence are being given over to wheat production. Lavender doesn't produce pollen, so the queen bee of the hive that produces the lavender honey lays no eggs —this, say the Lynns, is the price the beekeeper pays for the "rare treat." The lavender honey is not heated or filtered, and is a smooth, white crystallized honey, with the perfume of lavender.

Peter and Karen Lynn are now back in the United States, but Dottie Schoonmaker has a supply of their honeys for sale. When those supplies run out, the honey will no longer be available in this country.

In 1990, 2 250-gram jars of honey were $12, including shipping.

SMOOT HONEY COMPANY
P.O. Box 158
Power, MT 59468
(406) 463-2227
(406) 463-2217

Certified by: SELF
Catalogue/price list available
Minimum order: none
Order by: mail
Pay by: check
Ship by: UPS, parcel post
Gift pack available

SWEETENERS

Honey · Creamed honey

Donald Smoot started keeping bees in 1960 in California, and one of the reasons he left California for Montana in 1964—in addition to "blue sky"—was the frustration of losing bees to pesticides. "Nowadays we do come into a bee

yard and find some dead bees, but it's a bear that's been at them, not insecticide."

The eastern slopes of the Northern Rocky Mountains, where Donald and Ellen Smoot keep their bees, is "Glacier National Park country, some of the most pollution-free country remaining in the United States." These northern climates, says Donald Smoot, "seem to produce a lighter colored, lighter flavored honey."

Some insecticide is used on cereal grains in the area, says Smoot, but the bees don't get into those areas. Mostly, they are kept on clover, some northern weeds, and some irrigated, domestic alfalfa. The Smoot Honey Company does give antibiotics to the bees in early spring, but doesn't start making honey until early July. "There's a slight chance some of that might show up in the honey, but I doubt it," says Donald Smoot.

In 1990, a 1-gallon pail of honey was $16.50. Five pounds of honey were $9.50. Forty-five pounds of honey were $49.25. Prices include shipping. The gift pack contains orange-blossom honey from an area in California that does use insecticides.

TEAGO HILL FARM
Box 42
Barber Hill Road
South Pomfret, VT 05067
(802) 457-3507

Visits: yes; "wear rubber boots"
Certified by: SELF
Minimum order: none
Order by: phone, mail
Pay by: check
Ship by: parcel post

MAPLE SYRUP

Fancy · Medium A · Dark A

Glenn and Susan Benoit built their sugar house the year their son was born, which "is kind of a landmark for us in thinking about our history," says Susan Benoit. "We had a huge gathering here that day. A friend came up to do the timber-framing, and brought a group of friends to help. In one day they put up the sugar house and my husband's carpentry shop." The Benoits started sugaring their maples in 1981. "We put in 1,200 taps, and the sap ran by gravity through the lines to the sugarhouse, where we have a 1,500-gallon tank."

The Benoits had done some home-sugaring before, "with lots of smoke and soot falling in the syrup," says Susan Benoit. Glenn Benoit worked for another sugarmaker for two years, learning the trade. That sugarmaker used oil-firing, says Susan Benoit, "and my husband was upset that he just wanted to throw away any syrup that was slightly yellow. He didn't want to waste oil on it. He just wanted to make the Fancy-grade syrup." Although the Benoits do make Fancy and Medium A, they prefer the darker syrup, "and we know our friends prefer it. We're actually happier when we can make the darkest syrup. It takes just as much skill to make that as the Fancy. Not only is it a stronger maple taste, but it's thicker, so what you put it on doesn't soak it all up right away." I can imagine that their dark must be delicious, since their Medium A had a rich maple taste without being overly sweet.

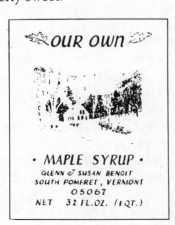

The Benoits use no chemicals on anything they grow. They do not put any formaldehyde pellets into the tap or additives in the syrup. In the early days, the Benoits did all their tapping by hand, which was "nice and quiet," says Susan Benoit. Today they have a less-than-quiet power tapper, but the syrup is still boiled over a wood fire. Glenn Benoit, an arborist and logger (their old label showed him on sled behind his team of logging horses) is responsible for "hefting the four-foot sticks onto the fire," says Susan. After the syrup is boiled, "canning is done hot on the spot," and the two Benoit children help out with the caps and labels.

In 1990, syrup was $7 for a pint, and you save by buying larger sizes. Shipping additional.

THISTLEDEW FARM
Route 89, RD 1
Box 122
Proctor, WV 26155
(304) 455-1728
(304) 455-1729

Visits: yes
Farmers' markets: Charleston; Center Square Farmers' Market in Wheeling
Certified by: SELF
Catalogue/price list available
Minimum order: $20 for credit-card orders
Order by: phone, mail
Pay by: Visa, check with order
Ship by: UPS

SWEETENERS

Honey · Honey straws · Comb honey

CONDIMENTS

Honey mustard

If you look closely at the photograph of Steve Conlon on ThistleDew Farm's flyer, you'll see that his old-style Pennsylvania Dutch beard is made entirely of bees. Why on earth does he do it? His wife, Ellie, explains that the point of the "bee beard" is that bees are not our enemies.

PURE WEST VIRGINIA
HONEY
THISTLEDEW FARM INC.
NEW MARTINSVILLE, W.VA.
26155-9774
304-455-1728
NET WT 32 OZ. (2 LBS)
TO LIQUIFY PLACE IN WARM WATER

Many local gardeners, says Ellie Conlon, put chemicals on everything, and don't understand that they are also killing beneficial bees. After all, pollination by bees is "responsible for every third bite of food that we consume."

The Conlons started beekeeping almost twenty years ago with one hive, a gift from Ellie's uncle, a beekeeper from Germany. In 1974, they moved from outside of Philadelphia "with one son, two dogs, a cat, and two beehives" to ThistleDew, which they describe as a "small, Quaker family farm," on the Ohio River.

The Conlons tried a variety of farming endeavors in their new home, including raising cattle, but West Virginia's soil was simply not conducive to that kind of intensive farming. They decided that beekeeping was the kind of agriculture that was least damaging to the environment—in fact, says Ellie Conlon, it's beneficial to the environment. They also became foster parents, so ThistleDew farm is now home to four sons, one dog, four cats, 500 hives, and a new honey house in a renovated school building. Their eldest son, who was in the Peace Corps when I spoke to Ellie, is contemplating going to England to study beekeeping. Their youngest, at age eight, has his own hive.

Their honey comes from wildflowers, and every year it's different, says Ellie Conlon. The predominant flowers are the tulip poplar, blackberries, raspberries, goldenrod, and aster, with some sumac and some locust. The Conlons remove the supers at different times of year, producing an early to midsummer honey, and a late summer or fall honey. The honey I sampled was an excellent, dark honey, spicy and aromatic. The honey mustard was extremely flavorful without the sharp sinus-clearing bite I've come to expect from honey mustards. In this version, you can actually still taste both honey and mustard, without obscuring the flavor of whatever you're spreading it on.

The Conlons have never had to use antibiotics on their hives. The mustard seeds in the honey mustard come from an organic distributor, but the mustard base is not necessarily organic. The honey that goes into the honey mustard is pasteurized, as required by the FDA.

In 1990, a 12-ounce honey bear was $1.95. Honey was $2.25 for a 1-pound jar. Honey mustard was $1.95 for a 6-ounce jar. Larger containers and gift jars available. A six-pack of honey straws was $1. A pound square of honey in the comb was $2.95. Shipping additional. The Conlons also sell beeswax candles, ornaments, pure beeswax, and fresh pollen. They also make a nut-and-honey topping, but the nuts are not organic.

UNCLE JOEL'S PURE MAPLE SYRUP
Route 1, Box 1580
Hammond, WI 54015
(715) 796-5395

Visits: yes
Certified by: SELF
Catalogue/price list available
Minimum order: none
Order by: phone, mail
Pay by: check
Ship by: UPS
Recipes available

SWEETENER

Maple syrup · Maple sugar candy (November– February)

A friend of mine who went to college in Canada, becoming a veteran of sugaring festivals in the process, poured some of Uncle Joel's rich, dark maple syrup on her pancakes and said it tasted "like it was fresh from the tree." Not bad for a man who started sugaring as a hobby with coffee-can buckets to collect the sap.

In 1975, says Joel Afdahl, "a friend of mine from high school owned a wood with her sister

and two brothers. They used to sugar as a hobby. My friend was the youngest of the bunch. When her brothers and sister were off in college, she wanted to keep sugaring, but she needed help. I volunteered. We learned together. We did that for about four years, then she went off to college, and I asked if I could keep going. I did it on a small scale for a few years and then it went from a hobby to commercial."

In the old days, Afdahl used a pan measuring three feet by three feet to cook sap down into syrup over a wood fire. He cut the wood and split it by hand with a two-man crosscut saw and an ax. Today, the sap runs from 1,000 taps through a network of plastic tubing to a collection area, is pumped into the new cookhouse, and cooks in a large evaporator. But some things stay the same. Nothing is sprayed or applied near the trees, and Afdahl does not use formaldehyde tablets to increase the flow of sap. "I never believed in the chemicals," he says. "I've heard that formaldehyde will boil out, but I don't believe it." Nothing is added to the syrup, and only butter is used as a defoamer.

In 1990, a half-pint of syrup was $2.75. A quart of cooking syrup was $5. You save by buying larger sizes or buying by the case. An introductory sample of 1 pint was $4. Shipping additional.

VERMONT COUNTRY MAPLE
Box 53
Jericho Center, VT 05465
(802) 864-7519

Certified by: SELF
Catalogue/price list available
Minimum order: none

Order by: phone, mail
Pay by: check, money order, Visa, MC
Ship by: UPS, parcel post

SWEETENERS

Maple Sprinkles · Maple syrup · Maple candy

Maple Sprinkles—maple syrup you shake, not pour—are the brainchild of W. Lyman Jenkins. Jenkins was working as a chemist for the Forest Service when he came across a method for dehydrating maple syrup into crystals. The process involves removing water from the sap (just as you do to make syrup); then stirring rapidly to start the crystals forming; and finally, air-drying. The patent for this process was held by Amstar, the world's largest sugar manufacturer. Jenkins bought a license from Amstar and started looking for investors. In the meantime, he would transport gallons of maple syrup from Vermont to Amstar's Brooklyn plant and drive the maple crystals back up to Vermont. Eventually, a Vermont maple company bought shares, and allowed Jenkins to use its processing plant, bringing the commute to Brooklyn to an end.

The granules are about the size of grains of sand, with intense maple flavor, like tiny versions of the maple candy that usually comes shaped like a maple leaf and says "Greetings from Vermont" on the box. Maple Sprinkles come in shakers the size of spice jars to use on hot or cold cereal, toast, pancakes, waffles, fresh fruit (particularly good on half a grapefruit), and on top of ice cream. I also recommend them straight out of the jar. For bakers, Maple Sprinkles come in larger canisters, bags, and boxes—you can substitute the Sprinkles for sugar in any cake or cookie; Vermont Country Maple also recommends using them on baked ham, chicken, and beans. You can get individual packets to carry when you travel. Hikers and campers take note—the dehydrating process is reversible—you can rehydrate the crystals into syrup for your campfire oatmeal.

Jenkins only buys syrup from growers who certify to him that no sprays are used near the maples, and no formaldehyde is used in the taps. In Vermont Country Maple's processing, nothing is added, and only water is removed.

In 1990, a 14-ounce canister or a package of 3 2.5-ounce shakers of Maple Sprinkles was $8.50. A 45-pound bag of Sprinkles was $40. A box of 250 individual packets was $20. Prices decrease if you order in quantity. Maple syrup was $11 a pint, and you save on larger sizes. Maple candy ranged from $7.50 to $11. All prices included shipping. Vermont Country Maple also sells whole-grain, but not organic, baking mixes.

LATE-BREAKING INFORMATION

PIERPONT MAPLE SYRUP
1434 Fairview Avenue
Columbus, OH 43212-2836
(614) 488-4547

Catalogue/price list available
Certified by: SELF
Minimum order: none
Pay by: check, money order
Ship by: UPS or USPS

MAPLE SYRUP

Grade B · Grade A Dark · Grade A Medium amber

No sprays are used near the maple trees, no formaldehyde is used in the taps, and no additives go in the syrup. "There's a fine line between being old-fashioned and maintaining high quality," says Pierpont's Cecil Wright. "I taste all barrels before packaging. The Medium amber, says Wright, is the grade most often sold on store shelves, with a medium flavor. The Dark amber has a stronger, more definite flavor; and grade B is "cooking grade," although "some people prefer it as table syrup because it has the right amount of flavor to them." Syrup is available in sizes from one cup to five gallons.

SUZANNE'S SPECIALTIES/ T&A GOURMET
I Kingsbridge Road
Somerset, NJ 08873
(908) 828-9565
FAX: (908) 545-4226

Rice certified by: OCIA
Minimum order: "Whatever the customer needs"
Pay by: COD or net thirty days
Ship by: UPS or USPS

BROWN-RICE SYRUPS

Strawberry · Raspberry · Blueberry · Original (no fruit) · Genmai

JELLIES

Strawberry · Blueberry · Raspberry

CANDIES

Lemon · Peppermint · Orange · Spearmint · Root beer · Cinnamon

Developed with the macrobiotic eater in mind, T&A Gourmet products start with organic brown rice, and use a process akin to rice-wine making to convert the rice into a syrup. You can use the original (full brown-rice syrup) or Genmai (partially polished brown-rice syrup) flavors in place of honey or malt syrups; the fruit flavors, with pureed fruit, are suitable for topping pancakes or ice cream. Or so say the folks at T&A; I found the blueberry flavor too gelatinous to be appealing—it was sort of like tasting an intermediate stage in the candy-making process. The candies are far more successful. They have no artificial coloring, and are less sweet than ordinary hard can-

dies, a virtue in my book. The folks at T&A say that the candies are suitable for people on sugar-restricted diets, but I'm happy to report that they do not have the medicinal flavor or powdery surface of artificially sweetened candies. The flavors vary in intensity: the peppermints are strong, the cinnamons red-hot, while the orange has a mild flavor that some will love and others will not.

Under the Suzanne's Specialty label, the same folks make fruit-juice sweetened conserves which have the consistency of jelly; I tasted the strawberry, which had a pleasing, if not strong, strawberry flavor, but I missed texture—no chunks of fruit. You can request OCIA-certified ingredients in the conserves.

SEE ALSO
The Apple Farm, Cascadian Farm, Cherry Hill Cannery, Chestnut Hill Orchards, Fiddler's Green Farm, Glorybee Natural Sweeteners, Lambsfold Farm, Malachite School & Small Farm, Minnesota Specialty Crops, North Hollow Farm, Ojibwe Foods, Rising Sun Farm, Seeds Blüm, Turkey Ridge Orchards, Wood Prairie Farm, Zebroff's Organic Farm

JAMS, JELLIES, AND PRESERVES

AMERICAN SPOON FOODS

P.O. Box 566
1668 Clarion Avenue
Petoskey, MI 49770
(800) 222-5886
(616) 347-9030
FAX: (616) 347-2512

Visits: Grand Traverse Resort in Traverse City;
and East Lake Street in Petoskey
Ingredients certified by: "nature"
Catalogue/price list available
Minimum order: $10
Order by: phone, mail, fax
Pay by: check, Visa, MC, Discover
Ship by: UPS
Gift packages available, including handmade
birch-bark baskets
Recipes available

JELLIES

Wild elderberry · Wild grape

PRESERVES

Wild thimbleberry · Wild blackberry · Wild
blueberry

DRIED FRUITS

Wild blueberries

NUTS

Black walnuts · Hickory nuts · Wild pecans ·
Butternuts

DRIED MUSHROOMS

Morels · Cepes

There can't be many people who list their occupation as "forager," but Justin Rashid is one
of them. When Rashid and his wife, Kate Mar-
shall, returned to Rashid's native Michigan
from the wilds of New York, where they had
worked as actors, the couple opened a store to
sell "Midwest exotics," which included fresh
mushrooms and fruit Rashid "foraged" in the
wild.

The business moved from fresh foods to preserves when chef Larry Forgione, owner of An
American Place in New York City, became a
partner. Forgione gave Rashid the first recipe
—for strawberry preserves—over the phone.
Rashid wrote it on a paper towel, and got to
work. When people first started making preserves, says Rashid, it was just a way of keeping
summer fruit around during the winter using
sugar as a preservative. People didn't use pectin, because they weren't aiming for a gelatinous consistency—liquid was just fine. In
Rashid's early preserves, the proportion of fruit
to sugar was unlike anyone else's: two-thirds
fruit to one-third sugar. You used a spoon, not
a knife, to get them out of the jar.

Rashid prides himself on the company's
techniques as well as its ingredients. The folks
at American Spoon Foods cut their strawberries, pit their apricots, peel their peaches, and

slice their nectarines by hand. After particularly
busy seasons, says Rashid, "we're pitting apricots in our sleep." The fruit is still cooked in
open copper kettles with very little sugar, and
only enough pectin to preserve the fruit. The
results have won acclaim from *Gourmet*—"extraordinarily good"—and *Vogue*, which called
American Spoon Foods "a national treasure."

As befits a forager, Rashid uses many wild
fruits and nuts. They aren't certified organic,
except, as Rashid says, by "nature." I sampled
the wild thimbleberry and wild blueberry preserves, both of which were dense with fruit.
Imagine the filling of the best fresh blueberry

pie you've ever eaten, and you'll have the blueberry preserve: an intense flavor, quite sweet, and far more berries than liquid. The thimbleberry preserve is the other end of the spectrum, a subtle flavor, both piquant and sweet, like a wild strawberry. In the wild, say the folks at American Spoon Foods, thimbleberries are salmon-colored with a tart flavor reminiscent of currants and raspberries. *Vogue*'s Jeffrey Steingarten called the thimbleberry preserve "rose-colored with crunchy, nutty little seeds and a complex winey perfume reminiscent of raspberries, sour cherries, or wild blueberries, but transcending them all."

I also sampled the beautiful, jewel-dark wild grape and wild elderberry jellies. Both had delicate flavors with the slightly musky taste of the woods. The elderberry was a dense spread, and the wild grape, semiliquid and slightly grainy. One friend compared the elderberry to a cross between a grape and a blueberry; I tasted a hint of spice and peppermint. Like the best fresh grapes, the wild grape combined the sweetness of the flesh with the puckery tartness of the skin.

I also sampled the wild pecans, hickory nuts, and black walnuts. The hickory nuts, although cousin to walnuts, were as sweet as pecans; a recipe from American Spoon produced a meringue-light nut cake. The pecans added a honey sweetness to a banana bread and had an almost alcoholic potency in American Spoon's recipe for caramel topping. The black walnuts made a dense, moist, fine-grained, and —as they say on Chinese menus—"Mysterious Flavor" cake. You bake it a day or two before serving, and let the nuts' flavor permeate the cake. Then play the game of making people guess what's in it. I can almost guarantee you that no one will guess walnuts—when I served it the guesses ranged from liqueur to cardamom.

In 1990, a 10-ounce jar of preserves was $6, except for wild thimbleberry, which was $9. The wild nuts ranged from $6 for 8 ounces to $5.95 for 4 ounces. Shipping additional. The beautifully illustrated catalogue contains dozens of other mouth-watering (but not necessarily organic) products, including hormone-free smoked meat, breads from French Meadow Bakery (page 33), Hard-scrabble Enterprises (page 69), and Gray's Grist Mill (page 134).

CASCADIAN FARM

P.O. Box 568
311 Dillard Street
Concrete, WA 98237
(206) 853-8175
FAX: (206) 853-8353

Visits: Produce stand in summer
Ingredients certified by: OR-TILTH, WSDA, CCOF, OCIA
Farm certified by: WSDA
Minimum order: none
Order by: mail, fax
Pay by: check in advance
Ship by: UPS
Gift boxes available

HONEY-SWEETENED CONSERVES

Apricot · Blackberry · Blueberry · Huckleberry · Strawberry · Raspberry · Orange marmalade (from unsprayed oranges) · Apple butter

FRUIT-JUICE SWEETENED CONSERVES

Raspberry-rhubarb · Strawberry-rhubarb · Grape jelly · Raspberry · Boysenberry · Marionberry

SWEETENER

White grape juice concentrate

SNACKS

Lightly salted potato chips · No-salt potato chips

PICKLES AND CONDIMENTS

Old-world sauerkraut · Low-sodium sauerkraut · Baby dills · Kosher dills · Spicy kosher dills · Spicy low-sodium kosher dills · Baby sweets · Genuine kosher dills · Dill pickle relish · Sweet pickle relish

In 1972, Chicago-born Gene Kahn started feeling a need to live on the land. He left a graduate program in English at the University of Wash-

CASCADIAN FARM

ington and found an abandoned farm surrounded by the glacier-covered peaks of the North Cascade National Park. With the help of volunteer labor who worked for room and board in a Mongolian yurt, Kahn made the land productive, and then some.

Today, Cascadian Farm, with sales approaching ten million dollars, is the largest organic farm in the Northwest. Kahn, whose license plate reads "ORGANIC," is famous for his methods, including the Chinese weeder geese that appear on the farm's label. Even secondary ingredients in Cascadian Farm products are organic: conserves sweetened with organic white grape juice concentrate; and pickles made with organic cider vinegar.

One friend of mine calls Cascadian Farm's apricot conserve "the best thing ever invented to put on bread." This essence of apricot is so thick it won't budge even if you hold your spoon upside down. I admit to eating it straight out of the jar, but it also makes a great pastry glaze, or a cookie filling.

The other flavors are no slouches, either. The apple butter is almost liquid, closer to a sauce than a jam, and is as flavorful as mulled cider. I sampled the blueberry and raspberry conserves, one sweetened with honey and the other with concentrated organic fruit juice, both dense with fruit. The raspberry is almost solid and not too sweet, allowing the berries' true flavor to come through. In the blueberry, honey and fruit flavors vie for attention.

And not for nothing does Cascadian Farm's sales manager, Roger Wechsler, sport the license plate "PICKLES." These are all first-rate, crisp, firm pickles. Cascadian Farm even managed to get me to like sweet pickles and sauerkraut. I usually find sweet pickles cloying, but these honey-sweetened pickles are crunchy and have a complicated flavor, spicy as well as sweet. My local sweet-pickle lover called them "great little gherkins" and threatened to finish the whole jar in one sitting. I think of sauerkraut as something limp and vinegary slung at you by a hot-dog vendor, but vinegar is almost incidental here: this is a true pickled cabbage, suitable as a side vegetable or salad, in place of cole slaw, with roots firmly in Austro-Hungarian cuisine. The kosher dills are sweeter and far less garlicky than the traditional pickle-barrel variety. The spicy dills were quite a hit, but be warned: they are fiery—the culprit is a jalapeño pepper floating in each jar.

The potato chips were a pet project for Kahn, a self-proclaimed potato freak. Kahn, who grows some 300 varieties of potatoes, chose Kennebecs for the chips, which are quick-cooked in safflower or sunflower oil, and lightly salted with sea salt. Kahn dedicates each run of chips to a notable person in botany or environmentalism, like Luther Burbank and Rachel Carson.

In 1990, pickles, relishes, and sauerkraut ranged from $11.50 to $17 for a half-case of 6 bottles. Conserves ranged from $18 to $25 for a half-case. You save by buying a full case. A gift pack of 1 jar each blackberry, raspberry, and strawberry conserves was $8. Potato chips were $19 for a case of 12 5.3-ounce bags. Some suppliers in the Under One Roof section carry Cascadian Farm's frozen fruits, vegetables, and outrageously good sorbets, which the company does not sell by mail order.

GRAFTON GOODJAM
Grafton Village Apple Company
Grafton, VT 05146
(802) 843-2276
FAX: (802) 843-2589

Visits: yes
Ingredients certified by: OR-TILTH, WSDA
Catalogue/price list available
Minimum order: none
Order by: phone, mail, fax
Pay by: check
Ship by: UPS

JAMS

Strawberry · Blueberry · Raspberry · Wild

blackberry · Apricot · Loganberry · Hunter's marmalade

CHUTNEYS

Hot gingered apricot · Popple dungeon cranberry · Windham county green apple

VINEGARS

Brown rice · Umeboshi (pickled plum)

When the Schoener family's berry bushes started producing a surplus, Mary Schoener took to the kitchen and started testing recipes until she came up with a jam that satisfied her. The demanding Schoener crossed pectin, sugar, and honey off her list of ingredients. Pectin shortens cooking time, she says, and increases the amount of sugar you need to use. You get a greater yield per pound of fruit, but the flavor of the fruit is diluted. Sugar, she says, actually increases the acid taste of the fruit. Honey drowns out the fruit's flavor. Maple syrup, on the other hand, "permits the fruit flavor to dominate, and results in a product that almost holds its shape, but is not jelly-firm."

The result of Schoener's experiments is Grafton Goodjam, which *Food and Wine* called "truly fruity and delicately sweet." Almost a pound of organically grown fruit and four ounces of maple syrup—from a neighboring family that's been sugaring its trees for 200 years—go into each 12-ounce jar. Schoener cooks small batches in open copper kettles. She describes her philosophy as "paralleling that of a small winery, which limits its production to maintain its quality." Schoener is responsible for everything inside the French jam jars and

WILD BLACKBERRY

out—using medieval woodcuts, she designed Grafton Goodjam's labels.

Schoener also sells organic umeboshi (pickled plum) and brown-rice vinegar. In addition, she combines white wine, red wine, champagne, and apple-cider vinegars (which are not organic) with herbs from her organic garden. Schoener uses hand-blown bottles, and the results are spectacular. You can see one of her dramatic infusions on the cover.

In 1990, a 10-ounce jar of jam or chutney was $10.25 plus shipping. The price of vinegar depends on the type of bottle.

KOZLOWSKI FARMS
5566 Gravenstein Highway
Forestville, CA 95436
(707) 887-1587
FAX: (707) 887-9650

Visits: yes
Ingredients certified by: CCOF, OCIA
Farm certified by: CCOF
Catalogue/price list available
Minimum order: none
Order by: phone, mail, fax
Pay by: check, MC, Visa
Ship by: UPS
Gift packs available

CONSERVES

Apple butter · Red raspberry · Blueberry · Blackberry · Boysenberry

JUICE

Apple cider · Raspberry cider

OIL AND VINEGAR

Apple cider vinegar

SAUCES

Chunky apple sauce

In 1947, Tony Kozlowski, just back from military service, married Carmen Lorenzo, and the couple began growing cherries, apples, and berries on Kozlowski Farms. Carmen and her mother, Julia, who had come to this country from the south of Spain, began turning the fruits of their orchard into jams, jellies, and fruit butters. When the family had an abundance of apples, says Carmen and Tony's daughter, Carol Kozlowski-Every, Carmen Kozlowski came up with a way to use apple juice to sweeten fruit preserves, instead of honey or sugar. Those recipes, using organic apples to make the juice, are part of Kozlowski Farms' line today.

The Kozlowskis' three children, Carol, Perry, and Cindy, carry on their parents' farm and business. They continue to make jams and preserves in small, open kettles, and say that "every batch of our products is individually supervised by a member of the Kozlowski family." No refined sugar is added to any product; calories range from six per teaspoon in the applesauce to ten per teaspoon for the conserves.

In 1990, a 9-ounce jar of conserves, applesauce, or apple butter was $3.39. A quart of cider was $2.99, and a bottle of cider vinegar was $3.69. Shipping and handling extra. The catalogue also lists wine jellies, mustards, and barbecue sauce, which are not organic.

MAD RIVER FARM COUNTRY KITCHEN
P.O. Box 155
Arcata, CA 95521
(707) 822-7150

Farmers' markets: Northern California crafts fairs; blackberry and raspberry popsicles and cheesecakes; call for information
Ingredients certified by: OR-TILTH, CCOF
Catalogue/price list available
Minimum order: none
Order by: mail
Pay by: check, money order, cashier's check

Ship by: UPS, parcel post
Gift packages in handmade redwood crates available

MARMALADE

Lemon · Sunshine (orange and lemon)

As a child, Susan Anderson learned to preserve from her mother in Ohio. Friends who tasted her jams asked her to make them for their bagel bakery and cafe, Los Bagels, in Arcata, California. The timing of the offer was perfect: Anderson had decided she needed a change from her life as a physician's assistant; she'd left the job and was just doing odd jobs to get by.

To finance the jam business, Anderson went to the "bank of Mom." Her equipment included a commercial stove her partner, Chris Ursich, found lying on the street in Berkeley which they sandblasted, repainted, and rewired. Their hard work and mom's investment paid off. Customers at Los Bagels started asking for jam to take home with them. "We proceeded to muddle through our first Christmas season," say Anderson and Ursich. "Imagine, if you will, a borrowed worktable full of hot blackberry jam suddenly collapsing. Jam jars literally cascaded to the floor! What could we do? A late-night blackberry skating party ensued. Fortunately, the blackberry lake was only temporary."

Anderson says she makes marmalades only from organically grown citrus. "No need to be concerned about the peels—no pesticides." All of her jams are lower in sugar than most commercial jams, which has actually gotten Anderson in trouble with the law. Because sugar is a preservative, there's actually a federal standard for how much sugar is required to call some-

Sunshine Marmalade
Oranges, Lemons, Sugar, Citric Pectin

thing a jam, and Anderson had fallen short. After being told to mend her ways, she bought a refractometer, which measures sugar content, to make sure she stays on the right side of the law.

Mad River Farm also makes a number of jams that use "the best quality fruit available, organic whenever possible, with juice from organic lemons." The flavors include blackberry, red raspberry, strawberry, boysenberry, blueberry, Montmorency cherry, red raspberry rhubarb, kiwi; and cranberry conserves. A year-long subscription is available.

In 1990, an individual jar was $4, and you saved by buying in larger quantities. A 6-jar gift pack in redwood crate, which holds cassette tapes when it's empty of jams, was $26, and 12 jars, mixed flavors, $46. The year-long subscription was $48. Postage and handling additional.

Mad River Farm Country Kitchen's products are also available through the Redwood Coast Gift Catalogue, 123 F. Street, Eureka, California, 95001, (800) 733-7700. Redwood Coast takes credit cards and phone orders. In 1990, the catalogue also offered a sampler of organic pasta, and a brunch sampler and a dinner sampler with many organic items. By 1991, the company hopes to carry other local organic foods.

PLAIDBERRY
P.O. Box 2546
Vista, CA 92083
(619) 727-1122

Farmers' markets: locations vary; call for information
Ingredients certified by: CHSC
Catalogue/price list available
Minimum order: none
Order by: mail
Pay by: check, money order
Ship by: UPS

PRESERVES

Plaidberry

Whenever Dennis Dickson takes his wares to a farmer's market, he puts out a sign that reads, "Ever taste a plaidberry?" Since no one ever has, customers line up. It turns out that a plaid-

berry is a "mythical creature—a blackberry that's been pickled with over twenty flavors." Scotch is the only one Dickson will mention; the others are hush-hush.

Dennis Dickson's love of food goes back to his childhood in Montreal, where he was "dragged around to pastry chefs and bakeries" by his upstairs neighbors, who were in the food business. Dickson came up with the idea of the Plaidberry, took it to the California State Fair, and took away a gold medal. He's filed for a patent on the name, and in 1990 modified his recipe to contain no sugar. The result is a garnet-colored, jelly-like preserve that rivals any blackberry jam you've ever tasted.

Dickson has gone "trekking to find organic blackberries" but hasn't had an easy time of it. He does have some sources and just hopes they will be able to meet demand. He won't label the preserves as organic until he's sure of a constant supplier—you can ask him about the status of the fruit when you order.

In 1990, a 12-ounce jar of Plaidberry was $5.75. Shipping additional for orders under $20.

SEE ALSO
The Apple Farm, Arjoy Acres, Aunt Nene's Specialty Foods, Bioforce of America, Ltd., Chestnut Hill Orchards, Emandal—A Farm on a River, Fiddler's Green Farm, Gourmet Fruit Basket, Haypoint Farm, McFadden Farm, Minnesota Specialty Crops, Ojibwe Foods, Persimmon Hill Berry Farm, River Bend Organic Farm, Smoke Camp Crafts, Sunshower Produce and Juice, Suzanne's Specialties/T&A Gourmet, Timber Crest Farms

FITZPATRICK WINERY
Famine's End Farm
7740 Fairplay Road
Somerset, CA 95684
(209) 245-3248
FAX: (209) 245-6838

Visits: yes; tasting room, restaurant, and lodge; seasonal events and dinners
Certified by: CCOF
Catalogue/price list available
Minimum order: 3 bottles
Order by: phone, mail, fax
Pay by: check, money order, Visa, MC
Ship by: UPS

JUICE

1989 Celtic Cider

NUTS

Walnuts (in shell or meats)

Everything at Fitzpatrick Winery—starting with the address—has a touch of whimsy about it, down to the winery's newsletter, which sports the banner "All the news that's Fitz." In a recent copy, Brian Fitzpatrick gleefully describes his victory at the 1989 World Championship Grape Stomp at the Sonoma Harvest Fair, a title he successfully defended in 1990. "Stompers smash the sixty pounds of slippery, red, staining grapes into a mash known as 'must'—a mixture of grape skins, seeds, stems, and juice—while staying upright in the barrel without aid of hands." Fitzpatrick describes his prize-winning technique as "controlled frenzy."

The Fitzpatrick Winery has just celebrated its tenth anniversary, and the World Championship is not the only prize Fitzpatrick has taken home recently. At the Amador County Fair, his Kings Red II won a gold medal, and his 1986 Cabernet Franc got a silver, which it also won at the El Dorado County Fair. The 1985 Cabernet Sauvignon claimed a silver medal from the San Jose *Mercury News* and the Orange County Fair. The wine writer David Rosengarten called it the "best wine" of a recent organic tasting. The hard cider, new in 1990, is made from CCOF-certified apples, aged in French oak, with no sugar added, and an alcohol content of roughly 5 percent.

In 1990, cider was $4.50 a bottle. Wines ranged from $6 to $13 a bottle. Contact the winery for out-of-state shipping on wine. In-shell walnuts were $1 a pound; shelled were a bit more expensive.

MOUNTAIN VIEW FARM
P.O. Box 636
Boonville, CA 95415
(707) 895-2364

Visits: yes
Certified by: CCOF
Minimum order: 1 case of juice or half-bushel of apples
Order by: phone, mail
Pay by: Visa, MC
Ship by: UPS

JUICE

Apple

APPLES

Red Delicious · Golden Delicious · Rome · Jonathan · Rayburn · Gala · Fuji · Jonagold

George Dyer has spent much of his professional life in the air: a commercial pilot, Dyer ran an air taxi service, took people "flightseeing," and gave flight lessons. But Dyer comes from a farming family (including an uncle who grows coffee in Kenya), and in 1985 he joined the family tradition. He now spends most of his time on the ground at Mountain View Farm, "a family farm in the traditional sense," says Dyer. "Everybody pitches in." His wife, Caroline, runs a commercial riding stable, which puts her "in charge of the manure and compost."

Growing apples organically, says Dyer, is not just a matter of taking a conventional orchard and stopping chemical use. "You need to make the canopies smaller so the trees get more light and air. You pretty much have to use trellises the way the Europeans do. Right now, I'm putting in 10,000 trees on trellises. It's very difficult, but the result will be a really good organic apple, which I don't think is out there on the market yet. Once people taste these apples, they'll come back."

Making apple juice is a natural part of being an organic apple grower, says Dyer. Every year, where a conventional grower might be able to pack 95 percent of his fruit, an organic grower will only be able to pack 70 percent because of

surface blemishes. In Dyer's case, that leaves some sixty tons of fruit to go into juice. "Aside from that," says Dyer, "I try to grow the apples that make the best juice. For example, with the apples I'm putting in now, the Jonagold has a nice tart flavor that offsets the sweeter varieties. The same is true of the blend of Red Delicious, Golden Delicious, Rome, and Jonathans. The combination makes an excellent juice."

Juice is sold in vacuum-sealed 44-ounce glass bottles. In 1990, a case was $15 plus shipping.

THE ORGANIC WINE WORKS/ HALLCREST VINEYARD
379 Felton Empire Road
Felton, CA 95018
(408) 335-4441

Visits: yes
Certified by: CCOF
Catalogue/price list available
Minimum order: 1 bottle
Order by: phone, mail
Pay by: Visa, MC, Amex, checks
Ship by: UPS (for wine, in state only)

GRAPE JUICE

Gewurtztraminer · Muscat White Zinfandel

John Schumacher studied enology at the University of California at Davis, so when he and his wife, Lorraine, bought the vineyard in 1987, he had every intention of making wine. He had no idea that the Hall family, who had planted Hallcrest Vineyard back in 1941, had developed a very loyal following for their nonalcoholic grape juices.

Schumacher says he believes in giving people choices. So, although juices pose a challenge to a winemaker, he accepted the challenge. Where winemaking is all about fermentation, juices have got to be made in under three days, to prevent fermentation. Schumacher uses varieties of grapes that make sweet wines, and in the juice, says Lorraine Schumacher, the "true flavors of the varietal grapes come through." By using cold-filtering and sterile bottling, Schumacher doesn't have to pasteurize the juice, and says that the flavor of the grapes remains stronger that way. Juices are available carbonated or noncarbonated. In 1989, the Schumachers took their White Zinfandel juice to the Riverside Farmers' Fair, which doesn't even have a category for juice, so they snuck it into the category of nonalcoholic wines. They won first prize.

John Schumacher does make wine, paying growers a bonus to grow their grapes organically, and acknowledging the name of the vineyard on each label. In spite of what he was

*The*Organic Wine Works

taught at the University of California at Davis, he doesn't use sulfur dioxide, either, and believes it's time we changed our thinking about wine and put it into a new category, like produce: something to be drunk while fresh.

Hallcrest Vineyards can ship juice anywhere. In 1990, grape juice was $4.50 a bottle, plus shipping. The Organic Wine Works can only ship wine within California. Wine ranged from $7.50 to $8.50 a bottle, plus shipping.

SUNSHOWER PRODUCE AND JUICE
48548 60th Avenue
Lawrence, MI 49064
(616) 674-3103

Visits: yes; organic vegetables and pears, and low-spray apples
Farmers' markets: Evanston and Oak Park, Illinois, Saturday mornings
Certified by: OGM
Catalogue/price list available
Minimum order: none
Order by: phone
Pay by: check
Ship by: COD, UPS

JUICE

Frozen pear

PRESERVES

Pear butter

Lynn and Mark Miller, and Lynn's sister, Lisa Groff, the owners of Sunshower Produce and Juice, have simple, practical aims: "to grow good, clean food." The Millers and their three children moved to the farm from Chicago, and carry on a tradition started back in 1973 by the founders of Sunshower, whom Lynn Miller describes as "a community of people from Chicago who had worked with the poor and decided they wanted to raise clean food at an affordable price."

The frozen pear juice is not a concentrate—once defrosted, it's juice. The Millers don't fill up the dairy-grade recyclable plastic jugs all the way, to allow for expansion when freezing, so a one-gallon jug, for example, will be labeled "120 ounces." Some people like to mix it with sparkling water, says Mark Miller, but then "they're not getting the full flavor of the juice," a blend of Bosc and Bartlett pears, with a smattering of Kiefers and Comice. If you want your pears in a spreadable form, they also make pear butter.

In addition to the frozen organic pear juice, Sunshower makes a number of frozen juices (apple-strawberry, apple-cherry, apple-

raspberry, and apple-grape) using its "ecological" apples—no herbicides or chemical fertilizers are used—but it does spray pesticides at low concentrations, stopping at least six weeks before harvest. Late-ripening apples may go as much as four months between the last spraying and picking.

In 1990, a case of frozen pear juice was $18, available in 9 60-ounce (half-gallon) containers, 16 30-ounce (quart) containers, or 25 15-ounce (single-serving) containers. Prices on other juices ranged from $13 to $27 a case. A mixed case of single-serving juices was $19. Shipping additional. Sunshower can also ship fresh pears if you don't live too far away. Contact the farm for information. It also sells Southern Brown Rice (page 224).

SEE ALSO
Cherry Hill Cannery, Flora, Inc.,
Healthland, Kozlowski Farms, Roseland
Farms, Zebroff's Organic Farm

MACROBIOTIC SPECIALTIES

The macrobiotic movement, founded by George and Lima Ohsawa, emphasizes combinations of grains and beans, and stresses eating foods that are in season. Rice is central to the macrobiotic diet, and these companies cater to rice connoisseurs. For example, the Richardsons of Gold Mine offer black sweet rice, "sweet and sticky," with a "very fruity, aromatic flavor, reminiscent of black raspberries." Other unfamiliar grains include Job's tears, a wild grass that resembles barley and has a "light, refreshing taste," say the Richardsons.

Many of the foods in this section are Japanese and may be unfamiliar to you. What follows is an introduction to some of these foods, courtesy of the suppliers listed below.

Mochi is made from sweet brown rice that has been hulled, steamed, coarsely ground, and then pounded into a paste, formed into small cakes and then dried. The cakes puff up when cooked, and can be eaten plain or stuffed. Ohsawa America recommends adding mochi to soups and stews, panfrying it with sesame oil, baking it and serving it with a soy-ginger sauce, toasting it in the oven for a snack, or using it as the base for a dessert topping. I remember eating mochi wrapped in nori leaves as a child at the home of a Japanese-American friend; its sweet stickiness made it a perfect food for kids.

Seitan is a meat alternative made from wheat gluten, first brought to Japan by the Zen monks of China. A wheat-flour dough is kneaded to activate the gluten. Then the dough is washed to remove the bran and starch. The remaining gluten is cooked slowly with tamari, kombu (a sea vegetable) and other seasonings, and can be used in soups, stews, sautés, or sandwiches. Lima Belgium's seitan pâté blends seitan with organic vegetables.

Umeboshi are Japan's traditional pickled plums, picked green and packed in salt, which makes a plum brine. Leaves of shiso, a mineral-rich plant, give the brine a deep red color and sweet taste. The plums are further pickled for seven days; each morning, they are sun-dried, and each evening returned to the brine. After that week, the plums age another four months. The plums add a salty, tart flavor to salad dressings, cooked vegetables, or sauces. The Athoses of Natural Lifestyle Supplies recommend trying a plum tucked inside a rice ball or spread thinly on corn instead of butter and salt.

Umeboshi plum paste is simply a puree of the salt plums; the ume concentrate is made by cooking the plums into a dark, concentrated syrup, The shiso condiment is made from the shiso leaves that are removed from the brine, sun-dried, and ground to a powder. Umeboshi vinegar is the "brines" in which the umeboshi plums or apricots have been cured.

As in the section on flour and grain, grains are listed first. An (F) means the grain is available as flour. A (C) means it is available as a cereal.

GOLD MINE NATURAL FOOD COMPANY

**1947 30th Street
San Diego, CA 92102
(800) 475-FOOD
(619) 234-9711**

Visits: yes
Certified by: various
Catalogue/price list available
Minimum order: none
Order by: phone, mail
Pay by: check, money order, MC, Visa
Ship by: UPS, parcel post, own truck

WHOLE GRAINS

Pearl short-grain brown rice (hulled or unhulled) (C) · Rose medium-grain brown riced (hulled) · Sweet long-grain brown rice (hulled) · Amaranth (F) · Brown teff (F) · Ivory teff (F) · Minnesota wild rice · Black sweet rice · Red rice · Rice bran · Job's tears · Barley · Millet · Whole oats (C) · Whole rye · Pastry wheat · High-gluten wheat · White high-gluten wheat · Quinoa · Raw white buckwheat groats · Rice bran · Yellow dent corn · Whole blue corn · Flint corn · Black Aztec sweet corn · Multi-colored flint corn · Blue flour corn · Yellow popcorn

OTHER CEREALS

Muesli · Three-grain

SEEDS

Black sesame · Brown sesame

BEANS

Adzuki · Anasazi · Bolita · Pinto · Whole yellow soy · Black soy · Lentil · Garbanzo · Black turtle · Green split peas · Kidney · Navy

NOODLES

Whole-wheat udon · Brown-rice udon · Somen · Kishimen · Soba · Mugwort soba · Buckwheat soba · Shizen soba · Jinenjo soba

MISO

Two-year barley · Two-year brown rice · Two-year soybean · Sweet barley · Brown rice · Soybean · Sweet white · Barley

SOY SAUCE AND TAMARI

Four-year shoyu · Two-year soy sauce · Wheat-free tamari

CONDIMENTS

Farmhouse tekka · Salsa (mild, hot, very hot, and killer hot) · Enchilada sauce (mild or hot)

PICKLES

Umeboshi plums (soft or firm) · Plum paste · Red ume paste · Light ume paste · Ume concentrate · Shiso powder · Pickled shiso leaves · Umeboshi with shiso · Umeboshi apricots · Tamari-daikon pickle · Takuan-daikon pickle · Amazake-daikon pickle · Shiso pickle · Sauerkraut

VINEGARS

Plum · Ume · Rice malt · Yuzu · Brown rice · Umeboshi apricot

BAKING SUPPLIES

Barley malt · Amazake concentrate · Hazelnut spread

READY TO EAT

Pinto beans · Garbanzo beans · Great northern beans · Adzuki beans · Tamari vegetable brown-rice dinner · Vegetable pâté · Seitan pâté

SEITAN

Fresh seitan (regular or spicy)

MOCHI

Brown rice · Brown rice with millet · Brown rice with mugwort

DRIED FOODS

Rare small wild shiitake · Sun-dried shredded daikon radish · Sliced lotus root

FRUIT SAUCES

Gravenstein apple

TEAS

Three-year twig-leaf tea · One-year twig-leaf tea · Twig tea · Green-leaf tea · Genmai cha ·

Lotus root powder tea · Yannoh coffee-substitute · Mugwort

SNACKS

Brown-rice Snackcracks (unsalted, lightly salted, vegetable mix, soy sauce, tamari)

Gold Mine's proprietors, Carlos and Jean Richardson, feel that other macrobiotic eaters are like their family. "When we share simple food, our blood quality becomes similar, so we become close, like family. We often harmonize much more with other macrobiotic eaters/ thinkers than we do with blood relatives who eat chaotically." The Richardsons' newsletter/ catalogue brings you into the life of their own family. In one issue, they described the home birth of their second daughter, Abbie; a later issue shows their two girls happily munching nori.

Gold Mine is the home of Ohsawa America's mail-order service, and in addition to their macrobiotic specialties, Gold Mine carries a variety of organic products from domestic producers, and aims to "respectfully pay them a fair price for their efforts, in order to help them grow." At a minimum, the organic products the Richardsons carry meet the standards of the California Health and Safety Code. In addition to the flours they list, they can mill any grain they sell into flour on site.

The Richardsons have many global environmental concerns, and their *Gold Mine Gazette* serves as a newsletter on these issues as well as a catalogue. Recent issues contained information on a campaign to link struggling black American farmers with processors in Nicaragua; a petition to save the Brazilian rainforest; a plea to recycle packing material; Greenpeace's list of alternatives to toxic products; and an appeal from the Ocean Sanctuary movement.

If you are unfamiliar with macrobiotic foods, be sure to ask for the product catalogue, which includes detailed descriptions, as well as the *Gold Mine Gazette.* Gold Mine sells a basic macrobiotic food kit, which contains five pounds of brown rice, one pound each of nine different grains and beans, assorted sea noodles, sesame oil, condiments, tea, a stainless vegetable knife, and a cookbook.

In 1990, the basic kit was $89.95, plus shipping. Gold Mine also carries the product of Southern Brown Rice (page 224), South River Miso (page 53), Ocean Harvest (page 242), Mendocino Sea Vegetable Company (page 241), and French Meadow Bakery (page 33). The catalogue also lists nonorganic foods, concentrates and food supplements, body-care products, books, saunas, water purifiers, and cookware.

MOUNTAIN ARK TRADING COMPANY
120 South East Avenue
Fayetteville, AR 72701
(800) 643-8909
(501) 442-7191

Visits: yes
Certified by: OCIA, CHSC, OOGA, other
Catalogue/price list available
Minimum order: none
Order by: phone, mail
Pay by: check, COD, Visa, MC, Amex
Ship by: UPS, parcel post
Discounts on bulk orders

WHOLE GRAINS

Brown rice (short-, medium-, or long-grain) (C) · Sweet brown rice · Basmati rice · Wild rice · Barley (pearled or whole) · Buckwheat groats · Dried corn (white, yellow, or blue) · Whole millet · Quinoa · Whole oats (C) · Red winter turkey wheat (F) · Popcorn · Brown teff (F) · Ivory teff · Amaranth · Spelt · Hato mugi · Rye berries

BEANS

Japanese adzuki · American adzuki · Black turtle · Chick-peas · Pinto · Green split peas · Black soy · Yellow soy · Green lentils · Anasazi · Black-eyed peas · Baby lima · Red lentil

OTHER CEREALS

Muesli · Belgian muesli

OTHER FLOURS

Yellow cornmeal · Unbleached white

SEEDS

Sunflower seeds · Sesame seeds · Sprouting alfalfa seeds

DRIED FRUIT

Apple slices · Apricot halves · Mixed fruits · Thompson raisins · Peach halves · Prunes · Turkish figs · Cherries

DRIED MUSHROOMS

Shiitake

PREPARED FOODS

Bean-grain soup mix · Refried beans · Cooked chick-peas · Cooked adzuki beans · Seitan stew · Seitan chili · Tempeh natto

FRUIT SAUCES

Gravenstein apple · Apple-sweet cherry · Apple-strawberry

FRUIT BUTTER

Apple

PICKLES, SAUCES, AND CONDIMENTS

Tamari daikon pickles · Sauerkraut · Kosher dill pickles · Pickled umeboshi plums · No-tomato pasta sauce (carrots, squash, onions, green pepper, garlic, olive oil, red miso, red wine vinegar, sea salt, natural herbs and spices)

OIL AND VINEGAR

Olive oil · Sesame oil · Ume vinegar

NOODLES

Buckwheat soba · Whole-wheat spaghetti · Sesame, rice, and wheat spirals · Vita-spelt pasta shells · Vegetable spirals · Paella ribbons · Provençal ribbons

MISO

Barley · Brown rice · Chick-pea with rice · Mellow white · Mellow barley

SOY SAUCE

Four-year shoyu · Tamari

SWEETENERS

Rice syrup · Maple syrup · Amazake

TEAS AND COFFEE

Bancha twig tea · Black tea (oolong) · Peruvian coffee · Colombian coffee

JUICES

Apple · Grape

CHIPS AND SNACKS

Blue corn chips · Black bean tortillas · rice cakes

NUTS AND NUT BUTTERS

Almonds · Sesame tahini · Almond butter (smooth or crunchy)

Frank Head, Jr., is a self-proclaimed anarchist who believes that change can only start with the individual and blossom from there. Mountain Ark grew out of that philosophy, to help people to take charge of their own diet and health. Head and his wife, Phyllis, have founded East West Centers in Austin, Houston, and Mexico City, and founded Mountain Ark in 1982 as a community enterprise.

While Head still holds to his original idealism, he admits that the founders were not all that practical when it came to making the business work. They had to learn, for example, that mail-order sales are not regular, month-in and month-out. Then came the realization that with the drop of the dollar against the Japanese yen, many of their imported macrobiotic products were becoming prohibitively expensive—which Head finds ironic, because in the company's early days, a macrobiotic diet was definitely cheaper than any alternative. One positive outcome of the drop in the dollar has been that Mountain Ark now searches out local growers and producers whenever possible.

If you're confused by the list of Mountain Ark's products, don't worry. Frank Head un-

derstands that most of his customers are just getting started with macrobiotic or organic eating, and sees Mountain Ark as providing more than food. Along with answering any questions you may have about individual products, the staff at Mountain Ark will educate you about the nutritional and environmental impact of your purchases. Head says the service is so personalized that he's had customers call up and start placing an order by rummaging through the cabinets and thinking aloud—I seem to be low on noodles (or rice, or tea)—what kind do you recommend?

Mountain Ark also sells the products of French Meadow Bakery (page 33) and South River Miso (page 53). The catalogue also contains cookware and water purifiers.

NATURAL LIFESTYLE SUPPLIES
16 Lookout Drive
Asheville, NC 28804
(800) 752-2775
(704) 254-9606

Certified by: various
Catalogue/price list available
Minimum order: none
Order by: phone, mail
Pay by: check, money order, COD, Visa, MC
Ship by: UPS, parcel post
Various samplers available

SWEETENERS

Brown-rice syrup · Barley malt syrup · Brown-rice syrup with pureed organic fruit (strawberry, raspberry, blueberry)

CANDIES (DROPS OR LOLLIPOPS)

Cinnamon · Lemon · Orange · Peppermint · Root beer · Spearmint

SNACKS

Popcorn with brown-rice syrup

COOKIES (RICE/MALT SNAPS)

Oatmeal · Carob · Cocoa with almond · Cocoa chip · Ginger · Sweet rice cookies

CHIPS

Carrot lites corn chips with carrots

COFFEE

Cafe Altura regular roast (ground or whole bean) · Cafe Altura decaffeinated (ground) · Instant Yannoh coffee alternative

OILS

Spectrum sesame

VINEGAR

Brown rice · Ume plum

MISO AND KOJI

Traditional barley · Brown rice · Mellow barley · Mellow white · Sweet white · Chickpea with rice · Soybean · Brown-rice koji

SOY SAUCES

Sakae shoyu · Nama shoyu · Mansan tamari

GRAINS

Amaranth · Pearled barley · Buckwheat · Brown rice (short-, medium-, and long-grain) · Millet · Whole oats (C) · Popcorn · Sweet brown rice (C) · Whole winter wheat · Quinoa · Brown basmati rice · White basmati rice · Wild rice

HOT CEREALS

Whole-wheat couscous

COLD CEREALS

Crispy brown rice · Amaranth flakes · Blue corn flakes · Healthy O's · Fiber 7 flakes · Millet-rice flakes with oat bran · Muesli · Wheat-free muesli

ORIENTAL NOODLES

Soba · Whole-wheat udon · Brown-rice udon · Whole-wheat somen · Mugwort soba · Jinenjo soba · Sobaya somen · Genmai udon

PASTA

Vegetable spirals · Vegetable shells · Parsley-garlic ribbons · Paella ribbons · Provençal ribbons · Extra-fine pasta · Sesame rice spirals · Spaghetti

BEANS

Adzuki · Black turtle · Chick-peas · Kidney · Pinto · Lentil · Navy · Split peas · Black soy

CONDIMENTS

Farmhouse tekka · Ketchup · Dijon mustard · Yellow mustard · Brown sesame seeds · Natto-miso chutney · Tofu-based mayonnaise · Tofu-based vegetable dressings (creamy dill, Italian, sesame-garlic, garden herbal)

SAUCES

Pasta sauce · Mild salsa · Hot salsa

PICKLES

Whole umeboshi · Ume plum concentrate · Shiso leaves · Takuan daikon · Tamari daikon · Amazake daikon

MOCHI

Brown rice · Brown rice with mugwort · Millet

PREPARED DINNERS

Brown rice with tamari and vegetables · Adzuki bean and brown rice

MISCELLANEOUS

Seitan · Refried beans · Tostada shells

DRIED FOODS

Lotus root · Dried shredded daikon

NUT BUTTERS

Peanut butter · Sesame butter · Sesame tahini · Almond butter

FRUIT SAUCES

Apple · Apple-wild blackberry · Apple-strawberry · Apple-cherry · Apple-raspberry

DRIED FRUIT

Golden Delicious apples · Bartlett pears · Apricots · Montmorency cherries · Raisins

BEVERAGES

Rice dream (almond, carob, chocolate) · Soymilk (original, vanilla, carob) · Soy malteds (carob, java, cocoa-mint, almond, vanilla)

TEA

Kukicha twig · Hojicha

When Debbie Athos met her husband-to-be, Tom, he was a natural-foods chef who taught macrobiotic cooking. Tom had been eating natural and macrobiotic foods since the age of nineteen. "Every time I'd eat something," says Debbie, "he'd say, 'Don't you ever read ingredients? Don't you know what you're eating?'" Eventually, the badgering worked, and Debbie Athos began to change the way she ate and eventually gave up animal products altogether. "After a while, I was sold because I was feeling so much better."

Together, the couple started a macrobiotic-cooking center in Tallahassee. When the Athos family—they have four children, all of whom were "born and raised eating good food"—moved to North Carolina, they brought their cooking classes with them. "People would come from two or three hours away to take our classes," says Debbie Athos, "and then they'd go home and call us and say they couldn't find the ingredients we'd used. They asked my hus-

Natural Lifestyle Supplies
Natural Food and Home Products for a Healthier Life

band to send them what they needed. So we put together a little catalogue, and put in it everything that we used in our lives, and before you knew it, we had a business running out of our house."

Natural Lifestyle's catalogue gives explanations of quite a few of the items, but if you need more information, or advice on cooking, just ask for it.

The company also carries the products of Cascadian Farm (page 172), Hardscrabble Enterprises (page 69), Bioforce of America, Ltd. (page 250), Maine Coast Sea Vegetables (page 238), Flora, Inc. (page 209), and Ocean Harvest Sea Vegetable Company (page 242). The catalogue also lists cookware, food supplements, environmentally sound household products, toys, and books.

MEAT, FISH, AND POULTRY

Until the 1990 Farm Bill takes effect in the fall of 1993, the USDA will not allow "organic" on meat labels. People get around this by calling their meat "natural" or "naturally raised." As one supplier observed, however, "even Perdue is using 'natural' these days," so it's important to have a definition as well as the name. All the farmers in this section raise their livestock without antibiotics (except for actual outbreaks of disease) and without hormones. In addition, they feed their livestock organically grown feed (exceptions are noted). Some of the purveyors in this section sell wild game that comes from animals who graze in the wild, in areas that are presumed to be uncontaminated. In the case of fish, the definition of "organic" is a bit fuzzy. Basically, it means that the fish come from unpolluted waters, and, in the case of fish raised on fish farms, the waters and fish can be tested for pesticide runoff and other chemical contaminants.

BANDON SEA-PACK
P.O. Box 5488
Charleston, OR 97420-0614
(800) 255-4370
(503) 888-4600
(503) 888-5525

Certified by: SELF
Catalogue/price list available
Minimum order: 1 case
Order by: phone, mail
Pay by: check, Visa, MC
Ship by: UPS, parcel post, freight COD

FISH

Pink salmon · Albacore tuna · Silver salmon

The first thing that will strike you about Bandon Sea-Pack tuna and salmon is that there's no can—it's in a glass jar. The unusual packaging came at the request of a doctor whose chemically sensitive patients were allergic to the linings in metal cans.

Then there's what's inside the glass. Every step of Bandon's process is designed to avoid chemical contamination. Bandon's tuna is caught in clean waters off the Oregon coast. During the summer months, salmon are brought in fresh daily. They are filleted to re-

move skin and bones. The fillets are cut by hand, never touching plastic pans or cutting boards, and packed uncooked in the glass jars. According to the folks at Bandon, large canner-

ies precook their tuna before canning to speed up the processing, and then have to add oil, broth, or water to regain moisture. At Bandon, the fish is cooked *inside* the jars in its own natural juices. Nothing is added, except for sea salt when requested.

In 1990, a case of 12 7.5-ounce jars ranged from $39 for tuna to $51 for silver salmon.

BRIGGS-WAY COMPANY
Ugashik
Via King Salmon, AK 99613

Certified by: SELF
Catalogue/price list available

Minimum order: 12 jars
Order by: mail
Pay by: check with order
Ship by: parcel post

FISH

Salmon

Roger and Emorene Briggs describe themselves as "a pair of eccentrics living in the wilderness of Alaska." The "wilderness" is Ugashik, a remote island whose winter population is only three families. The Briggses have lived in Ugashik since 1962, and educated their four children at home through correspondence courses. Later, the children traveled to Anchorage to attend high school and college.

Roger and Emorene Briggs now live in Ugashik only in the summertime, but they still run their "Mom and Pop operation" canning Red and Medium Red salmon, caught in the water around Ugashik, which is still pure and unaffected by the oil spill in Prince William sound, some 1,200 miles away. "Salmon avoid oil like the plague. We understand their sense of smell is so acute that the fish return to their river of origin through the smell of their natal stream."

The fresh-caught salmon is skinned, boned, filleted, and packed by hand. "The time from sea to jar is only a very few hours," says Emorene Briggs, "a feat impossible in large-scale commercial fishing operations." In a commercial operation, she says, the fish may languish for as long as two days, exposed to diesel oils and other engine fuels.

The Briggses pack their salmon in glass jars, at the request of Emorene's brother, a Chicago allergist, whose patients had trouble with chemically contaminated fish. The salmon in glass "bears little resemblance to salmon canned in a tin," says Emorene Briggs. "The flesh is so firm it is a joy to eat as it comes from the jar." The only addition to the fish itself is solar-evaporated salt. (You can also order salt-free.)

The Briggses begin shipping in mid-August, and continue for several months. "We only process enough salmon to fill the orders we have on hand by the middle of August. We take orders anytime, but ours is a once-a-year operation. Roger and I are both seventy years old and we have decided we need our winter free of packing and shipping. Once all of the orders are shipped, we leave Ugashik for the winter."

In 1990, 12 5-ounce jars of salmon were $30.96 plus postage and insurance. The jars come wrapped in styrofoam, in boxes of 12, 24, or 48 jars. The price per jar goes down slightly for 24 or 48 jars; postage and insurance for 48 jars is only slightly more than twice that for 12 jars.

BROKEN ARROW RANCH
Texas Wild Game Cooperative
P.O. Box 530
Ingram, TX 78025
(800) 962-4263
(512) 367-5875
FAX: (512) 367-4988

Visits: yes
Certified by: SELF
Catalogue/price list available
Minimum order: $30
Order by: phone, mail, fax
Pay by: check, Visa, MC
Ship by: UPS (in TX); Airborne Express
Recipes available

MEAT

Axis venison · Antelope venison · Venison smoked sausage · Wild boar smoked sausage · Venison salami · Wild boar salami · Smoked wild boar ham · Other meats may be available, including wild lamb

In the 1930s, Eddie Rickenbacker, the World War I flying ace, imported exotic zoo-surplus animals to his Texas ranch, let them loose and hunted them. By the 1970s, Texas was home to some 120,000 nonnative big-game animals, descendants of the "curiosities" men like Rickenbacker had brought to Texas for sport. While *native* wild animals are legally public property, and can't be raised for profit, *nonnative* game are private property; the distinction enabled Mike Hughes to turn the focus of big-game hunting from trophies to gourmet food.

Like Rickenbacker, Hughes, the founder of Broken Arrow Ranch, started his professional life as something of a daredevil—underwater. A commercial diver, Hughes ran a company that fought oil fires in the Persian Gulf, and which was also in charge of the recovery effort after the explosion of the space shuttle Challenger.

Hughes had lived in Europe, and he knew how popular venison was in European kitchens. In 1975, Hughes bought three Texas ranches, and went on to found the Texas Wild

Game Cooperative, home of the Broken Arrow label. Most of the member ranches joined because they were overrun with wild game. They thought of Hughes as a kind of population controller, and asked him to hunt only the female deer and antelope, leaving the bucks, and their impressive horns, for trophy hunters. As the market for venison has grown, Broken Arrow's strategy has shifted; now they hunt young bucks, leaving females for breeding.

Chefs are Broken Arrow's best customers, says Hughes; they like the meat's combination of rich, mild flavors and low fat content. But Hughes is eager to let everyone know about the nutritional qualities of venison. Broken Arrow advertises venison as having one-third the calories of beef and one-eighth of the fat. Their axis venison has "very mild flavor and the texture of veal," while the antelope venison is the "lowest in fat and calories and has a wonderful, beef-like flavor." To encourage you to try experimenting with venison, Broken Arrow has put together a venison cookbook, which includes not only recipes but general rules on how to substitute venison in recipes calling for other meats.

This meat is not certified organic, but all the game ranges freely on unsprayed land and is not fed hormones or antibiotics. The meat is inspected by the Texas Department of Health and the USDA.

In 1990, venison ranged from $3.98 a pound for ground meat to $17.98 a pound for scallopini. A venison sampler was $59.95. Shipping inside Texas was $10, and outside Texas was up to $15.

COUNTRY PRIDE MEATS
P.O. Box 6
Ipswich, SD 57451
(605) 426-6288

Visits: yes
Certified by: SELF
Catalogue/price list available
Minimum order: none
Order by: phone, mail
Pay by: COD, check
Ship by: UPS

MEAT

Bison · Bison jerky · Bison summer sausage · German sausage

Dominik Luond was raised on a dairy farm, and when he left, he swore he'd never own another cow—or any other livestock, for that matter. Luond, who's been a butcher since he was seventeen, moved in 1981 from the west coast to rural South Dakota, where he took over a butcher shop in the small town of Ipswich. The butcher shop's previous owner had sold bison, and Luond decided to give it a try.

At first, Dominik and Shirley Luond bought buffalo from other ranchers, but in 1985, frustrated with not being able to control the quality of the meat, they started raising their own. To his surprise, says Luond, it was a pleasure to work with them, and he now has some 200 head. The buffalo feed on unsprayed pasture;

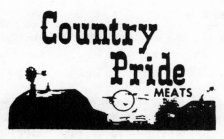

their water comes from dugout holes. They're given no shots. "Buffalo is real hearty," say Shirley Luond. "Heartier than beef. They don't hardly ever get sick." The buffalo meat, say the Luonds, is low in fat, and has no cholesterol; the sausage, they say, is low in salt, fat, and nitrites.

In 1990, bison ranged from $2.10 a pound for trim to $21 a pound for tenderloin portion cut. Jerky was $3 for a 3-ounce package. Summer sausage was $2.29 for 12 ounces and German sausage links were $2.89 a pound.

CZIMER FOODS
13136 West 159th Street
Lockport, IL 60441
(708) 301-7152

Certified by: SELF
Catalogue/price list available
Minimum order: none
Order by: phone, mail
Pay by: money order, certified check
Ship by: air freight, FedEx, UPS, bus
Prices and availability vary daily

GAME BIRDS

Pheasant · Quail · Partridge · Guineas · Mallard ducks · Muscovy ducks · Canada geese · Domestic geese · Squab · Wild turkey

GAME ANIMALS

Venison · Elk · Moose · Bear · Wild boar · Antelope · Buffalo · Lion · Eland · Kangaroo · Zebra · Yak · Water buffalo · Hippopotamus · Giraffe · Camel · Reindeer · Oryx (African antelope) · Wild goat/mountain sheep · Alligator · Rattlesnake · Beaver · Rabbit · Raccoon

FISH AND SEAFOOD

Catfish · Codfish · Clams · Crabmeat · Finn' Haddie · Flounder · Frog legs · Grouper · Haddock · Halibut · Yellow Lake perch · Mahi-Mahi · Monkfish · Orange roughy · Oreo dory · Oyster · Red snapper · Scrod · Shark · Shrimp · Smelts · Squid · Bay or ocean scallops · Sole · Swordfish · Trout · Tuna · Turbot · Snapping turtle · Wahoo · Alaskan whitefish

SMOKED MEATS

Pheasant · Goose · Turkey · Venison ham · Wild turkey · Buffalo tongue · Duck

While rabbit may be pretty exotic fare for most of us, John Czimer is not impressed. Rabbit's the kind of meat his grandfather, a Hungarian immigrant (also named John) first carried when he opened his meat market in Chicago in 1914. Back then, says the younger John Czimer, "We had the *common* types of game meats. Then we started raising pheasants, and getting deer and bear." In those days, explains John Czimer, if a restaurant wanted game, it had to agree to take the whole animal. A rabbit, a pheasant, or even a deer is one thing, but when you get to the bigger beasts, like lions, having to buy the whole animal could easily scare off the customers. So John Czimer's father and brothers started breaking the meat into cuts. When restaurants discovered this service, they started asking for ever more exotic meats, and the obliging Czimers provided them.

Today, all of the Czimers' wild meat comes from large game farms or ranches. The animals range on grass that has not been sprayed, and they are given no outside feed. As early as thirty

years ago, people with chemical sensitivities started coming to Czimer to get their meat.

Prices and availability change daily, but in 1990, pheasant was $4.25 a pound; Mallard ducks were $4.25 a pound; venison ranged from $3.95 for ground patties to $18.95 for tenderloin fillets; bison went from $3.95 a pound for ground patties to $25.95 a pound for whole tenderloins. Center-cut rattlesnake was $13.95 a pound.

D'ARTAGNAN
399-419 St. Paul Avenue
Jersey City, NJ 07306
(800) DAR-TAGN
(201) 792-0748

Certified by: SELF
Catalogue/price list available
Minimum order: none
Order by: phone
Pay by: MC, Visa, Amex
Ship by: UPS Next Day Air

GAME

Quail · Squab · Free-range pheasant · Guinea hen · Partridge · Rabbit · Wild boar · Buffalo · Venison

QUAIL EGGS

DOMESTIC ANIMALS

Chicken · Turkey · Poussin · Goose (mid-October–December) · Moulard duck · Moscovy duck · Pekin/Long Island duck · Wild turkey (October–December) · Whole baby lamb · Whole suckling pig · Whole kid goat

SCOTTISH GAME (FRESH OCTOBER 3–JANUARY 20; OTHERWISE FROZEN)

Grouse · Wood pigeon · Pheasant · Partridge · Wild rabbit · Hare · Venison

SMOKED MEAT

Magret · Poussin · Quail · Pheasant · Pekin duck · Venison

DRY CURED

Magret · Wild boar prosciutto · Duck sausage

SAUSAGES

Duck and foie gras · Venison with juniper berries · Wild boar with sage · Rabbit · Duck

Ariane Daguin says modestly that her parents own a hotel and restaurant in France, but what she calls a "small business" turns out to be perhaps the most famous restaurant in Gascony, a two-star in Michelin; her father, André Daguin, is consulting chef to the Louvre.

The younger Daguin came to this country to study political science and become a journalist. While at Barnard, she met her partner in D'Artagnan, George Faison, who, in spite of his name, is not French but Texan. The two met at Columbia University's International House, explains Daguin, "where there were all kind of foreign people—and Texans. I guess they are some kind of foreigner."

Daguin left Barnard and went to work for Les Trois Petits Cochons (The Three Little Pigs), the pâté company. When the company needed someone with a financial background, she introduced George, with his MBA, who happily traded international banking for international cuisine. After five years, the two decided to strike out on their own. With $15,000 in hand, they started D'Artagnan, named for the Gascon hero immortalized as Dumas's fourth musketeer.

Their original idea was to sell fresh foie gras from American ducks bred according to French tradition. *New York*'s Barbara Costikyan called their terrine "luscious." *Food and Wine* called their duck foie gras mousse "superb . . . splendidly silky and beautifully seasoned"; the *New*

York Times called their whole fresh foie gras "sheer indulgence"; *Vogue* called it "better than anything imported from France."

In 1989, Ariane Daguin even snuck some of her American foie gras into a dinner at the economic summit in Paris for which her father was the chef. The years of studying political science had not gone to waste. President Bush was so impressed by the foie gras that he gave her his lapel pin, an American eagle, and has become a regular customer of this half-Texan company's Scottish pheasant, rabbit, and foie gras.

But even with clients like these, "there's only so much foie gras you can sell at fifty or sixty dollars a pound," so Daguin and Faison branched out into fresh game, a natural move for Faison, who had been eating game since he'd learned to shoot—at age eight.

D'Artagnan sells both wild and domestic game, including poussin (spring chicken), three and a half weeks old; and magret, the breast of a moulard duck fatted for foie gras. Some of their meats may be unfamiliar, but their beautiful color booklet will give you a good idea of what you're getting.

Their game is shot or trapped in the wild; the Scottish game comes from the Scottish highlands and comes with the warning "Watch our for the shot!" For domestic meats, Faison and Daguin give farmers a chart of how to raise the animals: no antibiotics, no hormones, feed grown without pesticides, and clean water. They visit the farms to make sure their practices meet D'Artagnan's standards. Before starting any business with a farm, they have the meat analyzed to make sure it is free of chemicals. In addition, the smoked products contain no preservatives.

In 1990, chicken or turkey was $2.75 a pound; capon was $3.25 a pound; free-range pheasant from $6.50 to $7.50 a pound. Venison ran between $6.50 a pound for leg or shoulder to $19.95 a pound for boneless tenderloin. All products are shipped in insulated boxes. The company also has an extensive list of foie gras, terrines, and prepared entrées.

LONGHORN LEAN
RR I, Box 24
Lentner, MO 63450
(314) 588-2269

Visits: yes
Certified by: SELF
Catalogue/price list available
Minimum order: none
Order by: phone, mail
Pay by: MC, Visa, check, money order
Ship by: UPS
Gift boxes available

MEAT

Beef jerky · Summer sausage · Beef sticks · Ground beef

Longhorn Lean started with a wild bull chase. Rex Hollenbeck had bought several longhorn cattle as a hobby, and a neighbor who'd leased a bull from him called to say that the bull had gotten loose. He asked Hollenbeck to come and shoot the now-wild animal. Hollenbeck did, and then, out of curiosity, wanted to have the meat tested, to see how an animal living on its

own in the wild would compare to its domestic, grain-fed relatives. He called the nutrition department of the University of Missouri, his alma mater. The staff refused to test the meat, telling Hollenbeck it would look the same as any other beef. "They're not too big on organic," says Hollenbeck, "but then, that's not where their funds come from."

Hollenbeck was frustrated, but he was "bound and determined" to get that meat tested. He joined forces with a cardiologist in Joslin, Missouri, who also happened to raise longhorn cattle as a hobby. The two called around and found a lab in Chicago that would test the meat. Lo and behold, its cholesterol was less than half that of chicken—closer, in fact, to flounder than anything else. He also had the meat tested for fat levels, and discovered that it was lower in unsaturated fats than other beef. "The fat content labels of meat you buy in the supermarket are so far off, it's not even funny," says Hollenbeck, who's had that meat tested, too.

Hollenbeck had first seen longhorn cattle when he was in basic training during the Korean War; the cattle, considered an endangered national treasure, lived on a government wildlife refuge near his base. His own longhorns range freely on his farm, which hasn't seen chemicals since 1977. They are given no hormones or medication—longhorns are particularly hardy when it comes to parasites and diseases. They are descendants of animals brought to this country 500 years ago by the Spanish, which were soon roaming wild, giving them the resilience that make them valuable today.

Longhorn Lean sells hickory-smoked longhorn meat in various forms—plain beef jerky, barbecue-flavor jerky, Cowboy Cajun jerky, summer sausage, Hot-Hot jerky, spicy beef sticks—and they are available in a number of assortments. Fresh ground beef is also available frozen.

In 1990, sampler boxes ranged from $10.95 to $16.95. Ground beef was $2.29 a pound. Shipping additional.

MOUNTAIN SPRINGS
c/o Trophy Fish Ranch
3700 East Glenwood Road
Richfield, UT 84701
(800) 542-2303
(800) 542-2981 (in Iowa)

Certified by: SELF
Catalogue/price list available
Minimum order: 2 cans
Order by: phone, mail
Pay by: check, money order, MC, Visa
Ship by: UPS, parcel post

FISH

Smoked rainbow trout · Low-salt rainbow trout

If you're looking for a way to add more fish to your diet, but are concerned about the waters those fish come from, consider aquaculture—or fish farming, to the layperson. Fish farming may not seem sporting, but it actually gives the company almost complete control over the final product, which can't be said for fish caught in polluted waters. At Mountain Springs, for example, you can get rainbow trout hatched and reared in mountain spring water. The company monitors water quality, looking both for pesticides (from farm runoff) and the by-products pesticides create when they degrade. The water is tested at the parts-per-million level, and no contamination has ever been found.

The fish eat fresh-water shrimp, which gives their flesh a pink color in the late summer and early fall; they also eat some commercial (not organic) feed. The fish ranch is certified as disease-free by the Utah Division of Wildlife Resources, and no drugs are given to the fish themselves. Even so, because no certification standards exist for fish farming, David Young, president of Mountain Springs, says that he never uses the word "organic" in advertising. "Morally, we cannot call our fish 'organic'—we are not big, but we are honest."

The fish come to you skinned and filleted. I found both the smoked and the low-salt varieties juicy and tender. The low-salt made a delicious salad, sweeter than tunafish. The rich, lightly smoked trout has a more luxurious taste, not at all salty, delicious both straight out of the can and dipped in a hot horseradish sauce. As an added bonus, according to Mountain Springs, its trout are high in Omega-3 fatty acids, which "lower cholesterol levels, lower triglyceride levels, and slow the progression of atherosclerosis."

In 1990, a trial pack of 2 cans was $7.50, plus $1.50 for shipping. A case of 12 cans of low-salt fillets was $39, and 12 cans of smoked fillets were $44. Shipping was $4.

NORTH HOLLOW FARM
P.O. Box 218
Rochester, VT 05767
(800) 388-3597
(802) 767-3597
(802) 767-4255
FAX: (802) 767-3589

Visits: yes; farm stand in summer; other times by appointment only
Farmers' markets: Rutland, Wednesday afternoons; Norwich, Montpelier, and Burlington, Vermont, on Saturdays
Certified by: SELF
Catalogue/price list available
Minimum order: $25
Order by: phone, mail, fax
Pay by: check
Ship by: UPS
Gift packs of maple syrup, syrup and sausage, and half-hams available

MEAT

Chicken · Beef · Pork · Pork sausage

SWEETENER

Maple syrup

When Carroll Bowen bought North Hollow Farm in 1950, it hadn't been a working farm for years, and the Bowen family used it as a vacation home. Carroll Bowen bought his first few cows in 1974—mostly to keep the grass cut. Ten years later, he went into partnership with his son Mike to raise natural beef.

The beef cattle are Hereford, Hereford-Angus, and Hereford-Angus-Charolais, which make "lean, tender, and flavorful" meat, say the Bowens, with more protein than feed-lot beef —eighteen grams per three-ounce portion, compared with sixteen grams. The lower fat content means that the meat cooks faster than fattier beef, so you have to take care not to overcook it. The Bowens recommend searing the meat to maintain its moisture and flavor.

The cattle are fenced, but not confined. They eat feed raised on the farm, where the Bowens use no pesticides, insecticides, or weed killers.

They do use some commercial fertilizer as well as manure to raise the cereal grains. The animals' water comes from streams and springs. The cattle do not receive growth implants, antibiotics, or digestive stimulants. Medication is given only "when necessary for individual animal health, and never when on finishing feed."

The Bowens also sell pork, from Yorkshire-Landrace-Duroc breeding stock, fed no growth stimulants or antibiotics. They smoke the meat in traditional New England fashion—maple and corncob—without nitrites.

Valerie, Mike's wife, expanded the enterprise by raising free-range chickens while working full-time as a computer programmer. The Heavy White Cornish Hallcross chickens are given unmedicated grain after the first two weeks; they receive no medications or growth stimulants. During the day, the birds roam in a large fenced yard. At night, they share a split-level abode with a greenhouse (they get the first floor and the plants the second); the two support each other—chickens take in oxygen and give out carbon dioxide, and the plants, vice versa.

In 1990, chicken was $1.80 a pound, including shipping. Beef ranged from $2.95 to $8.95 per pound. Pork ranged from $1.95 to $3.99 per pound. Many sampler packages are available. Maple syrup was $10.99 for a pint, and less expensive in quantity. A gift pack of 2 1-pound packages of sausage and 1 quart of maple syrup was $19.99, including shipping Second Day Air.

OLD MILL FARM SCHOOL OF COUNTRY LIVING

P.O. Box 463
Mendocino, CA 95460
(707) 937-0244

Visits: yes; farm store in Mendocino; farm-visitation program; hikers' hut, family cabin, or getaway cabin; hay rides; farm-cooked meals; work-exchange rates available; readers of this book can receive a 25% discount, or will donate 25% of the cost to California Certified Organic Farmers, the Sierra Club, or the Ocean Sanctuary Coordinating Committee
Farmers' market: Mendocino, Saturdays
Certified by: CCOF
Catalogue/price list available
Minimum order: $50
Order by: phone, mail
Pay by: check
Ship by: UPS, parcel post
Apprenticeship program for 6-month stays available

MEAT

Lamb · Goat

GOAT CHEESE

Soft farmer's · Herbal pressed

Half an hour from the Pacific coast on a ridge 800 feet above sea level, the Old Mill Farm is a secluded, 100-year-old, 320-acre homestead. At the turn of the century, when a trip to the store in Mendocino was an all-day proposition, the farm was a family-owned lumber company and stock ranch. By the 1930s, the farm's inhabitants had opted for the conveniences of life in town—like electricity.

The farm and sawmill had been abandoned for twenty years when Chuck Hinsch bought it in 1974 and dedicated it to environmental education, which included turning forty of the farm's acres into a working organic farm. The Old Mill Farm School of Country Living, a nonprofit institution, is surrounded by 63,000 acres of Jackson State (Redwood) Forest, and is adjacent to the state-owned Mendocino

Woodlands environmental camp. "By car," says travel writer Robert Matson, "it takes forty minutes of slow driving on six miles of blacktop and on six miles of narrow gravel road that winds through a spectacular redwood forest" to reach the farm. "Most everybody, except senior citizens and nursery-school-age groups, is required to hike in."

At the Old Mill Farm, Chuck Hinsch and Eva Palm educate both children and adults about self-sufficiency and sustainable agricul-

ture. "Sustainable agriculture means voluntary simplicity and financial responsibility through self-sufficiency," says Hinsch, who teaches by example: the farm's water, electricity, hot water, and interior heat come from windmills, ram pumps, sun absorbers, and wood. Solar electricity replaced kerosene in 1987. (Draft horses, a former source of the farm's power, are still around to give hay rides.)

Children are central to the Old Mill Farm's mission. In the summer, groups of children camp out for two days and take classes in soap making, yogurt and cheese making, sheep shearing, spinning, dyeing wool, and woodworking. And if that's not enough, they get to eat ice cream made from the farm's own milk, berries, and eggs. Eva Palm, the farm's vegetable gardener, shakes her head at what "city-locked" children don't know. Sometimes, she says, they can't even name the vegetables in her garden—although it wouldn't really be fair to hold children accountable for the names of the Chinese vegetables she learned to grow on her family's farm in China's Suisun valley.

Both lambs and goats—for meat and cheese—are raised on the farm, without chemicals. The Robinson Crusoe Goat Dairy in Mendocino makes the sweet farmer's cheese and herbal pressed cheese from the milk of range-fed goats, whose diet is supplemented with organically grown sprouted grain and alfalfa hay.

In 1990, lamb and goat were sold by the half. Both were $4 a pound for a half-lamb or half-goat, including UPS air shipping. Cheese ranged from $10 to $15 a pound plus shipping. The farm also sells untreated colored wool, raw, carded, or handspun; quilt batting, hats, sweaters, scarves, and shawls.

RANCHO SAN JULIAN
Star Route
Lompoc, CA 93436
(805) 735-1535

Certified by: CCOF
Catalogue/price list available
Minimum order: $50
Order by: mail
Pay by: check with order, money order
Ship by: FedEx

MEAT

Beef (prime cuts available)

Jim Poett's family has been raising cattle at Rancho San Julian since 1837. The original land grant, says Poett, whose uncle has just written a history of the land, was given to a Spaniard who'd gone to Mexico in the late 1700s before heading north to California. He started raising cattle in the 1820s and left the land to four of his sons. "But they mortgaged it and lost it in the drought during the Civil War. In the 1870s, it was bought by a man who ended up marrying the daughter of one of the four sons. Her father was very involved in California's constitutional convention. One of the reasons California was a bilingual state until recently was because of that convention, and the compromises that were reached there."

The farm's organic history is almost as venerable. Jim Poett's uncle had read about raising cattle naturally back in the 1930s, and that's how the family has done it ever since. "I feel very strongly about the concept of integrated agriculture," says Poett. "Livestock, compost, and farming all go together."

ROSELAND FARMS
27427 M-60 West
Cassopolis, MI 49031
(616) 445-8769
(616) 445-8987

Visits: yes; farm market; meat and other organic foods
Certified by: OGM
Catalogue/price list available
Minimum order: none
Order by: phone, mail
Pay by: check, Visa, MC, food stamps
Ship by: UPS, Air Express
Gift packs available

MEAT

Beef (all cuts available, but Roseland Farms does not raise veal calves) · Chicken (whole roasters) · Turkey (whole) · Pork (chops, steaks, ground)

JUICE

Frozen wild apple (available in midwinter)

In the early 1970s, John Clark predicted that pesticides would soon turn up in groundwater. The prescient third-generation farmer refused to use chemicals, even when neighbors told him his 1,800-acre farm would soon be overrun with weeds. The land had been farmed chemically in the past, but Clark went "cold turkey," deciding to look at his farming career as "an ongoing experiment, mixing modern equipment and genetics with the good farming practices I had watched my grandfather and father use."

John Clark speaks as a scientist as well as a farmer. He has a PhD in biochemistry from Berkeley, has worked as a research scientist, and was on the chemistry faculty at Notre

Dame. You might think that his background would make him an enthusiastic supporter of chemical use, but Clark flatly rejects "scientific" models that reduce the hundreds of variables in farming to a single chemical solution. The "favorite ploy" of the pesticide industry, says Clark, is to leave one tree in a chemically farmed orchard unsprayed, and then photograph the results—a home for all the pests the chemicals had driven off the other trees. This picture, says Clark, has nothing to do with an orchard or field whose natural balances have been restored.

Clark knows first-hand that it takes time to achieve that balance. In his first year of farming, a cutworm invasion claimed all his soybeans. The county agricultural agent told him

he had two options: spray, or wait and replant. His neighbor chose to spray and had worms for the next four years. Clark replanted and never saw the worms again.

Merrill Clark, John's wife and the co-owner of Roseland Farms, is a leader of national and local campaigns against pesticide use, and John Clark used to serve on the Pesticide Advisory Committee of the Michigan Department of Agriculture—the only organic farmer on the committee—but his tenure was not renewed. As reported in the *Detroit News,* an acting director of the Department said that "we felt we needed to broaden the perspective of the committee, and the fact that we didn't reappoint Mr. Clark had nothing to do with organic farming." His replacement is a farmer who uses pesticides.

The Clarks' cattle are born on their own organic farm, nurse on their mothers for nine to twelve months, then eat feed the Clarks grow organically, with no antibiotics or hormones added. Their water comes from the farm's

ponds and wells. All of their beef is less than 13 percent fat. The Clarks also sell chicken, turkey, and pork raised organically at Welsh Family Farm in Iowa (see "Buying Clubs" section, page 291), and can cure bacon, spare ribs, or hams if you give them notice. The apple juice they sell comes from wild apple trees on the farm. These are "antique" apples—varieties that are no longer cultivated on a large scale.

In 1990, apple juice was $4 for a half-gallon. Beef ranged from $4.09 a pound for Swiss steak to $11.69 a pound for filet mignon. Ground meat ranged from $3.29 a pound to $6.99 a pound. Roasts ranged from $3.79 to $5.99 a pound. Gift packs were available for $20 or $40. You can also order beef by the quarter or the half. Whole roaster chickens were $2.19 a pound; turkeys were $1.89 a pound. A 10% discount for orders above 100 pounds, and 20% over 200 pounds. Shipping with dry ice additional.

WOLFE'S NECK FARM
2 Burnett Road
Freeport, ME 04032
(800) 346-9540
(207) 865-4469

Visits: yes; Recompence Shore Campground is open to the public
Certified by: MOFGA
Catalogue/price list available
Minimum order: none
Order by: phone, mail
Pay by: check
Ship by: UPS, air shipment, own truck

MEAT

Beef · Lamb

If you've ever driven through Freeport, Maine, you know that it's the outlet capital of the Northeast, not to mention the seat of the L.L. Bean empire. It's also home to Wolfe's Neck Farm, a 600-acre saltwater farm on the shores of Casco Bay. The farm has been in operation for over a century, and has produced organically raised beef since 1959.

Mr. and Mrs. Lawrence M. C. Smith started using "ecologically sound agricultural methods" in 1957, "long before the danger of doing otherwise became widely apparent," say the folks at Wolfe's Neck Farm. In the late 1950s, the Smiths went to court to stop public utilities from spraying power lines with pesticides, and won their case. After Mr. Smith's death, Mrs. Smith continued to fight to preserve the area down to the dirt roads, because, she says, what's childhood without a dirt road to walk on?

In 1985, the farm was given to the University of Southern Maine as a demonstration alternative farm and center for ecological studies. The farm's records, which document "both the problems and advantages of alternative farming," are organized to make information easily available to other farmers.

The farm's Angus cattle are pastured on clover and grasses, where there are no pesticides or chemically refined fertilizers. In the winter, the cattle are fed clover, grass, hay, wheat, and

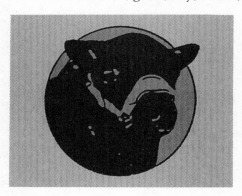

corn. Any purchased feed is tested for pesticide residues. In general, the farm's manager, Charles DeGrandpre, doesn't like to feed the cattle too much grain, in order to keep the meat lean. Although Angus cattle have a reputation for orneriness, Wolfe's Neck Farm's Angus are pretty docile, and DeGrandpre is pretty sure it's due to their healthy diet.

The cattle are given no medication in their feed; the only preventative Wolfe's Neck regularly uses is iodine, applied to the newborns' navels and to ears when they are tagged. The medical bills for the farm have been remarkably low: in some years, as little as 100 dollars for 300 head of cattle. The lamb for sale is raised organically at nearby farms.

The beef is aged ten to fourteen days in the hanging cooler before processing. Steaks are cut one inch to one-and-a-half-inches thick and trimmed of waste. Roasts are three to five pounds and trimmed of waste and boned, unless you want bones for cooking. The ground beef is double ground, and is 18 percent fat or less to make lean ground beef. All meat is flash frozen immediately after wrapping. All meat is USDA inspected.

Beef is available in a number of combination packages, or as ground beef or stew beef. In 1990, ground beef was available in 5 pounds for $12, and less expensive in quantity. Five pounds of stew beef were $13, and 5 packages of ground-beef patties were $13.50. Whole lamb was $3.25 per pound or $3.89 per pound for legs. Many combination and sampler packages are available. Shipping additional. The farm makes monthly deliveries in southern New Hampshire, Massachusetts, Rhode Island, and Connecticut. To other states, it will ship by air.

LATE-BREAKING INFORMATION

FOUR DIRECTIONS FARM
2690 O Road
Hotchkiss, CO 81419
(303) 835-3658

Farm certified by: state of Colorado
Catalogue/price list available in future
Minimum order: $25
Pay by: check, money order
Ship by: UPS, USPS First Class Mail

MEAT

Smoked pheasant · Frozen pheasant

The pheasants don't range freely—pheasants can fly—but they are fed only feed grown on this certified organic farm.

GREAT BEND ORGANIC FARM
P.O. Box 158
Port Clinton, PA 19549
(215) 562-5502

Farm and processing certified by: OCIA
Catalogue/price list available
Minimum order: $50
Pay by: 10% down at time of order; 15 days
remainder
Ship by: UPS

MEAT

Pork · Lamb · Poultry

Great Bend sells smoked ham and bacon without nitrates; as well as sausages containing only its own organic meat and herbs, with no MSG or casing agents.

SEE ALSO
Natural Beef Farms, Ojibwe Foods,
Organic Valley, Silver Creek Farm,
Welsh Family Farm

BLUE HERON FARM
P.O. Box 68
Rumsey, CA 95679
(916) 796-3799

Visits: yes
Farmers' markets: Marin County Farmers'
Market in San Rafael, not regularly
Certified by: CCOF
Minimum order: 5 pounds of nuts/1 box of
fruit
Order by: phone, mail
Pay by: check, money order
Ship by: UPS

NUTS

Nonpareil almonds (mid-September) · Ne Plus
almonds (mid-September) · Peerless almonds
(mid-September) · Mission almonds (mid-
October) · Hartley walnuts (late October)

FRUIT

Washington navel oranges (January–March)

John and Gretchen Ceteras do most of the
work on their small family farm by hand. The
almond harvest begins in the first week in August, and the nuts have to be "knocked, dried,
hulled, cracked, sorted, and boxed." All these
tasks take time, so the almonds aren't ready to
ship until mid-September. Between sorting and
shipping, the almonds are in cold storage to
assure freshness. "We don't freeze them, as this

BLUE
HERON
FARM

has a tendency to change the texture and flavor." Mission almonds are harvested later and
are available by mid-October; walnuts become
available at the end of October.

Even though the almonds' names—Nonpareil, Ne Plus, and Peerless—all seem to be competing for the same territory, the almonds do
differ in flavor, say the Ceterases. Gretchen
Ceteras recommends Nonpareil as the most attractive "and probably the sweetest" eating almond; the Ne Plus "are great for blanching";
the Peerless are "common in the shell at Christmas"; and the Mission are "a bit oilier, with
definite almond flavor, best for cooking and
sought out by gourmet cooks." Unless you
specify otherwise, you will be shipped Nonpareils.

The 1990 orange crop was "delicious," says
Gretchen Ceteras—it was sold out by the time
I got to them—"many of our mail-order cus-
tomers are on their third box."

In 1990, oranges were 49 cents a pound, plus shipping,
and a box tends to run to 35 pounds. A 5-pound box of
nuts was $24, including shipping.

CAPAY CANYON RANCH
P.O. Box 508
Esparto, CA 95627
(916) 662-2372
FAX: (916) 662-2306

Visits: yes; 4 kinds of almonds; walnuts, table
grapes
Farmers' markets: Davis and Sacramento
Certified by: FVO
Minimum order: none
Order by: phone, mail, fax
Pay by: check
Ship by: UPS, parcel post

NUTS

Nonpareil shelled almonds

Many of the almond trees at Capay Canyon ranch are over 100 years old. Until 1978, the orchard was cultivated with chemicals, but when Stan Barth and his wife, Leslie, took over, they decided that with 100-year-old trees, they simply couldn't make a go of the orchard financially if they had to spend money on chemicals, so they went organic. To add to their income, Stan Barth, who "likes being involved with machinery," according to Leslie, added a sheller to the orchard, and the couple started doing their own processing and distribution.

Even though the Barths are in the process of adding new trees to the orchard, organic growing is "part of our life now," says Leslie Barth. The new trees will be cultivated organically alongside the old. The Barths' nonpareils, says Leslie, are a large, light-colored flat almond, not a strong-flavored almond, but "the sweetest almond on the market."

In 1990, nonpareils were $2.70 a pound, plus shipping.

CHESTNUT HILL ORCHARDS
Route 1, Box 341
Alachua, FL 32615
(904) 462-2820
(512) 327-4107
FAX: (904) 462-4330

Certified by: affidavit
Certification pending from: Agricoltura Biologica
Catalogue/price list available
Minimum order: 1 kilo
Order by: phone, mail
Pay by: Amex, Visa, MC, check
Ship by: UPS Next Day Air
Recipes available

NUTS

Steam-peeled chestnuts

FLOUR

Chestnut

SWEETENERS

Wild chestnut honey

PRESERVES

Candied chestnuts · Chestnut jam · Chestnut-honey spread

When you bite into one of Chestnut Hill Orchard's sweet, steam-peeled Italian chestnuts, you may be tasting the fruit of a *very* old chestnut: a tree planted by the Romans, 2,000 years ago.

Sadly, all the "old chestnuts" on this side of the Atlantic had disappeared by World War II, victims of a blight first noticed in 1903 at the Brooklyn Botanical Garden. By the mid-1930s, the blight had reached the Blue Ridge Mountains and the Great Smokies, and was disastrous for the people of the Appalachians who had relied on chestnuts for food during the Depression.

Chestnut Hill Orchard is an outgrowth of Chestnut Hill Nursery, which is trying to repopulate the country with chestnut trees. Both are the brainchildren of Bob Wallace and Rick Queen, who met in a chemistry lab as students at the University of Florida. Queen, a student of sustainable agriculture, was fascinated by chestnuts because the "long-lived wonderful trees can grow in distressed soil and produce high-quality food; you can plant them on the side of a mountain and get the equivalent of a grain without having to plow up soil all the time for wheat or corn." Wallace's family history had been intertwined with chestnuts for centuries: one of his ancestors, says Queen, was an archbishop of Canterbury who insisted that the plague was caused not by vapors in the air but by uncleanliness and organisms. For this heresy, he was roasted at the stake—over a chestnut-wood fire.

In the 1950s, a closer relative, Bob Wallace's grandfather, Robert Dunstan, was sent two chestnut cuttings by a friend who'd stumbled across a surviving unblighted chestnut tree in a

CHESTNUTS

forest. He'd taken twelve cuttings, sending two each to six friends. Dunstan's were the only ones to take. The friend returned to the forest to get more, only to discover that the tree had been logged for timber. So Robert Dunstan, a professor of Romance Languages at the University of North Carolina, a man who "spoke nine languages and read fourteen," says Queen, worked with the cuttings he had, crossing and back-crossing to develop a blight-resistant chestnut tree.

After college, Queen and Wallace began working with Dunstan and traveled to Asia and Europe to study grafting techniques. While in Europe in 1987, they kept hearing about an Italian company that was producing "a wonderful chestnut," says Queen. They went to Italy and discovered that the company had developed a way of peeling the nuts with steam.

The steam-peeled chestnuts are immediately flash-frozen, shipped with blue ice. They should be stored frozen and can be thawed quickly in a microwave, if you're so inclined. As one grateful woman told Queen at a recent food show, "I remember having to peel twenty pounds of chestnuts for the turkey stuffing. You've taken the blood and guts out of chestnuts." You can roast the thawed nuts in the oven, make cream of chestnut soup or chestnut stuffing, put them in a stir-fry, or add them to pasta. You can also puree, spice, or sweeten them for dessert.

Using Chestnut Hill's recipes, I used one kilo of chestnuts to make enough rich, intoxicating cream of chestnut soup for ten people; enough sweet and savory chestnut–wild rice stuffing for a very large turkey (twenty-three pounds) and a large casserole besides. And I still had enough left over to roast for appetizers. My favorite of all these dishes were the firm, small, sweet nuts all by themselves.

The folks at Chestnut Hill Orchards sell chestnuts for health as well as convenience. They compare the nuts' nutritional value to wheat and brown rice, and say that you can substitute chestnuts for almost any grain. The nuts are also very low in sodium—one one-hundredth of the amount in brown rice. And, while other nuts, like almonds, are up to 50 percent fat, chestnuts are very low in fat—2 to 3 percent—and high in carbohydrates. Frances Moore Lappé, author of *Diet for a Small Planet*, gives chestnuts even higher marks than eggs for their content of a number of amino acids.

Chestnut Hill Orchards also sells chestnut flour. Most people, says Queen, mix the flour one-fourth to one-third with regular flour, but people who are allergic to wheat or gluten use it "straight up." Because the flour has no gluten, the result is a pretty dense bread. Chestnut jam is their newest product, sweetened with honey, using a reduced-pressure system to be able to pasteurize the nuts at sixty degrees centigrade so they retain their valuable enzymes and vitamins.

The chestnuts are certified by an Italian affiliate of Farm Verified Organic. They are not fumigated when imported, and have been tested in the laboratory to make sure that they were free of radiation (after Chernobyl).

In 1990, a kilo of steam-peeled chestnuts was $39.95, including shipping Next Day Air with blue ice.

EARL HIATT ENTERPRISES
13507 Quince Avenue
Patterson, CA 95363
(209) 892-8170

Certified by: CCOF
Minimum order: none
Order by: phone, mail
Pay by: check
Ship by: UPS, parcel post

NUTS

Walnuts (in shell or meats)

Earl Hiatt's five-acre walnut orchard stands next to the "old home place where I was born," says Hiatt. Hiatt's family had almonds even before planting the walnut trees, which are some twenty-five years old. Hiatt, who received certification in 1987, says that "organic was not a new item to me. I'd seen one of the first issues of *Prevention* magazine, and can remember hauling in organic stuff to put on the ground in the late forties or early fifties." When he decided to get certification, Hiatt made the few remaining changes necessary, like trading in herbicide and flame-burning the weeds around his trees instead. In 1990, he began shipping walnuts in the shell to Europe, the first whole organic walnuts from this country to be sold overseas.

In 1990, walnuts were approximately $2.50 a pound, plus shipping.

JARDINE ORGANIC RANCH
910 Nacimiento Lake Drive
Paso Robles, CA 93446
(805) 238-2365
FAX: (805) 239-4334

Visits: yes
Certified by: FVO
Minimum order: half-pound of nuts/1 case of almond butter
Order by: phone, mail
Pay by: check
Ship by: UPS

NUTS

Almonds · Pistachios · Walnuts

NUT BUTTER

Almond

"In its heyday, around 1945, before irrigation brought water into the Central Valley, this area was the almond capital of the world," says Duane Jardine, the fifth generation of his family to grow almonds at the Jardine Organic Ranch,

a family homestead for over 100 years. For now, his parents are still the farmers. "Someday they'll let me farm—maybe," says Jardine. In the meantime, he takes his job of marketing the almonds seriously. "We have the best-tasting almonds in the world. We've got customers in Europe and Japan who keep saying ours are the best. Even the Department of Agriculture inspectors say so."

In addition to their own almonds, pistachios, and walnuts, the Jardines buy nuts from over seventy orchards, all certified by Farm Verified Organic.

In 1990, almonds were $2.80 a pound, pistachios in shell were $4.75 a pound, and walnuts were $3.50 a pound. A case of 24 4-ounce jars of almond butter was $34.50. Shipping additional.

LIVING TREE CENTRE
P.O. Box 10082
Berkeley, CA 94709-5082
(415) 528-4467
(415) 420-1440

Visits: yes; no sales on site, but tastings of historic apple varieties
Certified by: CCOF
Catalogue/price list available
Minimum order: none
Order by: phone, mail
Pay by: check
Ship by: UPS

NUTS

Shelled almonds · Pistachios

NUT BUTTER

Almond

Dr. Jesse Schwartz, a former professor of economics, has a new career: "chief propagator" of the Living Tree Centre, which specializes in "antique" apple varieties. At the turn of the century, says Dr. Schwartz, one botanical listing named 878 different kinds of apples in this country. Today, you find three or four varieties in every supermarket—the ones that are easy to store and ship—and that's about it. Schwartz set out to remedy this situation. He began in his backyard, with scions of rare varieties from twelve different countries, and continues to search out endangered apples from around the world. Today, his catalogue contains more than sixty varieties of antique apple trees.

At Living Tree Centre, planting trees is not just a business—it's a spiritual mission. Alongside a map that compares the amount of virgin

forest in North America in 1620, in 1850, and in 1990, Schwartz observes that "the United States has done throughout its history what a righteous world denounces Brazil for doing today." Schwartz's tree-planting prayer goes like this: "I plant this tree by way of saying that I assume responsibility as a co-creator for this North American earth. I assume responsibility for the forests devastated by acid rain, for turning the Great Lakes into one 750-mile wide industrial sewer, for leaking nuclear power plants and the hole in the ozone layer. I dedicate myself to resurrecting the North American earth. As I am cultivating the secret garden of my soul so am I re-creating this earth. With this I plant a tree."

You may have sensed by now that the folks at Living Tree Centre are not your everyday apple growers. The catalogue, if you turn it over and upside down (sort of like playing the

Beatles backward), becomes a journal, with articles on such topics as "The Spiral Flame: A Study in the Meaning of D.H. Lawrence," "Effects of Orgonotic Devices on Tomato Plant Growth," and "Letting Go of Frozen History: An Orientation to Psycho-Orthopaedics."

All apples are plant-your-own; you can, however, order almonds and almond butter (from the apple's relative), and pistachios. The almonds are shelled and frozen immediately after harvest to preserve freshness. I can't say what effect the orgone boxes had, but the almonds I sampled were large, fresh, and sweet, and a big hit with a three-year-old friend who kept appearing at my side, hand out, saying, "Another almond." On her next visit, several weeks later, she went straight to the pantry to look for them.

In 1990, 8 pounds of almonds were $32. Almond butter was $15 for 3 pounds. Pistachios were 4 pounds for $20. You save by buying larger quantities. Shipping and handling adds 20% to your order. At holiday time, there is usually a discount on orders. A wide variety of fruit trees and plants are available for growers.

MIDWESTERN PECAN COMPANY
One Pecan Plaza
Nevada, MO 64772
(800) 433-NUTS
(800) 492-NUTS

Certified by: SELF
Catalogue/price list available
Minimum order: none
Order by: phone, mail
Pay by: check, money order, Visa, MC
Ship by: UPS
Gift boxes available

NUTS

Pecans halves · Pecan pieces · Pecan logs

Jim Bell and his wife, Camille, still live in the house his family built in 1909 when they moved to Missouri from Tennessee and started their pecan business. While the pecans are not

Midwestern Pecan Company inc.

certified organic, Bell says he has a letter from the state that says he is an organic grower. "I am not an organic person," says Bell, "but I don't spray and I don't use fertilizer because I don't have to. The Almighty was good to us when he put the trees here. The only place pecans grow this far north are in river bottoms that flood, and every time they flood, we get a rich silt fertilizer. Our winters are cold enough and severe enough that we don't have to spray; the cold takes care of any insect problems. The chemicals are just too expensive to use if you don't have to. Most pecan growers in the state started to use insecticides a few years ago, but I didn't, and I'm not going to start."

In Missouri, says Jim Bell, organic growers are looked at as "screwballs," and you won't find the word "organic" anywhere in Bell's catalogue. The ones Bell grows without chemicals are the Missouri Natives, which are larger, more flavorful, and contain more oil than the Papershell pecans, which he also sells but does not grow. All pecans are available plain or roasted and salted. By state law, the pecans are sterilized in a chlorine solution for a matter of seconds before they are cracked open, but this solution doesn't come into contact with the nut meats.

In 1990, 3 pounds of pecan halves were $17.70, or roasted and salted for $19.95. Shipping additional. The catalogue also lists many other nuts, but they are not grown by Bell, and are not necessarily organic.

ORION ORGANIC ORCHARDS
3220 Oak Way
Chico, CA 95926
(916) 345-8743

Visits: yes; apples, peaches, cherries, pears, tomatoes, basil, marjoram, and pepper
Farmers' market: Gold Country Market in Chico, Wednesday and Saturday mornings
Certified by: CCOF
Certification pending from: OCIA
Minimum order: none
Order by: phone, mail
Pay by: check
Ship by: UPS
Availability of varieties changes from year to year

NUTS

Nonpareil almonds · Hard-shell almonds · California mix (hard- and soft-shell almonds)

David Schell has an unlikely background for an organic farmer: a degree in chemistry from the University of California at Davis. Back in

1985, Schell was a believer, and a partner in an almond orchard that used chemicals. Schell admits that he got into organic farming "by default." Financial necessity, rather than conviction, changed his mind.

When Schell and his wife, Kathy Dailey, a financial analyst, bought their own farm, it was simply too costly for them to continue to farm chemically. Schell moved from pesticides to predators like the praying mantis and the ladybug, and today, Schell speaks with the faith of a convert, calling his former chemical use "a crime."

Schell credits his farm's rich soil with part of his success—he used to joke that you could even drop an H-bomb on it and get a good crop. Even so, the transition has been something of a struggle. His yields are still less than half of what chemical farmers are getting. What makes up for the difference is the price customers are willing to pay for organic produce— *more* than double what his chemical competition gets, and demand still exceeds supply. One reason for that demand, I'm willing to bet, is the taste—the California mix Schell sent me was truly addictive, almonds so flavorful and sweet that you'd barely need sugar to turn them into marzipan.

In 1990, nonpareils were $2.75 a pound, California mix was $2.65 a pound, and hard-shell mix was $2.60 a pound. Shipping additional.

PUEBLO TO PEOPLE
1616 Montrose Blvd.
Houston, TX 77006
(800) 843-5257
(713) 523-1197
FAX: (713) 523-1614

Visits: yes
Certified by: SELF
Catalogue/price list available
Minimum order: none
Order by: phone, mail, fax
Pay by: check, Visa, MC, Amex, Discover
Ship by: UPS

NUTS

Cashews (whole or pieces)

Pueblo to People is a nonprofit organization whose goal is to raise the living standards of small-scale producers of food and crafts in Latin America. Its founders, Marijke Velzeboer and Dan Salcedo, met at the University of Texas and worked together in Guatemala City as consultants for the Institute of Nutrition for Central America and Panama. That experience convinced them that traditional approaches to nutrition were inadequate; it didn't do any good to tell people to change their eating habits if they had no land and no money to grow new crops. But was there a way to get them more money?

While working in the Guatemalan highlands, Salcedo saw the hats made by the Maya Quiche Indians. In spite of the elaborate craftsmanship that went into the hats, the Indians got paid next to nothing. Salcedo and Velzeboer began selling the hats at the Common Market in Houston during their vacations, and Pueblo to People was born.

Since 1979, Pueblo to People has paid over four million dollars to producers of food and crafts in Latin America, over one million of that in 1989 alone. Out of every dollar in sales, forty to forty-five cents goes to the producers, and the rest goes toward operating expenses.

PUEBLO TO PEOPLE
A NON-PROFIT ORGANIZATION

Pueblo to People's cashews are grown in the Choluteca province, one of the poorest areas of Honduras, the second poorest country in the Americas. The lumber industry had completely deforested Choluteca, which led to serious erosion, with alternating floods and droughts. "The ground was just washing away and becoming like a desert," says Pueblo to People's Tracy Cramer. But cashew trees do well in poor soil and dry climates, and in 1977, at the instigation of the government, the local *campesinos* began buying and planting trees. The cashews grew "like weeds," says Cramer. "They are retaining and reinvigorating the soil."

The only problem was that the government had promised the *campesinos* a processing plant and never delivered, leaving them with mounting debts and no way to pay them. In 1981, they came to Pueblo to People. Several organizations gave technical support and funding— Peace Corps volunteers gave administrative help—and the *campesinos,* organized into 100 cashew-growing cooperatives—ninety-three to grow cashews and seven to process them—

generated jobs for more than 1,500 families. The cooperatives have also used their new-found income to create schools and health-care centers.

The cashew growers are organic by default, having no money for chemical inputs. The cashews are not currently certified organic, but Pueblo to People is working with Equal Exchange (page 254) to get them certified.

In 1990, a pound of whole cashews was $7, and a pound of pieces was $5. You save by buying in larger quantities. Shipping additional. Pueblo to People also sells coffee from Equal Exchange.

RANCHO SHANGRILA
9340 Ojai-Santa Paula Rd.
Ojai, CA 93023
(805) 646-1392

Visits: yes
Farmers' markets: Santa Monica, Wednesdays; Santa Barbara, Saturdays; Torrance, Tuesdays
Certified by: CCOF
Minimum order: none
Order by: phone, mail
Pay by: check, money order, COD
Ship by: UPS, parcel post

NUTS

Walnuts (whole or shelled)

Betty and Don DeBusschere bought their farm "cold turkey" in 1976, says Don. In their former lives, both DeBusscheres were teachers. Betty taught primary school, and Don taught metal shop and wood shop, skills he used to build their home, which just happens to incorporate an airplane hangar, since he and his son, Glen, also build and fly ultra-light aircraft.

The DeBusscheres raise "walnuts, weeds, and kids." They have three children and about 880 walnut trees: "Gloria, Rebecca, Frances, Mary. . . " Do they name all the trees after friends? "With that many trees, you're not picky," says Don. "You start naming them after your enemies, too."

As growers, the DeBusscheres follow "nature's own methods," says Don, who describes his wife as a "dyed-in-the-wool conservationist." Commercial nut growers, he explains, often use a chemical defoliant to soften the stems so the nuts will drop more quickly. At Rancho ShangriLa, the walnuts ripen on the tree. "The flavor changes depending on how much sun they get. The more sun, the more dehydrated they get on the tree, and the more flavor the nut has. The nuts can go from very light to amber to black. It's akin to roasted peanuts compared to raw—this is Mother Nature's

way of roasting the nuts in the shell. A lot of people look at a dark nut and say, 'Ugh, they're awful!' because people have been brainwashed into thinking they're not very good unless they're very light." In fact, says DeBusschere, commercial nuts can be bleached to suit this "brainwashed" taste. Commercial growers also routinely fumigate their nuts in storage. The DeBusscheres don't. Instead, they crack and shell the nuts in small batches so that the nuts don't sit around absorbing air and moisture before they're ready to package.

The trees are mostly Paynes and Eurekas—the Eurekas have the stronger flavor. Walnuts are high in protein, says DeBusschere, and they also reduce cholesterol in your diet, according to the Walnut Board. Like soybeans, walnuts can take on the flavor of meat. Debusschere recommends taking a small amount of meat and mixing it with walnuts—as much as three-quarter walnuts to one-quarter meat. The nuts take on the grain and texture and flavor of the meat—"You really don't know how much walnut is in there."

In 1990, walnuts were $3.75 a pound shelled and 3 pounds for $4 whole. Shipping additional.

LATE-BREAKING INFORMATION

NORTH VALLEY PRODUCE
P.O. Box 3527
Chico, CA 95927
(916) 345-8136
(916) 896-0606

Certified by: various
Catalogue/price list available
Minimum order: none
Pay by: COD
Ship by: UPS

NUTS

Walnuts · Pecans · Almonds · Pistachios

North Valley also sells a variety of dried fruits, and is considering shipping fresh mandarin oranges, figs, and persimmons.

SEE ALSO
Allergy Resources, American Spoon
Foods, Covalda Date Company, Eagle
Organic and Natural Food, Fitzpatrick
Winery, Lone Pine Farm, Minnesota
Specialty Crops, Noah's Ark, Specialty
Organic Source, Star Valley Farm, Yerba
Santa Goat Dairy/Poe Orchard

BLESSED MAINE HERB COMPANY
Box 4074
Chapman Ridge
West Athens, ME 04912
(207) 654-3994

Visits: farmstand in summers only
Farm certified by: MOFGA
Catalogue/price list available
Minimum order: none
Order by: phone, mail
Pay by: check, money order
Ship by: UPS

OIL AND VINEGAR

Elixir for a Long and Happy Life · Uncle Joe's hot oil

TEAS

Dancing Goddess (comfrey leaves, nettles, red clover blossoms, peppermint) · Balance and Well Being (wild red raspberry leaves, red clover blossoms, oatstraw, peppermint) · Brave and Free Amazon Tea (wild grape leaves, wild red raspberry leaves, red clover blossoms, peppermint) · Azure Heaven (borage leaves and flowers, lemon balm, oatstraw, rose hips) · Peaceful Child (chamomile, catnip, oatstraw, peppermint) · Blood Time (motherwort, ladies mantle, chamomile, peppermint) · Galatea's Brew (borage, fennel seed, oatstraw) · Breathe Deep (comfrey leaves, horehound, coltsfoot, mullein, peppermint) · Aunt Laura's cold cure (elder flowers, vervain, yarrow, rose hips, peppermint) · Beautiful Hair Strong Bones (comfrey leaves, nettles, horsetail, oatstraw) · Good Night (skullcap, lemon balm, chamomile, peppermint)

Gail Edwards's earliest memories of plants come from her grandparents, Italian immigrants in Hoboken, New Jersey. Hoboken may conjure up an industrial image, but Edwards remembers the feeling in her grandparents' small, backyard garden, full of vegetables and flowers, as peaceful and loving. Years later, Edwards read *Stalking the Wild Asparagus* and became fascinated by natural foods. Twenty years ago, around the time she moved to Maine, Edwards started making herbal teas for friends and family, who encouraged her to turn herbs into a business, which she did, with advice from the Women's Business Development Corporation, a private Maine foundation.

Blessed Maine **Herb Company**
West Athens · *Maine 04912*
Certified organic & wildgathered

All Blessed Maine's herbs are certified organic or gathered in the wild by Edwards and her children. In her own garden, Edwards visits her herbs as they grow, and is often sorry to have to harvest them. Elixir for a Long and Happy Life combines organic apple cider vinegar with fresh spring and summer herbs and dandelion leaves; the hot oil is a mixture of a cayenne and organic olive oil. "Watch out," says Edwards. "It's *hot.*"

In 1990, a 2.5-ounce bag of tea was $4.50. A 5-ounce bottle of vinegar and herbs or hot oil was $4.50. The catalogue also lists a line of herb teas, medicinal herbs, extracts, formulas, infused oils (including organic baby oil), salves, body care products, sachets, and smudge sticks.

DACH RANCH
P.O. Box 44
Philo, CA 95466
(707) 895-3173

Certified by: CCOF
Catalogue/price list available
Minimum order: none
Order by: phone, mail
Pay by: check
Ship by: UPS, parcel post

VINEGAR

Apple cider · Raspberry apple cider

While still in college, John Dach taught a course on wine- and beer-making that drew an enrollment of 180. As a junior, Dach convinced two wineries to fund him to conduct a year-long marketing study on the impact of their labels.

John Dach left college with a B.S. in marketing, took a job at a Jesuit winery, and started making wine on his own with two friends in an adobe horse barn on the property. Then Dach's parents bought land in the Anderson valley with plans of retiring there—on the condition that Dach move up and manage the apple orchard. "I said, 'Sure.' I didn't know *anything* about apples."

Dach had always grown grapes organically, but he called one of the chemical companies and made an appointment. "They sent a field

representative out here for a half-day appointment, and before I knew it, he had covered four legal-size pages with my spray schedule for the season. I thought to myself, 'I'm going to be *living* on that stuff.' My parents called the Department of Agriculture and Extension Service, and they just laughed. 'There's no way to grow apples organically,' they said. That really pushed my buttons. So I talked to someone who was doing Integrated Pest Management, which seemed much more sane and sensible. The first year we did five acres of apples organically and the rest with a very restrictive IPM program. We were really shooting from the hip —there was no one to ask."

Since 1977, Dach has grown all his apples organically, using some of his old skills to turn them into cider and cider vinegar. For cooks, Dach also sells Dach Ranch JAMIT, a low/no sugar pectin for jams and jellies, so you can make jam and jelly without adding sugar. By 1991, Dach hopes to be selling food grown by other organic producers through mail order. Contact him to find out if the catalogue is available.

FLORA, INC.
P.O. Box 950
Lynden, WA 98264
(800) 446-2110
(206) 354-2110
FAX: (206) 354-5355

Ingredients certified by: OCIA, OGBA, FVO, COPMC
Catalogue/price list available
Minimum order: none
Order by: phone, mail, fax
Pay by: check, COD
Ship by: UPS

OILS

Flax · Sunflower · Canola · Peanut · Sesame · Pumpkin seed · Safflower · Olive

JUICE

Elderberry

Thomas Greither takes his inspiration from the days before large-scale oil processing, when oil was fresh, perishable, and locally produced. In Germany, he says, corner oil mills turned flax seed into fresh flax oil, and the oilman, like the milkman, made weekly deliveries. Even though Flora sells on a national scale, Greither says he'd like to see the return of the small, local press. Greither's own first venture into fresh-pressed oil was in his health-food store, using a German press designed for home use.

The heart of Flora's line is flax oil—made from the same plant that gives us linen. Flax oil happens to be very high in omega-3s, a type of fatty acid that has almost disappeared from the typical Western diet. Back in the 1950s, the biochemist Dr. Johanna Budwig studied the connection between a diet low in omega-3s and atherosclerosis, arthritis, and cancer.

While oil from an olive is relatively easy to produce at low temperatures, seed-based oils like flax are much more difficult to extract, and often use chemicals or heat. The typical commercial process of making a seed-based oil can raise its temperature to 470 degrees. But heat destroys omega-3 fatty acids, so cold-processing is important to preserve what Flora calls the "nutritional gold."

After four years of experimentation, Greither developed a process to produce oils at temperatures under 85 degrees—anything below ninety-five degrees is considered "cold-pressing"—and in the absence of light and oxygen, which, like heat, can spoil the oil. Bottles of dark amber glass further protect the oils. The date of pressing is on the label. The flax oil is extremely perishable—Flora recommends using it within three weeks after opening, but

it can be frozen. Because the nutritional value of these oils depends on keeping them at low temperatures, they are not ideal cooking oils, but better for salads and other cold foods.

In 1988, *East West* magazine awarded Flora its "Best" in the category of specialty oils: "Freshness and flavor that is beyond compare." One *East West* writer called the oils "the best of the best," and said that "one taste and you'll realize you've never tasted truly fresh and cold-pressed oil before." To me, the safflower had a slightly cottony taste—you'd probably want to mix it with another flavor rather than use it alone on a salad. The flax oil had a nutty flavor, but a slightly bitter edge. The peanut and sunflower oils were delicate, yet only hinted at peanuts and sunflowers; the sesame oil had a darker taste, like toasted sesame seeds. The

canola had an oriental flavor I couldn't identify, reminiscent of incense and bamboo shoots, and the olive was, surprisingly, almost identical in flavor to walnut oil.

In 1990, oils in 8.5-ounce bottles ranged from $5.95 to $11.95 a bottle. A 16.9-ounce bottle of elderberry drink was $29.55. Flora sells food supplements and personal-care products. It also sells noncertified toasted sesame oil and almond oil.

FOUR CHIMNEYS FARM WINERY
RD 1, Hall Road
Himrod-on-Seneca, NY 14842
(607) 243-7502

Visits: yes; tasting room; seasonal events and celebrations; chamber music series
Farmers' market: Union Square Greenmarket in New York City, Wednesdays, Fridays, and Saturdays; Ithaca Farmers' Market, Saturday mornings
Farm certified by: NOFA-NY
Catalogue/price list available
Minimum order: none
Order by: phone, mail, soon fax
Pay by: check, money order
Ship by: UPS

VINEGAR

Red wine · White wine

Four Chimneys Farm Winery, named for the architecture of the Italianate chateau on the property, is the oldest organic winery in the country. In 1976, Walter and Dale Pedersen escaped from New York City—where Walter had been mugged three times—trading academia for twelve acres of wine grapes. While Dale Pedersen took charge of schooling their six children, Walter Pedersen, who has a master's degree in Slavic linguistics, studied European winemaking texts; he and Four Chimneys's winemaker, Scott Smith, traveled to France and Germany to learn how to grow grapes without chemicals (the ones used on grapes are some of the most toxic in agriculture) and produce wine without additives.

Four Chimneys's 1987 Late Harvest Vignoles won a silver medal at the 1989 New York State Wine and Food classic (no gold medals were awarded that year). The wines have been served at Woods and An American Place in New York City. Michael Turback, of Turback's in Ithaca, called their Cabernet Sauvignon "exceptional . . . round, full fruity character, bone dryness, and exceptional balance." They also introduced the country's first organic champagne.

The employees of Four Chimneys form a community, says Walter Pedersen, who also teaches the community's children in a school at

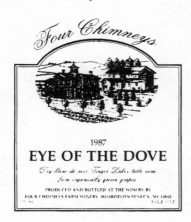

the winery. Part of the winery's profits go back into the business, and the rest goes to workers based on "productivity units." Pedersen, who has studied psychotherapy, says that employees rate one another on dedication, cooperation, and humility—because a humble person is more likely to see and correct his or her mistakes.

One member who must be earning lots of "productivity units" is Dongmee Smith, whose husband, Scott, is the winemaker. Smith, a pianist by training, has organized a summer chamber-music series in the vineyard's Victorian barn, followed by postconcert wine-tasting dinners. Four Chimneys pays the musicians in food and wine—a seven-course candlelight dinner, from organic ingredients, of course.

The white and balsamic-style red vinegars start with their own wines, which are not treated with sulfites or other preservatives during processing.

In 1990, organic vinegar, in a half-bottle size, was $2.95. Wines and champagne ranged from $5.95 to $22.95 a bottle. Vinegar can be shipped anywhere. Call to discuss out-of-state shipments of wine.

GAETA IMPORTS
141 John Street
Babylon, NY 11702-2903
(516) 661-2681
—or—
4 Anchor Drive, Suite 225
Emeryville, CA 94608-9991
(800) 669-2681
(415) 654-4639
FAX: (516) 661-7629

Farmers' markets: New York City, Saturdays at 68th Street between 1st and York; Sundays on Columbus at 76th Street; call for California locations
Certified by: SELF
Certification pending from: Agricoltura Biologica
Catalogue/price list available
Minimum order: $25 for credit-card orders
Order by: phone, mail, fax
Pay by: check, money order, Visa, MC, Amex
Ship by: UPS
Gift baskets available
Recipes available

OIL
Extra-virgin olive · Pure olive · X'tra light olive

DRIED MUSHROOMS
Porcini

CONDIMENTS
Dried capers · Olives

Deborah and John Fusco's father was born just south of Rome, in the town of Itri. Itri lies on the Appian Way in the Gaeta district, which, say the Fuscos, has been "blessed with fertile soil for olive growth since Roman days." When John Fusco graduated from Hampshire College in 1984, he went to visit his father's birthplace and discovered that his Italian cousins were leaving the land the family had been farming for almost 250 years. They were selling their olive oil to producers who wanted it for blends, where its extremely low acidity balanced more acidic, cheaper oils, enabling the producers to meet the legal requirement for the label "extra-virgin": less than 1 percent acidity.

John Fusco didn't think his relatives were getting a fair price for their oil. If they exported the oil to the United States, he thought, they'd do a lot better and might want to stay in the olive business. That, in turn, would save the family farms.

Gaeta X'tra Light
100% Pure Olive Oil™

But it's hard to start an import business if you don't speak the language, and John Fusco didn't. His sister, Deborah, had been studying Italian and loved the idea of starting a business where she could use it. She left a merchandising job with Avon's international division and joined forces with her brother. She says she's found dealing with Italian businessmen a challenge: they expect her to behave like their "passive female employees," and are surprised to find her both articulate and serious about what she does. But it's hard to imagine not taking her seriously when Gaeta's oils are on the shelves of Balducci's and Neiman-Marcus and grace the kitchen of the Waldorf-Astoria.

Gaeta's organic olive oil comes in three grades (the pomace is not organic). "Extra virgin" is the first pressing of the olive by stone mills, without heat. "Pure" is one-sixth extra-virgin oil combined with the second pressing

of the oil, which does use heat. "X'tra light" is the mildest-tasting oil of the three. I sampled the extra virgin, which had a remarkable, sweet flavor, like the oil of a flower—chamomile, perhaps—rather than an olive. It was delicious alone on bread, and drizzled over steamed vegetables in place of butter.

The Fuscos also sell their own olives, picked by hand by their Italian relatives. The *New York Times*'s Nancy Jenkins called their olives "small and tender, with a rich, smooth flavor that is delicately salty. A beautiful, pale purple-brown color, they look like little burnished beach pebbles." Their capers come from an Italian island near the African coast; the porcini mushrooms grow beneath chestnut trees in the forests of northern Italy.

The olives are certified organic in Italy. In addition, both olives and oils have been tested in American labs and show no pesticide or chemical residue. The capers and porcini mushrooms are either organically grown or picked in wild areas and forests.

In 1990, a quarter-liter bottle of extra-virgin olive oil was $2.99, and you saved by buying larger containers. Shipping additional. The catalogue also lists balsamic vinegar, pasta sauces, pasta, and conserves, which are not organic but contain no additives, preservatives, or colorings.

GREEK GOURMET, LTD.
195 Whiting Street
Hingham, MA 02043
(617) 749-1866
FAX: (617) 740-2005

Certified by: SELF
Certification pending from: Greek National Laboratories
Catalogue/price list available
Minimum order: 1 case
Order by: phone, mail, fax
Pay by: check
Ship by: UPS
Sampler available
Recipes available

OIL

Extra-virgin olive · Extra-virgin olive with herbs and edible flowers

CONDIMENTS

Calamata olives in olive oil

If you are an olive lover, you may want to pick a safe place to hide your Greek Gourmet Calamata olives before you order them. I made the mistake of leaving mine in plain sight. "I'll just have one," my friends said. They lied. Soon they were inventing excuses for returning to the kitchen. These olives produced rapturous descriptions—"smooth," "buttery," "like eating a fruit, not an olive." Everyone noticed the lack of a "metallic" or "harsh" or "sour" taste, and raved about the "luxurious" quality of olives packed in olive oil, which one friend described as "dissipating like a liquor."

Greek Gourmet olive oil, with its intense Mediterranean flavor, rich, green, and fruity, has become a favorite meal around my house —pour directly on a plate and swipe with fresh

bread. This "family-grown" oil has quite a tradition: at least ten generations have turned olives into oil at the Nassopoulos groves, eighty acres in the mountain village of Meropi. The groves themselves are some 2,000 years old, and hired hands are still paid in olive oil.

George Nassopoulos came to the United States in 1958 to go to college. Every year, he and his family would travel to Greece and bring home the next year's supply of extra-virgin olive oil from the family groves. The first time Diane Nassopoulos had to buy commercial olive oil, she got quite a shock—it was nothing like what she was used to. Terrible, in fact. She and her husband had always taken their oil for granted, but now they realized what it was worth.

In 1985, Nassopoulos was working as a naval architect, a profession befitting a Greek expatriate, but he was ready for a change. He and his wife felt that importing the family oil would perpetuate the bond between the family and the land so that his children would want to maintain it well into the future.

Alexandra and Christina Nassopoulos will have a fine tradition to uphold: Greek Gourmet won a gold medal in 1990 from Chefs in America. Their customers include Chez Panisse—it's the only olive oil Alice Waters uses—Jasper's and the Ritz-Carlton. Their oil was used during a 1989 tribute to Craig Claiborne.

Greek Gourmet sells only "extra-virgin" oil, which is the first cold pressing of the olive, using traditional millstones and no heat; the oil has an acidity of less than .5 percent. Only 5 percent of the annual yield qualifies as "extra virgin." The Nassopouloses warn against what they call "the black art of blending" in commercial oils: using oils of different acidity to end up with an "extra-virgin" level.

Chemical fertilizers are used when the olive trees are young, but not thereafter. Meropi is a mountainous region whose cool, dry climate means that insects are not as much of a problem as they are nearer the coast. In 1990, the government of Greece certified that Meropi was not sprayed aerially with any pesticides.

The Nassopouloses advise substituting olive oil for butter in most recipes, and even recommend bathing in it—as they do.

The standard size order is 1 case, but a trial gift box of 2 bottles, or 1 bottle and 2 jars of olives, is available. In 1990, a case of 12 1-liter bottles was $54. A case of 12 jars of olives was $33. Shipping additional.

NICK SCIABICA & SONS

P.O. Box 1246
Modesto, CA 95353
(800) 346-5483
(209) 577-5067
FAX: (209) 524-5367

Visits: yes
Farmers' markets: Modesto, Thursday and
Saturday mornings
Ingredients certified by: CHSC
Catalogue/price list available
Minimum order: none
Order by: phone, mail, fax
Pay by: check, money order, Visa, MC, COD
Ship by: UPS, parcel post
Recipes available
Gift boxes available

OLIVE OIL

Mission Varietal · Manzanillo

Nicola Sciabica (pronounced "Sha-bee-ka")
learned to press olives in his native Sicily and
brought that experience to California where he
went into business with his son, Joseph Sciabica, in 1936. Today, the third generation of
Sciabicas, Dan and Nick, is hard at work making varietal olive oils, which they compare to
making varietal wines. Looking at their beautiful bottles, the comparison doesn't seem extreme. The oils range from a pale gold to a deep
green, reminding you even before you taste
them that each batch is unique. The oils are
pressed in small batches, using only the first,
cold pressing of the olive. The Sciabicas use no
chemicals to extract the oil, and no additives or
preservatives.

Among their impressive collection are two
oils from organic olives, whose growers provide a signed affidavit of their growing practices. The olives in Mission oil are named for
the Franciscan missions that introduced the
olive to California. The Sciabicas describe the
oil's flavor as "clean and delicate," and recommend using it uncooked, either in salad dressing or drizzled over cooked vegetables. I found
it light, sweet, and delicate, excellent on salads.

Manzanillo has a "full-bodied fruitiness,
abundant flavor, with a slight tartness." The
organic Manzanillo is a golden oil, which the
Sciabicas recommend both for cooking and for
salads since it "imparts the fruitiest flavor of
the olives." But lest you think that olive oil is
only for salads, however, their catalogue comes
with recipes from Joseph's wife, Gemma, for
everything from minestrone to pumpkin bar
cookies.

In 1990, a case of 12 6-ounce bottles of Mission Varietal
oil was $42. Cases of larger-size bottles are available. All
oil comes with a money-back guarantee. The catalogue
also lists nonorganic olive oils and red-wine vinegar.

OMEGA NUTRITION USA, INC.

1720 La Bounty Road
Ferndale, WA 98248
   –or–
Omega Nutrition Canada Inc.
8392 Prince Edward Street
Vancouver, B.C.
Canada V5X 3R9
(800) 661-3529
(604) 322-8862
FAX: (604) 327-2932

Ingredients certified by: OCIA, FVO
Processing certified by: FVO
Minimum order: 1 case
Order by: phone
Pay by: check, COD
Ship by: UPS
Recipes available

OILS

Flax · Hazelnut · Sesame · Sunflower ·
Safflower · Olive · Canola · Pistachio · Almond

FLOUR

Defatted hazelnut

SNACKS

Nutri-snap organic treats

I wish I could remember the children's book—I think it must be *Charlie and the Chocolate Factory*—in which colorless substances magically taste exactly like roast beef or peanut butter or blueberries. That's exactly the experience I had sampling the oils from Omega Nutrition. Out of little black bottles (more on them later) come essentially colorless liquids, but put a few drops on your tongue, and the sesame couldn't be anything but sesame seeds; the sunflower is like liquid sunflower kernels; and (what luxury) the hazelnut is pure, out-of-this-world hazelnut. While I've never tasted flax seeds, I'm willing to guess they taste just like Omega's pleasantly nutty flax oil—with a little added crunch.

Flax oil is where it all started. The oil from flax seeds is particularly high in omega-3 fatty acids, which the body needs but does not produce by itself. Omega-3 are in short supply in the North American diet, which contains less than one-sixth of the amount our bodies need, and of what the average diet contained 170 years ago. (If you're interested, Omega Nutrition has an extensive file of medical research into the benefits of omega-3 fatty acids for a wide range of modern illnesses.)

Omega Nutrition

The trouble is that "flax oil is so volatile that even as you're making it in an ordinary environment it's starting to get rancid," and most commercial oils, say the folks at Omega, "are processed in huge volumes with heat, chemicals, and bleaches that strip them of live nutrients and leave them odorless, colorless, and often tasteless." The founders of Omega sought a way to make the oil without exposing it to heat, air, or light.

The venture was full of risk for this employee-owned company. "We had no deep-pocketed backers, and wound up on the fourth floor of an industrial walk-up in an impoverished Vancouver neighborhood. When we took our first truckload delivery of flax seed, we carried it up in a little elevator 1,000 pounds at a time—forty trips. It was a year and a half before anyone took wages. We considered it a major expense when we ordered a pizza big enough to keep everyone going through the late shift."

They eventually developed the "Omegaflo" process, which preserves the omega-3 fatty acids in nuts and seeds, using small presses and cold-pressing. The opaque black bottle, while not likely to be the most cheerful or decorative item on your shelf, continues to protect the oil during storage, while being "100% non-reactive with the oil." The oil is still a perishable product, stamped with a four-month expiration date.

East West magazine found Omega's flax oil "one of the finest edible oils, with a fresh, earthy aroma and a nut-like flavor that is very compelling." Since heat breaks down the omega-3s, it's important not to use flax oil for cooking. Omega recommends using the flax oil in salad dressings (you can use it in equal parts with olive oil and still get the olive taste), in fresh mayonnaise, and in blender drinks. Omega's oils are finding a following among gourmets, and its recipes include dishes like a mushroom risotto made with hazelnut oil.

In addition to oils, Omega makes the only defatted hazelnut flour in the country. The flour is rich in potassium, calcium, and vitamin A, but all that seems incidental when you taste that essence of hazelnut, ready to add to cakes, cookies, soups, and sauces. I made Omega's hazelnut butter cookies at Christmastime; they had an intense hazelnut flavor and were the closest I'd ever come to a real bakery butter-cookie texture. Omega will also send you recipes for muffins, hazelnut pie, hazelnut chicken, and hazelnut angel cake. If you don't own a kitchen scale that uses grams as well as ounces, be sure to specify that you want a version for measurement by volume.

Omega just started making almond oil and pistachio oil (the pistachios are free of pesticides and herbicides, but not certified organic) and will soon have hazelnut puree, pistachio puree, and almond puree, which can be "drizzled" on salads, added to sauces, or used in baking.

Omega really doesn't miss a beat: when the company decided to make a candy, it did a great job of that, too. Nutri-snap snack bars are the best version of sesame candy I've ever had, a wonderful combination of sesame and a sweet flavor I thought was honey or molasses but turned out to be brown rice syrup. If you've ever had Middle Eastern sesame candies, you know the texture, which starts out crunchy and turns chewy. A dentist's delight, but well worth it.

In 1990, a 12.75-ounce bottle of oil ranged from $4.97 to $16.18. A case contains 12 bottles, but you can mix and match. Hazelnut flour was $10 for a 17.5-ounce jar. (You don't need to order a full case of flour.) The Nutri-snaps were 65 cents for a packet of 3, and come 24 packets to a box. Also for sale is nutri-flax powder, a food supplement high in protein and fiber. If you ask for Mr. Gaffney and mention this book, you will receive a 10 percent discount on orders, and will avoid shipping costs. Larger orders will receive a wholesale price.

SEE ALSO
Allergy Resources, Diamond K
Enterprises, Emandal—A Farm on a
River, Grafton Goodjam, Kozlowski
Farms, Santa Barbara Olive Company

RICE AND WILD RICE

In this section you will find listings for both cultivated and wild rice, an aquatic grass native to the lakes of Minnesota and Wisconsin, and parts of Canada, America's only indigenous grain. Wild rice or *manomin,* meaning "gift of the gods," was a traditional staple of food and trade for several Native American peoples: in lean years, a cause for tribal battles over rice-bearing lakes; in times of plentiful harvest, the subject of songs, feasts, and ceremonies.

Some tribes used their surplus rice to trade with Europeans—French explorers knew it as "wild oats." In the 1950s, when wild rice became a delicacy, outsiders began buying up wild rice at roughly one-tenth to one-twentieth of what they would eventually charge for it. By putting a ceiling on the prices they would pay, these buyers practically guaranteed that harvesters would remain in poverty. Eventually, corporate interests found a way to circumvent the Native harvesters altogether, by growing "wild rice" domestically in diked paddies where, according to one Native American activist, the so-called "tame rice," often a hybrid strain, is grown with nitrogen fertilizers, fungicides, and 2-4 D.

By the 1980s, the vast majority of all rice sold as "wild" was this tame, paddy-grown variety. For many Native peoples, getting a fair price for this traditional crop by selling directly to the consumer their only avenue to financial independence.

GREY OWL FOODS
P.O. Box 88
Grand Rapids, MN 55744
(800) 527-0172
(218) 327-2281
FAX: (800) 527-0172

Visits: yes
Certified by: OCIA
Minimum order: 10 pounds
Order by: phone, mail, fax
Pay by: check
Ship by: UPS

RICE

Wild rice

FRUIT

Wild blueberries · Lingonberries

VEGETABLES

Wild mushrooms · Fiddlehead ferns

MEAT

Rainbow trout · Buffalo jerky

Grey Owl's wild rice comes from Saskatchewan lakes so isolated that they're inaccessible by road. Harvesters have to be flown into the lake area to gather the rice. The initial picking is still done in canoes, and is "open to anyone who wants to practice the ancient religious aspect of harvesting *manomin* (wild rice)," say the folks at Grey Owl. Subsequent pickings in modern airboats, like those used in the Everglades, skim the beds collecting the ripened seed in aluminum trays.

Grey Owl is entirely owned by the seventy-two bands of Indians of northern Saskatchewan, which produces more wild rice than any other Canadian province. Until the formation of Grey Owl, the wild rice harvesters' only outlets for their rice were marketers who blended their rice with cultivated wild rice raised in artificially diked paddies. Grey Owl's rice is entirely lake-harvested, and the entire process, from lake harvesting to processing and packaging, has been certified by OCIA; the rice is also kosher.

According to *Cooks* magazine, most wild rice grown today is "scarified, a process that removes some of the bran layer and roughs up the rest. Scarification creates a lighter-colored rice which cooks quickly. Because the seed is delicate, this process can also lead to a bitter, sour rice if the bran is mishandled." Grey Owl's drying process leaves the bran layer of the

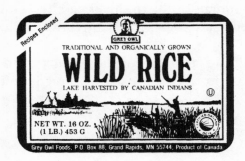

black rice intact. The resulting rice is high in protein, niacin, thiamin, and riboflavin. The rice cooks for an hour and expands to four times its volume. I made the rice with the extra water Grey Owl recommended. The result was quite tender, but with more than enough texture to differentiate it from white rice. The flavor was mild and nutty—my guests said it was the best wild rice they'd ever eaten.

In 1990, wild rice was $4.40 per pound in individual packages or $4.11 per pound in bulk packaging. Prices for the other foods had not been set.

IKWE MARKETING COLLECTIVE
Route 1, Box 286
Ponsford, MN 56575
(218) 573-3411

Certified by: SELF
Catalogue/price list available
Minimum order: none
Order by: phone, mail

Pay by: check
Ship by: UPS, parcel post

RICE

Wild rice

In 1985, Margaret Smith came home to the White Earth reservation. After twenty-two years in Minneapolis, she was ready to retire. But when she arrived at White Earth, she realized there was work to be done. Winona La-Duke, an activist for Native American rights and the environment whose work won her the 1988 Reebok Human Rights award, describes the situation Smith discovered at White Earth. "The Anishinabeg (Chippewa) have become almost refugees in our own land. Some 94% of the reservation is held by interests other than the tribe—indeed, most Indians are living in federal housing projects surrounded by, for the most part, non-Indian landholders. With 85% unemployment, dependency rates at 78%, and a host of other socio-economic problems, it was clear to local people that losing control over the rice crop [to producers who paid only a fraction of its value] was the last straw."

Margaret Smith began going door to door organizing rice harvesters and craftspeople into the Ikwe Community Education Project. Smith's idea was to get a fair price for the crafts and wild rice from the reservation, and to use the "Native-controlled project" to train people on the reservation "in the skills necessary to build this economy." Smith began to travel to regional tourist outlets, explaining to outsiders why they should pay a premium for Indian crafts. "What people don't realize is that our people have to buy food at the same stores everyone else shops at," she says. "Our prices should reflect at least minimum wage."

In the past, IKWE's rice has been certified organic, but in 1990, they did not receive the grant that had paid for certification in the past. Nothing about the harvesting or processing has changed. Even more than most organic crops, this rice is gathered without high-tech or gasoline-guzzling tools. In the traditional fashion, two people in a canoe use two

o'bawi'gana'tigog, or knocking sticks, to loosen the grains. LaDuke describes the process: "An Anishinabeg couple pulls their canoe towards the water's edge. The woman boards, sitting on her haunches in the front of the canoe. The man pushes the canoe off shore and jumps in. The man in back stands, head just above the *manomin.* The woman pulls the rice over her lap in a sweeping motion with one stick, and gently knocks it with a second." After harvest, the rice is finished on the reservation itself.

IKWE's catalogue also includes a variety of Native American crafts, mostly made by women—*Ikwe* means woman in the Anishinabeg language. "IKWE's important," says Margaret Smith, "because there's nothing else on this reservation for the traditional craft and wild rice producers to rely on. There is no other market. We are really isolated here—many of our producers don't have cars, and they certainly don't have access to a good market plan." Most of the profits go directly to the producers, with a small portion going to support development and training in marketing.

In 1990, an 8-ounce box of wild rice was $3.50; a 1-pound bag was $6.50. Shipping and handling additional. Prices decrease for bulk orders.

LUNDBERG FAMILY FARMS
P.O. Box 369
Richvale, CA 95974-0369
(916) 882-4551
FAX: (916) 882-4500

Visits: tours by appointment
Certified by: CCOF
Catalogue/price list available
Minimum order: none
Order by: mail

Pay by: check
Ship by: UPS

RICE

Short-grain brown · Long-grain brown · Sweet brown · California basmati brown · Golden Rose brown

FLOUR

Brown rice

SNACKS

Plain rice cakes · Mochi sweet rice cakes · Wild rice cakes · Popcorn rice cakes (with OCIA-certified popcorn)

HOT CEREAL

Creamy Brown Rice

SWEETENER

Sweet Dreams brown-rice syrup

You gotta love the Lundbergs. Their newsletter, *The Lundberg Rice Paper,* usually contains a shot of the four Lundberg brothers—Eldon, Harlan, Wendell, and Homer—above the caption "Out Standing in Our Field." Sometimes the grain is only waist-high; in other shots, only their heads and shoulders are visible. You get the feeling that one day you might see only the tops of their hats.

The Lundbergs, the first family of organic rice, came to California from Nebraska in 1937 as refugees from the Dust Bowl. Albert Lundberg helped found a local plant that made paper towels out of rice straw. The plant is defunct, but the family's connection to rice lives on. Albert's sons run the farm (its official name, Wehah, is an acronym of the five men's initials), and four of Albert's grandchildren work on or around the farm, either in the field or behind the scenes with computers and accounting.

Even during the chemical boom of the postwar period, Albert Lundberg used chemicals sparingly and looked for natural alternatives to chemical products. The Lundbergs have been growing a portion of their rice crop completely organically since 1967, when a maker of macrobiotic rice cakes asked them to grow organic rice. They started with seventy acres, and the years of trial-and-error began. They learned that by flooding the fields, they create an attractive habitat for waterfowl that mat down the rice straw as they search for seeds and insects —and fertilize the soil. The farm is now a winter home to egrets, herons, mud-hens, Red-

legged Dowitchers, Sand Hill Cranes, and even Bald Eagles.

Education is an important part of the Lundbergs' mission. They have created an extended family of rice growers who come together annually to share ideas and benefit from the Lundbergs' expertise. The conference round table is not the only medium the Lundbergs use to spread the word about organic rice farming. Harlan and Carolyn Lundberg have also been known to hold a seminar in the form of a puppet show, with characters like Millie Microorganism, Willie Worm, Billy Bittern, and Kernel Kelly.

But don't think the Lundbergs aren't serious about their rice. They handle it with extreme care from beginning to end of the process. The rice is milled on order and rarely sits more than two weeks in the warehouse, whereas conventional rice growers may let rice lie around for several years.

The Lundbergs currently grow some dozen varieties of rice. "We look to no *single* variety of rice, or any other crop, to suit all people," says Harlan Lundberg, the brother in charge of research into exotic and ancient strains. "We think that the more variety people have, the more interesting their lives will be. We don't spend much time trying to breed new strains," says Harlan. "There are lots of scientists doing that full time." Instead, Harlan looks for old strains that are genetically stable, avoiding hybrids or strains developed with radiation. The research is arduous because he often starts with only a handful of grain from a seed bank; it can take years of planting and replanting to produce enough grain to sell.

The Lundbergs also develop rice-based products, like their Sweet Dreams rice syrup. Enzymes break the rice starches down into sugars, primarily maltose, which the body absorbs more slowly than other sugars.

For economic reasons, the Lundbergs continue to grow their "premium" rice, which has "minimal application of chemicals." Often, say the brothers, "what we discover in our organic fields we later try to practice in our minimally treated fields, with the goal of someday being able to grow all rice for consumers at the same low price without the use of artificial applications."

In 1990, rice ranged from $12.65 to $15.53 for 25 pounds. Short-grain and long-grain brown rice was available in 12 2-pound boxes for $18.22. Twelve packages of rice cakes, 7 or 8 ounces each, were $14 to $15.20. Creamy rice cereal was $27.02 for 25 pounds or $14.49 for 12 12-ounce boxes. Brown-rice syrup was available only in 55-pound containers for $92.16.

MINNESOTA SPECIALTY CROPS
West Junction Highways 65 & 210
P.O. Box 86
McGregor, MN 55760
(800) 328-6731
(218) 768-4917

Visits: yes
Certification pending from: OCIA
Catalogue/price list available
Minimum order: none
Order by: phone, mail
Pay by: check, money order, COD
Ship by: UPS
Recipes available

RICE

Wild rice

NUTS

Wild hazelnuts

SWEETENERS

Maple syrup · Honey

DRIED FRUIT

Wild strawberries · Wild raspberries · Wild blueberries · Wild blackberries · Wild cranberries

JAMS

Wild strawberry · Wild raspberry · Wild blueberry · Wild blackberry · Wild cranberry

Minnesota Specialty Crops sells foods that grow wild in Minnesota but are rarely seen outside the state. The company, located in a severely depressed part of Minnesota, "puts money in the hands of those who need it most" by buying crops directly from the harvesters or wildcrafters (people who gather food in the wild).

Minnesota Specialty Crops sells wild rice harvested on the Leech Lake Reservation (see Ojibwe Foods, page 222). Because of Leech Lake's hand-parching techniques, the rice cooks in twenty-five minutes rather than forty-five minutes or an hour. Minnesota Specialty Crops includes recipes for a number of dishes

using wild rice, including hamburgers or meat-loaf with a proportion of a half-cup cooked rice to a pound of meat. The flavor is also milder than that of wild rice with the darker seed coat.

In 1990, wild rice was $8.95 for 1 pound, and decreased in price for larger quantities. Shipping included. Other crops were not yet available, but should be in 1991.

NORTHERN LAKES WILD RICE COMPANY
P.O. Box 592
Teton Village, WY 83025
(307) 733-7192

Certified by: SELF
Catalogue/price list available
Minimum order: 1 pound
Order by: phone, mail
Pay by: check, money order
Ship by: UPS
Recipes available

RICE

Wild rice

In the Ojibwe language, the August moon is known as the "rice-making moon." The traditional rice harvest takes place in August and September by two people in a canoe—one, the "poler," pushing the boat; the other, the "knocker," using sticks to knock the ripe kernels of grain off their stalks and into the boat. By Minnesota law, only grain harvested from lakes in this fashion can be labeled "hand-harvested." The rice from Northern Lakes, while not certified organic, is certified "hand-harvested." Ernest Anderson, the head of Northern Lakes, says this the best guarantee of purity.

When the rice comes out of the lake, says Anderson, it has a high moisture content. "Ducks love it." For people, it must be dried in large tumbling driers. Anderson's wild rice is aged for seven to ten days after harvest, and is parched to dry the grain and give it a toasted flavor. The seed coat is scratched slightly to allow water to penetrate during cooking, shortening the cooking time. The grains are gray-gold, not the shiny black of other wild rice. The

wild rice I sampled did cook quite quickly—half an hour, with an additional fifteen minutes in the pot but off the flame to expand fully. The grain had a satisfying balance of tenderness and crunch, but the flavor was fairly bland.

In 1990, a 1-pound bag of wild rice was $5.75. Prices decrease for larger orders. Shipping additional.

OJIBWE FOODS
Route 3, Box 100
Cass Lake, MN 56633
(218) 335-6341
FAX: (218) 335-8309

Visits: yes
Certified by: OCIA
Catalogue/price list available
Minimum order: none
Order by: mail, phone
Pay by: check, Visa, MC, money order
Ship by: UPS, parcel post
Gift packages available, including handmade birchbark baskets

RICE

Wild rice

MIXES

Wild-rice soup · Wild-rice pancake

SWEETENERS

Maple syrup · Chokecherry syrup

JELLIES

Wild chokecherry · Wild plum · Wild highbush cranberry · Wild grape · Wild blueberry · Wild blackberry (limited quantities)

MEAT

Smoked canned whitefish

Leech Lake, a reservation of 1,005 square miles in north central Minnesota, is home to some 4,800 Ojibwe people. Ojibwe Foods is owned and operated by the tribal government of the Leech Lake Chippewa people, which hopes that Ojibwe Foods will ultimately become a worker-owned cooperative.

"The traditional way of the Ojibwe people has been, and continues to be, tied to the cycle of the seasons," say the people at Ojibwe Foods. In the spring, the Ojibwe sugar their maple trees for maple syrup. In summer, they go into the thousands of acres of Chippewa National Forest that form part of the reservation to gather the wild fruits that go into their jellies, using only a small amount of sugar—"pure wild fruit juice is the primary ingredient in every jar." They also turn the chokecherry into a dark burgundy syrup you can pour on pancakes or ice cream.

In late August, the Ojibwe harvest wild rice, their traditional staple, which they parch by hand. The kernels are less uniform than wild rice processed by machine—the rice I sampled was not the dark, almost black grains I was expecting, but a lighter gray-green. The rice cooks in twenty-five minutes, quite fast for wild rice, and has a pleasing, mild nutty taste. A less expensive, machine-parched wild rice is also available, but it takes longer to cook.

Ojibwe Foods has combined the wild rice with organic vegetables, herbs, and spices to make a soup mix that cooks up in thirty minutes. They've also created a pancake mix of wild rice and with organic grains: whole wheat, rye, and buckwheat. I didn't get a chance to sample the mixes, but I cheer them on for going the extra mile to get all organic ingredients.

Leech Lake Reservation contains some of the largest lakes in the state of Minnesota, which provide both wild rice and whitefish, which the Ojibwe catch in nets between mid-September and the cold Minnesota winter. The fish are hand-filleted, frozen, and shipped to a custom packer where they are smoked slowly over alderwood. Ojibwe Foods describes the resulting flavor as "slightly roasted and rich, comparable to smoked salmon." The cans are hand packed to keep fillets intact, and are shelf-stable.

The wild rice is certified by OCIA. All other products are gathered in the wild.

In 1990, a half-pound of wild rice was $6, and a half-pound of machine-parched rice was $3. Jellies were $2.50 for a 5.5-ounce jar. Smoked whitefish was $3.75 for a 5.5-ounce can. Maple syrup was $4.50 for 8 ounces. Prices on rice and syrup decrease with larger orders. A 4-person serving of wild-rice soup mix was $4.75; a 1.5-pound package of pancake mix was $5. Shipping additional. The catalogue also lists a book on the Ojibwe people.

THE SECRET GARDEN
P.O. Box 544
Route 1, Box 404
Park Rapids, MN 56470
(218) 732-4866

Certified by: OGBA, OCIA, CHSC, OGM
Catalogue/price list available
Minimum order: none
Order by: phone, mail
Pay by: check, money order, Visa, MC, COD
Ship by: UPS
Internships in biodynamic agriculture available
Recipes available
Gift packages available, some with handmade Indian birchbark baskets

SOUP MIXES

Cream of Wild Rice · Wild Rice Vegetable · Twelve-Bean · Golden Grain Wild Rice

MAIN-COURSE MIXES

Minnesota Hearty Chili · Minnesota Black Beans and Rice · Almond-Apricot Wild Rice Stuffing · Spanish Rice Supreme · Super Stroganoff

RICE

Wild Rice

Anne and Dewane Morgan arrived in north-central Minnesota nearly twenty years ago. They had come from southern California by way of Utah, and even though it was a Minnesota January, they liked what they saw enough to purchase an abandoned 235-acre farm. Dewane Morgan had always dreamed of owning a farm, and this one was affordable. It was also in terrible shape. The neighbors looked on pityingly, recalls Anne Morgan, and offered plenty of advice.

The Morgans named their farm Midheaven, and Dewane Morgan attributes his success in revitalizing the farm to Rudolf Steiner's biodynamic methods, which include planetary and spiritual influences. Eventually, ground that had become hard and lifeless after years of corn planting came back to life, and is now home to raspberries, oats, corn, and an array of vegetables, herbs, and flowers. The neighbors, says Anne Morgan, finally stopped referring to the farm by the name of its former owner.

In 1985, Morgan and other members of a food-buying cooperative started packaging products from northern Minnesota for mail

The Secret Garden

order. Volunteers did the packing, using recipes that had worked well at the co-op's lunch counter. In 1986, fire destroyed the food co-op, and Anne Morgan continued the business on her own, as The Secret Garden.

Anne Morgan continues to promote Minnesota-grown and harvested products in her catalogue. The front page of a recent catalogue featured a map of Minnesota with points to show the origins of the various products in the catalogue (and even one to show where the catalogue itself was typeset).

Anne Morgan is a vegetarian, and so all mixes are vegetarian, and also contain no salt or preservatives. She uses organic ingredients in her mixes whenever possible. For example, I tried the Golden Grain Wild Rice soup, in which the barley, millet, buckwheat, and soy flour were organic. In future, Morgan hopes that all the vegetables will come from their own land.

The Golden Grain Wild Rice mix came with both an "Optional Quick Recipe"—basically mix with water, butter, and tamari, cook and serve; and a "Gourmet Recipe," which involved sautéeing some of the ingredients in butter before mixing everything together. I opted for the Gourmet Recipe, and the results were worth the small amount of extra effort. I allowed the soup to cook down even longer than recommended, and ended up with a very thick, flavorful, mushroom-and-barley soup—the other grains made the soup even heartier, but the dominant flavors were certainly the mushroom and barley. The soup had none of the powdery aftertaste you can get with soup mixes; one friend I served it to said it was the best mushroom-barley soup she'd ever had, and was particularly impressed with the seasonings, which didn't require any additions on my part to bring the soup to life.

In 1990, soup mixes ranged from $2.79 to $4.79. Entrée mixes ranged from $3.99 to $4.89. Lake-harvested wild rice was $8 for 1 pound or $5.50 for cultivated rice. A pound of wild-rice pieces for casseroles or soups was $4. The company pays shipping in continental U.S. for orders over $20. Otherwise, shipping is $2.50. The catalogue also lists cookbooks and some foods that are not necessarily organic, including popcorn, honey, boiled cider, and maple syrup.

SOUTHERN BROWN RICE
P.O. Box 185
Weiner, AR 72479
(800) 421-7423
(501) 684-2354
FAX: (501) 684-2226

Certified by: OCIA
Catalogue/price list available
Minimum order: 2 pounds
Order by: phone, mail
Pay by: check, money order
Ship by: UPS
Recipes available

RICE

Long-grain brown · Medium-grain brown · Short-grain brown · White basmati · Brown basmati · Brown and Wild · Southern Wild Blend (basmati, Arkansas Red, Minnesota wild) · Wild rice

CEREAL

Rice cream · Rice bran

FLOUR

Brown rice

BEANS AND GRAINS

Wheat · Soybeans

Back in 1907, Lewis Hogue began to experiment with growing rice in Arkansas. He harvested his first commercial crop in 1910, and Hogues have been raising rice in Arkansas ever since. Chemicals made their first appearance on the farm in the 1950s. "When we started farming in the sixties," says Willadean Hogue, whose husband, Ron, is Lewis's grandson, "we were interested in getting away from them, for health and the environment. This is a farming community, and I see lots of cancers and different illnesses. I'm convinced the chemicals are the cause of it." By 1978, the Hogues had entirely converted the farm back to organics. At first, says Willadean Hogue, "everyone thought we were crazy. But they don't laugh at us any more." The Hogues say that they are "much healthier, and sell our organic rice to the nicest people in the world."

Southern Brown Rice is whole-grain rice, including the bran layer, and spends no more than seven days between milling and delivery. The brown rice and the two blends—Brown and Wild contains Minnesota wild rice; the Southern Wild Blend adds Arkansas Red to the mixture—all have great texture, particularly the blends, but don't have the additional sweetness I expect from brown rice.

Basmati is a northern Indian rice with a rich flavor—not just a side dish, but a worthy ingredient of main dishes. Basmati is new to Arkansas, but the Hogues feel the Arkansas climate has only "enhanced its flavor and aromatic qualities." Their white basmati, which I had

never seen before, has the aroma of traditional basmati when cooking, and a milder version of the flavor; the rice was tender and plump; a good rice to try if you're used to white rice and are ready to be a little adventurous. A friend who has traveled widely in Southeast Asia said, "I don't usually like white rice, but I like this."

All of the Hogues' rice is ideal for people who've grown up with white rice and want a healthier alternative. Except for the white basmati, all varieties require more water and cooking time than a white rice; it took me a few tries to get the proportions right. I tried making the brown basmati rice for dinner, didn't give it enough water, and ended up with rice that was too crunchy to serve. Later that evening I rescued it in the form of a delicious, aromatic rice pudding.

Rice flour, hypoallergenic and low in sodium, offers an alternative to people with wheat allergies. Brown-rice cream cereal is "nutritious and easily digestible" by both adults and children, say the Hogues.

In 1990, rice and rice blends ranged from $1.85 to $4.50 for 2-pound bags. Brown-rice flour was $1.95 for 2 pounds. Prices decrease if you buy in quantity. Wild rice was $5 per pound. Rice cream cereal was $1 for a 1-pound bag. Rice bran was 35 cents for a 1-pound bag. Shipping additional.

ST. MARIES WILD RICE, INC.
P.O. Box 293
St. Maries, ID 83861
(800) 225-WILD
(208) 245-5835
FAX: (208) 245-4991

Visits: no on-site selling, but visitors are welcome by appointment
Certified by: OR-TILTH
Certification pending from: state of Idaho
Catalogue/price list available
Minimum order: none
Order by: phone, mail, fax
Pay by: check, money order, Visa, MC
Ship by: UPS, parcel post on request

RICE

Premium wild rice · Select wild rice

In 1952, a few duck hunters in Idaho decided to improve their odds by sowing wild rice seed from Minnesota—a duck's delicacy—in their local lakes. Thirty years later, these grasses had taken over the lakes: it was getting tough to dock a boat. The state of Idaho was looking for a way to clear the lakes, and auctioned off the right to gather the seed. Al Bruner, a former land manager for Idaho State Fish and Game, and Jeff Baker, an airline pilot, won the contract. In exchange for clearing the weeds and improving the wildlife habitat, they got to keep the wild rice.

Since 1984, their harvest has grown from the original twenty-five acres of Benewah Lake to over 1,500 acres. Bruner and Baker have convinced local farmers that their underused bottomland could be flooded and used to grow wild rice. This proved a boon to the local economy, which had been supported by the now-failing timber industry.

As a former wildlife manager, Bruner gets a great deal of satisfaction from being in a business that benefits wildlife. It's not unusual, he says, to see 10,000 swans, 20,000 Canada geese, and 20,000 ducks of varying species in the rice fields in a single year. His son, Steve, compares the fields to O'Hare International Airport during rush hour. But Bruner doesn't want to discourage the migratory birds. On the contrary, they help him out by stirring up the waters and fertilizing the plants.

In the forty years since it was sown, the wild rice has grown heartier; and produces longer,

fatter kernels than its Minnesota cousins. The rice contains about 14 percent protein, is high in B vitamins, and contains 130 calories per cup. Because part of his crop feeds wildlife, Bruner never uses chemicals on it.

Ducks are not the only ones who enjoy feasting on St. Maries rice. In 1990, Chefs in America awarded St. Maries a gold medal for both its Mild Wild rice and its Robust flavor; the judges gave the rice an "excellent" score on taste, appearance, and overall impression. *Cooks* magazine found St. Maries rice "dry but tender" and "very mild-flavored," and rated it third of thirteen brands sampled in a blind taste-test. I found the wild rice took more than the recommended amount of water, but once cooked, was sweet, nutty, both chewy and crunchy at once, and made a great complement to a chicken with wine sauce. The rice comes with a recipe booklet for pilaf, rice salad, rice stuffing, and a wild-rice-and-raisin breakfast cereal.

In 1990, premium grade wild rice was $4 for an 8-ounce gift box. Select grade wild rice was $3 for an 8-ounce poly bag. You save by buying larger quantities. Shipping additional. St. Maries also sells seed to improve wildlife habitats for birds.

SEE ALSO
Flours and Grains Section, Trout Lake Farm

SAUCES, PICKLES, AND CONDIMENTS

AUNT NENE'S SPECIALTY FOODS
Box 65
Lucerne, MO 64655
(816) 793-2100
FAX: (816) 793-2100

Visits: yes
Ingredients certified by: SELF
Catalogue/price list available
Minimum order: none
Order by: phone, mail, fax
Pay by: MC, Visa, check, money order
Ship by: UPS
Availability of products varies by season
Gift assortments available
Recipes available

PICKLES

Zesty sweet dill slices · Grandma's special lime pickles · Cracklin'-crisp bread-and-butter pickles · Curry and spice slices · Classic grape-leaf dills · Nine-day sweet pickle · Savory okra · Sweet-n-sour cukes · Sweet zucchini medallions · Sunshine honey spears · Five-alarm pickled peppers · Old-time garden relish · Candied cucumbers · Cornichons · Tea and cocktail sandwich filling (cucumber slices) · Cauliflower pickles

SAUCES

Chili sauce

JAMES, JELLIES, AND FRUIT SAUCES

Wild grape jelly · Wild jam · Wild plum sauce · Pear honey · Strawberry-honey sauce · Coriander-honey glaze · Autumn harvest marmalade (apples and fresh-pressed apple cider) · Gooseberry jam · Rhubarb conserve · Fruited zucchini marmalade · "Love apple" butter · Hot sweet pepper jam

As a child, Jeannine Williams got the nickname Nene from her four brothers; years later, their children would demand to know whether a pickle or jam was "Aunt Nene's" before they would take a bite.

Aunt Nene is a busy woman: whenever we talked, she was on the run, usually to her kitchen. Jeannine Williams doesn't have much time to spare because she specializes in the kind of time-consuming preserving that has largely been lost. The nine-day sweet pickle really takes nine days from the time the young cucumber is picked to the time the cap goes on the jar. The classic grape-leaf dills are "full sours" made in the classic crock method, skimmed daily for two weeks to a month, then packed with fresh grape leaves, dill, and garlic.

Williams had always put up preserves as a hobby, but she was trained as a music teacher. She had decided to stay at home when her sons were born, and when she and her husband, Bud, lost their farm to a series of disasters including hail, flood, and drought, she turned to her old skills for additional income. "I was out

in the garden one day—I've always loved to garden—and I thought, 'I've always given these things away, why don't I try selling them?' "

Williams had learned her recipes from her mother and grandmother. Where else will you find, for example, a rhubarb conserve made with citrus, golden raisins, spices, and pecans? Or "citrusy" zucchini marmalade? How about love-apple butter, combining apples and "love apples"—otherwise known as tomatoes—into a "rosy, fragrant spread"? Or cauliflower pickles, made without salt or sugar, where the florets turn pink naturally? I certainly can't think of another supplier of organic pickled okra—and for those who like that sort of thing, well, that's the sort of thing they like. Williams cooks in small batches and packs each jar individually. In 1988, her line of foods won the gold medal at the Missouri State Fair.

Williams, her husband, and their two sons, Chad and Codie, grow as much of the produce as possible in their own gardens—like her mother and grandmother, Williams gardens organically. All the products listed above use their own produce, but with the old-time garden relish, the strawberry-honey dessert sauce, the hot sweet pepper jam, and the cauliflower pickles Williams does turn to other growers when her own produce runs out. The honey is not from her own hives, but she says the beekeepers are "very strict" about their methods. Jeannine Williams uses no preservatives, artificial flavors, or MSG in her preserves and pickles.

In 1990, a crate of 4 jars was $15.95. Shipping additional.

CHERRY HILL CANNERY
Barre-Montpelier Road
MR 1
Barre, VT 05641
(800) 468-3020
(802) 479-2558

Visits: yes
Ingredients certified by: NOFA-VT
Processing certified by: NOFA-VT
Catalogue/price list available
Minimum order: none
Order by: phone, mail
Pay by: Visa, MC, check
Ship by: UPS
Gift packages available

PICKLES

Maple beet · Maple bread-and-butter · Dill pickles · Pickled fiddleheads · Pickled red cabbage

JUICE AND SAUCE

Tomato juice · Tomato sauce

SWEETENERS

Maple syrup · Maple granules

Cherry Hill Cooperative Cannery started as a place where Vermonters could turn their home-grown produce into jams and preserves for their own tables and as a way to make some extra money. The Cannery also developed a line of its own products, starting with sauces made from the wild apples in local abandoned orchards. Over time, the interest in community canning faded, but the cannery continued to expand its own line. Today, the cannery is a worker-owned cooperative of nine members, each of whom shares equally in the company.

Cherry Hill

According to Cherry Hill's general manager, Ken Davis, the cooperative is committed to supporting Vermont agriculture and uses Vermont-grown produce whenever it can. The beets, cucumbers, and cabbage pickled at Cherry Hill come from certified organic Vermont farms. The beet and cucumber pickles are "delicately maple-flavored," while the dills are "crisp and tart." Fiddlehead ferns, which grow in the wild, are a New England specialty: the ferns are picked when tiny and tightly curled

—like the scrolled top of a fiddle—and pickled "tart, hot, and wild." Cherry Hill also turns vine-ripened organic plum tomatoes into juice and into a thick puree from which only the seeds and skin have been removed.

Cherry Hill Cannery also sells the products of other small Vermont companies, including

Annie's Enterprises. Ann Christopher went to cooking school in New York and dreamed of becoming a professional chef. Then she married a Vermonter who brought her back to his family's 175-year-old dairy farm, fifty miles from the nearest restaurant fancy enough to need a chef. So Ann Christopher took her cooking degree and opened a gourmet barbecue stand. When she got pregnant, she gave up the fifteen-hours-a-day-on-your-feet life, but people kept asking for her barbecue sauce, and the Annie's line was born. The line now contains mustards, vinegars, and other cooking sauces, using healthy ingredients, like canola oil. In 1990, she began developing a recipe for her first all-organic product, a pasta sauce made from organic tomatoes, which made its debut in 1991.

In 1990, pickles ranged from $2.99 to $4.29 for an 8-ounce jar. Maple syrup ran from $4.89 for 8 ounces. You save by buying larger sizes. Maple granules were $3.89 for 4 ounces.

EMANDAL—A FARM ON A RIVER
16500 Hearst Road
Willits, CA 95490
(707) 459-5439
FAX: (707) 459-1808

Visits: yes; farm stays; summer camp; seasonal country weekends
Certified by: SELF
Catalogue/price list available
Minimum order: $20
Order by: phone, mail, fax
Pay by: check, money order
Ship by: UPS
Gift packages and samplers available
Orders accepted from the day the catalogue goes out, generally the beginning of November, until December 15

JAMS

Wild blackberry · Wild red plum · Wild blackberry—wild plum

JELLIES

Wild elderberry · Wild grape · Gewurztraminer grape

FRUIT BUTTERS

Wild plum

FRUIT BREWS

Peach · Apricot · Pear · Raspberry · Apple · Strawberry

PICKLES

Cucumber relish · Bread-and-butter pickles · Kosher-style dill pickles · Dill pickle slices

SAUCES AND CONDIMENTS

Chinese plum sauce · Tomato ketchup · Tomato salsa (mild or hot) · Green tomato salsa · Lasagna sauce

DRIED VEGETABLES

Dried tomatoes in olive oil

MISCELLANEOUS

Outrageous tomato soup · Green tomato mincemeat

VINEGAR

Apple cider

The short ordering season at Emandal reflects the nature of the enterprise—Tamara Adams and her family are not in the food business. They are simply maintaining the tradition of "putting up" the surplus of the summer and fall harvests of their farm on the Eel River.

As far back as 1908, Em and Al Byrnes began to invite friends to escape city life and spend time on their 1,000-acre farm, Emandal, two miles from the base of Sanhedrin Mountain, one of the highest points in the Coast Range. Guests would take the train to Willits and then reach the farm by horse-drawn wagon. At Emandal, they would eat farm-grown fruits and vegetables, meat and eggs, and homemade bread baked by Em Byrnes.

In 1946, Clive and Jessie Adams, two schoolteachers, bought the farm and opened it as a

camp during the summer. Clive Adams died in 1985, but Jessie Adams still lives on the farm, teaching children about astronomy and plants. Her son, Clive, Jr., and his wife, Tamara—a former camp counselor at Emandal—are now responsible for the farm. Their children, Buff, Zarya, Kashaya, and Malanyon, are the third generation of Adamses at the farm.

Tamara and Clive Adams strive for self-sufficiency on the farm. The jams started out as a way to make money in winter without having to take a job in town. Tamara Adams is in charge of the Emandal kitchen and likes to add and tinker with her recipes from year to year.

You can tell from her ingredients that she has the heart of an experimenter. Recently, for example, she added the Chinese plum sauce, which combines tart wild plums, Indian Blood peaches, red bell peppers, fresh ginger and fresh garlic, and a mix of other herbs and spices. Another newcomer to her list is the line of "fruit brews," pure fruit, blended smooth and condensed, sweetened with Emandal's own organic grape juice.

When it comes to tomatoes, Tamara Adams really goes to town. The dried tomatoes in olive oil have been "plumped" with Gewurtztraminer grape juice, marinated with garlic and herbs, and packed in jars with olive oil. The ketchup combines Emandal's tomatoes with onions, Gewurtztraminer grape juice, the farm's own apple cider vinegar—made from its own apples and aged up to three years—spices, and salt. The Lasagna sauce does indeed sound like a "Garden in a Jar," as advertised: tomatoes, mushrooms, carrots, purple and white eggplant, garlic, Gewurtztraminer grape juice, organic Cabernet Sauvignon, fresh oregano and basil, and a "luxuriant amount of fresh parsley." Adams also answers the perennial gardener's question: what do you do with green tomatoes? The answer is green tomato mincemeat, combining apples, pears, canteloupe, and green tomatoes, with dried fruit—apricots, peaches, prunes, cherries, pears, apples, dates, raisins, currants—and adding walnuts, almonds, butter, honey, and brown sugar. A jar is enough for one pie—Tamara adds brandy to hers before baking.

The farm is not certified organic, but has grown its produce without chemicals for twenty-three years. Most of its ingredients are grown on the farm or gathered in the wild.

In 1990, jams, jellies, and fruit brews were $4.40 to $5.25 for a 10.6-ounce jar. Cider vinegar was $4 for a 12-ounce jar. Pickles were $4 a pint and $6 a quart. Salsa was $3.50 for a 10.6-ounce jar. Ketchup was $5 for a 12-ounce bottle. Lasagna sauce was $4.50 a pint, green tomato mincemeat was $10 a quart, and dried tomatoes in olive oil were $8.50 for a 10.6-ounce jar.

LOAFERS' GLORY
RFD 3, Box 895
Westminster West, VT 05346
(802) 869-3148
(802) 869-2711 (Fridays)

Visits: yes
Ingredients certified by: various
Catalogue/price list available
Minimum order: none
Order by: phone, mail
Pay by: check in advance, money order
Ship by: UPS
For breads, place orders on Mondays

VEGANNAISE

Aioli · Fresh dill · Lemon curry

BREADS

Oat Bran Little Loaves · Butternut Babes

Gaelen Burns started baking in 1969 when she was pregnant with her daughter Alyson. She was trying to stay on a whole-grain diet, but had trouble finding whole-grain foods in the supermarket. A friend taught her to bake bread, and she fell in love with the process. In

1978, her husband built a twenty-two-by-fifty-foot bakery next to their home, but even though she's turned professional, her main interest is still to make the kinds of foods she and her family love to eat.

Vegannaise (pronounced "Vay-gun-aze"), the newest addition to the Loafers' Glory line, is a creamy condiment with the texture of may-onnaise that meets all the requirements of a vegan diet—no animal products whatsoever—and contains no cholesterol, no salt, no sugar, and no yeast. You can use Vegannaise in potato or tuna salads—but also as flavorful sauces for other dishes. The main ingredient in Vegan-naise is organic soymilk. The herbs are Vermont grown, and many are organic.

All three varieties of Vegannaise have enough flavor to jazz up any sandwich, even with a *very* thin layer. The aioli was my favorite. Vegetarians, cover your ears—put the aioli on a roast-beef sandwich and you'll get the effect of that wonderful combination: roast beef and Boursin.

The mustard dill was a close second, similar to the traditional sauce for gravlax, with plenty of dill and a pungent mustardy bite. It's a natural for fish, but also made a terrific dip for fresh green beans. Both the dill and the aioli were fabulous on boiled potatoes, and a dollop of either would be an impressive sauce for lightly steamed vegetables.

The lemon and curry flavors battle each other a bit—I prefer my curry straight—but lemon-curry Vegannaise did work in a tunafish salad with raisins, and I could see it on steamed or baked fish.

Gaelen Burns will send you recipes for Veg-annaise, including a squash soup and a curried cauliflower using the lemon curry; a garlic bread, a pizza, and a salsa with the aioli; and a salad dressing and a stuffed potato recipe you can make with any one of the three.

Of course, Loafers' Glory is still baking, and if you are sensitive to gluten, yeast, sugar, or dairy products, there is probably a Loafers' Glory bread or sweet treat for you—perhaps a shortbread sweetened with maple sugar, decorated with hearts and vines, and divided into eight wedges, which is available covered with Belgian chocolate at Christmastime. Most of the baked goods combine organic grain with unbleached and unbromated grain, but the Butternut Babes and Oat Bran Little Loaves use only organic flour, and the Butternut Babes use organic butternut squash. Burns describes the Oat Bran Little Loaves as "mega-muffins" and compares the Butternut Babes to her grandmother's spice cakes, "moist, sweet, loaded with raisins and toasted walnuts."

In 1990, a 7.5-ounce jar of Vegannaise was $2.40. Jars come in cases of 12. You can get an assortment. A 10-ounce package of Butternut Babes or Oat Bran Little Loaves was $2.40. Shipping (including blue ice for Vegannaise) additional.

PERSIMMON HILL BERRY FARM
Route 1, Box 220
Lampe, MO 65681
(800) 333-4159
(417) 779-5626

Visits: pick-your-own berries
Certified by: SELF
Catalogue/price list available
Minimum order: 3 jars
Order by: phone, mail
Pay by: MC, Visa, check, money order
Ship by: UPS, parcel post
Recipes available

SAUCE

Shiitake mushroom

Persimmon Hill's shiitake mushroom sauce comes under the heading of Amaze Your Friends, Astonish Your Enemies. I made the simplest of the recipes that came with the sauce. I won't embarrass myself by telling you how simple it is, but suffice it to say the only ingredients are chicken breasts and the miraculous sauce, and the result is as good as coq au vin from your favorite French restaurant. If you feel more daring, the sauce also comes with recipes for Glazed Cornish hen, Black Mushroom veal, and Beef Stroganoff shiitake, or simply add to a baked potato.

The sauce is the creation of Earnest and Martha Bohner. The Bohners were living in Seattle when a "love of the Ozarks" drew them back to Earnest's native Missouri. They bought a former dairy farm that was being turned into a subdivision. Local tobacco farmers tried to convince Earnest Bohner to join their ranks, but he and his wife, Martha, "had a strong commitment to producing something positive," says Bohner.

Earnest Bohner's training is in public health, where he often saw statistics "on birth defects and carcinogens in various vocations. The number one on both lists was chemical workers. The number two was farmers and their families." When the Bohners started their pick-your-own berry operation, he knew he wanted to go with as little spraying as possible: no pesticides at all, and herbicide only before blooms appear. Part of the fun of pick-your-own, says Bohner, "is to eat a handful while you're picking. We invite people to do it—we call it being your own quality control. I'd have a lot of trouble encouraging people to taste along the way if the berries had any pesticide residue."

Once the berry operation was in place, Earnest Bohner won a rural economic development grant to grow shiitakes and use them to improve the "struggling local economy." Shiitakes require little attention during the summer months, when farmers are busy elsewhere, but provide income during the winter. The crop took off and the Bohners realized they had a lot more fresh mushrooms than customers, so they came up with the shiitake sauce with

the aid of a local chef. The sauce contains no sugar and no preservatives.

The mushrooms have been certified organic by OOGA in the past, but are not currently certified. Bohner explained that OOGA withheld certification as an inducement for the Bohners to turn their entire operation into a strictly organic farm, but Bohner feels they simply can't afford to do so yet. In the meantime, nothing about the mushroom-growing methods has changed since they were certified. The other ingredients in the sauce are not organic.

By 1991, the Bohners hope to have a line of "Wild Ones" jams, using the wild fruit that grows around their farm: grapes, plums, blackberries, and, of course, persimmons, and much less sugar than commercial jams because, say the Bohners, they're in the business of selling fruit, not sugar.

In 1990, a gift crate of 3 jars of shiitake mushroom sauce was $14.95. A jar of sauce and an organic wild-rice blend was $14.95. Shipping additional. The Bohners also sell jam from their low-spray berries and starter logs for people interested in growing shiitake mushrooms.

RISING SUN FARM
2300 Colestin Road
Ashland, OR 97520
(800) 888-0795
(503) 482-5392

Visits: yes
Certified by: OR-TILTH
Catalogue/price list available
Minimum order: none
Order by: phone, mail
Pay by: check, COD, money order
Ship by: UPS, parcel post
Gift packs available
Recipes available

PESTO

Pronto · Garlic Lovers' · Pesto with Dried Tomatoes · Picante · Ultimate Classic Pesto · Fresh Sweet Basil in Olive Oil

SPICED HONEYS

Orange and spice · Almonds and spice · Ginger and lemon · Lemon thyme · Garlic-rosemary-sage

If I were writing a biography of Elizabeth and Richard Fujas, I'd want to call it "From Yacht to Yurt." Richard Fujas spent some thirty-eight years on the water in the merchant marine, as the skipper of a tuna boat, and running a yacht-charter business in the West Indies; Elizabeth Fujas was a "deck lizard and galley slave" who made her way around the world working as a shipboard chef. Their young daughter had logged nearly 10,000 sea miles by the time she was two, and the couple began to feel the need to put down some permanent roots. They bought some land in Oregon without knowing a thing about farming, except that, like living on the sea, it offered a chance to be self-sufficient.

Today the Fujas live in an authentic yurt in the shadow of Mount Shasta. They've found that herbs suit the climate and topography of their land, which is watered by melted mountain snow. Herbs are also fairly resistant to pests and disease, which was important, because they were determined to farm organi-

cally. Constantly confronting the elements at sea, says Richard Fujas, gave them both an enormous respect for the environment.

Even though restaurants and health-food stores were eager to buy their fresh-cut herbs, they still had far more than they could sell. Elizabeth's background as a chef made specialty foods the natural next step. Guests always complimented her pesto. In 1985, she took some down to the local health-food store in plastic jars with xeroxed labels. Soon, a fancier version of those jars was on the shelves at Bloomingdale's representing the best of Oregon foods, and Elizabeth Fujas was calling herself the "pesto-packing mama."

The Fujases grow twelve varieties of basil, which they turn into six different kinds of pesto, one for every taste. There's even a pesto for garlic haters: plain minced basil in olive oil. At the other end of the scale, Picante adds jalapeño and cayenne—"not a four-alarm, just full flavor," says Elizabeth Fujas. Lest you think pesto is just for pasta, they will send you recipes for pesto with seafood, with fish, pesto dip, butter sauces, and mayonnaise.

Rising Sun also makes a pesto-and-dried-tomato torta, a mixture of cream cheese, sour cream, butter, aged Parmesan and Romano topped with pesto and whole and minced dried tomatoes. Most of the tomatoes are organically grown, but late in the season, when supplies are low, the Fujases have to buy from off the farm, and have not yet found an organic farm able to fill their orders, so they don't market the tomato products as organic.

Rising Sun Farm also makes spiced honeys from its own wildflower honey, adding organic oranges to make orange-and-spice honey; organic almonds for the almonds-and-spice; organic lemon for ginger-and-lemon; and honey with organic lemon thyme. The Fujases recommend using these honeys in the traditional ways—in tea, or on muffins, but also as glazes for poultry and meat. They'll send you recipes for a ginger-lemon chicken, a shrimp in spicy orange sauce, and other herbed honey innovations.

In 1990, a 6-ounce jar of pesto ranged from $3.50 to $4.75. Honeys were $3.50 for an 8-ounce jar. A gift pack of 3 pestos was $19.25. A gift pack of 4 honeys was $17.50. The dried-tomato-and-pesto torta ranged from $22 for 3 8-ounce tortas to $78 for 12 tortas. Shipping additional. Pestos and tortas are shipped with ice in summer months. Rising Sun Farm also makes and sells a number of products whose primary ingredients are not organic, including herbed vinegars using Japanese rice vinegar, which is aged without any chemicals.

SANTA BARBARA OLIVE COMPANY
P.O. Box 1570
Santa Ynez, CA 93460
(805) 688-9917
FAX: (805) 686-1659

Visits: yes
Certified by: SELF
Catalogue/price list available
Minimum order: none
Order by: phone, mail, fax
Pay by: Visa, MC, Amex, Discover, check, money order, COD
Ship by: UPS, parcel post

GREEN OLIVES

Country style · Garlic · Mexican style · Hickory-smoked · Sicilian · Italian style · Wine-cured · Beer style · Oil-cured · Kosher · Dill style · Cajun · Plain green

BLACK OLIVES

California black · Greek black

PITTED OLIVES

Country · Garlic · Italian · Green · California black

CANNED OLIVES

California black

OLIVE OIL

Extra virgin

Craig Makela was working as a winemaker at the Santa Barbara winery when he decided to put his hand to a different kind of pressing: olives. In 1983, Makela took his extra-virgin olive oil to a statewide blind taste testing and beat all of the big names. "When they pulled the bottle out, everyone said, 'Who the hell is Santa Barbara Olive Company?'"

Makela still sells his oil, but the heart of his line is olives, seasoned any way you like them, from red chiles and garlic in the Mexican to olive oil, black pepper, and oregano in the Greek black. I sampled the mouth-puckering and tart green olives with garlic; the classic martini olive, a generous, juicy version; and the jalapeño, a fire-breather.

Makela describes Santa Barbara, which he runs with his wife, Cindy, as "natural-minded and health-minded," but does not label his olives or oil organic. He buys "chemical-free" olives from thirty to thirty-five growers, all of whom he knows, and most of whom have been in the business for five or six or seven generations. "The growers don't use any chemicals unless there's an infestation, and then it's widely publicized and everyone knows about it." Makela has encouraged his growers to get certified, but says that a clash of styles has made the process tricky. "You've got a guy

who's about sixty-two wearing army boots and a camouflage jacket and chewing tobacco, and here comes this young guy in Birkenstocks with no socks, and a beard and a ponytail. Even though the farmer's never used chemicals, he says, 'Get that hippie out of here.' It's the old versus the new thinking."

In the meantime, Makela will not use the label "organic" or try to "buffalo" anyone. "We're straight shooters and have always been that way." Santa Barbara uses no chemicals in the processing of olives; everything is packed cold and by hand. Its canned olives contain no ferrous gluconate. It also sells a line of no-sulfite-added vinegars. It even sells beauty products with an olive-oil base, which came about when Japanese stores put its oil in the cosmetics section by mistake. The oil was a hit.

LATE-BREAKING INFORMATION

MACDONALD FARM
RD 1, Route 227
Trumansburg, NY 14886
(607) 387-3058

Certified by: SELF
Price list available
Minimum order: none
Pay by: check, money order, COD
Ship by: UPS

PICKLES

Cucumbers · Sauerkraut

BEANS

Adzuki · Black turtle soup · Red kidney

Both cucumbers and sauerkraut are made in the "old European style," says Thomas MacDonald, using a sea-salt brine, and no vinegar. The sauerkraut is just shredded cabbage and sea salt. In the future, MacDonald Farm plans to make its own miso and soy sauces.

The pickles are available in 1- or 5-gallon containers. Dry beans come in 25-pound bags.

SEE ALSO
**The Apple Farm, Cascadian Farm,
Colonel Sanchez Traditional Foods,
Grafton Goodjam, Haypoint Farm,
Kozlowski Farms, Sandhill Farm**

SEA VEGETABLES

Yes, we're talking about seaweed. But this is seaweed with a history. "These marine vegetables," says Ocean Harvest's Betsy Holliday, "are the vegetal ancestors of all life forms on the planet today, dating back over 3.2 billion years."

Working with these ancient plants makes seaweed harvesters a mystical lot. To Maine Seaweed's Larch Hanson, seaweeds are "our elders, and deserve our respect. They developed strong internal polarity and established holdfasts to the earth long before humans knew which end was up. They live gracefully in the wave-moment, and they have done this through countless cycles of tides and seasons. As each vain human civilization has come and gone, they have remained constant, yet flexible and adaptable, offering humans a clear reflection of the energy and mystery of life." John Lewallen, of Mendocino Sea Vegetables, says that "seaweed has a deep spiritual consciousness. If you scorn seaweed consciousness, you get into trouble real fast." Every day, Lewallen throws back the first seaweed he harvests "as a kind of offering."

Seaweed harvesters' work is often dangerous, involving slippery surfaces in areas of powerful tides. Yet they describe the experience as a kind of oneness with the natural world. "I experience many of the parameters of life directly when harvesting in conditions that require absolute, breathing attention to staying alive and not doing harm; also conditions of great peace, gentleness, and comfort," says Cape Ann's Linda Parker. "All of the seaweed work is mantra work," writes Larch Hanson.

There is no process of certification for sea vegetables, but all these harvesters work in clean waters; some also test the seaweed and/or the water for chemicals. The vegetables themselves are "a veritable medicine chest of proteins, complex carbohydrates, and all forty-four trace minerals and vitamins," says Betsy Holliday, who recounts that once a year, the Sioux in Nevada would send runners to the Pacific coast to harvest and dry as much of the nutritious seaweed as they could carry back.

If you would like to include sea vegetables in your diet, here are some ideas, courtesy of the harvesters listed below.

Wild nori, or laver, is high in vitamin C and can contain as much as 25 percent protein. In Wales and Scotland, it's traditional to soak laver, mix it with rolled oats, and fry it. Nori can be toasted, dry roasted, or sautéed with peanut or sesame oil to bring out their nutty flavor. Roasted nori can be sprinkled onto soups, popcorn, and grains. One harvester likes to add it to eggs, another uses it in tempura. Maine Coast has recipes for a quick nori soup, sauteed cabbage with nori, fried rice with nori, an Indian dish of creamed corn with nori, and a nori salad dressing.

Alaria, which resembles Japanese wakame, is high in calcium and is a traditional base for miso soup. Fresh alaria can be sautéed in oil or eaten raw in salads; the dried alaria needs to be marinated or cooked at least twenty minutes in a soup stock, with rice and beans, or in a vegetable stew. Cape Ann's Linda Parker cooks alaria with red potatoes and black pepper. Maine Coast's recipes include an alaria succotash and an alaria-cucumber salad; it also recommends pan-frying alaria to make chips.

Dulse has more protein than chick-peas and is "the richest food source of iron in the world," says Cape Ann's Linda Parker. It requires little or no cooking. In New Brunswick,

Nova Scotia, and in Northern Europe, the soft, chewy vegetable is eaten raw as a snack, but cooking makes it milder and sweeter. You can add dulse to vegetables, grains, or beans shortly before serving; bake or steam it with potatoes; or add it to soups. Linda Parker likes to layer dulse with sweet potatoes in an oiled dish, drizzle the top with oil, then bake. Maine Coast recommends frying dulse into chips or baking it with cheese; its recipe book includes a dulse chowder, a vegetarian shepherd's pie, a Mediterranean salad, a dulse dressing, and even hot lemonade with dulse (for colds). The Lewallens of Mendocino Sea Vegetables even recommend adding dulse to your bagel and cream cheese—a vegetable version of the salty taste of smoked fish.

Kelp, or kombu, contains mannitol, a natural sugar, which gives it a slightly sweet taste. Kelp also tenderizes beans as they cook, making it a natural ingredient for soup stocks. Ocean Harvest's Betsy Holliday also makes kombu chips, bite-size pieces roasted briefly "until they turn bright green and begin to bubble—great with dips." You can also cook kelp and sprinkle it on popcorn. Maine Coast's recipes include black-eyed peas with kelp, kelp and potatoes, pickled cucumbers and kelp, and (yes) candied kelp.

CAPE ANN SEAWEEDS COMPANY

2 Stage Fort
Gloucester, MA 01930
(508) 283-9308

Certified by: SELF
Catalogue/price list available
Minimum order: none
Order by: phone, mail
Pay by: check
Ship by: parcel post

SEA VEGETABLES

Alaria · Dulse · Kelp (kombu) · Laver (nori) ·

Linda Parker and Janet Goto knew each other by sight—they had often passed each other jogging. One day, they were leaving the local food co-op together and got to talking. Parker was already a sea-vegetable forager, and Goto, who'd grown up in the country but spent many years in the city, started going with her as a way to get back to nature. On one of their walks in 1979—the summer solstice, to be precise—Cape Ann Seaweeds was born.

The two were having a picnic and foraging day on the beach, and the crop of laver was so large that Goto wondered aloud if they could sell it. Parker wasn't convinced, but they picked enough for their own kitchens and for a dozen one-ounce bags. While the laver was drying on Parker's porch, they called the manager of the local co-op. She agreed to let them sell it, and the two took down the bags with their carbon-copied labels. Total profit: six dollars. Undaunted, the two started doing research in cookbooks and in the sea itself. "The intertidal zone became our second home," says Parker.

The two also experimented with recipes. Janet Goto has spent time in Japan and uses

Cape Ann Seaweeds Co.

Alaria
Alaria esculenta

Thrive in delight and well being! Eat seaweed! Freshly picked seaweed has been sun or air dried. Wash to remove sea salt only if desired. Simmer Alaria in water for ½ hour to give tasty and hearty broth. Cooked seaweed can be chopped and stir fried. Especially good baked with carrots. Makes a delicious marinated salad with cucumbers. Add to rice and beans at beginning of cooking time. Use precooked Alaria in recipes calling for Wakame

NET WT. OZ.

2 Stage Fort Gloucester, Ma 01930 (617) 283-9308

seaweeds in oriental recipes; Linda Parker has what she calls a "more basic natural-foods style." Goto has since retired from the company to devote herself to medical school and mothering, but Cape Ann continues to benefit from "her joy and philosophy and cooking skills," says Parker.

In 1990, a 4-ounce bag of sea vegetables ranged from $1.80 to $2.25. You save by buying larger bags. Packages come with cooking ideas. Food co-ops interested in buying in bulk should contact Northeast Co-ops in the "Buying Clubs" section.

ISLAND HERBS
Waldron Island, WA 98297-9999

Visits: yes; weekend herbal retreats possible for small groups
Certified by: SELF
Certification pending from: WSDA
Catalogue/price list available
Minimum order: none
Order by: mail
Pay by: check
Ship by: UPS, parcel post
The price list gives seasonal availability so you can order in advance of the harvest; Island Herbs is closed December 20–February 20.

DRIED SEA VEGETABLES

Bladderwrack (whole or flakes) · Grapestone · Iridea cordata · Kelp (fronds or powder) · Nori · Sargassum mutica · Sea lettuce · Wakame

FRESH SEA VEGETABLES

Bladderwrack · Grapestone · Nori · Sea lettuce

TEA HERBS

Calendula · Rose hips · Red raspberry leaves · Wild raspberry leaves

Waldron Island, where Ryan Drum collects medicinal herbs and sea vegetables, is "sparsely inhabited," and more than two miles of treacherous water separate it from the nearest inhabited island. "I chose this isolated island hilltop as a safe, pollution-free—relatively speaking—place to live and raise my family with minimal environmental poison exposure," says Drum, who came to Waldron Island with a BS in chemistry, a doctorate in botany, postdoctoral work in cell biology, and ten years of university teaching behind him. The isolation of the island has meant a largely self-sufficient existence: Drum built his own house and has helped deliver his two children.

Waldron Island has "no pesticide spraying, no polluting industry, no road or ferry access, no stores, no utilities, and no safe harbor." Some people would consider these difficulties, but to Drum, they are advantages. "Many of my herbs come from never-tilled land, especially steep seaside meadows, and from forests far away from human habitation and machines." Waldron uses only "hands and hand tools" to gather and process herbs and sea vegetables, "which means fewer exhaust particles and incomplete combustion toxins." They are dried by wood heat "away from direct sunlight in rooms free of household and farm chemicals."

In 1990, sea vegetables ranged from $3 to $6 a pound fresh, and $13 to $24 per pound dry. There's a handling charge for orders under $20. Herbs ranged from $3 to $10 a pound fresh and $6 to $36 a pound dry. Waldron also gathers 30 varieties of medicinal herbs.

MAINE COAST SEA VEGETABLES
Shore Road
Franklin, ME 04634
(207) 565-2907
FAX: (207) 565-2144

Certified by: SELF
Catalogue/price list available
Minimum order: none
Order by: phone, mail, fax
Pay by: check, COD
Ship by: UPS, parcel post
Individual recipes and cookbook available

SEA VEGETABLES

Dulse · Kelp · Alaria · Nori · Digitata

SEA SEASONINGS

Dulse-garlic · Kelp-cayenne · Nori-ginger · Dulse granules · Kelp granules · Nori granules

SNACKS

Original Sea Chips (corn, dulse, kelp, onion, garlic, canola oil) · Saucy (corn, dulse, kelp, miso-onion, ginger, cayenne, canola oil)

SEA SWEETS

Kelp crunch (kelp, rice syrup, maple syrup, sesame seeds) · Kelp munch (kelp, puffed brown rice, raisins, pumpkin seeds, rice syrup, maple syrup, sesame seeds)

In 1971, Shep and Linette Erhart made a pot of miso soup using local alaria in place of imported Japanese wakame. To their surprise, they found they preferred the alaria, and Maine Coast Sea Vegetables was born. Today, from April to September, some eight to ten families wade out into the Atlantic in their hipboots to gather sea vegetables for Maine Coast Sea Vegetables. Hipboots or no, that hurts just to think of—have you ever felt the water off the Maine coast in April?

Maine Coast's literature lists many potential nutritional benefits of sea vegetables, including their high content of vitamins, proteins, and trace minerals, but adds that "dried sea vegetables are a concentrated and powerful food and may take some getting used to. A Japanese study indicates that assimilation improves as sea vegetables are more frequently consumed. We encourage people to try them more than once."

With those kinds of *caveat*s it's not surprising that Maine Coast has come up with ways to introduce sea vegetables to people who might be unlikely to crave dulse for dinner. Sea Seasonings combine flaked sea vegetables with familiar spices. I sampled all three blends. The dominant flavor in every case was the sea vegetable—the other herbs and spices really can't

compete—and while I can't really see them on popcorn, as Maine Coast suggests, they work well in oriental stir-fries or soups. Maine Coast also includes recipes for dulse-garlic dip, kelp-cayenne salsa, and nori-ginger tofu scramble.

Sea Chips are corn chips with dulse and kelp—the amino acids in the seaweed, say the folks at Maine Coast, complement the amino acids in the certified organic corn, making a more complete protein. The chips are baked before frying, so they don't have to spend very much time in the canola oil, which is also low in saturated fats and contains no cholesterol. The resulting texture is much fluffier than your usual corn chip. I sampled the Original Sea Chips, whose initial taste is dominated by corn, onion, and garlic adding a nacho accent. The second wave of flavor tastes the way ocean air smells. All in all, they're not going to replace other corn chips, but I could imagine serving them alongside a seafood- or fish-based meal.

The Maine waters are relatively unpolluted, and Maine Coast has had its seaweed tested for forty-seven different chemicals, of which no traces were found. With heavy metals, the story is not quite as simple. "We would like to report 'no traces,'" says Shep Erhart, "but that's an unrealistic expectation—these metals occur worldwide, both naturally, leached from exposed bedrock, and as industrial waste." All Maine Coast's plants "are harvested wild from their beds," says Shep, "and transported immediately to drying nets or racks for sundrying, or

MAINE COAST SEA VEGETABLES
Franklin, Maine 04634 • 207-565-2907
Nourishing products from the sea since 1971
■ SEA SEASONINGS ■ SEA CHIPS ■ SEA VEGETABLES

wood-heat drying in our special shed. There's no further processing before packaging."

Maine Coast includes recipes on each package, and sells an extensive cookbook.

In 1990, sea vegetables ranged from $1.80 to $2.60 for 2-ounce bags. Sea seasonings were 3 shakers for $8. Chips were $22.80 for a case of 12 6-ounce bags. Sea sweets were $8 to $10 for 4 3-ounce bags. You can order single bags of chips or sweets if you order other products. You save on most items by buying in bulk.

MAINE SEAWEED COMPANY
P.O. Box 57
Steuben, ME 04680
(207) 546-2875

Visits: yes; summer camp in August—write for details
Certified by: SELF
Catalogue/price list available
Minimum order: 3 pounds
Order by: phone, mail
Pay by: check
Ship by: UPS or USPS (specify)
Family pack available
Publications and recipes available
Apprenticeships available; if interested, write, don't call

SEA VEGETABLES

Kelp · Alaria · Digitata · Dulse

Over the years, Larch Hanson's life and the lives of plants have intertwined in mysterious ways. While living in San Francisco, Hanson worked as a typist for a company that built containment vessels for nuclear reactors. He replaced a secretary who had refused to type contracts dealing with nuclear power, and even though Hanson maintained the boycott, the company kept him on, "because I can type 70 words a minute on good days." While working there, Hanson met a woman who worked with Kevin, the psychic channel later made famous by Shirley MacLaine. He ended up "sitting in an office in the midst of the nuclear industry, typing a manuscript about healing flower essences that Kevin channeled from Dr. Bach."

Larch Hanson first tasted seaweed on a dare from the junior-high-school-age children in the summer camp where he was a counselor. In macrobiotic theory, says Hanson, this was first-level eating—"functioning at an unaware level of judgment." Since that first bite, he has spent nearly twenty years learning about—and from—the plants. His *Thoughts of a Seaweed Harvester* is a collection of poems (including one from Cape Ann Seaweed's Linda Parker), autobiography, and meditations on "paying atten-

tion," the "inner direction" required by seaweed harvesting.

Hanson works with the same wild plant beds every year, "in such a way that they can regenerate." After harvest, the plants are dried on lines outside or in a wood-fired "dryer." Hanson is distressed by the practices of harvesters in other parts of the world. For example, he believes that in Canada dulse harvesters "create potential sources of pollution when they spray their drying fields with herbicides, paint their boats with toxic marine paints, and refuse to build separating bulkheads between engine bilge-water and cargo space." (Hanson's boats are unpainted.) The Canadian harvesters' nets "may be treated with algicides, and the burlap bags used for containers may be treated with oil sprays. Some harvesters use aluminum boats that can react with the plants, just as aluminum cookware can react with the food."

Maine Seaweed Company includes recipes for soups, sautés, tempura, casseroles, and even

cookies, with the seaweeds. The recipes aren't anything of the "take a quarter-cup of this and a half-cup of that" variety—they're more like the base line for a jazz improvisation. More recipes are included in Hanson's *Thoughts of a Seaweed Harvester*.

In 1990, sea vegetables were $12 a pound. The family pack, a selected mix weighing at least 3 pounds, plus recipes and other literature, was $40. Shipping included. Kelp flake fertilizer is available for gardeners/growers and is $15 for 5 pounds.

MENDOCINO SEA VEGETABLE COMPANY

P.O. Box 372
Navarro, CA 95463
(707) 895-3741

Visits: yes
Certified by: SELF
Catalogue/price list available
Minimum order: none
Order by: phone, mail
Pay by: check
Ship by: UPS, parcel post
Recipes available

SEA VEGETABLES

Mendocino nori · Sea palm fronds · Mendocino wakame · Mendocino kombu · North Atlantic dulse

EXOTICS

Flaked nori · Sea whip fronds · Mendocino grapestone · Fucus tips · Mendocino dulse

Eleanor Lewallen was the first member of the Lewallen family to harvest sea vegetables, but wasn't quite sure what to do with them. So they hung around the kitchen—literally. At the time, her husband, John, was doing a stint in the real-estate business. One day, members of a commune called Love, Serve, and Surrender Corp. came to John looking for new property. They saw the seaweed in the kitchen and brushed aside the Lewallens' fears that some of it might be inedible, making their point by eating it all on the spot.

Eleanor Lewallen is a founder of the Ocean Protection Coalition, and is famous for coming to a hearing about offshore oil drilling partially draped in seaweed, which she tried to give to Donald Hodel, secretary of the interior. Hodel didn't know what he was missing. *East West* magazine has twice singled out Mendocino Sea Vegetables: in 1986, as "Best Sea Vegetable Supplier," and in 1987, as "Best Line of Sea Vegetables"—"fresh and tasty." Each package comes with recipes, and the Lewallens have written *Sea Vegetable Gourmet Cookbook and*

Forager's Guide, which also contains instructions for a seaweed picnic.

The Lewallens harvest sea vegetables "from unpolluted areas regularly monitored by biologists," says John Lewallen. He never uses plastic or metal screens for drying, for fear they might contaminate the sea vegetables.

John Lewallen, who used to edit and publish a counterculture newspaper, is not in the seaweed business to make money. The Stanford Law School dropout, who spent a year working with villagers in India and another two in a Montagnard village in Vietnam, says that even if you harvest 10,000 pounds a year, you're never going to get rich. At most, it supports "two environmental activists and our three kids (Rebecca, Shanti Shalom, and Loren) in economic low-income, with opulence of life," says John Lewallen. Opulence? Well, the Lewallens also sell (and use) the "Feather Boa for the Bath," a "feathered, sinuous, floating strip of seaweed" that is "very sensuous when rubbed on the skin." Although Lewallen does know people who eat the stuff, he's never tried it— even he draws the line somewhere.

In 1990, sea vegetables ranged from $1.80 to $2.40 for 1-ounce packages. You save by buying in larger quantities. Orders above $20 are postpaid; there is a mailing charge on smaller orders.

OCEAN HARVEST SEA VEGETABLE COMPANY

P.O. Box 1719
Mendocino, CA 95460
(707) 937-1923

Certified by: "Neptune"
Catalogue/price list available
Minimum order: none
Order by: phone, mail
Pay by: check, money order
Ship by: UPS, parcel post
Assortments available
Recipes available

SEA VEGETABLES

Sea palm · Silky sea palm · Wakame · Ocean ribbons · Sweet kombu · Kombu · Wild nori

Victor Marren had spent a dozen years foraging for sea vegetables on the "other" coast before he moved to California and founded Ocean Harvest Sea Vegetables. Marren says he left Gloucester, Massachusetts, for Mendocino for one reason: sea palm, a sea vegetable unique to this stretch of Pacific coast between Morro Bay, in California, and Vancouver Island, in British Columbia. At low tide, as Marren's partner, Betsy Holliday, described it for *East West*, the vegetable looks like a "miniature palm forest, a scene from *Gulliver's Travels*."

Sea palm has turned out to be Ocean Harvest's most popular sea vegetable. One reason for its popularity is its sweet taste, which comes from "natural complex sugars." Sea palm is also "high in trace minerals. Everybody enjoys sea palm—we've shared it raw with passers-by at the site of harvest, and every creature on the farm we inhabited last year—horses, goats, sheep, geese, ducks, chickens, hummingbirds, and bees, all adored sea palm." Holliday, who teaches macrobiotic cooking, has developed recipes for sea palm including tempura, soup, a salad with cucumbers, a stir-fry, a marinade, and lasagna.

As a rule, say Marren and Holliday, the sea vegetables of the West Coast are "a cross between the heavier, more medicinal flavors of Japanese sea vegetables and the lighter, thinner varieties of the Eastern seaboard." A distributor back on the East Coast wrote Victor and Betsy that "your seaweed has a strong, fresh, vegetable flavor, compared to other seaweeds which seem saltier and tougher."

Holliday and Marren attribute this difference in part to their conservative harvesting techniques. "We harvest our six species only in the peak of their growing season, even though it is possible to harvest about nine months of the year," says Holliday. "We are careful lest we imbalance this precious environment, and cut the algae so as to leave the reproductive functions intact. Our trimming and drying time, from ocean harvest to warehouse storage, is minimal—six to ten hours. We have nature to thank for this—a sunbelt adjacent to our damp coastal area whose extreme dry heat enables us to lock in the freshness of the algae under the sun's quick-drying eye."

Ocean Harvest gathers plants only from "pristine waters," says Betsy Holliday. "The area is classified by marine biologists as among the top five richest marine environments worldwide." She also points out that the steep continental shelf causes a tidal upwelling, which washes nutrients up to the sea vegetables. Offshore oil drilling would be a potent threat to that rich marine environment, and Ocean Harvest has named its two assortment packages after the House and Senate bills that will protect the coast if passed.

In 1990, single packages of sea vegetables (1 ounce to 1.6 ounces each) ranged from $3.70 to $4.50. A sampler pack of 3 varieties was $10.75; or 5 for $16.95. You save by buying in bulk. Shipping additional.

COLONEL SANCHEZ TRADITIONAL FOODS

P.O. Box 5015
Santa Monica, CA 90405
(213) 204-1137
FAX: (213) 204-1139

Ingredients certified by: OCIA
Catalogue/price list available
Minimum order: 1 case
Order by: phone, mail, fax
Pay by: check, money order, COD
Ship by: UPS
Cookbook available

SNACKS

Low-salt blue corn chips · No-salt blue corn chips · Chile and Spice blue corn chips

SALSA

Red chile · Green chile

FLOUR

Blue corn masa · Yellow corn masa · Tamale kit (corn husks, masa, chile, spices, recipes)

Born in Texas and raised in New Mexico, Kathryn Bennett has "a deep love of the traditional customs and lore of the Southwest." Bennett, who has run a health-food business and a soy-foods business, is a trained naturopath who describes herself as "a firm believer in living in tune with the forces of nature." So when it came time to choose ingredients for her line of southwestern specialties, she knew what she was looking for: organic ingredients, whose nutritional value had not been depleted by chemical fertilizers and overproduction.

Bennett chose blue corn not because it was "a fad or craze," but because the ancient, naturally blue strain, which southwestern peoples consider the "most nourishing" corn and use in their ceremonies and folk medicine, "yields a richer, more nutritious grain" than hybrids bred for easier harvesting, longer shelf life, or pest resistance. All the corn is organic and tested for aflatoxin. She also uses nonirradiated herbs and spices.

The beautiful, deep purple chips are delicate, crisp, and not at all oily—a group of us ate them while quilting, without worrying that we'd stain the fabric. The low-salt had a mild, slightly sweet flavor that would go well with guacamole or salsa. The chile and spice needs no dip at all. These are not nachos—there's no cheese involved. Instead, it's almost as if the chips had already been dipped in salsa, and pretty hot salsa at that, with just a twist of citrus. The chips come in opaque bags to reduce the effects of light and air on the oils. They are also available in decorator tins.

THE TRADITIONAL FOOD OF THE FUTURE

Bennett believes in preserving native methods of cooking as well as native grains. She sells corn masa to make tortillas from scratch, or the whole tamale kit, including corn husks, masa, chile, spices, and recipes.

In 1990, a case of 12 10-ounce bags of chips was $18. A box of 6 16-ounce decorator tins was $46.14. A case of 12 bottles of salsa was $24.32 for red and $25.96 for green. A case of 12 2-pound packages of masa was $23.16 for yellow and $38.40 for blue. A case of 6 gift-packaged tamale kits was $39.33 for yellow corn and $48.53 for blue corn. Colonel Sanchez also makes frozen foods, like tamales and burritos, which cannot be shipped. These use organic ingredients whenever possible. Contact the company for a store near you that carries them.

LEE'S ORGANIC FOODS
Running Springs Ranch
P.O. Box 111
Wellington, TX 79095
(806) 447-5445

Visits: yes; pick-your-own peaches, apples,
and Concord grapes
Certified by: SELF
Minimum order: $5
Order by: mail
Pay by: check
Ship by: UPS, parcel post

SNACK

Fruit jerky

Pemmican is a Cree word that originally meant
dried meat, often pounded with fruit and other
ingredients, into a handy food for explorers.
R. L. "Lee" Templeton makes fruit *pemmican*
from apples, peaches, and grapes he grows organically on his eighty-acre farm, which he
bought in 1960 because it had never been exposed to chemicals. "Not ever!"

The *pemmican* recipe changes from batch to
batch, says Templeton. "The taste of fruit jerky
varies according to the destiny of the fruit on
each tree, but the ingredients are always 50
percent shredded organic fruit, 20 percent
brown sugar, 15 percent oatmeal or pancake
mix, and 15 percent cornstarch."

Templeton picks apples when they're ripe,
which "gives a reddish color to our product,
particularly when winesap apples are added to
the mix." The "mix" includes Red Delicious,
Golden Delicious, Jonathan, Holland, Winesap,
and Templeton's pride—the Patrick Henry,
"which we think is the largest, best colored,
and best tasting apple in the world. Its aroma
is outstanding. We created this apple ourselves.
You can't get its flavor from anybody but us."

Templeton shreds the apples with the peel
on, finely enough so that the peel "will not be
caught between the teeth when eating." Ripe
peaches are put through a colander; they're so
ripe, says Templeton, "they come out as a bulky
peach batter." The skin gets thrown away. To
the apples and peaches, he adds oatmeal,
brown sugar, and "a bit of cornstarch to give
the batter a thick consistency." When he uses
honey, it comes from Running Springs Ranch's
own organic bee hives. This batter is baked,
cooled, and dried, and will last for three years
without refrigeration, says Templeton. I found
the flavor reminiscent of raisins and currants,
and would call it crunchy rather than chewy,
although I did refrigerate it before learning that
I didn't have to.

LEE'S ORGANIC FOODS
P.O. Box 111
Wellington, Texas 79095

"No Food is Better for Hungry Kids Coming
Home From School" proclaims Templeton's
package, but he also credits the jerky with
"mild laxative" properties and says that their
best customer is "a ninety-six-year-old tooth-
less widow, who 'gums' down our fruit jerky
after breaking it into small pieces with a pair of
pliers."

In 1990, a 10-ounce package of fruit jerky was $5.

OAK CREEK FARMS
Box 206
Edgar, NE 68935
(402) 224-3038
FAX: (402) 224-3536

Certified by: OCIA
Catalogue/price list available
Minimum order: none
Order by: phone, mail, fax
Pay by: check, money order
Ship by: UPS, parcel post

SNACKS

Blue corn chips · White corn chips · Yellow
corn chips

GRAINS

Amaranth (F) · Blue cornmeal · Yellow cornmeal · White cornmeal

CEREAL

Puffed amaranth · Roasted rolled oats

Ben Jones describes Oak Creek Farms as "neighbor working with neighbor." Oak Creek takes the grains of six or seven neighboring farms and adds value to them by turning them into pasta, chips, and flour.

One of the goals of Oak Creek, says Jones, is to repopulate the rural communities by offering more opportunities for people to get involved in farming, and "when neighbor works with neighbor, you build a good community relationship." Oak Creek Farms has been organic for ten years. It took three years to develop a market for its first organic crop, but Jones believes strongly that once you become "morally committed to organic growing and a clean environment, the financial success will follow." His faith has been justified: the farm has doubled its production, and its income, every year. Its packing material, by the way, is popcorn—the edible, not the styrofoam, variety.

Jones and his partner, Jack Horst, finance the operation "out of our own pockets," says Jones. "It's hard to get lending institutions to be interested in what we're doing. They'd be more than interested if we were spraying chemicals and growing corn and beans," but the unusual crops, like amaranth, a high-protein Aztec grain, and the unusual growing methods —organic—have made lenders wary. Whatever the bankers say, the folks at Oak Creek say using amaranth as one-quarter of the flour

in any recipe "adds sweetness and moistness" to baked goods.

One of Oak Creek's corn chips starts with blue corn, an ancient Hopi strain high in protein and much higher in the amino acid lysine than other corn. In Hopi legend, say the folks at Oak Creek, the mockingbird gave blue corn to humans, saying that the person who eats blue corn will have "a life of hard work, but his years will be many, and he will live into the time of his grandchildren." The violet-black chips made from the blue corn were an all-around hit, with a rich corn flavor and the light but dense texture of stone-ground grain. The yellow chips are close to the traditional tortilla, with a hint of roasted-corn flavor. The white chips are a bit oilier, and lighter and fluffier than either blue or yellow, with a mild flavor that cries out for a dip. The dominant flavor of the nacho-taco chips, which contain no cheese, was onion. All four varieties, as thick as taco shells, were extremely crisp, with just the right dash of salt.

In 1991, Oak Creek introduced a line of pastas, including several wheat-free varieties.

In 1991, an 11-ounce bag of chips ranged from $1.50 to $1.65. You save by buying in bulk. Flour ranged from $1.50 to $2 for two pounds. Shipping additional.

PLEASANT GROVE FARMS
P.O. Box 636
Pleasant Grove, CA 95668
(916) 655-3391

Certified by: CCOF
Catalogue/price list available
Minimum order: 1 case
Order by: phone, mail
Pay by: check
Ship by: UPS
Specialty gift packs available

POPCORN

Yellow · Popcorn on the Cob

NUTS

Almonds

Pleasant Grove's gorgeous butterscotch, amethyst, and garnet-colored popcorn comes on the cob, as decorative as Indian corn, but you don't have to hang it on your front door: it's completely edible. You have the choice of "cobbing"—twisting kernels off the cob before popping them in a pan, "the way they did in the old days," says Pleasant Grove's Ed Sills—or if you have a microwave, you can put the whole cob in a paper bag and pop it in about four minutes. I don't have a microwave, but took the popcorn to my cousins' house to try it. I particularly recommend the experiment if you have kids around, for the entertainment value alone. About half of the kernels fly off

PLEASANT GROVE FARMS

the cob, and the rest stay on, creating a cob covered with light, fluffy popcorn, ready for butter and salt.

Popcorn on the Cob is the brainchild of Ed and Wynette Sills. Ed Sills farms nearly 2,000 acres in partnership with his father, who started farming in 1946. In 1985, they converted forty-five acres to grow organic rice for Lundberg Family Farms (see page 219). Today, 95 percent of their acres are farmed organically. Wynette Sills, who has a master's degree in pest management, had worked as the Sacramento County farm adviser, and contributes her expertise. She divides her time between the office and the Sills's new daughter, and sometimes "the playpen comes right into the office."

Popcorn on the Cob comes in a handsome Mason jar, which makes it a beautiful gift, as well as a tasty one. The jar is tall enough to reuse for pasta, grains, or beans when you've finished your popcorn. This popcorn is also available in a cellophane bag for a slightly less expensive gift, and they do sell pre-cobbed kernels.

In 1990, a case of 12 22-ounce jars of yellow popcorn was $20. A case of 6 24-ounce jars of Popcorn on the Cob was $60. A case of 10 cellophane bags of Popcorn on the Cob (10 cobs per bag) was $40. Almonds were not yet available in 1990.

TABARD FARM POTATO CHIPS
1739 N Street, NW
Washington, DC 20036
(202) 785-1277
FAX: (202) 785-6173

Visits: yes
Farm certified by: VABF
Ingredients certified by: VABF, SELF
Catalogue/price list available
Minimum order: 1 tin
Order by: phone, mail, fax
Pay by: check, Visa, MC
Ship by: UPS

POTATO CHIPS

Yellow · Purple (available May–October)

Edward Cohen, who owns the Hotel Tabard Inn in Washington, D.C., has always had a strong personal belief that people need to know where their food is coming from. "When you have a restaurant in the middle of a city," says his daughter, Sarah, "you have to order all your produce. He always wondered, 'What *are* we serving people?'" To put an end to this question once and for all, Cohen and the staff of the Tabard Inn started a five-acre farm in Virginia's Shenandoah valley to provide organically grown food for the hotel.

Customers are "turned on" by having fresh, local produce, but so is the kitchen staff, says Sarah Cohen. "If the farm has a surplus of something, they know they have to use it, and it stimulates their creativity."

The potato chips grew out of just such a surplus. Edward Cohen is a "potato fanatic," says Sarah. "Potatoes are practically all he eats." So when a neighboring farmer found that the buyer he'd contracted his entire potato crop to had disappeared, leaving him with five tons of potatoes, Cohen stepped in and took some of the potatoes off his hands. He brought them back to the kitchen of the Tabard Inn and asked the cooks to experiment with chips. The result was so successful they soon had trouble getting enough potatoes to fill the demand.

Tabard Inn now has its own factory, but still makes chips using the "old-fashioned, hand-dipped kettle method," using sunflower oil. It makes its gold chips from Kennebec, Superior, and Yukon Gold potatoes, which, say the folks at Tabard Inn, "retain the least amount of oil and hold greater density and potato flavor than the average potato chips." The chips are re-

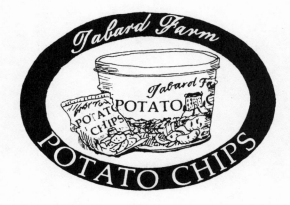

markably light, almost translucent, and completely addictive. Tabard Farm is also, thinks Sarah Cohen, the only place in the country making organic purple potato chips—undyed —from purple potatoes. Both chips come in a beautiful, reusable hat-box-sized tin.

Tabard Farm buys some potatoes from growers in states that do not have certification, but these growers provide a written statement of their organic practices.

In 1990, a 1.5-pound tin of yellow potato chips was $15, and a 1.5-pound barrel was $12.50. A 1.5-pound tin of purple chips was $20, and a 1.5-pound barrel was $12. Shipping included.

WYSONG CORPORATION
1880 North Eastman Road
Midland, MI 48640
(517) 631-0009
FAX: (517) 631-8801

Visits: yes
Ingredients certified by: various, including self-certified
Catalogue/price list available
Minimum order: none
Order by: phone, mail, fax
Pay by: check, COD, Visa, MC
Ship by: UPS

SNACKS

Blue corn chips

HERBS AND SPICES

Garlic Whole Salt

WHOLE GRAINS AND SEEDS

Quinoa · Flax seed · Wild rice · Whole brown rice · Whole wheat · Buckwheat · Alfalfa seed (for sprouting)

Dr. Randy Wysong markets his blue-corn Health Chips as "snacks without guilt." Dr. Wysong, a doctor of veterinary medicine, started the Wysong Corporation as a hobby, primarily to sell medical devices he'd developed in his practice. Then he had some "minor health problems" himself, and for the first time questioned his faith in technology to solve all medical problems. "The possibility of helping myself with simple foods or herbs seemed far more attractive than beginning to rely on various drugs," he says. Wysong began to study "a more gentle, less invasive, more natural, less harmful approach" to health. His catalogue expanded to include food supplements, vitamins, and a few foods—like organic whole grains and seeds.

It may seem strange that snacks get his top billing, but Dr. Wysong came up with the chips precisely because he knew how big a role snack foods play in the American diet. His Health Chips start with organically grown blue corn, a

W Y S O N G

particularly nutritious strain. Then he adds soybeans, ground sesame and flax seed, spirulina, and the dried juices of barley and wheatgrass. The chips are cooked in safflower oil, and lightly salted with Whole Salt, a combination of rock salt and trace minerals that Wysong says are missing from the diet of 60 percent of Americans. (For your own use, Wysong sells the Whole Salt plain or with organic garlic.)

To keep the oil in the chips stable, Wysong doesn't use commercial preservatives. Instead, he developed a natural preservative from vitamins, herbs, and natural resins. Wysong also sells an unskinned potato chip that is often, but not always, made from organically grown potatoes, and whose nutritional value, says Dr. Wysong, closely resembles the potato itself. The potato chips are thickly sliced, to reduce the amount of oil they absorb and, like the corn chips, cooked in safflower oil and lightly salted with Whole Salt.

Dr. Wysong ties personal health to the health of the environment—for one thing, he says, it's impossible to stay healthy in a decaying world. The Wysong Institute, a nonprofit subsidiary of the Wysong Corporation, is devoted to raising public awareness of environmental issues. Each month, the Institute compiles an audio tape of current research in the fields of health and conservation. The Wysong headquarters, surrounded by ten acres of woods, embodies its founder's ideas. Every room has a skylight, so employees can get natural sunlight; any artificial lighting in the building comes from full-spectrum fluorescent lights. Even the water in the air conditioners comes from a well on the property. The company has on-site day care, a fitness center for employees, and recycles all office materials.

In 1990, a 5-ounce bag of corn chips was $2.95. Garlic salt was $4.22 for 6 ounces. Grains ranged from $2.20 to $15.72 for 26 ounces and from $5.10 to $46.50 for 5 pounds. The catalogue also lists natural vitamins and minerals, food supplements, health and beauty products, and pet products.

SEE ALSO
Allergy Resources, Cascadian Farm, Eagle Organic and Natural Food, Omega Nutrition USA, Inc., Specialty Organic Source

TEA AND COFFEE

As with culinary herbs, the majority of tea herbs are imported, often grown in countries that allow heavy pesticide use, and routinely fumigated and/or irradiated. And, as one herb grower here points out, the accident at Chernobyl also contaminated much of Europe. This can make "healthy" herb tea not so healthy after all. The teas listed here come from herbs or tea plants that are grown organically or herbs that are "wildcrafted"—gathered in the wild. Some companies blend herbs from more than one source; "Certified by" refers to the sources of the herbs rather than the company.

AVENA BOTANICALS
P.O. Box 365
West Rockport, ME 04865
(207) 594-0694

Herbs certified by: MOFGA, TILTH
Farm certified by: MOFGA
Catalogue/price list available
Minimum order: none
Order by: mail
Pay by: check
Ship by: UPS

HERB TEAS

Day Break (oatstraw, alfalfa, calendula, nettles, spearmint) · Dancing Belly (peppermint, spearmint, alfalfa, fennel) · Mother's Blessing (blessed thistle, red raspberry leaves, nettles, fennel, peppermint) · Star Light (anise-hyssop, lemongrass, strawberry leaves, peppermint) · Winter's Wisdom (sage, yarrow flowers, peppermint, catnip flowers) · Yoni (red raspberry leaves, red clover blossoms, alfalfa, nettles, peppermint)

Deb Soule, born and raised in Maine, calls the wild herbs of Maine "my old, familiar friends." In 1985, Soule founded Avena Botanicals—named for the wild oat that "relaxes and strengthens the nerves"—to remedy the lack of chemical-free herbs on the market. Deb Soule has a busy teaching schedule, giving herb walks, workshops, and classes as far afield as Poland. Soule has published several books on herbs, including *The Whispering Weeds: Giving Voice to the Healing Herbs* and *Healing Herbs for Women.*

The names of Soule's teas give a sense of their purpose—Mother's Blessing is "safe and nourishing for nursing mothers"; while Day

PO Box 365
West Rockport, Maine 04865
207-594-0694

Break is "a nourishing and soothing tea to begin your day." Soule's description of Star Light is simply "Yummy!" All herbs in the teas are certified organic or wildcrafted.

In 1990, teas ran between $4.50 and $4.75 for a 3-ounce bag. The catalogue also contains simple extracts; compound extracts; extracts for women; women's herbs; oils and salves; flower essences; tonics, supplements, and products for animals; body-care products; bug repellent; home health chest; and books and pamphlets. The catalogue doesn't list uses for each herb; Soule suggests you direct your questions about herbs to a "well-trained herbalist."

BACK OF THE BEYOND
7233 Lower East Hill Road
Colden, NY 14033
(716) 652-0427

Visits: yes; bed-and-breakfast; greenhouse and "herbtique"; garden tours
Herbs certified by: SELF
Catalogue/price list available
Minimum order: none
Order by: phone, mail
Pay by: check, money order
Ship by: parcel post

TEA

Blend of lemon balm, chamomile, and calendula

GARLIC

Shallots (seasonal)

As a child, Shash Georgi "played store using silver dollars (Lunaria) or rose petals for money, and dried dock or coffee beans to trade and barter with other kids." Shash Georgi has turned her childhood "store" into a reality. In the 1960s, she and her husband, Bill, a doctor, moved from suburbs to the country, and built a greenhouse into their home. Bill "devoted

most of his spare time to designing the gardens, building compost heaps, tilling land, bartering with neighbors for hay and manure, and being totally supportive," while Shash developed her herbal recipes. The Georgis have been growing herbs organically for twenty-five years. Of

Shash Georgi's many herbal products, the herb tea is one of her biggest sellers. The Georgis also run an organic bed-and-breakfast with pond swimming and woods hiking in summer, and cross-country skiing in winter.

In 1990, a net bag of shallots was $2.50, and herb tea, enough for 10–12 cups, was $2.50.

BIOFORCE OF AMERICA, LTD.
P.O. Box 507
Kinderhook, NY 12106-0507
(800) 645-9135
(518) 758-6060
FAX: (518) 758-9500

Certified by: Schweiz Stiftung zur Forderung des biologischen Landbaus
Catalogue/price list available
Minimum order: $10 or $20 on credit-card orders
Order by: phone, mail, fax
Pay by: check, money order, VISA, MC
Ship by: UPS, parcel post

TEAS

Alpine blend (balm, raspberry, blackberry, strawberry, cornflower, peppermint) · Wild rose hip · Alpine peppermint

COFFEE SUBSTITUTE

Instant Bambu (chicory, figs, wheat, rye, barley, and acorns) · Whole Bambu (wheat-free)

CEREAL

Breakfast muesli

HERBS AND SPICES

Herbamare (celery bulb and leaves, leek, cress, onion, chives, parsley, basil, marjoram, rosemary, thyme, lovage, kelp, and sea salt) · Trocomare (same as herbamare, with red pepper, chile pepper, horseradish) · Alpamare seasoning with kelp

FRUIT SPREADS

Apricot · Strawberry · Rose hip · Blackberry · Blueberry · Raspberry

SWEETENERS

Carrot concentrate · Beet concentrate

When you look at the photographs of Bioforce's immaculate laboratories, you might well assume that they belonged to some high-tech realm of chemical agriculture: developing some potent pesticide, perhaps. Nothing could be further from the truth. These state-of-the-art scientific methods of research, analysis, and quality control are all in the service of herbal medicine and organic foods.

The founder of Bioforce, Dr. Alfred Vogel, was born near Basel in 1902. Dr. Vogel's first instructors in herbal lore were his parents and grandparents, and in 1925 he began publishing

books on medicinal plants and natural healing. After studying Europe's empirical folk medicine, he traveled to Africa, Asia, Australia, and the Americas to study the medicinal practices of tribal peoples. Dr. Vogel describes his stay among the Sioux of South Dakota as "among the most informative and inspiring" of his encounters, and credits it with deepening his "sense of man's union with nature." Dr. Vogel has lectured around the world; one of his books on natural medicine has been translated into eleven languages. In 1952, UCLA gave him an honorary doctorate in medical botany. Now ap-

proaching ninety, Dr. Vogel still works five hours a day.

Dr. Vogel founded Bioforce in 1963. Nearly thirty years later, Bioforce still grows herbs at its original site, the Swiss farming community of Roggwil, as well as elsewhere in Switzerland. The whole operation has an air of Swiss precision about it: photographs show perfectly neat rows of herbs in their gardens, shining stainless-steel instruments in the laboratories, and spotlessly white-coated technicians, even in the fields.

The herbs in the teas and seasonings are organically grown or gathered in the wild in Switzerland. The company is certified by a Swiss organization. When cultivating herbs, Bioforce doesn't use hybrids, starting its own plants from seed. I sampled their Herbamare seasoning, which contains an array of herbs but tastes primarily of celery and basil, and is a perfectly acceptable substitute for celery salt.

The fruit spreads contain only organically grown fruit and fructose, and are processed at a low temperature under a vacuum, leaving enzymes in the fruit intact. It takes pounds of organic carrots or six and a half pounds of organic beets to make one almost eight-ounce jar of concentrate, which can be stirred into cottage cheese or yogurt or added to cereal.

I was thrilled to learn that Bioforce made an organic version of muesli, the Swiss breakfast cereal. If you've never had muesli, the simplest way to explain it is that it's granola without the glue: a mixture of rolled oats, raisins, nuts, without any maple syrup or honey or peanut butter, or anything that gives granola its characteristic clumps. Muesli is not as good out-of-hand as granola, but with milk or yogurt and fresh fruit—heaven. Bioforce's version is delicious, sweet with almonds, chestnuts, dried apricots, and durian, a tropical fruit.

Bioforce's Bambu is not going to replace my favorite breakfast food—coffee—but made with hot milk, its sweet flavor, mellower than malted drinks like Ovaltine, might actually replace my late-night decaffeinated coffee. The night after I'd used my sample packet, I found myself wishing I had more around.

In 1990, fruit spreads ranged from $4.49 to $4.99 for a 7.76-ounce jar. Herb seasonings started at $2.29 for 3.2 ounces. Teas ranged from $3.49 for 1.4 ounces to $4.49 for 15.9 ounces. Breakfast muesli was $3.99 for 13.25 ounces. Juice concentrates were $10.99 for 7.76 ounces. Prices include shipping. Bioforce also sells a full line of herbal tinctures, combination herbal extracts, homeopathic medicines, vitamins, and body-care products.

BLESSED HERBS
Route 5, Box 1042
Ava, MO 65608
(417) 683-5721
FAX: (417) 683-3957

Visits: yes; no sales from the farm, but a family retreat house is available
Herbs certified by: various
Certification pending from: OOGA
Catalogue/price list available
Minimum order: $25
Order by: phone, mail, fax
Pay by: check, COD, Visa, MC
Ship by: UPS

TEA HERBS

Alfalfa leaf · Calendula flowers · Catnip · German chamomile · Elderflowers · Lemon balm · Lavender flowers · Linden flowers · Peppermint leaf · Red clover blossoms and leaf · Rosehips · Jamaican sarsaparilla · Sassafras root bark · Spearmint leaf

CULINARY HERBS AND SPICES

Ginger root · Juniper berries · Licorice root · Sage leaf

Martha and Michael Volchok and their four children live on the grounds of a Trappist monastery in Missouri, twenty-five miles from the closest town. The Volchoks, he from Seattle and she from Boston, chose Missouri as "a saner place" to raise their children, whom they teach at home. They first came to the monastery for a family retreat, and kept coming back. Eventually, the Trappist community (no longer

a completely silent order) took a vote and told them they could stay—but just for a year. The year elapsed, there was another vote, and the Volchoks got a second year. Now they have a twenty-five-year lease on 300 acres of land, and a contract in which they promise that their presence will not disturb the life of the monastery, where the Volchoks attend Mass and receive spiritual direction.

As their company's name suggests, the Volchoks believe strongly that herbs are "a blessing

from our Creator intended to nourish, heal, and soothe us." Martha Volchok is currently writing a book about the Christian use of herbs through time, to help Christians overcome negative associations of herbs with cults or fringe groups.

The Volchoks grew their first crop of organic herbs about fifteen years ago. One thousand pounds of fresh herbs turned into thirty-seven pounds dried. "We made something like twenty-seven dollars," says Michael Volchok. "After that experience, it took about ten years for us to get back to herbs as business. Our mentors are a number of smaller, genuine herbalists who directed and formed us, and taught us what constituted a high-quality herb, how to pick and dry herbs, and how to pick selectively to maintain the ecological balance of the area. Here in the Ozark woods, there are a tremendous amount of indigenous botanicals." The Volchoks grow some herbs themselves, buy herbs from certified organic growers, and also from people who gather herbs in the wild.

In 1990, the packets, from half-ounce to 2 ounces, ranged in price from $3 to $6 an ounce, depending on the herb. If you order 12 or more packets, you can qualify for wholesale prices. Many herbs are available fresh, shipped

Next Day or Second Day Air. Herbs are also available in bulk, starting at 1 pound, for buying clubs and other large-scale buyers. The Volchoks also sell an extensive line of medicinal herbs.

THE COFFEE CONNECTION
119 Braintree Street
Boston, MA 02134
(800) 284-JAVA
(617) 254-1459

Certified by: Demeter, University of Costa Rica
Catalogue/price list available
Minimum order: half-pound
Order by: phone, mail
Pay by: MC, Visa, Amex

COFFEE

Mexican Altura · Costa Rican Tarrazu

The Coffee Connection, Boston's coffee lovers' paradise, has recently added two organic coffees to an already overwhelming selection. You know you're dealing with serious coffee merchants when their catalogue rates each coffee on separate acidity and body scales, and indicates how the outer husk of the bean was removed (by drying or by washing). The Mexican coffee rated about a six on the acidity and body scales; the Costa Rican got about an eight on the acidity scale and a seven on the body scale. Both were washed, which means they have "crisper, cleaner flavor, more snap" than a dried bean.

The Mexican Altura, say the folks at Coffee Connection, has "the characteristic slightly spiced, milk chocolate nuance of fine Mexican coffees." These kinds of descriptions usually seem exaggerated to me, but I could actually taste what they were talking about—the rich flavor of cocoa made from real, unsweetened chocolate. On my acidity scale, the coffee rated very, very low.

The folks at The Coffee Connection describe the flavor of the Costa Rican coffee, grown on La Minita estate, as "an extraordinarily sweet, nutty fruitiness." I thought it had a spicy flavor, as powerful as many dark roasts even though the beans are fairly light, and definitely had more acidity than the Mexican.

The Mexican coffee is certified by Demeter, the biodynamic certification organization. The Costa Rican has been certified in a multi-step

process through the University of Costa Rica. An affidavit attests to the application of organic fertilizer, the soil and coffee were analyzed and no traces of twenty-four pesticides or herbicides were found. Finally, the total shipment was compared to standard yield for the number of hectares farmed, to make sure no other coffee beans were being added to the organically labeled shipment.

In 1990, a half-pound of the Costa Rican Tarrazu was $6.95. The Mexican Altura was $3.75 for a half-pound. You save by buying larger quantities. Coffee is available in whole beans or ground for any type of coffee maker. Shipping additional. You can also have a regular shipment of coffee, and you receive 20% off your first order.

DESERT MOUNTAIN TEA COMPANY

P.O. Box 328
Whitethorn, CA 95489
(800) 955-4832

Certified by: SELF
Catalogue/price list available
Minimum order: 1 can
Order by: phone, mail
Pay by: check, money order, MC, Visa
Ship by: USPS

TEA

Desert Tea

Desert Tea is just one of many names for the spidery Ephedra plant, native to the Southwest —among its other, more colorful nicknames are Mormon Tea (Mormons abstain from caffeine), Teamsters' Tea, Miner's Tea, Cowboy Tea, Mexican Tea, Squaw Tea, and Whorehouse Tea. I guess it's fair to assume we know who drank this tea, a free alternative to store-bought imported teas and coffees.

The folks at Desert Tea have been collecting wild ephedra in remote and clean locations since 1972—the exact spots remain the secret of the company. Brewing instructions are in-

cluded in the canister, which contains enough for 100 cups of tea. They say that you can keep renewing your cup by adding more hot water, and that the tea doesn't become bitter even if it steeps for hours.

In 1990, a 2-ounce canister was $9.95, including shipping.

EQUAL EXCHANGE

101 Tosca Drive
Stoughton, MA 02072
(617) 344-7227

Certified by: Naturland, OCIA
Catalogue/price list available
Minimum order: none
Order by: mail
Pay by: check
Ship by: UPS

COFFEE

Peruvian medium roast (whole bean or drip grind) · Peruvian French roast (whole bean) · Peruvian SWP decaffeinated, dark roast (whole bean) · Mexican medium roast (whole bean) · Mexican dark roast (whole bean)

The farmers who grow Equal Exchange's coffee are some of the poorest farmers in the world. Equal Exchange was founded in 1986 by "three veterans of the food-cooperative movement" to trade fairly with farmers like these and provide a "sympathetic marketing channel for Third World cooperatives." Equal Exchange seeks out democratically run cooperatives, and also trades with governments, as long as they "place a high priority on the well-being of all people through job creation, health care, literacy programs, and job reform."

The Peruvian coffee is grown by the Ashaninkas Association of Independent Coffee Producers, a farmers' cooperative in the mountainous rain forest west of Lima. Ashaninkas are the indigenous people of the area, and make up half of the cooperative's members. The other half are Peruvians new to the region. Co-ops like these, says Equal Exchange's Michael Rozyne, are particularly important in Peru's chaotic peasant economy, which has suffered terribly from years of civil war.

The Ashaninkas Association has a full-time agronomist who travels to the member farms and advises them on methods of organic growing. The entire process, including transportation, roasting, and storage, is certified by OCIA. Growing organically, says Michael Rozyne, one

of the founders of Equal Exchange, both helps the farmers get a higher price for their coffee and protects them from exposure to toxic pesticides.

The Mexican coffee is grown by a cooperative of 2,000 Indian coffee farmers in twenty-eight villages in the mountainous southern section of the state of Oaxaca. These farmers traditionally grew coffee without pesticides; now they are working actively to build up the organic content of their soil. Their soil is certified by Naturland of West Germany, which requires that growers abstain from chemical use for one year prior to initial certification. The 1990–91 season is the fourth year of certification for this coffee.

"Each family," says Rozyne, "works five to eight acres of land, including garden space for maize and beans, which many families grow for home consumption. The co-operative is run on a democratic basis. Each small village elects a representative to the general assembly. The co-operative has started a training facility to enable children of the farm families to get a supplementary education beyond elementary school. The training facility will teach children about gardening and organic methods of growing home vegetables, as well as the basics of coffee production. In 1990, the school enrolled girls for the first time."

In 1990, Peruvian coffee ranged from $6.35 to $7.95 a pound for whole beans. An 8-ounce can of ground coffee was $3.85. The Mexican coffee was $6 a pound. Coffee is sold in 4- to 5-pound bags. Orders over $50 receive a discount of 10%. The Equal Exchange catalogue also lists nonorganic coffees: Cafe Nica, arabica coffee from Nicaragua; and Cafe Libre, from "the frontline states in southern Africa."

FINCA DEL SETO CAFE
P.O. Box 30
Jayuya, PR 00664-0030

Visits: yes
Certified by: SELF
Minimum order: 1 pound
Order by: mail
Pay by: check, money order, COD
Ship by: Priority Mail
Harvest time is approximately August–November; supplies of coffee are limited

COFFEE

Arabica (whole beans or ground)

Coffee arrived in Puerto Rico in the 1750s. The Jayuya area, where Suzanne and Ed Jorgensen run a five-acre coffee plantation, is known for its coffee, and many of the Finca del Seto's Arabica trees are fifty years old.

The Jorgensens, originally from Chicago, live "in the shadow of Mt. Morales of the Cordillera Central, the mountainous backbone of Puerto Rico." The size and methods of their plantation are typical of the area. "From cultivating to picking to roasting, we do the job ourselves," says Suzanne Jorgensen. "We are very small-time, very much a cottage industry. In this day and age of freeze-dried, mass-

Finca del Seto
POB 30
Jayuya, Puerto Rico
00664-0030
Coffee Growers

produced coffees, our—literally—handmade coffee is a practically extinct product. We personally handpick our own beans when they're big, red, and juicy. No immature green beans. We pulp and sun-dry the beans, following traditional methods. And we always fresh roast each order, in an open kettle, to your specifications, although we do recommend our own dark, rich 'finca roast.'"

Indeed, when the Finca del Seto coffee arrived, it did not look even remotely like a mass-produced product. The beans varied in size and shape, and instead of being a shiny brown, were charcoal black. The coffee had a dark, smoky aroma and flavor reminiscent of food cooked over a wood fire.

Puerto Rico has no certification program, but the Jorgensens grow without synthetic chemicals or pesticides, and use no preservatives.

In 1990, coffee was $8 a pound, plus shipping, for orders under ten pounds. You save by ordering in bulk.

GRANUM, INC.
2901 N.E. Blakely
Seattle, WA 98105
(800) 882-8943 (orders only)
(206) 525-0051
FAX: (206) 523-9750

Visits: yes; complete macrobiotic specialty store
Certified by: SELF
Minimum order: 1 case
Order by: phone, mail, fax
Pay by: check, money order, COD
Ship by: UPS

CHOICE TEAS

Twig · Ban-Cha · Green · Oolong · Breakfast

Granum's teas are grown at the mountaintop Nagata Family Tea Gardens in Uji, Japan, where tea growing has a Zen feel: the Nagata family does not prune all the tea plants into identical forms; instead, they believe that every tea bush must be allowed to grow according to its own pattern. The Nagatas, says Granum's Ron Hanson, are known throughout Japan for their "nature farming"—growing without chemicals. Nature farming, say the folks at Granum, makes Nagata's plants much healthier

than commercially farmed tea. "The average lifespan of a commercial tea plant is only twenty years, while the Nagatas' nature-farmed plants can provide excellent tea for up to forty years."

The Choice tea line includes teas for both Western and Eastern tastes. I tried the Breakfast tea out on an English friend, who gave it his understated seal of approval: "It could almost be English." His American wife liked the "smoky flavor" of the Oolong, which I found smooth as well as smoky, with a slightly fruity taste.

The other teas are decidedly Eastern in flavor. The green tea is made from the first, tender spring leaves of the harvest season, steamed briefly immediately after picking. Steaming prevents fermentation and darkening of the leaves, which are then slowly oven-dried. In the bag, the leaves are distinctly green, with a rich smell reminiscent of fresh spinach. The tea itself has a tangy, almost acidic flavor. One friend described it as "strong, clear, and pungent."

Hanson explains that although other natural-food retailers call their twig tea Ban-Cha, in Japan the name means 'everyday tea,' so Granum reserves its use, in the Japanese style, for its roasted leaf tea. I found the flavor musky and decidedly oriental. I tried it out on a friend who'd grown up in Japan; she found it "mellow, not too acidic, which some Ban-Chas can be. It needs to steep a good four or five minutes. If you want more oomph, let it steep longer."

Granum's twig tea comes from the aged twigs and stems of the tea plant, harvested late in the season, when the caffeine level in the plants is at its lowest. The twigs are steamed and dried before resting for several years to bring out their flavor. Twig tea is rare in Japan, because the Japanese associate it with the poverty of wartime and the Occupation, but macrobiotic eaters know it as a good balance to the vegetables and grains of their diet. Twig tea may take some getting used to. One friend compared it to sassafras. Another said it was like "leaves, but not necessarily the ones you'd think of making into tea." I found it medicinal and slightly fishy, but Granum's Rod Hanson says he knows people who can't live without it.

In 1990, the price for one case (12 boxes) of tea was approximately $3 per box. Orders above $150 receive wholesale prices.

HERB AND SPICE COLLECTION
P.O. Box 118
Norway, IA 52318
(800) 365-4372

Herbs certified by: OR-TILTH, WSDA, OGBA
Facilities certified by: OGBA
Catalogue/price list available
Minimum order: none
Order by: phone, mail
Pay by: check, money order, Visa, MC
Ship by: UPS

TEA HERBS

Alfalfa leaf · Catnip · Lemongrass · Peppermint leaf · Raspberry leaf · Red clover · Spearmint leaf

HERB TEAS IN TEA BAGS

Alfalfa-mint

CULINARY HERBS

Lemon thyme · Sage

SPROUTING SEEDS

Alfalfa · Cress · Mung beans

In 1976, Frontier Cooperative Herbs was a two-person enterprise in a small cabin on the Cedar River in Iowa. Today, Fontier has a staff of over 125 and a licensed child-care facility for the employees' children. Sixty acres of farmland are devoted to organic herbs, wildlife plantings and habitat, and the employees' own gardens.

The Herb and Spice Collection, the retail catalogue of Frontier Cooperative Herbs, offers single tea herbs in foil packets that keep the herbs fresh for months. The single herbs allow you to enjoy the individual flavors or create your own blends. One whiff of the peppermint, fresh out of the foil bag, was as potent as the strongest English peppermints I'd ever eaten; brewed, the tea grew milder, but still had both the sweetness and kick of true peppermint. The raspberry leaf was sweet, with an oriental flavor reminiscent of jasmine tea. The red clover was not unlike a mild chamomile; the alfalfa had a clear, grassy flavor that would blend well with other herbs, and was very refreshing iced. If you prefer a preblended tea in bags, you can purchase a blend of alfalfa, peppermint, and spearmint.

Among its vast collection of herbs and spices, Frontier carries forty-nine that are certified organic. Not all are listed in the retail catalogue; but Frontier will make any of the organic herbs in its wholesale catalogue available to you in one-pound quantities. Garlic is available in five- or forty-pound quantities.

As of 1990, Frontier was growing six organic herbs in quantity on its own land. For all other herbs, it requires affidavits from all its organic suppliers. You can obtain these affidavits from them at any time. The company also will not sell any herbs or spices that have been irradiated.

You can also order the Cafe Altura organic coffee listed in the wholesale catalogue. Cafe

Altura is grown on the several small, family farms in the Sierra Mountains of southern Mexico. The coffee is imported directly from the farm, without brokers or middlemen, and is certified organic by the Demeter Association.

The Arabica beans are sorted by hand, soaked in rainwater, and sun-dried. One roastmaster has supervised the roasting of the coffee for the past ten years. The decaffeinated coffee is produced with the Swiss water process, which uses only water and steam to remove the caffeine.

Cafe Altura has plenty of flavor, but even the dark roast is lighter than most European roasts. The Kona blend is wonderfully, even dangerously smooth.

In 1990, culinary herbs ranged from $1.69 to $1.75 for a half-ounce. Tea herbs ranged from $1.65 to $2.25 for six-tenths of an ounce. Seeds for sprouting ranged from $1.89 to $3.25 for 4 ounces. You save considerably by buying in bulk. The catalogue also contains medicinal herbs, nonorganic seasonings and mixes, potpourri, dried fruits and vegetables, cheese powders, and natural flavorings and extracts.

LONG LIFE HERB CLASSICS
P.O. Box 69
Basking Ridge, NJ 07920
(908) 580-9252

Herbs certified by: CHSC
Catalogue/price list available
Minimum order: none
Order by: phone, mail, fax
Pay by: check, MC, Visa, money order, COD
Ship by: UPS

HERBAL TEAS

Dr. Chang's Original · Early Morning Riser · Sweet Oriental Lemon · Royal Chinese Chamomile · Vanilla Spice

Long Life teas have certainly earned their name: the "Original" Long Life tea has been around for 400 years. The story begins during the Ming Dynasty, when the royal family asked

the court's herbal physicians to create a tea that would have a delicious taste, a pleasant aroma, be visually attractive, and be both healing and nutritious. The resulting blend of licorice root, peppermint, ginseng, cinnamon, honeysuckle, poria, chrysanthemum, chamomile, and astragalus was handed down through the generations, and eventually ended up in the hands of Dr. Stephen Chang. Dr. Chang, who has written many books on herbal medicine, self-healing, the Tao, and I-Ching, passed the formula on to Kevin Lindseth, one of his students. Lindseth, who is both a medical doctor and a Chinese doctor, founded Long Life Herbal Classics in 1981. His wife, Katherine Lindseth, assured me that Dr. Chang is alive and well and living in San Francisco, and serves as an advisor on all Long Life's products.

Ordinary herbal teas, say the people at Long Life, are blended according to a fixed percentage of ingredients. By contrast, Long Life reblends teas every time it gets a new crop of herbs to maintain the taste and balance of the herbs, a process that can take days to accomplish. I sampled Dr. Chang's Original, which has a many-layered flavor; the first wave of taste is dominated by the peppermint; the second is a wave of sweetness—licorice, yes, but something more—that rolls over your palate. If you normally enjoy your herb tea with honey, you will find it completely unnecessary with this one. I can't explain it, but the sweetness is right there in the tea. When iced, the flavor has a touch of cinnamon and even a hint of coconut.

All the herbs are primarily certified organic or wildcrafted. If not certified, growers provide a statement of their organic practices. Some imported ingredients, like the vanilla bean, are certified by the government of the country they are grown in. The teas contain no caffeine, sugar, or flavorings. In addition, the bags are not bleached with chlorine or dioxin; the boxes are entirely made of recycled paper; and the cellophane wrapping is biodegradable.

In 1990, all teas were $3.25 a box, with a free box of the tea of your choice if you order all five. Long Life also sells medicinal teas in powder form, health and beauty products, and literature on the Tao.

ROOSTER FARMS COFFEE COMPANY
P.O. Box 471
Honaunau, HI 96726
(808) 328-9173

Certified organic by: Demeter
Catalogue/price list available
Minimum order: none
Order by: phone, mail, fax
Pay by: check, Visa, MC
Ship by: Priority Mail

COFFEE

Kona dark roast · Kona medium roast

The only thing wrong with Rooster Farms coffee is how smooth and sweet it is: a coffee addict like me could easily drink far too many cups before realizing what I'd done. I was just as happy drinking the medium as the dark roast, which is unusual, because it usually takes a darker roast to give coffee enough flavor for me. Both the medium and dark roasts were miraculously free of acidity or bitterness. Mike Craig, the owner of Rooster Farms, says that his coffee's "distinctive touch of sweetness is characteristic of high-mountain—mauka—beans."

The volcanic soil of the Kona region is ideal for coffee, says Craig. Coffee was first planted on Kona around 1828, "to supply Hawaiian royalty. We carry on some of the older cultivating practices," says Craig, "like handpicking, sun drying, and keeping the beans in small batches."

Craig has been an organic farmer since 1978, and has been "cultivating and promoting an organic program at every level of the Kona coffee industry." Some of the fertilizer for Rooster Farms comes—not surprisingly—from the Kona Poultry Farms.

Rooster Farms is certified by the Demeter Association, which certifies Biodynamic growers. An independent laboratory test showed its beans to be free of pesticides to the .01-parts-per-million level; free of insecticides to the .01-parts-per-million level; and free of herbicides to the .05-parts-per-million level.

In 1990, a half-pound of coffee was $6.95. You save considerably by buying larger quantities. Shipping additional.

ROSETTA TEAS

P.O. Box 4611
Berkeley, CA 94704-0611

Herbs certified by: various
Catalogue/price list available
Minimum order: none
Order by: mail
Pay by: check, money order
Ship by: UPS, USPS

TEAS

Solstice (rosemary, sage, thyme, gotu kola, red clover, spearmint) · Siesta (valerian root, chamomile, passionflower, lavender) · Revery (kava kava, damiana, gingko, passionflower, motherwort, peppermint, spearmint, lemongrass) · Max-Immune (pau d'arco, echinacea, red clover, prickly ash, licorice root) · Geronimo Red (kola nut, mate, rose hips) · Aphroditea (kava kava, damiana, saw palmetto, gotu kola, lavender, orange, spearmint)

In the spirit of the Rosetta stone, which helped archaeologists decipher Egyptian hieroglyphics, the folks at Rosetta Teas seek to unlock the

"benefits of the Earth's herbal heritage." They are also, incidentally, crusaders for "religious freedom," specifically, the right to use peyote in religious vision quests. (They will send you a pamphlet on the traditional uses of peyote, if you're interested.) I sampled their Siesta,

Solstice, and Max-Immune teas. The Siesta had a mild chamomile flavor. I preferred the Solstice, a light, refreshing tea, and liked the natural sweetness—from licorice—of the Max-Immune.

Whenever possible, the herbs are organically grown or harvested in the wild. The teas are sold loose, and are not ground, heated, or oxidized, so that the herbs retain their volatile oils and potency.

In 1990, teas were $4 for a 2-ounce bag or $20 for all 6 teas. You save by buying larger bags. Shipping free for orders over $20. Rosetta also sells reusable cotton tea bags, bamboo tea strainers, and steel mesh tea balls.

SATORI TEAS

401-B Ingalls Street
Santa Cruz, CA 95060
(800) 444-7286
(408) 429-1708
FAX: (408) 429-9899

Herbs certified by: OR-TILTH, WSDA, CHSC
Catalogue/price list available
Minimum order: none
Order by: phone, mail, fax
Pay by: check, COD
Ship by: UPS

HERBAL TEAS

Peppermint · Spearmint · Lemongrass · Red clover · Lemon thyme · Alfalfa

According to the *American Heritage* dictionary, satori is "a state of spiritual enlightenment sought in Zen Buddhism." Satori Teas are the creation of Steve Steigman, a former bartender and a pharmaceutical engineer whose own quest for enlightenment led him to develop the first herbal tea that provided a significant amount of vitamin C.

Steigman says freshness is the most important quality of an herbal tea. He advises his customers to take the "smell test" when they open a package of herb tea. The *San Jose Metro*'s

"Mr. Taste Test" took up Steigman's challenge and gave Satori's teas his highest rating—four stars, "for gourmet quality, aroma, and full-bodied flavor." Satori ensures freshness by offering the "herbs of the season," so selection and availability depend on what's being harvested at the time.

I can vouch for the freshness of Satori's products: a whiff of the peppermint will clear your sinuses, even before you brew it into tea with strong, clean, pure peppermint flavor. The

SATORI® FINE HERBAL TEAS

pungent spearmint doesn't carry *quite* the same kick. The lemongrass is mild and sweet tea, more grassy than lemony. If some of the teas are unfamiliar to you, you can order a two-bag sampler to try them out.

Most of the herbs are grown or wildcrafted (gathered in the wild) at Trout Lake Farm in Washington (page 303).

In 1990, a box of 20 tea bags was $2.95. A 2-bag sampler was 25 cents. Shipping additional. Satori also sells medicinal teas. Loose herbs are available on request.

SMOKE CAMP CRAFTS
Route I, Box 263-SS
Weston, WV 26452
(304) 269-6416

Visits: yes
Certified transitional by: MSOGBA
Certification pending from: MSOGBA
Catalogue/price list available
Minimum order: none
Order by: phone, mail
Pay by: check in advance
Ship by: UPS, parcel post
Gift boxes available

TEA HERBS

Bee balm · Chamomile · Lemon balm · Lemongrass · Lemon verbena · Peppermint · Sassafras root bark · Spearmint

TEA BLENDS

Appalachian mint (mints, persimmon, strawberry, and sassafras leaves, sumac berries) · Chamomile rose (chamomile, apple mint, hibiscus, rose hips, and rose geranium) · Cinnamon rose hip (rose hips, lemongrass, cinnamon, and lemon peel) · Colonial tea (bee balm, lemon balm, mints, raspberry leaves, sassafras root bark, fennel seed) · Cool mint (mints, alfalfa, eucalyptus, wintergreen leaves) · Day's End (chamomile, rose hips, mints, hops, orange peel, anise, fennel seed) · Elderblossom (elderblossoms, alfalfa, anise seed, orange peel, clove) · English rose (rose petals, lavender mint, rosemary, rose geranium leaves) · Lemon lavender (lemongrass, lemon balm, lavender mint, lemon verbena, lavender, rosemary) · Lemon mint (mints, lemon balm, lemongrass, lemon verbena, hibiscus, sassafras leaves) · Mint medley (mints, lemongrass, alfalfa, nettles, rose hips, orange peel) · Red clover (clover blossoms, cinnamon, orange peel) · Rosy mint (mints, lemongrass, hibiscus) · Spiced jasmine (black teas, jasmine flowers, spices) · Spicemint (peppermint, wintergreen, raspberry leaves, sassafras leaves, cleavers) · Thin mint (mints, cleavers, yerba mate, cornsilk, rose hips, fennel seed)

CULINARY HERBS AND BLENDS

Anise seed · Basil · Whole bay leaves · Cilantro · Dill weed · Crystallized ginger · Lemon thyme · Marjoram · Greek oregano · Mexican oregano · Parsley · Whole rosemary · Sage · French tarragon · Thyme

HERB BLENDS

Roastmeat seasoning · Salt-free seasoning · Curry powder · Herbal blend · Herb butter mix · Italian blend · Lemon pepper · Bouquet garni

JELLIES

Sassafras · Cinnamon apple · Dandelion blossom · Apple-geranium · Elderberry apple · Corncob · Lavender blossom · Chamomile · Rose petal · Violet blossom

BUTTERS

Grape-apple · Pumpkin

JAM

Lemon honey · Seedless blackberry · Seedless gooseberry · Green pepper · Raspberry rhubarb · Blueberry cinnamon · Rhubarb apple · Peach nutmeg · Sour cherry · Quince apple · Hot pepper · Strawberry rhubarb · Spiced tomato · Plum · Persimmon apple · Elderberry grape

Dorothy and Robert Montgillion got into the herb business when they "escaped" from Maryland to West Virginia, says Dorothy Montgillion. A number of their new neighbors were elderly people who depended on herbs for medicines but were no longer able to go out in the woods and collect what they needed. They heard that the Montgillions knew something about herbs, and asked whether they would mind doing the collecting.

It wasn't long before the Montgillions found themselves in business. Today they sell some eighty herbs and herb blends, and some thirty jams and jellies, but it's still strictly a family business, with some help from a granddaughter, and some from an apprentice who is "learning by doing."

All of the herbs are organically grown or wildcrafted except for a few tropical/desert species. Dorothy Montgillion says that they're very lucky to live next door to a 5,000-acre nature preserve where "nobody lives, and nobody sprays—not even the right of way gets sprayed," and where she is able to gather many of her herbs without worrying.

In addition to her teas, Dorothy Montgillion makes such rare delicacies as flower jellies. Like teas, they start out with blossoms infused in boiling water. None of the flower jellies is

too sweet, she says, because you have to add a fair amount of lemon juice to make them jell. The dandelion, she says, has a honey flavor; the apple-geranium combines apple juice with scented geranium leaves. The lavender is a delicate flavor that makes a good dressing for a fruit salad.

She also makes corncob jelly, a recipe that dates back to the 1880s. "It was developed out in the Midwest. I guess they were pretty hungry, and the only things they had to make jelly from were corncobs." She used red field corn, which gives the jam a reddish color; she says the sweet flavor is reminiscent of maple syrup.

Dorothy Montgillion also makes hot pepper jam, a recipe from her mother's Ball canning book, written back in the 1940s. It's a base of bell peppers, with a bit of hot pepper added. If it were all hot pepper, she says—"Wow, you couldn't eat it." She recommends it with cream cheese or as a relish for meats.

She doesn't call her jams organic, because the sugar and the pectin are not organic, but except for cranberries and tropical fruits like pineapple, orange, and banana (not listed above), all flowers, fruits, and vegetables in the jams and jellies are gathered in the wild or locally grown, almost all organically.

In 1990, tea blends were $1.50 apiece, and a gift box of 4 was $6. Culinary herbs and blends in plastic bags were 85 cents to $1.50. A gift box of 3 jars of herbs was $4. Postage additional. A 5-ounce jar of jam was $2.50. Prices decrease if you order in quantity. A gift box of 3 jams was $7.50. Prices of jam include postage. The Montgillions also sell medicinal herbs, medicinal blends, and books on herbs. Limited quantities of other herbs are available, so if you're looking for something else, ask whether it's for sale.

WAHATOYA HERB
P.O. Box 169
Gardner, CO 81040
(719) 746-2370

Visits: yes
Herbs certified by: various
Catalogue/price list available
Minimum order: none
Order by: phone, mail
Pay by: check, money order, COD
Ship by: UPS

HERB TEAS

Breathe-Free (chamisa; anise; alfalfa; red, yellow, and white clover; peppermint; comfrey; mormon; rosemary; juniper berry; sunflowers; sage; willow bark) · Flow-Thru (lemongrass, nettles, cornsilk, Uva Ursi, mint, parsley, burdock root, cleavers, barley straw, hollyhock flowers, dandelion leaf, horsetail, alfalfa) · Geronimo (dandelion root, chicory root, sprouted barley, carob, amaranth, mushroom, flax seed, blue corn, yellow clover) · Just for Fun (peppermint, elderberries, rosehips, red raspberry leaves, strawberry leaves, pine needles, elderflowers, violet leaves and flowers, rose petals, calendula flowers, plantain) · Soothe-Me (chamomile, coriander, catnip, borage, hops, wild lettuce, skullcap, comfrey, valerian root, spearmint, cultivated and wild licorice root)

The Huerfano Valley, or Valley of the Orphan, in southern Colorado, is one of the highest mountain valleys on the North American continent. The founders of Wahatoya Herbs settled in the valley because it had never seen pesticide use; the land surrounded by mountains was completely clean. *Wahatoya,* an Indian word meaning "Breast of the Earth," is the name of the mountains that mark the valley's entrance.

As that poetic name suggests, the two founders of Wahatoya Herbs look to the earth for nourishment. Bella Hecht-Cloud is an herbalist who has been blending herbs for over fifteen years. Her partner, Juleen Gliko, describes Hecht-Cloud as "a typical sixties drop-out who'd left New York for the Southwest and lived off the land for a long, long time." Gliko shuttled back and forth, living part-time in the Southwest, and returning to New York City, where she worked as an art director, whenever she needed to make some money. "The only way to live in the middle of nowhere," says Gliko, "is to be independently wealthy—or start a business," which is exactly what she and Hecht-Cloud did in 1986. Two years later, *East West* magazine awarded their Just for Fun tea, a light, citrusy blend, its award for "Best New Tea."

The blends start with herbs that are abundant in the Huerfano Valley. Hecht-Cloud experimented for years to combine the often bitter medicinal herbs with culinary herbs to achieve appealing flavors. Except for anise,

chamomile, and cultivated licorice root, the herbs are "wildcrafted from sheltered places in the mountains" or grown organically by neighbors. The blended teas are not irradiated and come in resealable bags. All teas come in tea bags, except Geronimo, an instant beverage that comes in bulk.

In 1990, each bag (16 individual tea bags) was $3.50, plus shipping.

LATE-BREAKING INFORMATION

RANUI GARDENS
1459 Hoytsville Road
Coalville, UT 84017
(801) 336-2813

Certified biodynamic by: Demeter
Minimum order: none
Pay by: check
Ship by: USPS

TEA

Chamomile

Ranui Gardens grows tea at an altitude of 6,000 feet, which produces a higher oil content, says owner Jennifer Erikson—you need much less tea to make a cup.

In 1990, tea was $2.50 a packet (1.5 ounces), plus shipping. The company also sells catnip products.

SEE ALSO
Big River Nurseries, Blessed Maine Herb Company, Cottage Garden Herbs, Eagle Organic and Natural Food, Elderflower Farm, Island Herbs, Meadowbrook Herb Garden, Mountain Butterfly Herbs, Richters, Riverbluff Farm, Rose Eagle Enterprises, Inc.

The companies in this section sell foods in many, many categories—one-stop shopping, if you will. Many ship fresh produce as well as dry and packaged items. They carry too many items to list individual prices, but all have catalogues or price lists available.

At the end of this section you'll find a list of local natural-foods stores that will ship organic items. Most will ship only nonperishable foods, but exceptions are listed.

When companies sell both grains and flours, grains are listed first. An (F) next to the grain means that flour is also available. A (C) means that cereal is also available.

In most cases, these companies sell produce/products from many different suppliers. "Certified by" indicates the organizations that certify their suppliers.

CARR'S SPECIALTY FOODS
Box 1016
Manchaca, TX 78652
(512) 282-9056

Sells items certified by: CHSC, TDA
Catalogue/price list available
Minimum order: $25 for credit-card orders
Order by: phone, mail
Pay by: check, Visa, MC
Ship by: UPS

DRIED FRUIT

Apples · Apricots · Bing cherries · Black Mission figs · Calimyrna figs · Zante currants · Medjool dates · Deglet Noor dates · Halawi dates · Monukha raisins · Thompson raisins · Peaches · Pears · Prunes · Mixed fruit sampler

NUTS AND NUT BUTTERS

Almonds · Walnuts · Filberts · Cashew butter · Sesame tahini

SEEDS

Flax · Sesame · Sunflower · Quinoa

BEANS

Anasazi · Baby lima · Black-eyed peas · Black turtle · Chick-peas · Kidney beans · Lentil (red or green) · Mung · Pinto

GRAINS

Pearled barley · Hulled millet (F) · Whole rye (F) · Wheat bran · Long-grain brown rice · Amaranth (F)

OTHER FLOUR

Stone-ground whole wheat · Blue cornmeal · Yellow cornmeal · Unbleached white

BAKING MIXES

Multi-grain biscuit · Bran muffin · Multi-grain pancake and waffle

SNACKS

Yellow popcorn · Blue corn curls · Yellow corn curls · Cheese corn curls

CUPCAKES (CAROB OR YOGURT TOPPING)

Brownie · Carob chip

SOUP MIX

Beans, lentils, barley, and spelt

HERBS

Sage

While working for a life-sciences institute, Ruby Keegan met many people who couldn't find the natural and organic foods they wanted. Keegan started the business with her brother, Don Carr, in 1987. In addition to what's in the catalogue, says Mrs. Keegan, "established customers often request certain fresh produce or other items they haven't been able to find. We get it." In coming years, Carr's will place a greater emphasis on carrying foods grown locally in Texas. It currently carries the Arrowhead Mills line of flours and grains, one of the most venerable organic suppliers, based in Texas. It also carries products from Timber Crest Farms (see page 64).

DEER VALLEY FARM
RD 1
Guilford, NY 13780
(607) 764-8556

Visits: yes; picnic facilities
Foods/ingredients certified by: NOFA, CCOF
Catalogue/price list available
Minimum order: $10
Order by: phone, mail
Pay by: check
Ship by: UPS, parcel post
Fresh fruit available November–May

BREAD

Whole wheat · Whole-grain rye · Whole-grain raisin · Whole-wheat frankfurter rolls · Whole-wheat hamburger buns · Three-grain sprouted bread (wheat, rye, and oats)

CAKES

Flourless nut · Whole-wheat fruit (November–December only) · Whole-wheat pound · Whole-wheat sponge

COOKIES, PASTRIES, AND BUNS

Carob chip · Molasses · Fruit-filled tea ring · Maple nut buns · Danish buns (fruit filled) · Apple turnovers · Sticky buns · Whole-wheat date-nut bread · Bran muffins

PIES

Apple · Raspberry · Pumpkin · Blueberry · Strawberry

DRIED FRUITS

Apples · Apricots · Deglet Noor dates · Dehydrated dates · Black Mission figs · Calimyrna figs · Prunes · Thompson seedless raisins

APPLES

McIntosh · Spy · Cortland · Red Delicious · Winesap

CITRUS

Oranges · Grapefruit · Lemons

BEANS AND SEEDS

Adzuki · Alfalfa seeds · Navy · Lentils · Baby lima · Marrow · Mung · Red kidney · Soy (yellow or green) · Yellow split peas · Turtle soup

GRAINS

Barley (whole or pearled) (F,C) · Buckwheat · Popcorn · Brown rice (long- and short-grain) (F) · Whole kernel rye (F) · Wheat kernels (C) · Whitmer wheat kernels (F) · Triticale (wheat-rye cross) (F)

OTHER FLOUR

Yellow corn · Graham · Soy · Soft wheat · Pancake mix

OTHER CEREAL AND MEAL

Yellow cornmeal · Corn grits · Sesame seed meal · Soy (grits or meal)

HONEY

Buckwheat · Wildflower (liquid or crystal) · Tupelo

WHOLE-WHEAT PASTA

Spaghetti · Elbows · Noodles · Shells · Lasagna

SPINACH PASTA

Fettucini · Linguini · Spaghetti · Elbows · Noodles

JUICE

Grape

MEAT

Beef (many cuts) · All-beef frankfurters · Veal (many cuts) · Lamb (many cuts) · Pork (many cuts) · Ham slices · Pork sausage · Bacon · Canadian bacon · Turkey · Turkey sausage · Chicken

OTHER DAIRY

Eggs · Soymilk

FISH

Cod · Perch · Turbot

FRESH VEGETABLES

Potatoes · Carrots · Onions · Rutabaga · Cabbage (red or green) · Beets · Turnips · Acorn squash · Butternut squash

Deer Valley Farm, in the rolling hills of New York State's Chenango County, is a family farm, says its owner, Robert Carsten. "We do hire outsiders, but then we consider them to be family." The Carstens are among the pioneers of organic farming in this country. Robert Carsten says that his father "had always been interested in natural foods, and read J. I. Rodale's *Pay Dirt* in the early 1940s." When the family moved from Long Island to Deer Valley Farm, the elder Carsten "went all the way."

The senior Carsten's interest was "accentuated by serious health problems" which he "pulled through" by switching to a natural diet with plenty of raw juices. When we spoke, Robert Carsten's father was about to celebrate his ninety-fifth birthday. "There's no doubt about it," says his son. "He wouldn't be around today if he hadn't made the switch."

In the 1940s, the Carsten family converted a "regular commercial farm" to an organic dairy farm; after fifteen or twenty years of raising dairy cows, they added beef cattle, pork, veal, and chickens. Today, in addition to selling their own meat and vegetables, Deer Valley has an on-site bakery that bakes bread, cookies, and cakes from stone-milled organic grains,

fresh eggs, milk, organic raw honey, maple syrup, nuts, and dried fruits. Its yeast breads contain no sugar, sweetened only with honey, maple syrup, and unsulphured molasses.

GARDEN SPOT DISTRIBUTORS
438 White Oak Road
New Holland, PA 17557
(800) 829-5100
(717) 354-4936
FAX: (717) 354-4934

Visits: yes; to visit Shiloh Farms, write P.O. Box 97, Sulphur Springs, AR 72768
Ingredients certified by: OCIA, private labs
Catalogue/price list available
Minimum order: $25
Order by: phone, mail, fax
Pay by: check, MC, Visa
Ship by: UPS, Second or Next Day Air, USPS

BREADS

Seven-grain · Gluten · Sprouted rye · Sprouted wheat · Wheat-free rye · Ten-grain sandwich loaf · Sprouted five-grain · Sprouted seven-grain · Bran · Whole wheat · Whole-wheat raisin · Whole-wheat sunflower seed · Whole-wheat hot dog rolls · Whole-wheat hamburger buns · Whole-wheat pita

MEAT

Uncured beef hot dogs · Uncured chicken and beef hot dogs · Beef brown 'n' serve sausages · Beef sandwich loaf · Beef with garlic sandwich loaf · Chicken · Turkey · Chicken pies · Turkey pies

JUICE

Apple · Carrot · Boysenberry · Homegrown punch · Martha's Vineyard · Peach nectar · Strawberry cooler · Concord grape

FROZEN VEGETABLES

Corn · Peas

SNACKS AND CHIPS

Blue or yellow corn tortillas · Whole-wheat

tortillas · Nachos · Corn chips · Blue corn chips

BEANS

Adzuki · Black soy · Black turtle · Green lentil · Mung · Navy · Pinto · Soybeans · Sprouted peas

PREPARED FOODS

Refried beans

GRAINS

Amaranth (F) · Hulled or hull-less barley (F,C) · Whole seed corn (F,C) · Buckwheat groats (F,C) · Whole kamut (F) · Kamut pasta · Millet (C) · Whole oat groats (F,C) · Popcorn · Rye · Rice (long- or short-grain) (F) · Triticale · Spelt · Hard wheat (F,C) · Soft (pastry) wheat (F)

OTHER FLOUR

Rye · Soybean · Unbleached

OTHER CEREALS

Blue cornmeal · Oat bran raisin delight · Soybean grits

BAKING MIXES

Whole-wheat pancake · No-salt whole-wheat pancake

PASTA

Kamut

DRIED FRUIT

Thompson seedless raisins

SEEDS

Alfalfa for sprouting

SWEETENERS

Date sugar

OILS

Corn · Olive · Safflower · Sesame

TOFU/MEATLESS PRODUCTS

Tofu · Tofu burgers · Vegetarian burger mix

CHEESE

Jack · Cheddar · Colby · Life farmer's

CONSERVES

Peach butter

Shiloh Farms was founded in 1942 as a Christian community on a farm in western New York, where relationships were based on "integrity, honesty, hard work, and care for others." A bakery and food-distribution center supported the community. After twenty-six years, Shiloh, which means "Place of Peace," moved to the Ozark Mountains in northwest Arkansas.

Garden Spot is the exclusive East Coast distributor of products from Shiloh Farms. The owner of Garden Spot, John Clough, is the former president of Shiloh Farms. His wife, Kathy, explained that most of the families at Shiloh have been there for forty years; but "people are free to come and visit or stay for a day, a week, or a lifetime, at no charge. They just become part of the family. It's interdenominational—you need to follow the rules, but no one is coerced into anything." The bakery at Shiloh

still produces all of the sprouted-grain breads that carry the Shiloh Farms label. Shiloh has always used organic grains, says Kathy Clough, but by 1991, every ingredient, including the gluten flour, will be organic.

I sampled the sprouted seven-grain and ten-grain breads. Both are American-style sandwich loaves, with a bit more substance and a more interesting texture, a slight crunchiness from the whole grains, than a standard American bread. I preferred both breads toasted, particularly as a base for grilled cheese. They'd probably be a good choice if you have a lot of children's sandwiches to make; they're close enough to their nonorganic counterparts not to cause a ruckus. I gave some to a neighbor to test on her four-year-old and nine-year-old; she reported that both breads were versatile and "easily disguised" for children; hers ate them happily in sandwiches, as toast, and as French toast.

The newest additions to the Shiloh Farms line use kamut, an ancient Egyptian grain related to wheat. Kathy Clough explains that "because it has twenty-eight chromosomes, 99 percent of the people with wheat allergies can eat it. The pasta turns light-colored when cooked, so even children or people who are not interested in health food will eat it. Unlike spelt pasta, which turns to mush if you overcook it, this pasta holds its shape. The flour is close to a soft wheat flour, so it's better for pastry than for bread." I sampled kamut macaroni, which was sweeter and denser than a white-flour macaroni, without macaroni's traditional bounce; it made a satisfying bowl of pasta, with a slightly spicy flavor.

The breads contain only whole sprouted grains, pure water without chlorine, fluoride, or trihalomethanes, and natural sweeteners. The meats are free of hormones, stimulants, antibiotics, nitrates, and nitrites. Shiloh Farms requires that all its products be grown and processed without synthetic chemicals for at least three years. The products undergo lab testing for twenty-nine different insecticides and pesticides. The products may not have a residue in excess of 5 percent of the level regarded as safe by the FDA. The products must also be continuously refrigerated rather than fumigated. Copies of lab reports are available.

Also for sale are products from Specialty Organic Source (page 281), Tabard Farm Potato Chips (page 246), French Meadow Bakery (page 33), Sno-Pac Frozen Foods (page 300), and Cascadian Farm (page 172), including the frozen foods that Cascadian Farm doesn't ship. Five percent discount on orders over $100. Frozen foods shipped with dry ice at an extra charge. Cheese is shipped only in cold weather. Many products are also kosher and are marked as such in the catalogue.

JAFFE BROTHERS, INC.
P.O. Box 636
Valley Center, CA 92082-0636
(619) 749-1133
FAX: (619) 749-1282

Visits: yes
Sells foods certified by: various
Catalogue/price list available
Minimum order: 5 pounds
Order by: phone, mail, fax
Pay by: check, MC, Visa, COD
Ship by: UPS, parcel post, PUC truck
Samplers available
Gift certificates available
Recipe collection available

DRIED FRUIT

Apples · Apricots · Sun-dried apricots · Cherries with pits · Black Mission figs · Calimyrna figs · Peaches · Pears · Santa Clara jumbo prunes · Pitted prunes · Monukka raisins · Thompson seedless raisins · Zante currants · Fuyu persimmons · Unsweetened persimmons (processed without bleach or preservatives) · Mixed fruit pack (apples, pears, peaches, pitted prunes)

DATES

Khadrawi · Deglet Noor · Halawi · Zahidi · Medjool · Bread date · Honey date · Empress · Date-coconut confection · Date-pecan logs

PEAS AND BEANS

Black-eyed peas · Whole sprouting peas · Soy · Mung · Lentils · Red kidney · Pinto · Adzuki · Navy · Black turtle · Great northern · Garbanzo · Green split peas · Baby lima · Anasazi

SEEDS

Hulled sunflower · In-shell striped sunflower · In-shell black sunflower · Hulled sesame · Flax · Cabbage · Onion · Kale · Yellow mustard · Alfalfa · Red radish · Red clover

GRAINS

Amaranth (F) · Whole yellow kernel corn (F) · Millet · Sprouting millet · Rolled oats · Hulled oats · Sprouting oats · Sprouting wheat berries · Wheat berries for baking (F) · Pastry wheat berries (F) · Rye berries (F) · Whole-kernel sprouting buckwheat · Buckwheat groats · Popcorn · Hulled barley · Sprouting barley · Quinoa · Oat bran · Brown rice (long- and short-grain) · Wild rice

CEREAL

Multi-grain (whole wheat, millet, barley, corn, rye, triticale)

PASTA

Whole-wheat lasagna · Elbows · Veggie elbows (tomato, spinach, celery) · Medium shells · Flat noodles · Spinach flats · Spirals · Whole-wheat spaghetti

CONDIMENTS

Low-salt sauerkraut · Sweet pickle relish · Low-salt kosher dills · Baby sweet pickles

JUICES

Prune · Apple · Apricot · Strawberry-apple

JAM

Apricot · Blueberry · Wild blackberry · Raspberry · Strawberry · Apple butter

FRUIT SAUCES

Apple · Cherry-apple · Strawberry-apple

OIL

Extra-virgin cold-pressed olive

NUT BUTTERS

Peanut · Almond · Sesame tahini

NUTS

Almonds (in shell or shelled) · Peanuts (shelled) · Pecans (in shell or shelled halves) · Filberts (in shell or shelled) · Walnuts (in shell or shelled halves and pieces) · Macadamias (in shell)

CANNED

Olives, Sun-dried black olives in olive oil, oregano, and pepper · Pitted Italian olives

SNACKS

Tamari corn chips · No-salt corn chips · Snack bar (oats, peanut butter, honey, dates, figs, brown-rice syrup, malt-barley syrup, sunflower seeds, vanilla, and lecithin)

SWEETENER

Maple syrup

The first Jaffe at Jaffe Brothers was Sid, who established the business in 1948. His sister-in-law, Emmy Jaffe, describes Sid as "the original nature boy." Long before other people had made the connection, Sid Jaffe observed that people were "burdened by illness" because they didn't understand nutrition, and had lost their instincts about good food. He was also skeptical about the new chemical farming. He knew he wanted to eat food without chemicals, but he was living in upstate New York and "having a terrible time getting organic foods," says Emmy Jaffe. "So he decided to come out to California. The first thing he found was organic dates, so he started to sell those by mail order."

Back then, says Sid Jaffe, "The stock was stored in a small, unused garage." Today the Jaffes ship to all fifty states, as well as Norway, Singapore, the Philippines, and Japan. Sid's brother Alan joined him in 1959, and today Alan's wife, Emmy, and their son, Larry, are part of the crew. Emmy Jaffe describes the family's commitment to organic foods as "a way of life." She and Alan Jaffe raised their children without any shots, and their first grandchildren were raised that way, too.

JAFFE BROS.
INC.

P.O. BOX 636
VALLEY CENTER
CALIFORNIA 92082-0636

(619) 749-1133

Every pound of Jaffe Brothers' dried fruit starts out as eight pounds of fresh fruit. The dried fruit is never sulphured or fumigated. No chemicals or preservatives are added, so don't be surprised if these fruits look darker than what you're used to, say the folks at Jaffe Brothers. If they need softening, you can rinse them in cool water. The jams contain no sugar: just organically grown fruit, honey, lemon juice, and pectin.

Jaffe Brothers also sells the products of Vermont Country Maple (page 168).

KRYSTAL WHARF FARMS
RD 2, Box 2112
Mansfield, PA 16933
(717) 549-8194

Foods certified by: various
Catalogue/price list available
Minimum order: 10 pounds
Order by: mail, then phone
Pay by: check, money order
Ship by: UPS, own truck
Fresh produce shipped September–May; other goods shipped year-round

FRESH VEGETABLES

Beets (red or gold) · Cabbage (red or green) · Carrots · Daikon root · Garlic · Onions · Parsnips · Potatoes (red, russet, Yukon Gold, Yellow Finn, purple) · Sweet potatoes · Garnet yams · Rutabagas · Squash (acorn, butternut, red kuri, spaghetti, delicata, sweet dumpling, turbin)

APPLES

Red Delicious · Golden Delicious · Granny Smith · McIntosh · Cavendish

CITRUS

Ruby grapefruit · Lemons · Valencia oranges

GRAINS

Barley (hulled or pearled) · Raw or roasted buckwheat groats · Corn kernels (F) · Millet · Oat bran · Rolled oats · Popcorn · Rice (F) · Rye berries (F) · Spring wheat berries (hard or soft) (F) · Wheat bran

OTHER FLOUR

Unbleached white

BEANS

Adzuki · Black turtle · Garbanzo · Great northern · Kidney · Lentil · Mung · Navy · Pinto · Red chili · Soybeans (green or yellow) · Split peas

NUTS

Raw almonds · Filberts · Walnut halves

SEEDS

Alfalfa · Sesame · Sunflower

DRIED FRUIT

Dry, shredded, or chipped coconut · Apples · Apricots · Cherries · Currants · Pitted Deglet dates · Barhi dates · Medjool dates · Calimyrna figs · Mission figs · Turkish figs · Peaches · Pears · Pitted prunes · Thompson raisins · Red flame raisins · Sultanas · Trail mix (raisins, dates, apples, almonds, sunflower seeds)

PASTA

Macaroni · Fidilini · Flats · Lasagna · Shells · Spinach flats · Spinach spaghetti · Veggie elbows · Veggie spirals · Chow mein noodles

CEREALS

Muesli · Creamy maple rye · Creamy rice and rye · Maple raisin oats · Porridge oats · Five-grain cereal · Wheat-free muesli · Brown rice and barley · Multi-grain flakes · Multi-grain flakes with raisins

SNACKS AND CHIPS

Wheat-free millet-rice cakes · Popcorn · Yellow corn chips · Blue corn chips · Popcorn with canola oil · Yellow taco shells · Blue taco shells

PREPARED FOODS

Refried beans

SWEETENERS

Date sugar · Maple syrup

Burt Israel has been gardening since he was seven years old; as an adult, he grew organic food for his own family, supplementing that with organic produce from other sources. "Those were the days when just about all you could get were organic potatoes, onions, and carrots." Friends heard about what he was doing, including one who ran a store, and soon Israel was supplying him with organic produce. The business grew from filling a pickup truck to a van, to a refrigerated truck, and now Krystal Wharf Farms distributes some 5,000 pounds of organic produce and goods each week. Burt Israel has been a professional musician, but nowadays there's no time for anything but organic produce. "Some distributors only work during the summer season, but we're committed to supplying chemically sensitive customers year-round."

Many of Krystal Wharf's customers are "environmentally disabled," a term for people who have reactions to chemicals in the environment, whether in the air, the water, or in food. Israel described one customer who can't even order by phone because of a reaction to the plastic handset. "In the modern age we're constantly assaulted by toxins. These reactions sometimes come on suddenly. I've talked to a medical professional who said the sudden onset actually comes from overexposure to the toxin over a long period of time. The liver simply can't get rid of them any more." Israel himself suffers from several such reactions, including an allergy to the formaldehyde used to process permanent-press clothing. We share an allergy to MSG, which he says has even made him hallucinate. "When the walls in the restaurant started vibrating, I knew there was something wrong with the food."

Israel and his wife, a rehabilitation counselor, are entering the next phase of their commitment to organics: a counseling service for people with environmentally induced disabilities. "The conditions are not usually reversible," says Israel, "but you can get some control over your life, and eating clean food is one of the ways you can do it. I don't make any health claims for organic food, but in some places doctors are actually beginning to prescribe it for people with recurrent allergies the pharmaceuticals just don't help. It's fascinating to see the doctors seeking out these alternatives."

Israel sells only certified organic produce, except for some transitional apples when the supply is low. Among organic growers, he says, "I've even gotten to know which growers' produce is cleaner than others." He also forages for herbs in the wild in the mountains around Krystal Wharf Farm—ask about herbs, if you're interested.

Most goods are shipped in 5- or 10-pound units. Fresh produce is priced weekly. Krystal Wharf also sells products of Southern Brown Rice (page 224), Lundberg Family Farms (page 219), and Cascadian Farm (page 172). For co-ops and health-food stores in Pennsylvania, western New York, western New Jersey, Ohio, and West Virginia, Krystal Wharf Farms has a larger list of items available by refrigerated truck delivery.

MILLSTREAM NATURAL HEALTH
1310-A East Tallmadge Avenue
Akron, OH 44310
(216) 630-2700

Visits: yes
Foods certified by: OR-TILTH, CHSC
Catalogue/price list available
Minimum order: none
Order by: phone, mail
Pay by: check, Visa, MC
Ship by: UPS

FRESH VEGETABLES

Asparagus · Avocados · Green beans · Beet roots · Beets with tops · Bok choy · Broccoli · Burdock · Cabbage (red or green) · Carrots · Cauliflower · Celery · Chard · Collards · Cucumbers · Daikon radishes · Eggplant · Garlic · Kale · Leeks · Lettuce (red leaf, green leaf, and romaine) · Mustard greens · Onions (yellow or green) · Parsley · Snow peas · Green peppers · Potatoes (red, russet, or yellow) · Radishes · Spinach · Acorn squash · Zucchini · Cherry tomatoes · Turnips · Watercress yams

FRESH FRUIT

Red Delicious apples · Granny Smith apples · Bananas · Grapefruit · Seedless red grapes · Kiwi · Lemons · Limes · Canteloupe · Navel oranges · Valencia oranges · Pears · Tangelos · Tangerines

DRIED FRUIT

Apricots · Prunes · Raisins · Dates

BREAD

Whole-wheat sliced · Whole-wheat Italian · Sprouted · Wheat-free spelt · Rye Essene (yeast-free) · Bible pocket

NUTS AND NUT BUTTERS

Walnuts · Peanut butter (smooth or crunchy) · Almond butter · Cashew butter

SNACKS

Corn chips · Nacho chips · Blue corn chips · Brown rice chips · Cookies

JUICE

Apple · Grape · Pear · Prune · Tomato

CEREAL

Multi-flake wheat and rice · Millet with rice flakes · Crispy brown rice · Blue corn flakes

SOY PRODUCTS

Soy milk (original, carob, or vanilla) · Tofu

Millstream's president, Jonathon D. Miller, has been in the health-food business since 1974, and has written several books on health, including *Nutrition, Health and Harmony*. Most foods Millstream sells meet the California Health and Safety Code standards; some are certified by other organizations, and Miller has letters and certificates on file for many of the growers.

Millstream cautions you not to order anything too perishable outside its overnight radius, which includes Buffalo, Pittsburgh, Charleston, Cincinnati, Fort Wayne, Grand Rapids, and Detroit. Millstream also carries products from Lundberg Family Farms (page 219), Cascadian Farm (page 172), and Pronatec (page 162).

NATURAL BEEF FARMS
4399-A Henninger Court
Chantilly, VA 22021
(703) 631-8705
(703) 631-0881

Visits: yes; fresh produce available
Foods certified by: various
Catalogue/price list available
Minimum order: 15–25 pounds
Order by: phone, mail
Pay by: VISA, MC, UPS, COD
Ship by: UPS, FedEx
UPS shipping goes out twice a month

MEAT

Beef · Chicken · Lamb · Pork · Bacon · Hot dogs (turkey, beef, or chicken) · Lunch meat (plain or garlic) · Hot Italian sausage · Sweet Italian sausage · Applesauce sausage · Kielbasa · Breakfast sausage · Smoked sausage

FISH AND SEAFOOD

Salmon · Swordfish · Halibut · Tuna · Mahi-mahi · Cod · Shrimp

CHEESE

Mozzarella · Provolone

FROZEN ENTRÉES AND DESSERTS

Vegetarian pot pie · Broccoli and cheese pot pie · Macaroni and cheese · Cheese pizza · Apple pie

DRIED FRUIT

Apples

CANNED VEGETABLES

Crushed tomatoes · Refried beans

COOKIES

Barley wafers

BREAD

Whole wheat · Whole-wheat sandwich rolls · Sprouted wheat · Whole-wheat pita · Whole-wheat croissants

RICE

Chesapeake basmati · Long-grain brown · Wild-rice blend

CHIPS AND SNACKS

Yellow corn chips · Blue corn chips · Nacho corn chips · Trail mix · Popcorn · Yellow tortilla or taco shells · Blue tortilla or taco shells · Whole-wheat tortilla or taco shells

CEREALS

Muesli · Creamy rice and rye · Maple raisin oats · Quick oats · Multi-grain (plain, with raisins, or millet)

SWEETENERS

Maple syrup

COFFEE

Cafe Altura regular (beans or ground) · Cafe Altura dark roast (beans or ground)

FROZEN JUICE

Apple cider · Orange juice concentrate

Suzanne and Stefan Donner are concerned about the implications of chemical farming and food processing, both for their customers and for the world as a whole. They use their catalogue to raise some of these issues and list resources for alternative agriculture and health care. A recent copy, for example, recounted Suzanne's attempts to get straight answers from the FDA about food irradiation. She learned that poultry was being exposed to between 300,000 to one million times the radiation of an X-ray, and that the processing plants were approved by the Nuclear Regulatory Commission. "The nuclear industry must find something to do," was her wry observation. "Hey, why don't they nuke bacteria in poultry?"

The Donners own a farm where beef cattle are raised on unsprayed pastureland and certified organic corn, without hormones or antibiotics. All meat they sell comes from animals raised to Natural Beef Farms' specifications, although not all are raised at the farm itself. All animals must be documented from birth; never

given antibiotics, hormones, or sulfa drugs; and never given feed that was treated with synthetic herbicides or pesticides. "The poultry and pigs are housed, but have plenty of room," says Suzanne Donner. The seafood is from Alaska, processed on factory ships, flash frozen, cut, and vacuum packed without preservatives. The shrimp comes from South Carolina and contains no additives, preservatives, sulfites, or sodium tripolyphosphate. The hot dogs and sausage contain no nitrates or nitrites.

All meat is shipped frozen; all other items in their catalogue can be shipped, with the exception of products in glass jars. All shipments come in returnable styrofoam coolers.

The Donners offer discounts for 25-pound, 50-pound, split side, or side orders on meat, and for whole cases on other products; UPS shipping twice a month. They offer free delivery for orders above $50 to metropolitan D.C., Baltimore, Annapolis, Fredericksburg, Williamsburg, and Newport News. They also carry the products of Sucanat (page 162); Tabard Farm Potato Chips (page 246); Lundberg Family Farms (page 219); French Meadow Bakery (page 33); Cascadian Farm (page 172), including frozen produce, which Cascadian Farm doesn't ship; Morningland Dairy (page 47); Garden Spot Distributors (page 267); Walnut Acres Organic Farms (page 284); and Bioforce of America, Ltd. (page 250).

ORGANIC FOODS EXPRESS
11003 Emack Road
Beltsville, MD 20705
(301) 937-8608

Visits: yes
Foods certified by: various

Catalogue/price list available
Minimum order: 1 pound
Order by: phone, mail
Pay by: MC, Visa, check
Ship by: UPS
Orders are taken Mondays; if you cannot call on Mondays, special arrangements can be made; if you plan to shop regularly, someone at the company can also call you each week to take your order

FRESH VEGETABLES

Beet root · Broccoli · Cabbage (red or green) · Carrots · Cauliflower · Celery · Red chard · Collards · Corn · Cucumbers · Daikon · Garlic · Kale · Leeks · Lettuce (romaine or leaf) · Onions · Parsley · Peas · Peppers (red or green) · Potatoes (red, russet, or yellow) · Sweet potatoes · Spinach · Alfalfa sprouts · Summer or winter squash · Tomatoes · Turnips · Watercress

FRESH FRUIT

Apples · Avocados · Bananas · Canteloupe · Grapefruit · Kiwi · Lemons · Limes · Melons · Valencia oranges · Navel oranges · Peaches · Pears · Pineapples · Tangerines

PASTA

Whole-wheat elbows · Fidilini · Sesame-rice spirals · Shells · Spaghetti · Spinach spaghetti · Veggie spirals

SWEETENERS

Brown-rice syrup · Maple syrup

PRESERVES

Apricot · Blackberry · Blueberry · Raspberry · Strawberry · Strawberry-rhubarb

SNACKS

Blue corn chips · Yellow corn chips · Blue nacho chips · Nacho chips · Cheese popcorn · Potato chips · Taco shells · Rice cakes · Wafers (barley, apple, or apple-pear)

OIL AND VINEGAR

Olive oil · High-oleic safflower oil · Sesame oil · Apple cider vinegar

CHEESE

Mild white Cheddar · Medium white Cheddar · Colby · Lite farmer's · Monterey Jack

OTHER DAIRY

Extra-large eggs · Plain yogurt

BOTTLED JUICES

Apple · Apple-blackberry · Apple-boysenberry · Apple-raspberry · Apple-strawberry · Grape · Kauai punch · Lemonade · Pear · Prune · Raspberry lemonade · Strawberry lemonade · Strawberry-guava · Vegetable cocktail

CANNED SODAS

Apple · Grape · Lemonade · Raspberry lemonade

BREADS

Whole wheat · Eight-grain sourdough rye · Sourdough rice · Sourdough raisin · Croissants · Bran muffins · Pita · Whole-wheat dinner rolls · Whole-wheat sandwich rolls

COOKIES

Chocolate chip · Ginger molasses

GRAINS

Hulled barley · Buckwheat kasha · Cornmeal · Millet · Oat bran · Rolled oats · Popcorn · Quinoa · White basmati rice · Brown basmati rice · Brown rice (long- and short-grain) · Wheat berries (F)

SEEDS

Sunflower · Sesame

DRIED BEANS

Adzuki · Baby limas · Black turtle · Garbanzo · Great northern · Lentil · Navy · Pinto · Green split peas

OTHER FLOUR

Unbleached white

MIXES

Buckwheat pancake · High-bran pancake · Twelve-grain pancake · Blueberry muffin

NUTS

Almonds · Walnuts

DRIED FRUIT

Apricots · Figs · Pitted prunes · Raisins

CEREAL

Quick oats · Healthy "O"s · Multi-grain flakes

SOUPS

Cream of watercress · Corn chowder · Vegetarian vegetable · Chicken corn · Chicken stew · Cream of celery · Chicken rice · Vegetable beef (no salt) · Clam chowder · Tomato

NUT BUTTERS

Almond · Peanut (smooth or crunchy) · Sesame tahini

COFFEE

Regular grind · Dark grind · Breakfast-blend grind decaf

FRUIT SAUCES

Apple · Apple-raspberry · Apple-blackberry · Apple-cherry

PICKLES AND RELISHES

Dill low salt · Dill regular · Pickle relish · Low-salt sauerkraut

SAUCES

Mild salsa · Hot salsa · Spaghetti sauce · Spaghetti sauce with mushrooms · Tomato puree

CANNED VEGETABLES

Yellow sweet corn · Garbanzo beans · Kidney beans · Peas

MISCELLANEOUS

Refried beans · Sunburgers

The order form from Organic Foods Express comes with customers' comments on the tastiness of the produce and the efficiency of the packing—including eggs. Scott Nash, one of the founders, is particularly proud of the quality of his fruits and vegetables, and says that "the prices are pretty good, too." Case quantities of some items are available at a 10 percent discount. Availability of fresh produce varies with the season. Use discretion when ordering perishables during the warm weather months.

RISING SUN ORGANIC FOOD

P.O. Box 627
PA 150 & I-80
Milesburg, PA 16853
(814) 355-9850
FAX: (814) 355-4871

Visits: yes
Foods certified by: various
Catalogue/price list available
Minimum order: none
Order by: phone, mail, fax
Pay by: check
Ship by: UPS
Place orders between 10 A.M. and 2 P.M., or 4 and 6 P.M., leave message on answering machine; shipments go out every other week

FRESH VEGETABLES

Globe artichokes · Jerusalem artichokes · Asparagus · Beans · Beets without tops · Broccoli · Cabbage (green or red) · Bok choy · Collards · Corn · Cucumbers · Daikon · Eggplant · Endive · Escarole · Garlic · Ginger · Kale · Leeks · Lettuce (romaine, red leaf, green leaf, bibb) · Onions · Parsley · Parsnips · Peas · Peppers (green, red, and hot) · Potatoes (russet or red) · Sweet potatoes · Radishes · Spinach · Summer squash · Tomatoes · Turnips · Watercress

FRESH FRUIT

Apples · Bananas · Cherries · Grapes · Grapefruit · Kiwi · Kumquats · Lemons · Limes · Melons · Nectarines · Oranges · Papayas · Persimmons · Plums · Pomegranates · Sapotes

DRIED FRUIT

Apples · California apricots · Turkish apricots · Cherries · Currants · Deglet Noor dates · Medjool dates · Calimyrna figs · Mission figs · Peaches · Pears · Prunes (whole or pitted) · Raisins

NUTS

Almonds (whole or shelled) · Filberts · Roasted pistachios · Walnuts

NUT BUTTERS

Raw or roasted almond · Peanut · Tahini

BEANS AND SEEDS

Alfalfa · Adzuki · Black turtle · Garbanzo · Great northern · Green split peas · Kidney · Lentils · Mung · Navy · Pinto · Sesame · Sunflower

GRAINS

Amaranth · Barley (hulled or pearled) · Buckwheat groats · Corn for grinding · Millet · Oat (groats or rolled) · Popcorn · Brown rice (short-grain or long-grain) (F) · Brown basmati · Mochi sweet brown rice · Whole rye (F) · Wild rice · Hard winter wheat (F) · Soft spring (pastry) wheat (F)

OTHER FLOURS

Blue cornmeal · Yellow cornmeal

CEREALS

Porridge oats · Five-grain cereal · Muesli · Wheat-free muesli · Multi-grain millet and rice · Crispy brown rice

PASTA

Whole-wheat elbows · Lasagna · Sesame-rice spirals · Spaghetti · Veggie spirals · Chow-mein noodles

JUICES

Apple · Apple-blackberry · Apple-strawberry · Cherry lemonade · Lemonade · Strawberry-guava · Pear · Prune · Gravenstein apple cider · Boysenberry cider

OIL AND VINEGAR

Olive · Safflower · Sesame · Veg-omega 3 · Vinegar

FRUIT SAUCES AND CONSERVES

Peach butter · Apple butter · Applesauce

SWEETENERS

Maple syrup

SNACKS

Corn chips · Nachos · Blue corn chips · Rice cakes · Sesame rice cakes

PREPARED FOODS

Refried beans

DAIRY PRODUCTS

Eggs · Biodynamic yogurt (plain, maple, or vanilla)

SOY PRODUCTS

Soy cheese, Soymilk (carob, original, or vanilla)

MISO

Mellow barley · Country barley · Sweet white · Mellow white

COFFEE

Cafe Altura dark roast (ground) · Cafe Altura regular roast (ground or beans) · Cafe Altura decaf (beans)

CONDIMENTS AND SAUCES

Horseradish · Sauerkraut · Sauerkraut and beets · Macrokraut · Raw kim-chi · Pasta sauce

MEAT (MANY CUTS AVAILABLE)

Chicken · Beef · Pork · Lamb

Hope Woodring started shipping organic produce in 1979 at the request of a friend who had severe food allergies and was paying more to have his food flown to him than the food cost. Woodring hasn't had to advertise her shipping service—word of mouth has worked just fine —"customers just seem to come to us through the cosmos."

Although Woodring ships food far and wide, she finds it painful to do, because she knows the food is never in quite as good a condition when it arrives as when it leaves. She's working hard to develop better connections between consumers and their local growers. "We all have to eat, and we all have to have good food. But we're relying far too much on imported oil. We need to become locally independent for our food."

Woodring, who was an organic gardener for years before she got into the food business, is doing more and more growing herself, and would like to see as many people as possible growing their own food or finding local growers to raise it for them. She has developed something like a subscription service, where customers give her a rough list of what they want and get a shipment of thirty or forty dollars' worth of produce each week—whatever's in season locally. If you live in her area, you might also contact her about that and another idea she's developing: a well-stocked truck, like a bookmobile, that would serve local communities with organic food.

All produce in the catalogue that is labeled organic is third-party certified. Perishable products are shipped in insulated boxes; a deposit is required for the box, and credited when you return it. Rising Sun also sells products from Cascadian Farm (page 172), Maine Coast Sea Vegetables (page 238), Morningland Dairy (page 47), Sprout Delights (page 41), Lundberg Family Farms (page 219), Pronatec (page 162), and Earth's Best Baby Food (page 29). It also sells food supplements and nontoxic household products.

SIMPLY DELICIOUS
243 A North Hook Road
Box 124
Pennsville, NJ 08070
(609) 678-4488

Visits: yes
Foods certified by various
Catalogue/price list available
Minimum order: $25 for credit-card orders
Order by: phone, mail
Pay by: check, Visa, MC, Discover
Ship by: UPS

JUICE
Apple · Pear · Peach cider

CEREAL
Creamy rice and rye · Blue corn flakes · Rice cream

NUT BUTTERS
Sesame tahini

SNACKS
Blue or yellow tortilla chips · Popcorn with canola oil and sea salt · Rice cakes · Peanut butter bars · Spice raisin bars

PASTA
Whole-wheat elbows · Shells · Lasagna · Ribbons · Spaghetti

SALAD DRESSING
Crazy carrot · Summer scallion · Sweet beet

BABY FOOD
Five-grain cereal · Barley rice cereal

SOYMILK
Original · Vanilla · Carob

SAUCES
Spaghetti sauce

GRAIN
Amaranth · Barley (hulled or pearled) (F) · Buckwheat groats (F) · Yellow popcorn · Corn grits (F) · Hulled millet · Whole oat groats (F,C) · Rice (long- and short-grains) (F)

OTHER FLOUR

Rye · Soy · Whole wheat · Whole-wheat pastry · Unbleached white

BEANS

Adzuki · Chick-peas · Red kidney · Green lentil · Green split peas · Pinto · Soy · Black soy · Soy grits · Black turtle

BAKING MIX

Whole-wheat pancake

SEEDS

Hulled sesame · Hulled sunflower

DRIED FRUIT

Apple rings · Mixed fruit · Peaches · Pears · Pineapple · Thompson raisins · Trail mix

HERBS

Basil · Bay leaf · Lemon thyme · Marjoram · Oregano · Rosemary · Sage · Tarragon · Thyme

SWEETENERS

Maple syrup

FRESH FRUIT

Apples · Cherries

Simply Delicious opened in 1988. Organic items are scattered throughout its price list. Everything is organized by brand, however, so that if you know you're looking for a particular item from a particular company, you're all set. Otherwise, you may have to browse a while. The company also sells products from Pronatec (page 162), Earth's Best Baby Food (page 29), and Cascadian Farm (page 172).

Free delivery is offered to anyone in Salem County who is housebound, with orders over $20.

SPECIAL FOODS
9207 Shotgun Court
Springfield, VA 22153
(703) 644-0991

Foods certified by: various
Catalogue/price list available
Minimum order: none
Order by: phone, mail
Pay by: check
Ship by: UPS, parcel post
Recipes available

MEATS (MOST CUTS AVAILABLE)

Beef · Lamb · Pork · Chicken · Turkey

FLOURS, BAKING POWDERS, PANCAKE MIXES, CREAMED CEREALS, CRISPY CEREALS, IMITATION MAYONNAISE, MASHED POTATO SUBSTITUTES, IMITATION NUT BUTTERS, NOODLES AND PASTA, LOAF BREADS, COOKIES, CRACKERS, TORTILLAS, CHIPS, ARE AVAILABLE IN SOME OR ALL OF THE FOLLOWING

White sweet potato · Cassava · Malanga · Yam · Artichoke · Lotus · Amaranth · Milo · Water chestnut · Rice · Oat · Barley · Millet · Rye · Mung bean · Buckwheat

NUT BUTTERS (WITH SUNFLOWER OR SAFFLOWER OIL)

Pecan · Pumpkin seed

JAMS

Papaya · Mango · Guava · Star fruit · Pomegranate

FRUIT ROLL-UPS (FRUIT AND DISTILLED WATER)

Papaya · Mango · Star Fruit

MISCELLANEOUS

Amaranth seeds · Whole-grain milo · Quinoa seeds · Cottonseed oil · Green jackfruit, packed in water

Karen Slimak has lived through what must be every parent's nightmare. Slimak's first child "never seemed to be well." By the time he was five, "he'd had thirty-six ear infections, and bronchitis and pneumonia frequently enough for them to become commonplace. He was having difficulty with other children his age, and was royally flunking kindergarten." The Slimaks became convinced their son's problems were their fault. "Could it be that we didn't wash our hands enough? Took him out too much? Not enough? Was it because he was born a month early? Would he outgrow it?"

The story repeated itself in slightly different versions with her next two children—the third was the worst. He would "writhe in pain" after nursing and acted "like he was being poisoned." When he ended up in the hospital, unable to eat formula, the doctors finally gave her the diagnosis: food allergies. But instead of handing her something her child *could* eat, they simply said, "There's food out there somewhere you child can eat, and we know you'll find it."

If anyone was equipped for the job, it was Karen Slimak, who had a degree in environmental chemistry. She put aside the consulting firm she had founded, and devoted herself full-time to figuring out what the "food out there somewhere" might be. She went through the grocery store and came up with one food the children could eat: sweet potatoes. Meat seemed out of the question. "In desperation, we made arrangements with the local fire department, and my husband and a group of firemen traveled to a deserted island off the coast of Virginia, where they shot a wild bull. They field-dressed it, transported it across eight miles of open water, and brought it back to us to try." No luck. Finally, venison worked, and with sweet potatoes and sunflower oil, she developed a "reasonably well-balanced diet." The baby became "essentially symptom-free, and began a calm, almost businesslike exploration of his world that was simply wonderful to watch."

But then the sweet-potato diet started turning the baby "bright orange." Slimak started looking for alternatives in the only place left: "local ethnic markets. I walked up and down the aisles looking for something strange." Frozen *poi* was the first success. With each new food, Slimak would try to get other customers to explain what to do with it. "It was a hilarious situation—nobody could speak much English, and I couldn't speak any Korean or Japanese or Spanish."

When her children became bored with a steady diet of boiled tubers, Slimak developed flour from tubers, then pancakes, and even breads. It wasn't easy, and 99 percent of the foods she's developed are now covered by patents.

Recipes are included with orders, so that you can learn how tuber-based flours behave differently from wheat or other grain flours. "For example," says Slimak, "when making a pie crust, the dough will seem much more tough than wheat-flour dough, and it takes more effort to roll out. But it tastes just fine when cooked, and isn't a tough crust in a finished pie."

Each of the fruits and tubers that go into Special Foods comes from a different family and tastes different in different products. "If someone doesn't like the taste of something as a noodle," says Slimak, "they can try another product, because the flour will taste completely different in, for example, a cookie. Sweet potato flour noodles taste ever so slightly like

sweet potatoes, the imitation nut butter tastes like peanut butter, the cookies taste like peanut butter cookies, and the bread tastes simply bland." Malanga, a relative of the taro root, says Slimak, "is probably the most hypoallergenic food in the world," a good place to start.

The products made from artichoke, amaranth, quinoa, milo, barley, rye, rice, buckwheat, millet, oat, lentil, papaya, and pomegranates are organic, certified by their growers. All other items are "naturally grown, in traditional ways without the use of pesticides," says Slimak. The flour is packaged and mailed on the day it is ground. The jams are made from fruit and distilled water, without sweeteners, and are shipped as soon as they are cool. Products do not contain milk, eggs, yeast, or sugar. In any product that contains oil, Special Foods will substitute another oil at your request.

Slimak explains that Special Foods can qualify for a medical deduction on your taxes if prescribed by a physician or other health professional for alleviation or treatment of an illness, but not if they are simply for nutritional needs.

SPECIALTY ORGANIC SOURCE
P.O. Box 1628
Champaign, IL 61824-1628
(800) 782-5581
(217) 687-4810
FAX: (217) 687-4830
    –or–
P.O. Box 3114
Estes Park, CO 80517-3114
(303) 586-0533

Grains and storage facility certified by: OCIA
Catalogue/price list available
Minimum order: none
Order by: phone, mail, fax
Pay by: check, money order, COD
Ship by: UPS

GRAINS

Amaranth · Barley (hulled, pearled) (C,F) · Hulled Buckwheat (F) · Whole blue corn (F) ·
Hulled Millet (F) · Yellow Popcorn · Peruvian Quinoa (F) · Brown rice (short-, medium-, long-grain) (C,F) · Rye berries (C,F) · Hard red winter wheat (F, C) · Soft white winter wheat · Spelt · Ivory teff

OTHER CEREAL

Kamut · Soy · Oat (rolled, steel-cut, bran)

OTHER FLOUR

Soy · Unbleached · Oat · Flax meal · Sesame meal

EDIBLE AND SPROUTING SEEDS

Alfalfa · Flax seed · Mung bean · Radish · Sesame (hulled, toasted) · Red clover · Sunflower (whole, hulled)

BEANS

Adzuki · Black turtle · Garbanzo · Great northern · Baby lima · Red kidney · Green lentil · Navy · Green split peas · Yellow split peas · Pinto · Corsoy soybeans

OIL AND VINEGAR

Flax seed · Sesame · Toasted sesame · Safflower · Sunflower · Corn · Gern · Soy

SWEETENERS

Sucanat · Barley malt

DRIED FRUITS

Thompson raisins · Sultana raisins · Golden Delicious apples · Rome apples · Apricots · Tangy cherries · Pears · Sunshine blend (apples, raisins, peaches, pears) · Fruit leather bars (apple, blueberry, raspberry, tangy cherry)

DRIED VEGETABLES

Sun-dried tomatoes

JAMS AND PRESERVES

Apple butter · Carrot-mint jelly · Ginger-carrot jam · Lemony-Gold beet jelly · Veggie jam · Red beet and herb jelly · Champe wild rose hip jelly

SAUCES

Chunky applesauce with raisins

HEALTH-RICH SNACK BARS

Strawberry-banana · Blueberry-sesame · Cinnamon-raisin · Peanut butter · Apple-oat bran

PASTA

Brown rice broad udon noodles · Vita-spelt pasta · Kamut pasta

Specialty Organic Source is the mail-order retail supplier of Specialty Grain, which not only sells organic grains and flours but also turns organic grains into delicious snacks. One of Specialty Grain's more unusual products is microwaveable popcorn. I took the popcorn to a friend's house and in four minutes: fluffy, light popcorn, not at all dry, and good even without butter or seasonings. One friend, who's eaten plenty of air-popped popcorn in her day—especially during exam time—said this one outdid all the others. Specialty Grain's bag

contains no susceptors, metallicized plastic film strips that help heat foods, but also, in all likelihood, transmit chemicals.

Specialty Grain is also proud of its Oats for Life, which it calls "the Ultimate Oatmeal." Rolled oats are usually heated with steam, rolled, steamed again, and then dried and toasted for two to three hours. This process, say the folks at Specialty Grain, drains vitamins, minerals, and flavor out of the oats. By contrast, the Oats for Life process uses "only dry radiant heat for less than forty-five seconds at low temperatures. More of the natural flavor

and nutrition are retained. You can even taste the delicious, wholesome flavor of whole-grain oats—no more bland, flavorless oatmeal." I'm here to tell you they're not kidding. The oatmeal cooked in half an hour and was light and smooth, nothing like the gluey porridge "oatmeal" can conjure up. They use the same process on the whole line of Country Grown Flakes hot cereals.

They've also used some of their grains in Health-Rich snacks, which are not dry and crunchy, like granola bars, but moist and chewy snacks. The Goldilocks report: the blueberry-sesame bar is too bitter—sesame dominates, and only a hint of blueberry flavor comes through. On the other hand, the strawberry-banana bar is far too sweet for my taste; the strawberry flavor is overpowering, and the texture, perhaps from the oat bran, has an odd, unexpected grainy crunch to it.

The other three, I'm happy to say, are just right—snacks I'd be happy to have on any outing. The only problem is that the dominant flavor is never the one listed on the label. Both the oat-bran with apples and honey and the cinnamon-raisin bar are delicious, although both have more peanut flavor than either apples or cinnamon. In the peanut butter bar, also delicious, honey dominates. Go figure.

SOS was just getting under way in early 1991 and promises to carry organic sourdough breads, soup mixes, snack mixes, nuts, and nut butters in the future. In addition to its organic foods, it carries some products that are not organic but are tested for pesticide residue; these are marked on the order form.

In 1991, whole grains ranged from 31 cents to $2.17 a pound and flaked cereals ranged from 56 cents to $1.18 a pound. Stone-grinding added 6 cents per pound to the price of grains. Beans and seeds ranged from 35 cents to $2.59 a pound. Dried fruit ranged from $4.60 to $9.25 a pound. Oils ranged from $2.28 to $9 for 16 ounces. You save on most commodities by buying in bulk. SOS also carries Sucanat from Pronatec (page 162). Shipping additional.

THE GREEN EARTH

2545 Prairie Avenue
Evanston, IL 60201
(800) 322-3662
(708) 864-8949

Visits: yes
Foods certified by: Demeter, OCIA, CCOF, OGBA
Catalogue/price list available
Minimum order: none
Order by: phone
Pay by: check, Visa, MC, COD
Ship by: UPS, FedEx

FROZEN

French fries · Waffles

DAIRY

Cheese · Eggs

BAKERY

Biodynamic bread · Wheat-free, yeast-free bread · Whole-wheat bagels

COFFEE AND TEA

Coffee (regular and decaf) · Bancha-Kukicha tea · Herbal tea

JUICES

Carrot juice

WHOLE GRAINS

Brown rice · Oat bran · Rice · Wheat bran

FRESH VEGETABLES

Alfalfa sprouts · Beans · Beets · Bok choy · Broccoli · Brussels sprouts · Burdock roots · Cabbage (green, red, savoy, or nappa) · Carrots · Cauliflower (white or purple) · Celery · Chard (red or green) · Chestnuts · Collard greens · Corn · Cucumbers · Daikon · Dandelion greens · Eggplant · Endive · Escarole · Garlic braids · Garlic · Ginger · Jalapeño peppers · Jerusalem artichoke · Kale · Leeks · Lettuce (butter, romaine, red leaf, and green leaf) · Lotus root · Mushrooms · Mustard greens · Onions (green, red, yellow, and white) · Parsnips · Peas (English, snow, and sugar) · Peppers (green, red, and yellow) · Potatoes (red, russet, Yellow Finn, Yukon Gold, white, yellow rose) · Radishes · Rutabagas · Shallots · Spinach · Sunflower greens · Sweet potatoes (garnet, Japanese, Jersey, and jewel) · Taro root · Tomatoes (red, cherry, New Zealand pear, yellow cherry, yellow taxi) · Turnips

SQUASH

Acorn · Golden acorn · Buttercup · Butternut · Delicata · Gold nugget · Hokkaido · Patty pan · Kobocha · Red kuri · Spaghetti · Sweet dumpling · Turban · Yellow · Zucchini

APPLES

Anna · Gala · Golden Delicious · Granny Smith · Gravenstein · Jonathan · Jonathan Gold · McIntosh · Pippin · Red Delicious · Rome · Spartan

OTHER FRUIT

Apricots · Hass avocados · Red and yellow bananas · Blueberries · Cherries · Dates · Figs · Red and white grapefruit · Grapes (Concord, Flame, Ribier, and Thompson) · Kiwi · Kumquats · Lemons · Melons · Nectarines · Oranges · Papayas · Peaches · Pears · Persimmons · Plums · Pomegranates · Raspberries · Sapote · Strawberries · Tangerines · Tangelos

MEAT

Beef · Pork · Lamb · Chicken · Buffalo · Turkey

Kyra Walsh and Karin Dittmar, who founded The Green Earth in 1970, see their function as "educators" as well as shop owners. "We are always checking ingredients, analyzing growing as well as food processing methods monitoring the policies—politically—of larger companies that we buy from. Whenever possible we support socially responsible and environmentally safe companies; likewise, we have discontinued products for ethical considerations, either related to the product line or to their policies."

Green Earth has an enormous variety of fresh produce available by mail. (The catalogue

green earth
natural and organic foods

doesn't give a complete listing of the other goods they carry, but they'll be happy to answer questions on the phone. All the produce is organic. Most is grown in California, according to the California Health and Safety Code standards; in the summer, The Green Earth also buys from certified local farms. It also sells —and labels as such—transitional produce, and produce that is grown with the Integrated Pest Management system, which uses natural predators whenever possible and chemical pesticides only as a last resort.

The livestock is local, ranges freely, is fed organic feed, and is free of drugs and hormones. The Green Earth also sells "natural" buffalo, chicken, and turkey, which means that while the animals themselves have been given no hormones or antibiotics, commercial feed is used. Walsh and Dittmar visit and interview the farmers who raise the meat to make sure they are following these practices.

Most produce is flown in from California and goes out daily to mail-order customers, so that even though it makes a stop in Illinois on its way to you, it hasn't been on the road very long. The people at The Green Earth clearly understand how to ship fresh produce—the boxes are lined with styrofoam. My box arrived with all of its varied contents intact, including a fruit spritzer that did not explode when I opened it, lettuce as crisp as if I'd bought it that day at a local market, and a bag of unbroken corn chips. The company has a recycling program for the containers.

The Green Earth also carries Earth's Best Baby Food (page 29). Its catalogue also lists vitamins and personal-care products.

WALNUT ACRES ORGANIC FARMS
Walnut Acres Road
Penns Creek, PA 17862
(800) 433-3998
(717) 837-0601
FAX: (717) 837-1146

Visits: yes; picnic tables and room for trailers; Walnut Acres will happily provide you with information about nearby campsites and places to stay
Foods certified by: SELF, OCIA, FVO, OGBA
Catalogue/price list available
Minimum order: none
Order by: phone, mail, fax
Pay by: check, MC, Visa
Ship by: UPS, parcel post
Samplers available

CANNED VEGETABLES

Whole tomatoes · Tomato puree · Sweet corn · Beets · Pumpkin · Green beans · Kidney beans · Pinto beans · Garbanzo beans · Great northern beans · Peas · Sauerkraut

NUT BUTTERS

Raw almond · Dark roast almond · Sesame tahini

HOT AND COLD CEREALS

Corn grits · Brown-rice cream · Whole rye · High-fiber cereal · Indian meal · Twenty-grain porridge · Twelve-grain cereal · Four-grain cereal · Oatmeal · Flaked oatmeal · Steel-cut oatmeal · Early-riser oatmeal · Date-nut oatmeal · Oat bran with raisins and spice · Oat bran · Bran flakes · Corn bran · Fiber-rich cereal

WHOLE-GRAIN MIXES

Twelve-grain pancake · Whole-wheat and soy pancake · High-bran pancake with oat bran · Buttermilk Johnnycake · Wheatless pancake · Oat bran muffin · Bran muffin · Four-bran muffin · Corn muffin · Blueberry muffin · Spicy apple nut muffin · Maple granola muffin · High-lysine cornbran muffin

JAMS AND PRESERVES

Blueberry · Strawberry · Wild elderberry · Black raspberry · Red raspberry

CANNED FRUIT

Peaches · Applesauce · Apple Essence apple butter

SWEETENERS

Tupelo honey · Grade A maple syrup · Cooking maple syrup · Fruit sweetener, made from grapes · Barley-malt syrup · Rice syrup

COFFEE

Cafe Tierra decaffeinated breakfast blend (beans or ground) · Golden Pecan decaffeinated (beans or ground) · Guatemalan (beans or ground) · Guatemalan breakfast blend (beans or ground)

WHOLE GRAINS

Amaranth (F) · Spring Wheat (F) · Winter wheat (F) · Deaf Smith wheat (F) · Millet · Barley (F) · Raw buckwheat groats · Quinoa

OTHER FLOURS

Twelve-grain · Unbleached bread · Unbleached pastry · Cornell bread · Cornmeal · High-lysine cornmeal · Corn · Oat · Rice · Soy · Rye

OIL AND VINEGAR

Extra-virgin Spanish olive oil · Sesame oil · Apple cider vinegar

PASTA

Whole-wheat rigatoni · Spaghetti · Elbows · Egg noodles · Vegetable spirals · Corn pasta

SAUCES

Spaghetti · Marinara · Chunky garden marinara

CONDIMENTS

Ketchup · Zucchini relish · Dilled zucchini spears

HERBS

Basil · Celery · Chives · Dill leaves · Fish herbs · Marjoram · Oregano · Parsley · Poultry seasoning · Rosemary · Sage · Salad herbs · Savory · Soup herbs · Tarragon · Thyme

RICE AND RICE BLENDS

Three-grain rice blend · Rice pilaf · Bombay rice · Oriental rice · Cajun rice · Herbed Bulgur rice · Near-east kasha · Red beans and rice · Amaranth medley · Paul's eight-grain medley · Brown rice (long- or short-grain) · Basmati rice · Wild rice

SEEDS AND BEANS

Hulled sunflower · Flax · Sprouting seed mix (alfalfa, mung, green lentil) · Alfalfa · Sesame

BEANS

Mung · Green lentil · Navy · Pinto · Garbanzo · Great northern · Soy · Sprouted green peas · Bean soup mix · Split green peas · Kidney · Quick-cook adzuki · Red split lentil · Sprouted bean medley · Rice and sprouted beans

DRIED SOUP MIXES

Split pea and barley · Beef barley · Lentil soup

CANNED SOUPS

Cream of watercress and potato · Cream of pea · Cream of carrot · Cream of celery · Cream of chives · Corn chowder · Vegetarian vegetable · Vegetarian minestrone · Lentil · Tomato · Navy bean · Black bean · Tomato rice · Three-bean vegetarian chili · French onion · Chicken rice · Chicken gumbo · Scotch broth · Vegetable beef · Chicken corn · Chicken broth · Lentil soup with hot dogs · Chicken curry · Beef gumbo

PREPARED FOODS

Chicken stew · Beef stew · Chili con carne · Noodles and ground beef · Beans and hot dogs · Braised beef hash · Ground beef

DRIED FRUIT

Hunza apricot halves · Super apricots · Monukka raisins · Sun Ray large prunes · Moyers prunes · Thompson seedless raisins · Medjool dates · Deglet Noor dates · Turkish apricots · Black Mission figs · Calimyrna figs

SNACKS

Yellow popcorn · Tamari sunflower seeds · Unsalted sunflower seeds · Wafers in maple or apple-pear spice

JUICES

Apple · Purple grape · Vegetable cocktail

BREADS

Pumpernickel hearth · Whole wheat · Salt-free whole wheat · Oatmeal hearth · Cornell formula · Twelve-grain · Three-grain · Cinnamon raisin · Rye · Sourdough

CHEESE

Colby · Monterey Jack · Pennsylvania creamy Cheddar

MEATS

Hamburgers · Hot dogs · Chicken · Turkey

FRESH VEGETABLES

Yellow globe onions · White potatoes · Carrots · Beets

Paul and Betty Keene, the founders of Walnut Acres, started growing organic foods in 1946 and shipping them through the mail not long after that. Paul Keene was born the son of a rural preacher; in the 1930s, he was the head of the mathematics department of a small New Jersey college. On a two-year leave of absence, he traveled to India, where he taught in a mission school. He studied agriculture, rural living, and nutrition; and spent time at a rural school run by Mahatma Gandhi and his disciples. He also met and married Betty Morgan, who was born and educated in India.

Paul Keene's interest in mathematics couldn't compete with his newfound passion for farming and rural life. Back in the United States, the Keenes worked at a school that taught back-to-the-land homesteading, and at an organic farm school. After a disastrous experience on a rented farm, they bought a place of their own in Penns Creek, in a valley formed by an ancient seabed and bordered by a moun-

tain stream. The abundant black walnut trees gave the farm its name.

"We were practically destitute," says Paul Keene. "We had borrowed every cent to purchase the farm and simple equipment." The farm's only source of power was two horses. Their house was a simple, wood-heated, no-plumbing affair.

It was tough going until a writer from the *New York Herald Tribune* discovered that the Keenes were making apple butter from unsprayed, worm-free apples, and doing it the old-fashioned way: over an open fire. She wrote a column about Walnut Acres, and suddenly they were in the mail-order business with their first product, Apple Essence.

Today, Walnut Acres has grown beyond the Keene family to some seventy staff members, all of whom are part-owners of the company. Members of neighboring Amish families help out with the extensive project of weeding fields that haven't seen a weed killer in forty years. Paul Keene has built a recreation center for the town and established the Walnut Acres Foundation, which funds schools and hospitals both in the United States and abroad. Betty Keene died in 1987; Paul Keene turned eighty in 1990 and shares the running of the company with his daughter and son-in-law. He still opens each catalogue with an introductory essay, "Greetings from the Farm."

Whatever the farm and its kitchens can't supply, Keene seeks out from other growers who meet Walnut Acres standards. Among those suppliers are Lundberg Family Farms (page 219), Timber Crest Farms (page 64), Cascadian Farm (page 172), and Pronatec (page 162). Walnut Acres will not call a product organic unless the farm has not used chemicals for five years. The catalogue scrupulously distinguishes among the products, using symbols for "strictly organically raised"; "claimed by grower to be organically grown"; and "have no poisonous chemical sprays used in growing."

Unlike many catalogues, the one from Walnut Acres gives you full-color photographs of the products—not just from the outside, but what they look like cooked up. I sampled a few of the 250 products in the forty-eight-page catalogue. The whole-wheat vegetable spiral pasta, if a tiny bit grainy, was hearty and far more substantial than ordinary wheat pasta. The Garden Marinara sauce is rich and flavorful with herbs; it outdoes any commercial pasta sauce and can hold its own against homemade. I didn't have the urge to doctor it, although it could take meat well if you were so inclined.

Some of the company's other prepared foods seem to have been made on the theory that it's easier to spice up than spice down. The vegetarian chili is bland; you'd have to add something hot if your taste runs to two-alarm or three-alarm chili. The chicken curry is a fine, vegetable-rich chicken soup, but barely curried. The minestrone is almost a stew, rich in tomatoes and beans, but even that can use some jazzing up with your favorite herbs.

The twelve-grain pancake mix was a nice surprise. With a name like "twelve-grain," I was expecting something heavy, but instead, the pancakes were light, rose impressively high, and had their own sweetness, even before I put maple syrup on them.

Flour is ground the day before it is shipped, and stored in refrigerated bins; peanut butter is ground daily; mayonnaise and dressings are prepared fresh every few days; soups are made with the farm's own well water; canned fruits are peeled by hand, not with the lye-and-hydrochloric-acid combination in use in traditional canneries. The company's pantry-plan allows you to create a standing monthly order. With one week's notice, you can add or subtract items. Even though sales have grown to some 100,000 orders a year, Keene still promises his customers "a friendliness and a genuine concern which go far beyond a cold business relationship."

The catalogue also lists vitamins, minerals, food supplements, skin- and hair-care products, and cookware.

SEE ALSO
Fiddler's Green Farm

LOCAL NATURAL-FOODS STORES

In most cases, these stores do not have catalogues and tend to ship to people who've been in their stores and know what they carry. Your best bet is to call (or even better, visit) the one nearest you. Unless specified, there is no minimum order.

ALABAMA

PEARLY GATES NATURAL FOODS
2308 Memorial Parkway SW
Huntsville, AL 35801
(205) 534-6233

Bulk herbs (over 700); full line of beans, grains and flour, pasta
Ship by: USPS
Pay by: MC, Visa, check

CALIFORNIA

CALIFORNIA HEALTH FOODS
115 East Commonwealth
Fullerton, CA 92632
(714) 525-4260

Ship by: USPS
Bill sent with order, pay by check or money order

NATURE'S FOOD CENTER
601 North Forbes
Lakeport, CA 95453
(707) 263-5359

Ship by: UPS, parcel post
Pay by: bill sent with order, return check or money order
In addition to nonperishable items and dried fruit, the company will also ship a gift box of vine-ripened organic tomatoes by Federal Express "for the person who has everything"; greenhouse-grown tomatoes shipped out-of-season
A catalogue is being developed

SUNFLOWER NATURAL FOODS
726 Sutter Street
Yuba City, CA 95991
(916) 671-9511

Ship by: parcel post
Pay by: Visa, MC, check in advance
Supplements and food items

CONNECTICUT

GREENWICH HEALTHMART
30 Greenwich Avenue
Greenwich, CT 06830
(203) 869-9658

Ship by: UPS
Minimum order: $25
Any nonperishable natural foods, vitamins, supplements, herbs
Pay by: Visa, MC, Amex, personal check

ILLINOIS

NATURES CORNUCOPIA
1259 North Green
McHenry, IL 60050
(815) 385-4500

Ship by: Priority Mail
Minimum order: $25
Pay by: Visa, MC, Discover, or check prior to order

NEW CITY MARKET
1810 Halstead Street
Chicago, IL 60614
(312) 280-7600

Ship by: UPS
Pay by: Visa, MC, Amex

SALT OF THE EARTH NATURAL FOOD
1340 North Cedar Road
New Lenox, IL 60451
(815) 485-6525

Ship by: UPS or parcel post
Pay by: check, cashier's check, money order

SUNRISE FARM HEALTH FOOD STORE
17650 Torrence Avenue
Lansing, IL 60438
(708) 474-6166

Ship by: UPS
Pay by: check, credit card

MASSACHUSETTS

BREAD & CIRCUS WHOLEFOOD SUPERMARKETS
392 Harvard Street
Brookline, MA 02146
(617) 738-8187
FAX: (617) 738-5145

Ship by: UPS
Pay by: check or money order in advance
Nonperishable items only; gift baskets available

MINNESOTA

CAYOL NATURAL FOODS
811 LaSalle Avenue
Minneapolis, MN 55402
(612) 339-2828

Natural vitamins and packaged food items
Pay by: Visa, MC, Discover, Amex, check, money order
Ship by: UPS, parcel post

NORTHERN NATURAL FOODS
13 South 4th Street
Box 66
Moorhead, MN 56560
(218) 236-5999

Minimum order: $10/$20 for credit cards
Pay by: check, money order, Visa, MC
Ship by: UPS, parcel post

Northern Natural has been in business for 25 years, and has a mail-order price list with many organic grains, seeds, and flours, as well as vitamins and food supplements; the proprietor, Sharon Price, notes that she can get almost any organic grain, nut, seed, or flour on request

MONTANA

THE GOOD FOOD STORE, INC.
920 Kensington
Missoula, MT 59801
(406) 728-5823

Pay by: Visa, MC, check, money order
Ship by: UPS, USPS
Catalogue available; also for sale are flour and grain from Montana Flour and Grains, Inc. (page 296)

REAL FOOD STORE
1090 Helena Avenue
Helena, MT 59601
(406) 443-5150

Ship by: UPS
Pay by: check or money order in advance
Nonperishables only

NEVADA

IRA'S ORGANIC FOODS MARKET
5643 West Charleston Boulevard #3
Las Vegas, NV 89102
(702) 258-4250

Pay by: MC, Visa, check in advance
Ship by: UPS
You can get looseleaf inserts of what fresh food, packaged food, and alternative medicines are available. You can also call to find out what's fresh
Will send fresh fruits and vegetables, nuts and seeds, rice, beans and pasta, grains, flour oils, vinegar, spices, and environmentally sound household products; stock is entirely organic, and specializes in products for people with allergies and on alternative therapies; the owner, Ira Lovitch, spent two years checking out the sources he buys from

NEW JERSEY

NUTRITION CENTER
Route 130
Warren Plaza West
Hightstown, NJ 08520
(609) 448-4885

Will ship: vitamins and supplements,
nonperishable foods
Ship by: UPS
Pay by: Visa, MC; prepay or charge the first
order, after that a bill can be sent with the
order

NEW YORK

INTEGRAL YOGA NATURAL FOODS
229 West 13th Street
New York, NY 10011
(212) 243-2642

Pay by: MC, Visa, check with check-cashing
card established
Ship by: UPS
In 1990, the store shipped only case lots, but
was working on a catalogue with no minimum
order

TENNESSEE

HONEYSUCKLE HEALTH FOODS
4741 Poplar
Memphis, TN 38117
(901) 682-6255

Ship by: UPS or parcel post
Pay by: MC, Visa, Amex
Will ship nonperishables; many bulk items
available

VIRGINIA

EATS NATURAL FOODS
1200 North Main Street
Blacksburg, VA 24060
(703) 552-2279

Ship by: UPS or USPS
Minimum order: $25
Pay by: check, Visa, MC
Will ship produce, depending on season

WEST VIRGINIA

MOTHER EARTH FOODS
1638 19th Street
Parkersburg, WV 26101
(304) 428-1024

Ship by: UPS
Pay by: COD, check in advance, MC, Visa
Will send out "almost everything"

WYOMING

WYOMING NATURAL FOODS
242 South Walcott
Caspar, WY 82601
(307) 234-4196

Ship by: UPS
Pay by: bill with order "to people we know";
otherwise, COD, Visa, MC, or check in
advance
"We'll ship anything they want"

In this section, you will find suppliers whose minimum order is large, and therefore more appropriate for co-ops, groups of friends buying together, schools, and individuals buying for large occasions. The first part is devoted to suppliers of specialty items, and the second part to wholesalers who, unless otherwise specified, carry a full line of products. These wholesalers generally sell to buying clubs and co-ops. If they will also ship smaller orders to individuals by UPS, that information is listed. Most have both pick-ups at the warehouse and truck delivery (of large orders) to their local area, and often deliver to neighboring states. Entries are organized by state to help you find the supplier nearest you, and most can send you information to help you start a buying club if you don't already belong to one.

SPECIALTY ITEMS

ADAPTATIONS
P.O. Box 1070
Captain Cook, HI 96704
(808) 328-9044

Certified by: affidavit
Minimum order: $50
Order by: phone, mail
Pay by: check
Ship by: parcel post, FedEx
Adaptations also sells medicinal herbs

CULINARY HERBS

Basil · Stick oregano · Broad-leaf oregano · Marjoram · Thyme · Peppermint · Italian parsley · Garlic · Garlic chives · Nasturtium flowers

DRIED FRUIT

Bananas · Papayas · Pineapples

Tane Datta formed Adaptations to "gather all the different growing climates we have here in Hawaii and market them all together." Among Datta's gourmet specialties is white pineapple, which is available only three months out of the year; most of his crop goes to local restaurants, but he may be willing to ship in the future. He also hopes to have organic macadamia nuts, perhaps chocolate or carob-covered, in the future.

Datta's farm is virgin land that's never been sprayed. Because Hawaii has no certification program, Adaptations combines the Oregon, Maine, Texas, and California standards and requires signed affidavits from farmers. The state is interested in defining organic, says Datta, "but things move slowly out here. Most of Hawaii is pineapple and sugar, and that's massive agricultural business."

BLACK RANCH
5800 Eastside Road
Etna, CA 96027
(916) 467-3387

Visits: yes
Catalogue/price list available
Certified by: CCOF
Minimum order: 25 pounds
Order by: phone, mail
Pay by: check
Ship by: UPS, parcel post

GRAINS

Hard red spring wheat (F) · Soft white pastry wheat (F) · Rye (F)

CEREAL

Six-grain cereal · Three-grain cereal · Wheatless cereal

TEA HERBS

Alfalfa leaf · Rose hips

Black Ranch has been around since the early days of agricultural chemicals, but it's been spared the worst of their effects. Dave and Dawn Black have been farming Black Ranch, where Dave Black grew up, since 1972. Black's parents, who started the ranch in 1941, "used very little chemicals," says Dawn Black, "so the land wasn't in bad shape when we started." The Blacks mill their own flour, and every order is milled fresh, the day before it is sent out. You can specify how you'd like the grain milled: fine, medium fine, medium, or coarse.

Flours and grains are primarily sold in 50-pound bags. In 1990, a bag of flour was $12.50, a bag of whole grains was $10, and a bag of cereal was $25. Alfalfa leaf and rose hips can be ordered in 1-pound quantities; prices were not available. Black Ranch also has a delivery route on I-5 from Grants Pass, Oregon, to Sacramento, California.

CAMAS GRAIN
219 Soldier Road
Box 337
Fairfield, ID 83327
(208) 764-2254
(208) 764-2615
FAX: (208) 764-2254

Visits: yes; Fairfield, Idaho, and Gooding, Idaho
Catalogue/price list available
Certified by: CHSC
Minimum order: $50
Order by: phone, mail, fax
Pay by: check
Ship by: parcel post

SEEDS AND BEANS

Alfalfa · Flax · Yellow field soy (C,F)

GRAINS

Whole millet · Brown rice (long- or short-grain) · Whole rye (F) · Flaked rye · Whole triticale (F) · Hard red wheat berries · Soft white wheat berries (F) · Durum wheat berries (F) · High-protein wheat berries (C) · Cracked wheat · Wheat bran · Amaranth (F) · Pearled barley (F) · Sprouting barley · Whole raw buckwheat (F) · Unhulled buckwheat · Yellow whole corn (F) · Yellow popcorn

OTHER FLOUR

Pumpernickel rye · Unbleached · Whole-wheat fine

OTHER CEREAL

Vita six-grain cereal

DRIED FRUIT

Raisins

The grain elevator is a familiar site in midwestern towns. It's often the tallest building in town, and in some cases the only building in town. The Camas Prairie Grain Growers, founded in 1940, was a co-operative grain business that stored, sold, and processed grain. By 1982, the cooperative was defunct, two of its four facilities sold off. The current owners, whose families had lived in the community since 1901 and 1904, respectively, worried about the impact on the community if the business were to close permanently. They leased the business, and then purchased it in 1984.

The new owners' philosophy has been to "make sure the grower gets a fair shake." The company pays a premium—as much as fifty cents a bushel above market price—to get organically grown grain, and works hard to expand the market for organic grain. Reuben Miller, manager of the Camas Prairie Grain Company, explains that local growers make most of their money from alfalfa hay but that every alfalfa field has to be planted with grain periodically to combat disease in the alfalfa crop. Camas Grain Company has made that off-year profitable. It's relatively easy to maintain the organic practices when they return to al-falfa: the plant suppresses weeds naturally, and minimizes the need for artificial fertilizer by attracting bacteria that "fix" nitrogen in the soil.

One of the company's suppliers says, quite honestly, that he and his fellow farmers in the Camas valley are not idealists—they're agribusinessmen, complete with college degrees, computers, and offices. The bottom line is dollars. But even he admitted to the local paper that it was "kind of nice" to have a reason not to have to use chemicals.

All organic growers meet the standards of California and Oregon, and affidavits are available on request.

Grains, seeds, flours, and raisins are available in 25- and 50-pound bags. A few are available in 5- and 10-pound bags. In 1990, a 50-pound bag of whole-wheat flour was $14.60.

FACKLER FAMILY FARMS
65 Plymouth Street
Plymouth, OH 44865
(419) 687-7665

Visits: yes
Certified by: OEFFA
Minimum order: 25 pounds
Order by: phone, mail
Pay by: check in advance, COD
Ship by: UPS, parcel post

BEANS

Adzuki · Black soy

Todd Fackler first became interested in farming without chemicals in the 1970s for social and political reasons: the so-called Green Revolution, which was supposed to feed the world through advanced hybrids, "just wasn't doing anything for the Third World," says Fackler. When his wife, Holly, became pregnant, he started to consider the health aspects. He stopped using chemical fertilizers, cut down on

herbicides, and eventually went all the way to organic farming.

Because adzuki (sometimes spelled aduki) beans are often a part of macrobiotic and vegetarian diets, there was a natural market for an organic adzuki bean. The Japanese use the beans in a sweet bean paste, says Fackler. They cook the beans and add about 50 percent sugar, take the paste, mold into a cake, bake it, and—as if it weren't already sweet enough—pour a sweet sauce over it. Fackler uses the beans, which have a hint of bitterness in their natural state, in burritos, in soups, and in chili.

GLORYBEE NATURAL SWEETENERS
P.O. Box 2744
Eugene, OR 97402
(503) 689-0913
FAX: (503) 689-9692

Visits: yes
Catalogue/price list available
Certified by: SELF
Minimum order: 1 case
Order by: phone, mail, fax
Pay by: check, Visa, MC
Ship by: UPS, parcel post
Gift assortments available

HONEY

Alfalfa · Blackberry · Clover · Cranberry · Fireweed · Huckleberry · Orange blossom · Raspberry · Wildflower · Comb

OTHER SWEETENERS

Molasses · Brown-rice syrup · Maple syrup

GRAINS AND SEEDS

Whole oat groats (C) · Oat bran · Sunflower seeds

DRIED FRUIT

Raisins

Richard Turanski is a fifth-generation bee-keeper. The first year he taught beekeeping at the local community college, over eighty people attended the first night of the course. "The school didn't have a classroom big enough, so I had to use the auditorium. Fortunately, all of these students became customers for 'Dick's Bee Supplies.'"

Turanski sells a range of honeys, each with a distinct flavor: alfalfa produces "rich, sweet-tasting honey"; honey from blackberries is "not as sweet but has a definite bouquet"; and raspberry, while similar to blackberry, is "more sharp and tangy." Clover is "very sweet" and "much milder in taste." Fireweed is "tangy or spicy," and huckleberry is "darker and stronger, but tangy tasting." Orange blossom, the country's most popular honey, has a "distinct" orange flavor.

Although the honey is not certified organic, a 1990 lab report on the honey and honey stix (honey and pure flavor extracts) showed no antibiotics, cadmium, or lead. A 1989 test on the molasses showed no pesticides and less than 0.1 parts per million of lead. The maple syrup, from Vermont, is certified by OCIA, contains no lead, formaldehyde, or other chemical additives, and is certified kosher.

Honey is available in cases of 4-, 12-, 16-, or 32-ounce jars. In 1990, a case of 12 4-ounce jars of honey was $8.40. You save on larger sizes. Honey is also available in buckets or drums and can be decanted into smaller jars.

HAZELRIDGE FARM
Box 268
Shelbrook, Saskatchewan
Canada, SOJ 2EO
(306) 747-2935

Visits: yes
Certified by: OCIA
Minimum order: 5 kilograms
Order by: phone, mail
Pay by: check, money order, approved credit
Ship by: parcel post

SEEDS FOR SPROUTING

Alfalfa · Radish

Most farmers who raise alfalfa grow it for live-stock feed. Ironically, that means the alfalfa sprouts you buy in a health-food store are not necessarily healthy: they may have been

sprayed with insecticides or drying agents, or any one of a number of other chemicals. Jim and Maggie Mumm recognized the need for organic alfalfa seed for human consumption and have added radish seed, another popular sprout. To produce your own alfalfa or radish sprouts, you can buy a sprouter at a health-food store.

In 1990, a 10-kilogram bag of alfalfa seed was $50. A 10-kilogram bag of radish seed was $24.50. Ten percent discount for orders above $100.

JACOBS FARM
Box 508
Pescadero, CA 94060
(415) 879-0580
FAX: (415) 879-0930

Farmers' markets: Marin, Palo Alto, and
Santa Cruz
Catalogue/price list available
Certified by: CCOF
Minimum order: $100
Order by: phone, mail, fax
Pay by: first order COD/check in advance
Ship by: UPS, FedEx

CULINARY HERBS

Chervil · Tarragon · Rosemary · Thyme ·
Lemon thyme · Sage · Oregano · Marjoram ·
Savory · Chives · Garlic chives · Variegated
chives · Dill · Cilantro · Sorrel · Comfrey ·
Spearmint · Peppermint · Apple mint · Orange
mint · Grapefruit mint · Lemon balm · Lemon
verbena · Lavender · Lovage · Salad burnet ·
Anise hyssop · Curled parsley · Italian parsley

EDIBLE FLOWERS

Mixed · Calendula · Borage · Nasturtium ·
Violet · Pansy · Johnny jump-up · Sweet violet ·
Bachelor's buttons · Marigold · Geranium ·
Dianthus · Chrysanthemum · Garlic chive
blossom · Chive blossom · Hollyhock

VEGETABLES

English pod peas · Sugar snap peas ·
Artichoke · Russian kale · Curled kale ·
Collards · Mache · Red orach ·
Chrysanthemum leaves · Horseradish

Sandy Belin and Larry Jacobs met on an organic farm in Maine and moved to California to farm, but in recent years, they've turned much of their attention south of the border. In 1985, Jacobs and Belin were taking a vacation in San Jose del Cabo, the southernmost tip of Mexico's Baja California peninsula. They saw the possibility of growing crops like tomatoes organically in the off-season, but rather than competing with the local farmers, or simply

Jacobs Farm

hiring local farmers as employees, they proposed a joint effort.

Jacobs was particularly eager to bring organic growing to Mexico, where he had seen growers mixing toxic poisons without any protective gloves or masks. The couple took their idea to the local *ejido*, or land cooperative, in which members share tools and water, but have the right to sell the produce of their own small parcel—usually between two and five acres. Many members were already farming without chemicals, and eight agreed to farm their land according to the California organic standards, which Jacobs and Belin had translated into Spanish.

The couple spent the first year of the project living with the farmers, learning as much about their growing methods as possible, and helping them to make the gradual transition to completely organic practices. Within a few years, 120 growers had joined the project. Some California growers have felt threatened by the competition, but others agree that it's inherently good for the organic business to have produce available year-round.

LAMBSFOLD FARM

Route 2, Box 1720
Columbus, NC 28722
(704) 863-4253

Visits: yes
Certified by: CFSA
Minimum order: 50 pounds (vegetables)
Order by: phone, mail
Pay by: money order
Ship by: not determined

FRESH VEGETABLES

Sweet potatoes · Acorn squash · Butternut squash

CANNED FOODS

Tomatoes

SWEETENER

Sorghum molasses

For David Rowe, organic farming is a religious commitment. Rowe says he'd "like to feel we can be of some service to mankind, growing food that won't tear down people's bodies and minds and souls." When Rowe was a small child, his father was "a one-horse farmer," and he never forgot what it was like living on the farm. His own farm is in the foothills of North Carolina, where the piedmont comes up to the mountains. Columbus, says Rowe, "is a large city—with two red lights—population, 700, and we live twelve miles out of there."

In addition to root vegetables, Rowe raises three different varieties of tomatoes, which his wife cans for the family's use, and will probably have enough to ship. They're also planning to sell sorghum molasses. "All your little farmers

used to make it. It's like sugar, but instead of sugarcane it's sorghum cane. You boil the juice in an evaporator pan. It takes nine gallons of juice to make one gallon of molasses. It's high in vitamins and iron, and it'll keep for a couple of years, like sugar."

Lambsfold Farm is just getting into mail order. Rowe does not yet have a price list, but will send you a list of what he has available.

MONTANA FLOUR AND GRAINS, INC.

Ferry Route Box 808
Big Sandy, MT 59520
(406) 378-3105
(406) 622-5503

Grain and mill certified by: OCIA
Catalogue/price list available
Minimum order: 50 pounds
Order by: phone, mail, fax
Pay by: COD, check in advance
Ship by: UPS

GRAINS AND SEEDS

Hard red winter wheat (F) · Hard red spring wheat (F) · Hard white wheat (F) · Soft white wheat (F) · Durum (F) · Kamut (F) · Hull-less barley · Triticale · Millet · Rye · Flax · Hull-less oats · Montana seven-grain mix

"We know that a little stress and adversity will often bring out hidden strengths and qualities in a person," says Bob Quinn of Montana Flour and Grains. "The same is true with wheat." Quinn credits the tough climate of Montana with producing the high-protein bread wheat he grinds into flour.

Bob Quinn's grandfather, Emmet, came to Big Sandy, Montana, in 1919. "He rented a place and had a milk cow," says Bob Quinn, who returned to the family farm when his father retired in 1978. Today the Quinn family's wheat-and-cattle operation covers 2,400 acres. Bob Quinn began experimenting with alter-

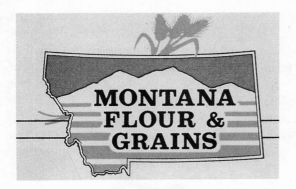

MONTANA FLOUR & GRAINS

native agriculture in the mid-1980s, and by mid-1991 will have completed the lengthy transition to complete organic certification. "We are committed to the ideals of the family farm," says Bob Quinn, "and intend to work in harmony with the resources the Lord has given us to perpetuate the opportunity to produce high-quality, nutritious food in a sustainable way for the generations of the future."

Hard red winter and spring wheats make up the bulk of what Quinn sells. He's also excited about kamut, a 4,000-year-old relative of wheat that some people claim was first discovered in an Egyptian tomb. Quinn says that the "mild-flavored" kamut seems not to cause a reaction in people who are allergic to wheat—he says he won't make any claims for it until he's got some scientific studies in.

Quinn stone-grinds his grain "pretty much to order, not more than a week in advance," and says that most of his customers don't worry about storage because they use it fairly quickly. He does recommend that you keep it cool and dry for extended storage, particularly in warmer, damper parts of the country. If you are interested in smaller orders of his grain or flour, contact The Good Food Store in Missoula (page 289).

NATURAL WAY MILLS, INC.
Route 2, Box 37
Middle River, MN 56737
(218) 222-3677
FAX: (218) 222-3408

Visits: yes
Catalogue/price list available
Grains certified by OCIA
Mill certified by: OCIA
Minimum order: none
Order by: phone, mail
Pay by: prefer prepaid, 15 days net
Ship by: UPS

GRAINS

Hard red spring wheat berries · Soft winter (pastry) wheat berries (F) · Hard white spring wheat berries (C) · Rye berries (F,C) · Durum wheat berries (F) · Whole buckwheat (F) · Whole corn (F,C) · Flax seed · Triticale berries (F) · Barley (hulled, unhulled, pearled) (F,C) · Brown rice (short-, medium-, long-grain) (F) · Hulled millet (C,F) · Whole oat groats (C,F)

OTHER CEREALS

Seven grain · Cracked wheat · Whole-wheat cream of wheat

OTHER FLOUR

Whole wheat · Gold 'N' White Flour with germ · Gold 'N' Lite pastry · Golden graham · Golden 86 whole wheat · Gold 'N' White 86 · Gluten · Flax meal

BEANS

Soy (C, F) · Navy

MISCELLANEOUS

Vegetarian meatless burgers · Herb seasoning

Ray and Helen Juhl are farmers who began milling as a "home hobby," says Helen Juhl. "We were always interested in healthful living, and the business just grew out of that." The Juhls are still farmers, although, says Helen Juhl, "we don't grow a fraction of what we mill." The distinctive quality of Natural Way Mills's flour, says Helen Juhl, is that it is much

NATURAL WAY MILLS INC.

drier than most flours on the market, "which makes it less expensive. You're paying for product, not for moisture. The dryness also gives it a longer shelf life. We guarantee the shelf life for up to one year."

Most items available in 25- or 50-pound bags only. Whole-wheat flour is available in 5 10-pound or 10 5-pound bags. In 1990, flours ranged from $3.75 to $14.25 for 25 pounds and from $7 to $28 for 50 pounds.

PALLAN APPLE ORCHARD
30535 Anthony Road
Valley Center, CA 92082
(619) 749-1168

Visits: yes; cider, Asian pears, Red Bartlett pears, Arkansas Black apples
Certified by: CCOF
Minimum order: 40 pounds
Order by: mail
Pay by: check
Ship by: UPS

APPLES

Granny Smith · Red Delicious · Golden Delicious · Criterion

Every year from 1976 to 1981, Frank and Alberta Pallan planted several hundred fruit trees, says Pallan, who retired several years ago from a job in computer systems at General Dynamics. They chose the popular Granny Smith and Red and Golden Delicious varieties, as well as Criterion, a cross between a Red and a Golden Delicious that looks like a Golden, but has the firmer flesh of the Red.

Frank Pallan was born and raised on a farm in Oklahoma, but his family "sure didn't use chemicals." From the beginning, the Pallans farmed organically, says Frank Pallan, who feels that "DDT was the biggest mistake ever made. You can't get rid of it. It's got a half-life of several hundred years, and the only thing you can do is plow it under—way down deep.

We're just poisoning ourselves with chemicals. You look around and it's not just the country, it's the world. People keep saying, 'This isn't hurting us,' but then there's acid rain, the air's polluted, the water's polluted, we're chopping down the rain forests. It's tragic."

In 1990, a 40-pound box of apples was $20, plus shipping.

PAVICH FAMILY FARMS
Route 2, Box 291
Delano, CA 93215
(805) 725-1046
FAX: (805) 725-1216

Certified by: CCOF
Ship by: UPS
Minimum order: 30 pounds
Pay by: check, money order

DRIED FRUIT

Raisins

The Pavich family bills itself as the "world's largest grower and shipper of table grapes." The elder Paviches, Stephen, Sr., and Helen, began growing table grapes back in 1953. Even then, they used few agricultural chemicals; in the 1960s, their son, Stephen, Jr., became con-

= PAVICH FAMILY FARMS =

vinced that organic was the way to go when he was "overcome by pesticide fumes from a washed vineyard tank." Stephen and his brother, Tom, began converting the family land, and they now grow both grapes and melons on 1,000 acres of organic land—one brother in California and one in Arizona.

Grape-picking is often done by migrant workers, but the Pavich family takes pride in the continuity of its work force—some have stayed as many as eight years, and one family for twenty years. And, at the Pavich farm, workers don't have to worry about pesticide exposure, which is often cited as one of the main dangers of the grape-picker's life.

I live on Pavich grapes in summer, and was not surprised to learn that by popular demand, the Pavich family is now shipping seedless raisins that start as juicy Red Flame grapes. They recommend freezing raisins for up to a year; or pureeing them to make a sweetener for cooking or baby food.

In 1990, a 30-pound carton of raisins was $49.50, including shipping.

RANCHO SANTA MADRE
32929 Lilac Road
Valley Center, CA 92082
(619) 742-1801
FAX: (619) 742-1814

Visits: yes
Certified by: SELF
Certification pending from: CCOF
Minimum order: 40 pounds
Order by: phone, mail, fax
Pay by: check
Ship by: UPS, parcel post

FRUIT

Valencia oranges · Pink grapefruit · White grapefruit · Mineola tangelos

When Jim Nolan took over the family ranch in 1985, he "inherited a pretty bad situation. The grove wasn't dead but pretty close to it. I admitted to myself that I didn't know anything about what to do, so I got myself the best advisors about how to fix it. After we got the problems cleared up, the farm adviser said to me, 'Now it's time to start spraying for mites.' I asked, 'Start? When do we stop?' We had just spent twenty-seven thousand dollars on insecticides. He said, 'You don't stop,' and I said, 'I don't think so.' I just wasn't that pleased with working with respirators and rubber gloves. So I started reading and talking to other growers about alternative methods. It's worked out pretty well." Nolan's involvement in organic growing has led him to the presidency of his local chapter of CCOF.

RONSSE FARMS
P.O. Box 117
Chicago Park, CA 95712
(916) 346-2918

Visits: Yes
Certified by: CCOF
Minimum order: 1 box
Order by: phone, mail
Pay by: money order, cashier's check
Ship by: UPS, own truck

APPLES

Early Girl · Bright and Early · Double Red · Newtowne Pippin · Golden Delicious · Granny Smith

Jim and Ann Ronsse both come from apple-growing families in the Santa Cruz mountains. The Ronsses, who are now in their fifties, planted their own eight-and-a-half acre orchard fifteen years ago. They currently grow three red and three yellow apples, with the Newtowne Pippin a particular favorite among their customers.

The couple decided to go organic several years ago. "I don't want to say that before that we were too young to care," says Ann Ronsse, "but we weren't really aware of the dangers. Of course, growing up with all that spray, we knew about the effect on health as far as our own families. We had sensitive stomachs, and allergies, and there's cancer on both sides of our family. You just have to wonder if the sprays contributed to it." The Ronsses aren't the only growers in their family to make the switch. "I have two or three uncles who've switched and gone organic. The consumer is tired of sprays. The change should have happened long ago."

The Ronsses are just getting into mail order and would prefer large orders—but are happy to ship small orders on the West Coast, or by UPS elsewhere if they get "a regular customer, who wants some good organic apples on a regular basis." Call them to discuss it.

SNO-PAC FROZEN FOODS
379 South Pine Street
Caledonia, MN 55921
(507) 724-3984
(507) 724-5281

Farmers' markets: Cub Foods in LaCrosse, Wisconsin; Cub Foods in Decorah, Iowa; Sugar Loaf Garden in Winona, Minnesota
Catalogue/price list available
Certified by: OGBA
Minimum order: $100
Order by: phone, mail
Pay by: check prior to shipping
Ship by: UPS (winter); air freight (summer)

FROZEN VEGETABLES

Peas · Sweet corn · Beans · Broccoli · Cauliflower · Butternut squash · Carrots

Ramon Gengler's father started freezing peas for a canning company in 1943, says Ramon's wife, Darlene, then went into business for himself. "He had a butter and vegetable route, and just added the frozen peas to it." Gengler was organic from the beginning. "He'd read about people growing organically in England and liked the sound of it. This was just when they were coming out with DDT. I guess that makes him a pioneer. It's been kind of exciting to watch everybody else get the idea, but we're still the first ones growing, processing, and freezing organic vegetables." Sno-Pac processes its vegetables without salt, sugar, sulfites, or food coloring.

In 1990, a case of 12 packages (between 8 and 10 ounces per package) ranged from $10.50 to $10.90. A case of 6 packages (32 to 40 ounces per package) ranged from $16.50 to $18. There was a flat charge for ice and transportation to the airport of $20, and shipping is additional, so large orders are more economical than small ones.

STAR ROUTE FARMS
95 Bolinas-Olema Road
Bolinas, CA 94924
(415) 868-1658
FAX: (415) 868-9530

Minimum order: 5 flats
Certified by: CCOF
Catalogue/price list available

SALAD GREENS

Rocket · Mustard · Mizuna · Cress · Tatsoi · Red kale · Radicchio · Chicory frisee · Baby spinach · Baby leeks · Baby garlic · Coastal Garden Mix · Mesclun

HERBS

Cilantro · Dill · Burnet · Epasote · Lemon balm · Lovage · Marjoram · Oregano · Rosemary · Sage · Summer savory · Winter savory · Sorrel · Tarragon · English thyme · Lemon thyme · Silver thyme · Spearmint

EDIBLE BLOSSOMS

Anise hyssop · Borage · English daisies · Johnny jump-ups · Lemon gem marigolds · Mixed blossoms · Nasturtiums · Radish · Rocket · Roses · Sage · Pineapple sage

FRUIT

Fraise des bois

Warren Weber came to farming in 1974 with a Ph.D. in English from Berkeley. It was a dry time in academia, says Weber. Jobs were scarce, and you could send out hundreds of résumés without getting one call. Weber had studied agricultural economics at Cornell, and had always wanted to farm, so he and his wife took the plunge. They got caught up in the wave of organic farming, which he recalls as being something like a religious movement. Although Weber was never a zealot, you can see him standing in his fields and arguing quite elo-

quently on behalf of organic farming in Les Blank's documentary, *Garlic Is as Good as Ten Mothers*. Today, Weber primarily supplies restaurants and natural-food retailers in the Bay Area.

In 1990, 5 pounds of specialty greens were $20; herbs by the dozen bunches ranged from $5.40 to $10.08. Three pounds of mesclun or Coastal Garden Mix were $19.50.

SUMMERCORN FOODS
1410 Cato Springs Road
Fayetteville, AR 72701
(501) 521-9338
(501) 443-5771

Ingredients certified by: OOGA, KOP
Visits: yes
Catalogue/price list available
Minimum order: none
Order by: phone, mail
Pay by: check, money order, COD
Ship by: UPS, parcel post

COOKIES

Amazin' Raisin · Almond macaroon · Peanut butter

BREAD

Whole wheat · Whole-wheat burger buns · Whole-wheat sourdough · Rye sourdough · Cinnamon currant · Italian

SOYFOOD

Tofu · Baked marinated tofu · Savory soysage · Okara tempeh · Tofu onion dip · Soymilk · Tofu jerky · Tofu in sweet-and-sour sauce

GRAINS AND BEANS

Soybeans · Whole-wheat berries (F) · Rye berries (F)

OTHER FLOUR

Unbleached white

Summercorn Foods, a collectively owned and managed company, began as a bakery in 1974. Summercorn continues to bake breads, cookies, and granolas using organic grains. Its cinnamon currant bread, says Summercorn's David Druding, draws orders from all over the country. In 1990, Summercorn moved to a new location and put in a wood-fired oven for sourdough breads.

Summercorn does its own milling on two French-granite stone mills. The millers at Summercorn learned to dress the millstones "from an elderly gentleman here in northwest Arkansas," says Druding. The flour that goes into the cookies and breads is milled fresh for each baking, and if you order flour, it is freshly stone-ground to your order. Custom milling is available.

Summercorn has been making soyfoods since 1980 and is constantly expanding its line, using only organic soybeans. In 1990, it began adding "shelf-stable" and ready-to-eat foods, like a tofu jerky, and a tofu in sweet-and-sour sauce.

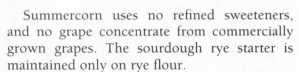

Summercorn uses no refined sweeteners, and no grape concentrate from commercially grown grapes. The sourdough rye starter is maintained only on rye flour.

All grains and soy products, as well as baked products, can be nitrogen-flushed (to drive out the oxygen) and vacuum-packed to preserve their freshness. Summercorn is also considering using canning jars, because the plastic pouches in the vacuum packaging are not at all recyclable, and last forever.

In 1990, a 50-pound bag of flour ranged from $15.50 to $18.50. A case of 24 cookies ranged from $13.80 to $16.30. A case of 8 1.5-pound breads ranged from $14.25 to $20.25. A case of tofu, marinated tofu, or tofu products ranged from $10.80 to $22. Shipping additional. Volume discounts for orders over $250.

TKO FARMS
101 East Manor Drive
Mill Valley, CA 94941
(800) 232-0507
(415) 389-0507
FAX: (415) 389-8137

Certified by: SELF
Minimum order: $200
Order by: phone, fax
Ship by: Airborne Express

SALAD AND SPECIALTY GREENS

Field mix · Upper Cut mix · Straight lettuce mix · Warm braising mix · Arugula · Young spinach · Radishes · Beets · Asian greens

Imagine the best-looking and best-tasting salad you've ever served in a fancy restaurant. Now imagine opening a box and finding enough of that salad to serve you and a dozen or more friends. I opened the box of field mix—a gorgeous assortment of arugula, chicory, watercress, and several greens I couldn't identify, already "triple-washed" and cut, ready to serve. When Todd Koons calls his produce "knockout" salad greens, it's not just a pun on the name of his farm (TKO), but the honest truth. You may not want to order one every week, but it would be perfect for a large, special occasion.

Todd Koons grew up on a self-sufficient organic farm in Oregon. His parents grew everything, right down to the wheat, says Koons. But what got him interested in starting TKO Farms was his experience as a chef at Chez Panisse. He gardened for the restaurant, and calls TKO Farms a natural extension of his "passion for salads and lettuce greens." Although he now supplies restaurants, wholesalers, and distributors, he says that one of the main reasons he became a grower was "to get products out to the folks who don't have thirteen organic markets, like in Berkeley." Koons is working hard to be able to supply specialty greens year-round, but still finds time to do some cooking, usually for the benefits to raise money for local charities like Meals on Wheels and the Open Hand project, which provides food to AIDS patients.

TROUT LAKE FARM
149 Little Mountain Road
Trout Lake, WA 98650
(509) 395-2025
FAX: (509) 395-2645

Herbs certified by: OR-TILTH, WSDA, CCOF, OCIA
Farm certified by: WSDA
Catalogue/price list available
Minimum order: 10 pounds
Order by: phone, mail, fax
Pay by: COD for first order, check, money order
Ship by: UPS, parcel post

CULINARY HERBS AND SPICES

Anise · Basil (dried or fresh-frozen) · Bay leaves · Black pepper · Celery seed · Chervil · Chicory · Chives · Cilantro · Coriander · Dill seed · Dill weed · Fennel · Fenugreek seed · Ginger · Gingko · Lemongrass · Licorice root · Marjoram · Mustard seed · Parsley · Parsley root · Rosemary · Sage leaf · Tarragon · Lemon thyme

DRIED VEGETABLES

Carrot powder · Dehydrated beet root · Celery flakes · Sweet corn powder · Garlic powder or granules · Leek · Dehydrated onions (minced or powdered) · Quick-frozen diced onions · Potato flakes · Red pepper · Spinach · Tomato powder

TEA HERBS

Alfalfa · Anise hyssop · Astragalus · Calendula flowers · Catnip · Chamomile · Spearmint · Peppermint · Raspberry leaf · Strawberry leaf

OTHER COOKING INGREDIENTS

Wild rice · Dried orange peel · Dried lemon peel · Sesame seeds (hulled or natural)

After graduating from the University of Colorado with a degree in sociology and anthropology, Lon Johnson went to work for the fledgling Celestial Seasonings tea company as an herb buyer. Within six months, he'd discovered that most of the herbs in the United States actually come from Europe, and that they are not even the best of the European crop—he

calls them "the dregs," old and stale by the time they reach our shelves. Many of these herbs are grown with chemicals and are irradiated and fumigated as a matter of course, first when they leave their home port and then when they arrive in this country.

Johnson had grown up on a farm, which prompted him to start growing herbs himself. He spent three years looking for land and ended up in the Cascade Mountains of Washington State, where he founded Trout Lake Farm in 1973. Johnson chose the area because of its pure, glacial water, its isolation from pollution, and its climate, ideal for growing herbs. The farm's 190 acres provide about two dozen of the medicinal and culinary herbs Trout Lake sells: the company contracts with other certified growers to provide herbs and vegetables of other climates. Johnson's success has even earned him a two-page, four-color spread in *The Furrow*, a magazine for owners of John Deere Tractors—not the people I'd vote most likely to be interested in organic herbs.

The freshness and potency of both the herbs and dried vegetables is extraordinary. I sampled the peppermint and the dehydrated minced onions. Each came in a sealed ziplock bag, packed in its own UPS cardboard box— and I didn't even have to open the box to identify the contents.

In 1990, tea herbs ranged from $2.80 to $13.80 a pound. Dried culinary herbs ranged from $9 to $10.25 per pound. Drive or powdered vegetables ranged from $2.80 to $10.95 a pound. Prices are lower for 5 pounds of each herb or vegetable. Be sure to specify that you want the bulk price list, with 10-pound minimum, and not the wholesale price list—unless you're interested in 200 pounds of herbs.

WELSH FAMILY FARM
℅ **David Feldman**
402 North Pine Meadow Drive
De Bary, FL 32713-2307
(407) 668-6361
FAX: (904) 775-4220

Visits: Contact Mr. Feldman
Farm certified by: OGBA
Catalogue/price list available
Minimum order: $250
Order by: phone, mail, fax
Pay by: check
Ship by: UPS Second Day Air
Shipments made on Mondays

MEAT (MANY CUTS AVAILABLE)

Beef · Pork · Chicken

Bill Welsh became aware of the hazards of chemicals and biocides during his years as an instructor of atomic, biological, and chemical warfare in the Air Force. Doubtless, whatever he learned there is classified—but we can certainly guess, given that it prompted him to make his family farm "completely organic," an effort that began in 1979.

Welsh Family Farm, some 200 acres in Iowa, grows feed for its animals without pesticides or herbicides. If the Welshes need to buy feed from off the farm, it's certified organically

grown. David Feldman, who represents the farm for mail-order sales, says the Welshes "are convinced that a healthy soil produces a healthy plant, a healthy plant produces healthy feed, healthy feed produces healthy animals, and healthy animals provide for healthy humans."

The livestock are hand-fed twice a day, says Bill Welsh. "Automatic waterers supply clean drinking water twenty-four hours a day. When old enough, all animals are free range with access to outside and shelter." The animals are not treated with any chemicals or antibiotics for other than therapeutic purposes. William Welsh also works with the state extension service to provide material to any farmer interested in sustainable agriculture.

All meat is shipped frozen. In 1990, beef ranged from $2.20 per pound to $6.29 per pound for T-bone steak. Hamburger was $2.50 per pound. Pork ranged from $2.40 to $3.15 per pound. Chicken ranged from $2.10 to $4.95 per pound for parts, or $1.78 per pound for whole chickens. Shipping by UPS Second Day Air is extra. For smaller orders from Welsh Family Farm, see Roseland Farms, page 195.

LATE-BREAKING INFORMATION

BREAK-A-HEART RANCH
2450 Blucher Valley Road
Sebastopol, CA 95472
(707) 823-8046

Certified by: CCOF
Brochure/price list available
Minimum order: $50
Pay by: COD
Ship by: UPS Next Day Air or Ground

FRESH VEGETABLES

Tomatoes · Peppers · Dry beans · Snap beans · Squash · Corn · Mesclun · Carrots · Eggplant · Garlic

EDIBLE FLOWERS

Nasturtiums · Dianthus · Calendulas · Violets · Primroses · Johnny jump-ups · Day lilies · Hibiscus · Borage · Gladiolas · Geraniums · Fuschias · Sweetheart roses · Pelargonium · Petal Confetti TM

Petal Confetti TM is an alternative to rice to throw at weddings, and many chefs use it as a garnish.

RIVERVIEW FARM

35218 S.E. David Powell Road
Fall City, WA 98024
(206) 391-0393

Certified by: SELF
Minimum order: $100
Pay by: COD
Ship by: UPS, FedEx, Airborne Express
Call for availability; prices fluctuate with season

HERBS

Basil · Babydill · Chives · Italian parsley · Lemon thyme · Marjoram · Mint · Oregano · Rosemary · Sage · Savory · Sorrel · Tarragon · Thyme

The herbs are shipped fresh-cut from this farm, which was profiled on the PBS cooking show "The Frugal Gourmet," and chosen as a model organic farm by the national association of county extension agents. The farm was certified by the Tilth Producers' Cooperative and by the state until certification became too expensive.

SONOMA ORGANIC GROWERS

8209 Starr Road
Windsor, CA 95492
(707) 838-9559
FAX: (707) 838-8548

Certified by: CCOF
Catalogue/price list available
Minimum order: none
Pay by: check, money order, credit cards in future
Ship by: UPS air/ground

FRESH VEGETABLES

Salad greens · Prepared salad mix · Mesclun mix · Specialty lettuce mix · Baby vegetables · Summer squash · Varietal small tomatoes

HERBS

English thyme · Lime thyme · Lemon thyme · Italian oregano · Rosemary · French tarragon

Lettuces are shipped washed and ready to eat. The herbs are shipped fresh. The company also grows and ships keeping vegetables: ask for current availability. Although there is no minimum order, shipping costs make larger orders a better value.

The following companies also give discounts for bulk orders: American Forest Foods Corporation, Colonel Sanchez Traditional Foods, Community Mill and Bean, Cross Seed Company, Diamond K Enterprises, Dirnberger Farms, Do-R.-Dye Organic Farm, Ecology Sound Farms, Gaeta Imports, Garden Spot Distributors, Granum, Inc., Great Grains Milling Company, Greek Gourmet, Ltd., Green Earth Farm, Greensward/New Natives, Hanson Farms, Hawaiian Exotic Fruit Company, Herb and Spice Collection, Living Farms, Lundberg Family Farms, Maskal Forages, Morningland Dairy, Mosher Products, Mountain Star Honey Company, Natural Beef Farms, Ocean Harvest Sea Vegetable Company, Paradise Ranch, Roseland Farms, South River Miso, Southern Oregon Organics, Starr Organic Produce, Inc., Three Sisters

ARIZONA

TUCSON COOPERATIVE WAREHOUSE
350 South Toole Avenue
Tucson, AZ 85701
(602) 884-9951

Minimum order: $50 (buying clubs only)

ARKANSAS

OZARK COOPERATIVE WAREHOUSE
P.O. Box 30
Fayetteville, AR 72702-0030
(501) 521-2667

Minimum order: $100 (buying clubs only)

CALIFORNIA

MOUNTAIN PEOPLE'S WAREHOUSE
P.O. Box 1027
Nevada City, CA 95959
(916) 273-9531

Minimum order: $300–$500; $200 on pickups

SIERRA NATURAL FOODS
440 Valley Drive
Brisbane, CA 94005
(415) 468-8800
FAX: (415) 468-8801

Minimum order: $125-$250 for Northern California; $500 for nonstandard stops and for Southern California
UPS available on macrobiotic products from Ohsawa and Soken: $100 minimum

SIERRA NATURAL FOODS

WEST VALLEY PRODUCE COMPANY
726 South Mateo Street
Los Angeles, CA 90021
(213) 627-4131

Minimum order: Under consideration
Fresh produce

WHOLEFOOD EXPRESS
3134 Jacobs Avenue
Eureka, CA 95501
(707) 445-3185

Minimum order: $500 for buying clubs, $50 for pickups
UPS available: $50 minimum, COD only

FLORIDA

ORANGE BLOSSOM COOPERATIVE WAREHOUSE
1601 N.W. 55th Place
P.O. Box 4159
Gainesville, FL 32613
(904) 372-7061
FAX: (904) 372-7988

Minimum order: $300–$500
Pickup: $100

ILLINOIS

SALT OF THE EARTH BUYING CLUB
127 Branchaw Boulevard
New Lenox, IL 60451
(815) 485-3333

Minimum order: none, but smaller orders pay a premium
As of 1990, only set up for pickup; delivery/ shipping possible in the future

SEYMOUR ORGANIC FOODS
P.O. Box 190
Seymour, IL 61875
(800) 782-5581
FAX: (217) 687-4830

Minimum order: 25 pounds

IOWA

BLOOMING PRAIRIE WAREHOUSE
2340 Heinz Road
Iowa City, IA 52240
(319) 337-6448
FAX: (319) 337-9940

Minimum order: $400

MICHIGAN

COUNTRY LIFE NATURAL FOODS
Oak Haven
Pullman, MI 49450

Minimum order: $250
UPS: no minimum

MICHIGAN FEDERATION OF FOOD COOPERATIVES
727 W. Ellsworth #15
Ann Arbor, MI 48108
(313) 761-4642

Minimum order: $250

MINNESOTA

**BLOOMING PRAIRIE
NATURAL FOODS**
510 Kasota Avenue SE
Minneapolis, MN 55414
(612) 378-9774
FAX: (612) 378-9780

Minimum order: $250–$800

NEW HAMPSHIRE

ASSOCIATED BUYERS
P.O. Box 207
Somersworth, NH 03878
(603) 692-6101

Minimum order: $250

NEW YORK

CLEAR EYE NATURAL FOODS
RD 1, Route 89
Savannah, NY 13146-9790
(315) 365-2816
FAX: (315) 365-2819

Minimum order: $500/500 pounds

**HUDSON VALLEY FEDERATION
OF COOPERATIVES, INC.**
P.O. Box 367
Clintondale, NY 12515
(914) 883-6848
FAX: (914) 883-9044

Minimum order: $250
UPS available—$25 minimum

NORTH CAROLINA

MOUNTAIN WAREHOUSE
1400 East Geer Street
Warehouse #3
Durham, NC 27704
(919) 682-9234

Minimum order: $350

OHIO

**FEDERATION OF OHIO RIVER
COOPERATIVES**
320 Outerbelt Street, Suite E
Columbus, OH 43213
(614) 861-2446

Minimum order: $200 plus $50 delivery
charge; over $600, no delivery charge; local
people can pick up

PENNSYLVANIA

FRANKFERD FARMS FOODS

318 Love Road
RD 1
Valencia, PA 16059
(412) 898-2242
FAX: (412) 898-2968

Minimum order: $200–$250; none on pickup
UPS: no minimum
Pay by: check; hope to have credit cards by 1991
Frankferd Farms has been growing and grinding organic grain since 1978 and is an OCIA-certified farm, as well as a distributor; included in the farm's catalogue are breads baked from its own grain

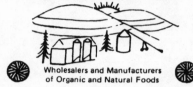

FRANKFERD FARMS FOODS

Wholesalers and Manufacturers
of Organic and Natural Foods

"Good food from the Ferderber Family"

GENESEE WHOLESALE NATURAL FOODS

RD 2, Box 105
Genesee, PA 16923
(814) 228-3205
FAX: (814) 228-3638

Minimum order: $250
UPS: no minimum

GENESEE WHOLESALE
NATURAL FOODS
W.VA. PA. N.Y. N.J. OHIO

NESHAMINY VALLEY NATURAL FOODS

5 Louise Drive
Ivyland, PA 18974
(215) 443-5545
FAX: (215) 443-7087

Minimum order: $200–$400 for delivery; $100 on pickups

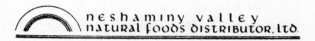

neshaminy valley
natural foods distributor, ltd.

VERMONT

NORTHEAST COOPERATIVES

P.O. Box 1120
Quinn Road
Brattleboro, VT 05302
(802) 257-5856

Minimum order: $400

VIRGINIA

HATCH NATURAL FOODS

P.O. Box 888
Warrenton, VA 22186
(800) 548-6792 (orders only)
(703) 987-8551
FAX: (703) 987-9359

Minimum order: $200
UPS: no minimum; contact Robert Wagg

Hatch Naturals

WASHINGTON

BEAR FOODS WHOLESALE
P.O. Box 2118
125 East Woodin Avenue
Chelan, WA 98816
(800) 842-8049 (orders only)
(509) 682-5535

Ship by: parcel post; shipments to Alaska
using barge lines out of Seattle
Minimum order for free delivery by the
company's truck: $50
Order one day in advance for pickups at the
warehouse

NUTRASOURCE
4005 Sixth Avenue South
Seattle, WA 98108
(206) 467-7190

Minimum order: $350 for delivery; 15%
surcharge for orders under $500; 10%
surcharge for orders under $1,000;
5% surcharge for orders under $1,500;
over $1,500, no surcharge; $100 on
pickups UPS available for nonfood
items

WISCONSIN

COMMON HEALTH WAREHOUSE COOPERATIVE
1505 North 8th Street
Superior, WI 54880
(715) 392-9886
FAX: (715) 392-4517

Minimum order: $500; $100 on pickups

NORTH FARM COOPERATIVE WAREHOUSE
204 Regas Road
Madison, WI 53714
(608) 241-2667

Minimum order: $500; $100 on pickups by
arrangement
Cash-and-carry store on site

GROW YOUR OWN

Clearly, one of the easiest ways to ensure that your food is organic is to grow it yourself. Growing your own food is also environmentally sound: you are reducing the amount of fuel that goes into transporting food to your table. It opens up a world of variety that simply isn't available at your local store.

The companies listed here differ from large, commercial seed companies in a number of important ways. In the 1930s, the U.S. Plant Patent Act created the first patents for hybrid plants. Hybrids often sacrifice taste and nutritional value for characteristics that benefit the large-scale farmer like easy storage and shipping. Hybrid seeds also tend to need large quantities of water.

Hybrids are either sterile, like mules, or do not breed true in the second generation, so you can't save seed from one generation of plants for the following year, so both home gardeners and large-scale farmers have become dependent on the seed companies for seed, year in and year out.

Because hybrid plants are genetically identical, they may even ripen on the same day. That's wonderful for large-scale growers who have to pay pickers, but terrible for the home gardener who wants to have tomatoes on the table over a long period. Growing genetically identical plants also issues a tempting invitation: if a pest can figure out how to attack one of them, it's got the whole crop, so hybrid seeds increase growers' dependence on chemicals.

Plants from open-pollinated seeds, on the other hand, will provide seeds for the next generation. They also contain a range of genetic material, so that the growers can choose the two or three best tomatoes from the first year, and use their seeds for the next year's crop, and so on, developing the best tomato for his or her soil and climate, and the one most resistant to local pests.

Most of the seed companies listed here sell only open-pollinated strains, or indicate which ones in their catalogues are hybrids. In addition, many of them sell "heirloom" varieties of plants, older varieties that have been crowded out of the large seed catalogues by the more popular hybrids. The vegetables and fruits these heirloom varieties produce are generally higher in nutrients than those of plants raised from hybrid seeds.

This is not just nostalgia. It's important for growers, both small-scale and large-scale, to keep these heirloom varieties alive. Plant species can be as endangered as animal species, and if we stop growing them, they're gone forever. In this country, we grow very few varieties of the major grains and produce on a large scale. If one of them is wiped out by a disease or pest, as nearly happened in the corn blight of 1970, we will need to turn to other strains to resist the blight. If no one is cultivating those strains any more, there simply won't be any alternatives. The federal government's seed bank is not doing its job to preserve genetic diversity; one geneticist referred to the seed banks as "seed morgues" because the seeds are drying from improper storage. Forest Shomer of the Abundant Life Seed Company points out that the Irish Potato Famine is a perfect example of the danger of having only two or three strains of a crop feed an entire country.

Finally, many large seed companies are owned by multi-national oil and chemical companies, and routinely coat their seeds with pesticides, which makes them potentially fatal for birds, and not the sort of thing you'd want to hand to small children to plant. Some of these fungicides are so deadly that the EPA forbids companies to burn leftover seeds: the emissions don't pass EPA requirements. The companies listed here sell untreated seeds.

ABUNDANT LIFE SEED FOUNDATION
P.O. Box 772
Port Townsend, WA 98368
(206) 385-5660
(206) 385-7192

Visits: Yes
Certified by: various
Catalogue/price list available
Minimum order: $15 for credit-card orders
Order by: phone, mail
Pay by: check, money order, MC, Visa
Ship by: USPS, UPS, Second Day Air

SEEDS FOR

vegetables · small grains · edible seeds · culinary herbs · flowers · wildflowers · trees · shrubs

Abundant Life specializes in plants and seeds of the North Pacific Rim, with particular emphasis on those species not commercially available, including rare and endangered species. Abundant Life sells only open-pollinated seeds. Roughly 60 percent of the Foundation's seeds are organically grown, and no seeds are coated with fungicides or pesticides. Accessories and extensive selection of books on organic, biodynamic, and sustainable agriculture.

Membership in the Foundation is on a sliding scale, from $5 to $25 per year, and entitles you to a year's subscription to the catalogue and book list, as well as periodic newsletters.

BUTTERBROOKE FARM
78 Barry Road
Oxford, CT 06483
(203) 888-2000

Certified by: NOFA-CT
Catalogue/price list available
Minimum order: none
Order by: phone, mail
Pay by: check, money order
Ship by: UPS, parcel post
Catalogue/price list free with SASE only

Full line of short-maturity fruit and vegetable seeds; some flowers; gardening guides and videotapes

Most of Butterbrooke's varieties are particularly chosen for northern gardeners, but can be used in the South for succession plantings of two or three crops a season. All seeds come from organic gardeners and seed savers. Seeds are not coated.

If you join the Butterbrooke co-op, you receive a discount on seed orders, a quarterly newsletter, a gardening advice service, a role in selecting the seed varieties, an opportunity to purchase rare or heirloom variety seeds from a members-only list, and invitations to meetings and workshops.

In 1990, seed packets ranged from 45 to 95 cents. Members receive a 15% discount on orders. The home garden collection assortment, 16 vegetable varieties, and a planting guide, was $7.50 including postage and handling.

CIRCLE HERB FARM
Route 1, Box 247
East Jordan, MI 49727
(616) 536-2729

Visits: yes; cooking classes
Certified by: SELF
Minimum order: none
Order by: phone, mail
Pay by: COD
Ship by: UPS

CULINARY HERB PLANTS

All plants are greenhouse-grown from seed, organically. You can also buy dried culinary herbs: oregano, soup seasoning, Italian seasoning, rosemary, and sweet marjoram.

HUMMINGBIRD HILLS HERBAL NURSERY
RR 2, Box 351a
Ashland, MO 65010
(314) 657-2082

Visits: yes; greenhouse, two strip gardens, a large perennial and herb garden, and a woodland shade garden for display; classes and demonstration days
Farmers' market: Columbia, on Saturdays
Certified by: SELF
Catalogue/price list available
Minimum order: 4 plants
Order by: phone, mail
Pay by: check
Ship by: UPS

FULL LINE OF CULINARY AND TEA HERB PLANTS

The herbs are all greenhouse-grown from seed, and only organic methods are used to fertilize the soil and control insects.

In 1990, 4-inch herb pots ranged from $1.75 to $3. Also for sale are medicinal herbs, ornamentals, and perennials, everlastings, trees and shrubs, and dried flowers. The catalogue costs $1, but contains coupons worth $12.50. All plants and flowers come with an unconditional guarantee.

NATIVE SEEDS/SEARCH
2509 North Campbell Avenue #325
Tucson, AZ 85719
(602) 327-9123

Visits: yes; demonstration garden, annual seed sale, special seasonal events
Certified by: NONE
Catalogue/price list available
Minimum order: none
Order by: mail
Pay by: check, money order
Ship by: UPS, USPS

SEEDS FOR DESERT PLANTS

grains · beans · chiles · corn · fruit · herbs · vegetables · specializing in threatened and wild plants

Native Seeds/SEARCH cannot guarantee that all seeds come from plants raised organically. It grows its own seed organically, but also gets seed from Native farmers and from volunteers who may or may not use organic methods.

Part of the mission of Native Seeds/SEARCH is cultural: to preserve the crops and foods that are intertwined with Native American identity, to give Native Americans "a superior set of resources and greater self-esteem" than do "welfare programs, trading posts, and fast-food outlets."

In 1990, seed packets were $1.25. Native Seeds/SEARCH also sells Native American and Mexican foods, herbs, and spices. When possible, these are organically grown, and listed as such in the catalogue. The catalogue also lists baskets and crafts, T-shirts, cassettes, and publications, including cookbooks.

PEACE SEEDS
2385 S.E. Thompson Street
Corvallis, OR 97333
(503) 752-0421

Visits: yes
Certified by: OR-TILTH
Catalogue/price list available
Minimum order: none
Order by: mail
Pay by: check, money order, bank transfer
Ship by: UPS, USPS, Express Mail

SEEDS FOR

high-nutrition vegetables · heirloom varieties · medicinals · herbs · flowers · conifers

All seeds are organically grown or gathered in the wild. The catalogue is organized according to the International Taxonomic system rather than by common name, although a common-name index is there to help out. This scheme is designed to help growers see which plant species are endangered and must be preserved at all costs.

In 1990, the seed catalogue was $3.50. Articles and papers available.

REDWOOD CITY SEED COMPANY
Box 361
Redwood City, CA 94064
(415) 325-SEED

Certified by: NONE
Catalogue/price list available
Minimum order: none
Order by: phone, mail
Pay by: check, money order in advance
Ship by: USPS

SEEDS FOR

vegetables · fruit · herbs · books on unusual plants, native plant ecology, and recipes

The Redwood City Seed Company

Redwood specializes in heirloom varieties that are not available elsewhere. The proprietors are also pepper experts, and have trademarked their "Hotness Scale." All seeds are open-pollinated.

In 1990, the catalogue was $1. Seed packets ranged from 35 cents to $2.50. Shipping was $1 for the first packet, and 10 cents for each additional packet.

SEED SAVERS EXCHANGE
RR 3, Box 239
Decorah, IA 52101

Visits: yes. Heritage Farm, the demonstration farm for Seed Savers, displays heirloom and endangered food crops; tours available; seasonal weekend celebrations; write for information
Catalogue/price list available
Minimum order: none
Order by: mail
Pay by: check

The SSE does not sell seeds directly. Members save seeds from their best vegetables and protect them from cross-pollination. Each member receives an annual listing of over 800 members and the seed varieties they have to share, many

of which are not available in any seed catalogue and are threatened with extinction. Members receive the summer and harvest editions of the listing, which contain articles, a plant-finder

service for people looking for rare plants, and profiles of the SSE's heirloom varieties.

The SSE also publishes the Garden Seed Inventory, which compiles the offerings of 215 mail-order seed catalogues, and the Fruit, Berry, and Nut Inventory, which compiles the listings of 248 mail-order catalogues. It also offers books on seed saving. Profits from these sales go to buy and preserve endangered plant species.

In 1990, membership was $25 with reduced rates of $15 or $20 for those who cannot afford $25, no questions asked.

SEEDS OF CHANGE
621 Old Santa Fe Trail #10
Santa Fe, NM 87501
(505) 983-8956
FAX: (505) 983-8957

Visits: by appointment; the 250-acre farm covers 8 types of growing regions
Certified by: OR-TILTH
Catalogue/price list available
Minimum order: 5 packets
Order by: mail, fax
Pay by: MC, Visa, check, money order
Ship by: UPS, parcel post

SEEDS FOR

heirloom vegetables · traditional Native American vegetables · high-nutrition vegetables · unusual salad vegetables · drought-tolerant vegetables · edible organic flowers

All seeds are organically grown. The Seeds of Change seed bank contains 6,500 varieties of native seeds. Seeds of Change also offers consultancy services in sustainable organic farming, organic native seeds, organic herbs, sustainable agro-forestry, drought-tolerant crops and agro-forestry, marketing and promotion, and environmental restoration—including the use of wetlands plants to remove toxins from water systems. Consultancy services are available by phone, mail, or fax.

In 1990, the catalogue was $5.

SOUTHERN EXPOSURE SEED EXCHANGE
P.O. Box 158
North Garden, VA 22959

No phone
Pay by: check, money order
Ship by: USPS, UPS

SEEDS FOR

herbs · vegetables · fruits · grains · shrubs · trees · flowers · books and gardening supplies

Southern Exposure Seed Exchange specializes in open-pollinated, nonhybrid seeds, and plans to add a second seed catalogue to focus on rare and endangered varieties.

SOUTHERN OREGON ORGANICS
1130 Tetherow Road
Williams, OR 97544
(503) 846-7173

Visits: yes
Farmers' markets: Grants Pass, 8th and L streets on Saturday mornings
Certified by: OR-TILTH
Catalogue/price list available
Minimum order: none

Order by: phone, mail
Pay by: check, money order
Ship by: First Class mail

SEEDS FOR

vegetables · melons · culinary and tea herbs and flowers; some heirloom varieties

All seeds are open-pollinated and come from plants grown on this organic farm. None are treated with chemicals. Seeds are available in garden seed spectrum sets: pick twelve or more packs of seeds from a list of fifty-four varieties, amaranth to zinnia.

In 1990, the price for a spectrum set was $1.25 per pack.

TINMOUTH CHANNEL FARM
Town Highway 19 Box 428 B
Tinmouth, VT 05773
(802) 446-2812

Visits: yes
Farmers' Markets: Rutland Shopping Plaza in downtown Rutland, Saturdays
Certified by: NOFA-VT
Catalogue/price list available
Minimum order: 6 plants
Order by: phone, mail
Pay by: check, MC, Visa
Ship by: UPS
Recipes available

Full line of herb plants and seeds, ideal for northern gardeners

All plants grown organically at Tinmouth Channel Farm.

In 1990, the catalogue was $1. Plants in 3-inch pots were $3 each, and seed packets of 100 seeds were $1.

WILTON'S ORGANIC PLANTS
357 Catherine and Harlem Avenues
Pasadena, MD 21122
(301) 544-5746
(301) 647-1561

Visits: yes
Farmers' markets: Annapolis, Saturdays from 7 A.M. to 2 P.M. or until plants are sold out; Baltimore Herb Festival in May; Inner Harbor Annapolis Wine and Food Festival in June
Certification pending from: state of Maryland
Catalogue/price list available
Minimum order: $5
Order by: phone, mail
Pay by: check, money order
Ship by: under consideration

Full line of herbs and vegetable plants; organic fertilizers

In 1990, the catalogue was $2, refundable with first order; a price list was free with SASE of 45 cents postage.

In addition, the following farms/companies sell seeds, starter plants, or fertilizers: American Forest Foods Corporation, Cheyenne Gap® Amaranth, Filaree Farm, Good Earth Association, H-S Farming Company, Hardscrabble Enterprises, Inc., Herb and Spice Collection, Living Tree Centre, Maine Seaweed Company, Meadowbrook Herb Garden, Nu-World Amaranth, Inc., Orange Blossom Farm, Organicly Yours/Aldo Leopold Agricultural Institute, Persimmon Hill Berry Farm, Richters, Ronniger's Seed Potatoes, Seaside Banana Garden, Seeds Blüm, The Sprout House, Wood Prairie Farm

APPENDIX: CERTIFICATION ORGANIZATIONS

The following organizations certify growers and/or processors listed in this book. You can contact them for details of their certification procedure and standards.

CALIFORNIA CERTIFIED ORGANIC FARMERS (CCOF)
P.O. Box 8136
Santa Cruz, CA 95061
(408) 423-2263

CAROLINA FARM STEWARDSHIP ASSOCIATION (CFSA)
P.O. Box 511
Pittsboro, NC 27312
(919) 968-4076

COLORADO DEPARTMENT OF AGRICULTURE (COLORADO)
Division of Plant Industry
700 Kipling Street, Suite 4000
Lakewood, CO 80215-5894
(303) 239-4140

DEMETER ASSOCIATION, INC.
4214 National Avenue
Burbank, CA 91505
(818) 843-5521

Demeter certifies at three levels: organic, biodynamic, and Demeter quality.

FARM VERIFIED ORGANIC (FVO)
P.O. Box 45
Redding, CT 06875
(203) 544-9896
FAX: (203) 544-8409

Note: Producers pay for FVO to certify farms and processing plants, and license the right to use the FVO symbol. The farms certified for those producers do not have the right to use the symbol (because they did not pay for the service).

FLORIDA ORGANIC GROWERS' ASSOCIATION (FOGA)
1204 NW 13th Street
Gainesville, FL 32601

MAINE ORGANIC FARMERS' AND GARDENERS' ASSOCIATION (MOFGA)
P.O. Box 2176
Augusta, ME 04330
(207) 622-3118

MOUNTAIN STATE ORGANIC GROWERS' AND BUYERS' ASSOCIATION (MSOGBA)
Route 10, Box 30
Morgantown, WV 26505
(304) 296-3978

NATURAL ORGANIC FARMERS' ASSOCIATION (NOFA) (SIX STATES)

CONNECTICUT:
Route 2, Box 229
Durham, CT 06422
(203) 349-1417

MASSACHUSETTS:
RFD #2, Sheldon Road
Barre, MA 01005
(508) 355-2853

NEW HAMPSHIRE:
150 Clinton Street
Concord, NH 03301
(603) 648-2521
(603) 654-2270

NEW JERSEY:
RD 2, Box 263A
Pennington, NJ 08534
(609) 737-6848

NEW YORK:
P.O. Box 454
Ithaca, NY 14851
(607) 648-5557

VERMONT:
15 Barre Street
Montpelier, VT 05602
(802) 223-7222

OHIO ECOLOGICAL FOOD AND FARMING ASSOCIATION (OEFFA)
65 Plymouth Street
Plymouth, OH 44865
(419) 687-7665

OREGON TILTH (OR-TILTH)
P.O. Box 218
Tulatin, OR 97602
(503) 691-2514

ORGANIC CROP IMPROVEMENT ASSOCIATION (OCIA)
3185 Township Road 179
Bellefontaine, OH 43311
(513) 592-4983

ORGANIC GROWERS' AND BUYERS' ASSOCIATION (OGBA)
1405 Silver Lake Road
New Brighton, MN 55112
(612) 636-7933
FAX: (612) 636-4135

ORGANIC GROWERS OF MICHIGAN (OGM)
3928 South Sheridan Avenue
Lennon, MI 48449
(313) 621-4977

VIRGINIA ASSOCIATION OF BIOLOGICAL FARMERS (VABF)

Box 252
Flint Hill, VA 22627
(703) 456-6106

OZARK ORGANIC GROWERS' ASSOCIATION (OOGA)

Box HCR 72, Box 35
Parthenon, AR 72666
(501) 446-5783

WASHINGTON STATE DEPARTMENT OF AGRICULTURE (WSDA)

406 General Administration Building
Olympia, WA 98504
(206) 753-5043
FAX: (206) 753-3700

TEXAS DEPARTMENT OF AGRICULTURE (TDA)

P.O. Box 12847
Austin, TX 78711
(512) 463-7602

ALPHABETICAL INDEX

Welsh Family Farm, 304
White Mountain Farm, 146
Williams Creek Farms, 92
Wilton's Organic Plants, 317
Wolfe's Neck Farm, 196

Wood Prairie Farm, 108
Wysong Corporation, 248

Yerba Santa Goat Dairy/Poe Orchards, 49

Zebroff's Organic Farm, 66

INDEX OF LOCAL STORES AND WHOLESALERS

STATE-BY-STATE INDEX

(V) after the name indicates that the farm or company has on-farm sales, a retail store, or gives tours. In all cases, call or write ahead for hours and directions. (M) indicates that products are sold at local farmers markets. Listings of wholesalers and local natural-foods stores, organized by state, can be found under "Buying Clubs" and "Under One Roof."

ALASKA

Briggs-Way Company (V), 186

ARIZONA

Arjoy Acres (V), 110
Native Seeds/SEARCH (V), 313

ARKANSAS

Dharma Farma (V), 75
Eagle Organic and Natural Food (V), 130
The Good Earth Association (M, V), 133
Mountain Ark Trading Company (V), 182
Southern Brown Rice, 224
Summercorn Foods (V), 301
War Eagle Mill (V), 145

CALIFORNIA

Ahler's Organic Date & Grapefruit Garden (M, V), 55
Ancient Harvest Quinoa, 123
The Apple Farm (V), 73
Big River Nurseries (V), 147
Black Ranch (V), 291
Blue Heron Farm (M, V), 199
Break-A-Heart Ranch, 304
Capay Canyon Ranch (M, V), 199
Capay Fruits and Vegetables (M), 69
Colonel Sanchez Traditional Foods, 243
Covalda Date Company (V), 56
Dach Ranch, 208
Desert Mountain Tea Company, 254
Earl Hiatt Enterprises, 201
Ecology Sound Farm, 76
Emandal—A Farm on a River (V), 229
Fitzpatrick Winery (V), 177
Four Apostles Ranch (M), 57
GEM Cultures, 51
Gold Mine Natural Food (V), 181
Gourmet Fruit Basket (V), 59
Gravelly Ridge Farms (M, V), 98

Great Date in the Morning, 60
Green Hills Farms (M), 77
Green Knoll Farm (V), 78
Greensward/New Natives (M), 98
H-S Farming Company, 99
Jacobs Farm (M), 295
Jaffe Brothers, Inc. (V), 269
Jardine Organic Ranch (V), 202
Javianjo Kiwifruit (M, V), 78
Johnson's Kiwis and Produce (V), 78
Kozlowski Farms (V), 174
Living Tree Centre, 202
Lundberg Family Farms (V), 219
McFadden Farm (V), 151
Mad River Farm Country Kitchen (M), 175
Medicine Hill Herb Farm (M), 115
Mendocino Sea Vegetable Company (V), 241
Mountain View Farm (V), 177
Munak Ranch (M, V), 80
Nick Sciabica and Sons (M, V), 214
Noah's Ark, 91
North Valley Produce, 207
Ocean Harvest Sea Vegetable Company, 242
Old Mill Farm School of Country Living (M, V), 242
The Organic Wine Works/Hallcrest Vineyard (V), 178
Orion Organic Orchards (M, V), 204
Pallan Apple Orchard (V), 298
Paradise Ranch, 81
Pato's Dream (M), 62
Pavich Family Farms, 298
Plaidberry (M), 176
Pleasant Grove Farms, 245
Poncé Bakery (V), 38
Rancho San Julian, 195
Rancho Santa Madre (V), 299
Ranch Shangrila (M, V), 206
Redwood City Seed Company, 314
Ronsse Farms (V), 299
Rosetta Teas, 260
Santa Barbara Olive Company (V), 234

Satori Teas, 260
Seaside Banana Garden (M), 84
Sleepy Hollow Farm (V), 86
Sonoma Organic Growers, 305
Sowden Bros., 63
Star Route Farms, 300
Star Valley Farm, 63
Sun Angle, 120
Three Sisters (V), 64
Timber Crest Farms (M,V), 64
TKO Farms, 302
Valley Cove Ranch, 88
Van Dyke Ranch (M, V), 65
Weiss's Kiwifruit (V), 89
Yerba Santa Goat Dairy/Poe Orchards (V), 49

COLORADO

Allergy Resources, 122
First Fruits Organic Farms, 91
Four Directions Farm, 197
Green Earth Farm (M, V), 136
Malachite School & Small Farm (V), 52
Wahatoya Herb (V), 263
White Mountain Farm, 146

CONNECTICUT

Butterbrooke Farm (V), 312
Cricket Hill Farm, 112
Panacea Plantation (V), 72
Sill House Bakery (V), 40

DELAWARE

Organicly Yours/Aldo Leopold Agricultural Institute (M, V), 102

DISTRICT OF COLUMBIA

Tabard Farm Potato Chips (V), 246

FLORIDA

Chestnut Hill Orchards, 200
Dirnberger Farms, 90
Glaser Farms, 91
How-Well Organics, 109
Rosslow Groves, 92
Sprout Delights Bakery (V), 41
Starr Organic Produce, 87
Welsh Family Farm, 304

HAWAII

Adaptations, 291
Hawaiian Exotic Fruit Company (V), 61
Rooster Farms Coffee Company, 259

IDAHO

Camas Grain (V), 292
Maskal Forages, 139
Mountain Star Honey Company (M, V), 161
Ronniger's Seed Potatoes (M, V), 103
Seeds Blüm, 105
St. Maries Wild Rice, Inc. (V), 225

ILLINOIS

Czimer Foods, 189
The Green Earth (V), 283
Nu-World Amaranth, Inc., 144
Specialty Organic Source, 281

INDIANA

Dutch Mill Cheese (V), 44
Lone Pine Farm (V), 80

IOWA

Banwart Family Foods (M, V), 93
Herb and Spice Collection, 257
Seed Savers Exchange (V), 315

KANSAS

Cheyenne Gap® Amaranth (V), 125
Cross Seed Company, 127

KENTUCKY

Gracious Living Farm (V), 97

LOUISIANA

Rein Farms, 102

MAINE

Avena Botanicals, 249
Blessed Maine Herb Company (V), 208
Crossroad Farms (V), 94
Diamond Organics, 95
Fiddler's Green Farm (V), 131
Maine Coast Sea Vegetables, 238
Maine Seaweed Company (V), 240
Morgan's Mills (V), 141
New Penny Farm, 100

Wolfe's Neck Farm (V), 196
Wood Prairie Farm, 108

MARYLAND

Chesapeake Center Farm (V), 111
Organic Foods Express (V), 274
Wilton's Organic Plants (M, V), 317

MASSACHUSETTS

Baldwin Hill Bakery (V), 30
Bread & Stuff, 31
Cape Ann Seaweeds Company, 237
The Coffee Connection (V), 253
Equal Exchange, 254
Greek Gourmet, Ltd., 212
South River Miso, 53
The Sprout House (V), 106

MICHIGAN

American Spoon Foods (V), 171
Circle Herb Farm (V), 313
Eugene and Joan Saintz (V), 104
Haypoint Farm (V), 159
Roseland Farms (V), 195
Sunshower Produce and Juice (M, V), 179
Wysong Corporation (V), 248

MINNESOTA

Diamond K Enterprises, 129
Forest Resource Center, 72
French Meadow Bakery (M, V), 33
Grey Owl Foods (V), 217
IKWE Marketing Collective, 218
Living Farms (V), 138
Mill City Sourdough Bakery (M, V), 35
Minnesota Specialty Crops (V), 220
Natural Way Mills, Inc. (V), 297
Ojibwe Foods, 222
The Secret Garden, 223
Sno-Pac Frozen Foods (M, V), 300

MISSOURI

Aunt Nene's Specialty Foods (V), 227
Blessed Herbs, 252
Glackin's Organic Acres (V), 59
Hummingbird Hills (M, V), 313
Longhorn Lean (V), 191
Midwestern Pecan Company, 203
Morningland Dairy (V), 47
Persimmon Hill Berry Farm (V), 232

Plumbottom Farm (M, V), 117
Riverbluff Farm (M, V), 155
Sandhill Farm (V), 163
Schaeffer Family Farm (M), 118
Shepherdsfield Bakery, 39

MONTANA

Great Grains Milling Company (V), 135
Hanson Farms (V), 137
Montana Flour and Grains, Inc., 296
Mountain Butterfly Herbs (V), 152
Smoot Honey Company (V), 165

NEBRASKA

Do-R.-Dye Organic Farm (V), 129
M & M Distributing (V), 139
Oak Creek Farms (V), 244
Rose Eagle Enterprises, Inc. (V), 156

NEW HAMPSHIRE

Pronatec International, 162

NEW JERSEY

D'Artagnan, 190
Long Life Herb Classics, 258
Simply Delicious (V), 278
Suzanne's Specialties/T&A Gourmet, 170

NEW MEXICO

Seeds of Change, 315

NEW YORK

Back of the Beyond (V), 250
Bioforce of America, Ltd., 250
Bread Alone (M, V), 32
Chesnok Farms (V), 111
Community Mill and Bean, 126
Deer Valley Farm (V), 266
Four Chimneys Farm Winery (M, V), 210
Gaeta Imports (M, V), 211
Hawthorne Valley Farm (M, V), 45
Little Rainbow Chevre (M, V), 46
MacDonald Farms, 235

NORTH CAROLINA

American Forest Foods Corporation (V), 68
Lambsfold Farm (M, V), 296
Natural Lifestyle Supplies, 184
Nature's Storehouse (V), 36

OHIO

Daisy Dell Fruit Farm (M, V), 74
Fackler Family Farms (V), 293
Millstream Natural Health (V), 272
New Morning Farm Pasta (M, V), 143
Pierpont Maple Syrup, 169
Silver Creek Farm (V), 119

OREGON

Bandon Sea-Pack, 186
Cottage Garden Herbs/Windy River Farm (M, V), 148
Earthshine Farm (M, V), 112
Elderflower Farm (V), 150
Glorybee Natural Sweeteners (V), 293
Honey Grove Farm (V), 114
Mountain Meadow Farm (M), 116
Peace Seeds (V), 314
Rising Sun Farm (V), 233
River Bend Organic Farm (V), 82
Schoonmaker/Lynn Enterprises, 164
Simply Wonderful Organic Products (V), 106
South Oregon Organics (M, V), 316
Williams Creek Farms, 92

PENNSYLVANIA

David's Goodbatter, 128
Dutch Country Gardens (V), 95
Garden Spot Distributors (V), 267
Great Bend Organic Farm, 198
Krystal Wharf Farms, 271
Rising Sun Organic Food (V), 276
Walnut Acres Organic Farms (V), 284

PUERTO RICO

Finca del Seto Cafe (V), 255

RHODE ISLAND

Gray's Grist Mill (V), 134
Meadowbrook Herb Garden Catalog (V), 151

SOUTH DAKOTA

Country Pride Meats (V), 188

TEXAS

Anderson Acres (V), 93
Broken Arrow Ranch (V), 187
Carr's Specialty Foods, 265

Lee's Organic Foods, 244
Orange Blossom Farm (V), 101
Pueblo to People (V), 205
S. M. Jacobson Citrus (V), 84
South Tex Organics, 92

UTAH

Mountain Springs, 192
Ranui Gardens, 264

VERMONT

Brewster River Mill (V), 124
Brookside Farm (V), 157
Cherry Hill Cannery (V), 228
Earth's Best Baby Food, 29
Grafton Goodjam (V), 173
Loafers' Glory (V), 231
Maverick Sugarbush (V), 160
North Hollow Farm (M, V), 193
Shelburne Farms (V), 49
Teago Hill Farm (V), 166
Tinmouth Channel Farm (M, V), 316
Vermont Country Maple, 168

VIRGINIA

Golden Acres Orchard (V), 76
Golden Angels Apiary (M), 158
L'Esprit de Campagne (M), 70
Natural Beef Farms (V), 273
Southern Exposure Seed Exchange, 316
Special Foods, 279

WASHINGTON

Abundant Life Seed Foundation (V), 312
Blueberry Lake Farm, 90
Cascadian Farm (V), 172
Filaree Farm (V), 113
Flora, Inc., 209
Granum, Inc. (V), 256
Healthland, 137
Island Herbs (V), 238
Omega Nutrition USA, Inc., 214
Rattlesnake Ranch, 117
Riverview Farm, 305
Royal Organic (V), 83
Trout Lake Farm, 303

WEST VIRGINIA

Brier Run Farm (V), 43
Hardscrabble Enterprises, Inc., 69

Mountain Spirit Organic Farms, 71
Smoke Camp Crafts (M, V), 261
ThistleDew Farm (M, V), 167

WISCONSIN

Nokomis Farms (V), 37
Organic Valley (V), 48
Turkey Ridge Orchards, 88
Uncle Joel's Pure Maple Syrup (V),
    168

WYOMING

Mosher Products, 142
Northern Lakes Wild Rice Company, 221

CANADA

Hazelridge Farm (V), 294
Mountain Path Farm (V), 142
Opeongo Maple Products (M, V), 162
Richters (V), 154
Zebroff's Organic Farm (V), 66